For Kirit

With the good wishes
of Feroza H. Seervai
and of Navroz.

January, 2006.

"He has achieved success who has lived well, laughed often and loved much, who has enjoyed the trust of pure women, the respect of intelligent men and the love of little children; who has filled his niche and accomplished his task; who has left the world better than he found it, whether by an improved poppy, a perfect poem or a rescued soul; who has never lacked appreciation of earth's beauty or failed to express it; who has always looked for the best in others and given them the best he had; whose life was an inspiration, whose memory a benediction."

Bessy Anderson
Cited in a letter to H. M. Seervai
from Maj. Ruzbeh Mehta (22-10-1944)

EVOKING H. M. SEERVAI

Jurist and Authority on the Indian Constitution

H. M. SEERVAI

EVOKING H. M. SEERVAI

Jurist and Authority on the Indian Constitution

1906-1996

A Compilation
for his Centenary
By
FEROZA H. SEERVAI

Edited and Published
By
FEROZA H. SEERVAI

Universal
Law Publishing Co.
New Delhi

First printing 2005

Price: Rs. 525/- in India.

Published by
Feroza H. Seervai, Maison Belvedere, 107, M. Karve Road, Mumbai 400 020.

Printed by
Arun K. Mehta at Vakil & Sons Pvt. Ltd.,
Industry Manor, Appasaheb Marathe Marg, Worli, Mumbai 400 025.

ISBN No.: 81-7534-478-4

Cover design
from a photograph by Hamilton Studios, Mumbai.

Distributors:
Universal Law Publishing Co. Pvt. Ltd.
C-FF-IA, Dilkhush Industrial Estate,
(Opp. Hans Cinema, Azadpur), G. T. Karnal Road,
Delhi-110 033,
Tel : 011-2721 5334, 2743 8103, 5238 1334
Fax : 011-2745 8529
E-mail : sales@unilawbooks.com
Website : www.unilawbooks.com

CONTENTS

ACKNOWLEDGEMENTS

THIS BOOK CONTAINS several Recollections of Seervai. Some of them have been contributed specially for this book at my request by distinguished persons. I thank them all very sincerely, they are extremely busy persons and their having taken time off to write their recollections in response to my request, is greatly appreciated by me. My first thanks go to The Hon'ble Lord Mackay of Clashfern, M.P., the former Lord Chancellor of England, former Chief Justice Raghunandan S. Pathak, Supreme Court of India, and former Judge International Court of Justice (The Hague), Justice Sujata Manohar, Retired Judge Supreme Court of India and former Chief Justice Kerala High Court, Soli J. Sorabjee, former Attorney-General for India, Fali S. Nariman, Member of the Rajya Sabha, former Additional Solicitor General of India, Ashok H. Desai, former Solicitor General of India, Anil B. Divan and Rohinton F. Nariman, Senior Counsels, Supreme Court of India, Venkat Iyer, Bar-at-Law and Professor of Law, Ulster University, and the distinguished writer Gillian Tindall. My grandson Jehangir P. Madon who is an Accountant in New Jersey, U.S.A. also has my thanks.

Next I thank Iqbal M. Chagla, Senior Counsel, Supreme Court of India, and Adil S. Kajiji, Solicitor, whose Court References at the Bombay High Court are published in this book. They readily agreed to their republication here.

I thank Tehmtan R. Andhyarujina, Senior Counsel, former Advocate General of Maharashtra and former Solicitor General of India for permission to re-publish his two tributes which appeared respectively in an issue of *The Elphinstonian* dedicated to Seervai, and in *Constitutional Perspectives* a festschrift published by Universal Book Publishers Pvt. Ltd., edited by Dr. Venkat Iyer, which is slightly modified for publication here. Likewise I thank Atul M. Setalvad, Senior Counsel, Supreme Court of India, whose tribute also appeared in the same issue of *The Elphinstonian*. Both Setalvad and Andhyarujina had been Seervai's devils.

For permission to re-publish the above I thank the Principal of the Elphinstone College and Universal Book Publishers Pvt. Ltd., respectively, the latter being thanked also, along with Dr. Venkat Iyer, for their permission to re-publish the Recollections by Dr. Sheryar K. Ookerjee, former Head, Dept. of Philosophy, Wilson College and by my daughter, Dr. Meher J. Pocha, Consultant Paediatrician, Bedford Hospital, Hertfordshire, which is slightly modified for publication here. I thank them as well.

The piece by the late Dr. Homai J. Shroff, former Principal, Elphinstone College is published with the permission of the Principal of Elphinstone College, to whom I express my thanks.

The remaining Recollections, one written by my son, and others in the form of letters by my niece, Mrs. Shanoor S. Forbes, the late Advocate Shanti Shah, Ms. Sashi N. Thakar, and Mrs. Persis P. Kothawalla are part of our family papers. I am grateful for their recollections.

In another part of this book I have published correspondence commencing 1927 and going on until 1996 and beyond. The correspondence upto 1996 is part of Seervai's and my personal papers and the later letters are part of my papers. I acknowledge the friendship and regard which animates these letters, with genuine feelings for my husband.

As always, my son took time off to discuss various points with me, to look at the material I compiled, to help with reading proofs. For his careful guidance and for his inputs, and for providing the background for some letters (headnotes), I thank him, as I thank him for sparing the time of his secretary to do my typing, where my own effort in that direction was inadequate. I thank Mrs. Padma Nagarajan for her assistance in typing.

As in the case of *The Seervai Legacy*, so for this book, Vakil & Sons Pvt. Ltd., who have printed both books, have been very co-operative, careful and helpful to me. Unlike on the earlier occasion, when I used to be often at their printing press or their Ballard Estate office, for discussion and finalisation, this time round, their people Mr. Meher G. Marolia and Mr. Shivaji P. Jadhav have been good enough to meet me at my residence, understanding my difficulty in visiting them. For this and for their courtesy, I thank them, as well as for the production of a handsome volume.

Feroza H. Seervai

INTRODUCTION

THE TITLE OF THIS BOOK precisely conveys what the book does, for its purpose is to evoke my husband as he was. It is not a biography but it is a biographical book. What manner of man was he? The aim of my endeavours has been that in going through these pages, the reader may almost feel Seervai's breath, as he is seen in photographs, as his thinking and his feelings are revealed in his articles and speeches, as people who knew him closely relate their impressions of him, and as the varied correspondence discloses a rarely experienced aspect of him.

A factual Note is re-published from *The Seervai Legacy*. An idea of Seervai's non-professional associations can also be had from it.

This book has been compiled and published in anticipation of the Centenary of H. M. Seervai's birth. He was born on 5th December, 1906. He was for many years, an admired and honoured public figure.

Seervai died in January, 1996, following which I published a book *The Seervai Legacy* containing a selection of his papers, which was distributed by Universal Law Publishing Co. Pvt. Ltd.

That book having been well received and welcomed, our children wanted me to publish more of Seervai's papers for his centenary. Although the material with me is extensive, I have made a small selection. It gives a rounded picture of the man, especially when read with the previous publication, and because of the selected material, Seervai is readily evoked, seen completely.

I did not want to publish bulky volumes, because readers generally have little time today, to spend on reading. I also wanted to make the material in the book as little repetitive as possible. Seervai's own advice was — and he acted on it — "know what to omit rather than what to include".

In going through the papers, I found a "Birthday Forecast" for 5th December.

I reproduce the Forecast just as it was published in a newspaper.

Forecast for Monday, 5th Dec. (By Havrah Durkeet)
ZODIAC SIGN: SAGITTARIUS

If to-day is your birthday, you have no enemies, and hosts of friends, as a result of your quiet, unassuming disposition, and your ever present desire to hurt no one, either in word or deed. You have the happy knack of saying the right thing at the right time; whilst not brilliant or talented, your intuition enables you to "hit the nail on the head". In everything too, in every relationship of life, you are sincere, and always mean what you say. Your optimism is also of a high order, and it undoubtedly inspires those with whom you come in contact. It is rather strange that with such outstanding and endearing characteristics you have only been able to achieve moderate success; this, however, is brought about by entire lack of ambition for the world's material rewards. You are not built along the lines of those who find happiness in fighting and struggling; you are, morally too much of a pacifist and a philosopher. Provided you have sufficient to gratify your very moderate tastes, no earthly power can persuade you to vary your activities, even though greater emoluments may be the prize of other efforts. Your home life is happy, only if your mate is contented with a simple life; if, however, this is not the case, a great lack of harmony and congeniality will be experienced."

I must say that my husband and I did not believe in astrology in the least. However, I am reproducing what can only be an astrological "forecast". Admittedly, it is true to life in the case of my husband (except where it says "whilst not brilliant"). And his life was very successful indeed, in terms of both achievement and happiness. What else denotes success?

This book is issued somewhat in advance of the centenary date, because of my wish to see it published in my lifetime, as I near the end of my journey and while health and faculties allow.

Feroza H. Seervai

12 A Maison Belvedere,
107, M Karve Road,
Mumbai 400 020
fseervai@vsnl.net

H. M. SEERVAI

H.M. SEERVAI SERVED Maharashtra as Advocate-General, from 1957 to 1974, when he resigned (with no word of appreciation from the Government, for 17 years of outstanding work for the State, although by general consent, he added lustre to this great Office). He resigned on finding the high Office denigrated by the actions of the Minister for Law and Judiciary.

In 1981, the British Academy elected Seervai to be its Corresponding Fellow. After his death in 1996, in a letter from the Academy, the Secretary stated that "The Corresponding Fellowship of this Academy is reserved for scholars of the highest academic distinction, and we were proud to number H.M. Seervai among them. ...His election to the British Academy in 1981 paid tribute to his outstanding contribution as Jurist, Law Officer, and Advocate to Constitutional Law, primarily in India, where he fearlessly and dispassionately maintained the Constitution, of which he was the principal exponent and interpreter; but also as a comparative scholar recognised as of outstanding merit throughout the jurisdiction which participates in the British and American legacies."

In 1994, the International Bar Association awarded Seervai a beautiful trophy "in recognition of outstanding service to the legal profession internationally": an award called Living Legend of Law Award of Recognition.

The President of India conferred on Seervai, the Padma Vibhushan, in 1972, recognising the work in his books, especially *Constitutional Law of India*.

In 1991, the Asiatic Society of Bombay, formerly the Royal Asiatic Society, elected Seervai to be an Honorary Fellow, in a long line of distinguished Fellows from all over Europe and later, India.

The Committee administering the Dadabhai Naoroji Memorial Prize which commemorates a most distinguished Indian, gave the Prize for 1980, to Seervai.

Distinguished Parsis, some of them with international fame, J.R.D. Tata, Zubin Mehta, and others, were honoured by the Bombay Parsi Panchayat. Among them was Seervai.

Successively, Seervai was invited to be a judge of the High Court at Bombay, and a judge of the Supreme Court of India, and also, to be the Attorney General for India. Had Seervai accepted judgeship of the Supreme Court, he would have been Chief Justice of India for 5½ years. For personal reasons and for reasons that had to do with his book *Constitutional Law of India, A Critical Commentary*, Seervai declined the invitations.

Seervai, whose degrees were in Philosophy, taught English Literature at the Elphinstone College in 1932. He was at different times, President of the Bombay Philosophical Society, and of the People's Union for Civil Liberties in Bombay. He was a founder of both societies. He was the sole Founder Patron-Trustee of the Bombay International School. For forty years until his death, he was a trustee of the Elphinstone College, managing the Trust's business. From its inception, Seervai was a trustee of the Chief Justice Chagla Memorial Trust, taking a very active part in its business, until he died. His legal career spanned nearly seventy years, during which he continued to give time, thought, legal advice and money for the causes among others, of education, and of civil liberty. He continued to have an active concern in literature, history, philosophy, biography, essays, and belles-lettres, constantly buying books and reading them, both by himself, and with members of his family.

Books written by Seervai include *Partition of India: Legend and Reality*, *The Position of the Judiciary under the Constitution of India* (Sir Chimanlal Setalvad Lectures delivered at the University of Bombay), *The Emergency, Future Safeguards and the Habeas Corpus Case: A Criticism*, and an essay on Federalism and the Indian Constitution, being an essay commissioned by the University of Mexico. It was published in Spanish to form part of a 4-Volume treatise on Federalism. Seervai was invited to deliver the Tagore Law lectures but declined to do so since at the time when he was invited to deliver these lectures, he was too busy with his professional commitments and felt that he would not be able to devote the time necessary to meet the exacting standards required of one invited to deliver so prestigious a lecture series.

In 1967 a member of the Bar complimented Seervai, mentioning Aldous Huxley's complaint, that intellectually we are all 21 years of age — that after University we remain stagnant, going on to say "This did not happen to you. You were growing all the time, and still are growing. ...At the age of 61, your enthusiasm, zest, passion for life, law, and other things that matter, is admirable... You were all kindness to me the other day. In the midst of heavy work, you gave me one precious hour. I learnt so many things. I learnt how a great lawyer is made up (sic). I learnt that he has read a good deal in his life-time — Gibbon, Goldsmith, Hazlitt, Macaulay, Dickens, Thackeray, Trollope, Morley, Barrie, Maughan, Churchill, Holmes, Cardozo, Frankfurter ...I learnt that to him life is not purposeless, to be spent away in mere gossip, but a ceaseless struggle towards perfection."

Seervai's ancestor Lovji Nusserwanji Wadia (1734-1774) was the first of a long line of Master Builders of the Mazagaon Docks in Bombay, Seervai's mother being the daughter of the last, the Assistant Master, Hirjibhai Meherwanji. One ship built by them is still afloat — now a museum in England — after 183 years. The Master Builders were noted for inflexible integrity, as were the Seervai ancestors in Navsari, noted particularly for great courage. Sher-vai means "like a lion". Legend has it that one ancestor, called upon to kill a lioness that terrorised the "mohalla", first woke the sleeping beast, and when it leapt on him, severed its head with one stroke of his sword. Seervai's grandfather Nusserwanji Bachaji Seervai was for many years, Rajvaid at the Royal Court in Baroda, the sovereign honouring him with the silver anklet. As a child, Seervai, like his forbears and his brother, was ordained a priest of the Zoroastrian religion. He was eight years old, his brother ten.

He was known for the family traits, strong in him, of moral courage and inflexible integrity and for the simplicity of his life. Seervai's was a philosophical and creative mind with high intellectual capacity. It made him a stoic, an optimist, and a man of compassion, so that, given time, he brought himself to forgive even disloyalty, which in his view was the worst of human failings, especially in those who owed loyalty.

Seervai was not to be encountered in the city's social whirl, declining when he could, even the invitations of the Head of State. He never left India till he was 66. He repeated that he was happiest in his home, at all times. Barely 14, he had lost his father suddenly. To his mother he gave extraordinary devotion until she died in 1938. At his birth, his mother was 42.

In 1945, aged 39, Seervai married. His joy was to make his family laugh. His wife as well as the smallest child of the family enjoyed very great freedom of thought and action. He neither preached about nor "taught" the qualities he valued. His life held the lesson — learn it or leave it.

Seervai died very soon after the celebration of his Golden Wedding. A few weeks earlier, the presence of his three children and their families made him immensely happy, his daughters and their families coming from abroad, specially for the occasion. He also enjoyed the Navjote, a few days before he died, of his youngest grand-daughter. They both had been eager that he should be present for her initiation ceremony.

Seervai was forever quoting lines of verse or prose from memory, and was very fond of these lines of Walter Scott, because they summed up everything that he believed in and stood for: "Without courage, there cannot be truth; And without truth, there can be no other virtue."

Feroza H. Seervai

Republished from *The Seervai Legacy*.

RECOLLECTIONS BY LAWYER FRIENDS

Some Recollections have been specially written in response to my request for them for this book. Others were written when Seervai died in 1996, spontaneously expressing the writer's feelings and thoughts, in the form of an essay or a letter. Some were previously published in a College Magazine dedicated to Seervai, and in a festschrift for him.

Court References were given to Seervai in the Supreme Court of India, and in three High Courts — Bombay, Delhi, Gujarat. I have chosen two of them.

Some Recollections are in the form of letters. The Recollections are not formal in spirit, and the Recollections of family members are, as may be expected, very personal and intimate.

These Recollections present my husband from many different points of view, therefore in many aspects, thus bringing alive the personality of Seervai as vividly and as completely as it is possible to do on paper.

FULL COURT REFERENCE

Iqbal M. Chagla

President, Bombay Bar Association

February 1, 1996

In the death of Hormasji Maneckji Seervai, one of the brightest stars in the legal firmament has gone out, leaving a shadow that casts itself, not only over the legal world, but over every one of us who had the good fortune of knowing him.

To say he was the last of his kind would be to speak a lie; for Seervai could never be one of a kind; he was *sui generis*, he was unique. For him there were in life no shades of grey: there was only black and white, right and wrong. He set for himself the highest standard of moral integrity and in that he was totally inflexible and uncompromising, at times unreally so. When a young colleague asked what could be wrong about charging high fees when clients were willing to pay them, unhesitatingly came the answer: "If a man is willing to be robbed, would you be a thief?"

His integrity of purpose was coupled with immense courage: when Sir Jamshedji Kanga (who venerated the office of judgeship) was appalled that Seervai was contemplating a complaint against a sitting Judge of this Court, Seervai said he would not embarrass Jamshedji and would leave his Chambers. But do his duty he must. Jamshedji appreciated the courage of his conviction and supported Seervai who succeeded in unseating the Judge. Seervai was to show the same daunting and fierce courage throughout his life: his credo is reflected in the lines of Sir Walter Scott — I can almost hear him recite them in his stentorian voice:

> "Without courage, there cannot be truth, and without truth there can be no other virtue."

For over 17 years Seervai brought to the office of Advocate-General dignity, forthrightness and a fierce independence. During those luminous years, Government had the benefit of sage and objective advice, the citizen an opponent who fought keenly but never unfairly, and the Court the advantage of an argument as well-constructed as it was balanced; and as a bonus the Bombay Bar Association a President who commanded the respect and affection of its members.

Sitting on the first floor in what was then the Advocate-General's chamber, Seervai was accessible to one and all — the juniormost member could enter and no problem of his was too small or too insignificant. He was incapable of being derisory of anyone or of any argument, whether it came in conference from the juniormost counsel or even the client. It would be examined, discussed and reasoned with a patience that was truly heroic.

This virtue which enabled him to suffer even fools, is best typified by the vagabond at the Oval who mischievously suggested that the flask Seervai was carrying contained illicit liquor. Anyone else would have ignored it, but not Seervai: he stopped and explained in detail how one section contained tea and the other milk as the two should not be pre-mixed. The vagabond departed, a chastened but a wiser man.

Over a career at the Bar that spanned some 65 years, Seervai could justly claim that his most abiding contribution to the law, greater than all his arguments in the most important constitutional cases, greater than all the awards and distinctions he received, was his *magnum opus, The Constitutional Law of India*. It was and is the greatest work of Indian scholarship and hailed as such, not only in India, but throughout the world. This was, indeed, his great labour of love and one that engaged him from 1961 until his death, and at times to the exclusion of all else save his family.

Seervai and my father had a special relationship: counsel and puisne Judge, Advocate-General and Chief Justice, author and critic and, finally, comrades who fought the common cause of democracy and civil liberties. They could not meet over dinner: Seervai would want an early meal without any pre-prandial refreshment, my father precisely the opposite. Compromise was reached: Seervai would drop in for tea, sharp at 4 o'clock. Even as it approached 5.30, my father would steal a glance at his watch when Seervai would say "Yes, Chagla, I know. It's time for your bridge at the Club — we can go down together." I once remonstrated with my father that this was very rude when I was told "Nothing of the sort — Seervai and I have known each other much too long for either of us to take offence." When we established the Chief Justice Chagla Memorial Trust, Seervai and Nani Palkhivala were the automatic choice for trustees. Happily, the Trust helped to bridge the gulf that sometimes occurs in the greatest of friendships.

Seervai was known to say that in his life the priorities were Family, Literature and the Law — strictly in this order.

His love of reading encompassed the great prose and poetry of the English Language — the range was formidable and included the great philosophers, the classics, the entire works of Churchill (whom he idolised), Milton, Shakespeare, Tennyson, Byron, Keats, his favourite Wordsworth. He would say that he had read, re-read and re-re-read them all; indeed he could quote extensively and at will, and was always ready with the right quotation for the occasion.

On his very first visit to England in 1973 his knowledge of English history sometimes proved an embarrassment to the guide who took them around historical sites; it prompted a visitor to ask whether he was a Professor of History in an English University and was surprised at the answer that he was only a lawyer from India.

But there was nothing in his life, no briefs in Court, no conferences, no pressing engagements that would ever prompt Seervai to say to his beloved wife Feroza or his children Meher, Shirin or Navroz "Not now — I am busy". There could have been no more loving or devoted husband — of course, Seervai would have said he was only reciprocating a love as great as his own; or a father who devoted as much love, time and attention on his children, and, latterly, his grandchildren.

It was all-pervasive and all-encompassing love for the family that dictated that he refuse, in 1956, a judgeship of the Supreme Court: he would have had a tenure of 15 years, 5½ of them as Chief Justice of India; it was for the same reason that he declined, in 1971, the office of Attorney-General for India. He believed that the move to Delhi would disrupt his family life and nothing could be more precious and no sacrifice too great to preserve that unity and harmony.

My lords, Seervai lived as he believed a man should; he died, I believe, as he, himself, would have wished. He had only just celebrated his golden wedding anniversary, he had attended the Navjote ceremony of a grandchild; even the 4th Edition of *The Constitutional Law of India* was complete. In the fitness of things, Seervai chose to leave us on the anniversary of the birth of our Constitution and the Republic. My lords, we shall feel the lack of him more than words will ever express; but our consolation is that he will continue to live in the minds and hearts of all those who were privileged enough to know him.

I should like to end with his favourite lines from Milton — they are appropriate to the man we remember today:

> "Unmoved
> Unshaken, unseduced, unterrified,
> His loyalty he kept, his love, his zeal
> Nor number, nor example with him wrought
> To swerve from truth, or change his constant mind."

On behalf of myself and the members of the Bombay Bar Association, I convey my heartfelt condolences to Feroza, to Meher and Shirin, to Navroz and to his grandchildren.

FULL COURT REFERENCE

Adil S. Kajiji
President, the Bombay Incorporated Law Society
February 1, 1996

THE MANAGING COMMITTEE, the members of the Bombay Incorporated Law Society and myself, associate with the sentiments expressed by my Lord the Chief Justice, Mr. Sawant, the Advocate-General, Mrs. Ranjana Desai, the Govt. Pleader, Mr. Sandeep Ghogre the Vice Chairman of The Bar Council of Maharashtra and Goa, Mr. Iqbal Chagla the President of the Bombay Bar Association, and Mr. Shirish Gupte the President of the Advocates Association of Western India, on the demise of Mr. H. M. Seervai.

Just a week ago we had assembled to mourn the demise of a great lawyer and a fine human being. Today we have assembled to mourn the demise of another and in doing so we are slowly bringing down the curtain on an era which is coming to an end.

Already much has been said about Mr. Seervai but it matters not if one is repetitive, for enough will never be said of him. For it was this scholar Jurist:

(a) who at an early age inbibed from his mother Zoarastrian tenets of "good thoughts, good words, good deeds" and the value of being inflexible in the pursuit of right, a lesson he never forgot,

(b) who was ever so proud of being an Elphinstonian and of which college he was a Dakshina Fellow and for almost 40 years a Trustee,

(c) who under the influence of the likes of Prof. A. C. Covernton and Prof. E. A. Wodehouse developed an abiding love of English Literature, more so poetry, and till the end, one of his most joyful pastimes was reciting from memory, the English Poets,

(d) who, by association with Sir Patrick Geddes, the great sociologist, learnt that, "Great thoughts spring from the heart, but must be circulated through the head", and which ideology he carried with him both in his work and his personal life,

(e) who having majored in Philosophy, never tired of putting it to practice, and was the President of The Bombay Philosophical Society founded by his revered mentor Prof. J.C.P. d'Andrade,

(f) who with his stern exterior, as was expected of a man of books, had the genuine appreciation of the needs and necessities of others,

(g) who always rose to a deserving cause as evidenced by his being for 20 years or more a stanuch and active civil libertarian, and who started his destiny with law and its practice when he joined the Chambers of Sir Jamshedji Kanga in 1929.

The initial lean years notwithstanding Mr. Seervai strode the precincts of this Court like a colossus. His was the personality of a lawyer, in the true sense. He brought to law, as he said of his friend the late Mr. Karl Khandalavala, "gifted speech, a first class mind and an immense capacity for hard work".

Rao v/s. Advani, the Prohibition Cases, the *Chamarbaugwala Case, Sodhi Sukhdev Singh v/s. the State of Punjab, Keshav Singh Case, the Keshavananda Bharati Case, the Judges Transfer Case,* all come to mind.

Be it in the matters of the Indian Constitution before the Judges of the Supreme Court of India, be it in his appearances before the late Chief Justice Chagla, be it in the tax references before the late Mr. Justice N. A. Mody, be it in the matter of the celebrated land acquisition reference of Suleman Zaver before the Palekar and Kotwal Bench which eventually led to the amendment of the Land Acquisition Act, his was a point well taken, his was a balanced argument, his was a voice to reckon with and as late Mr. Justice Chagla said of Mr. Seervai in his remarkable autobiography *Roses in December* and I quote "Judges can always depend on him not to mislead them or to lead them astray".

To this brilliant lawyer recognition came in the form of his appointment as the Advocate-General of Maharashtra and he made the finest Advocate-General of his time and if I may make bold to say so, may be, of all times to come.

He undoubtedly has given to this Court some of its proudest moments.

His study of and keen insight into the Constitution of India is legendary and his book on the Indian Constitution bears testimony. The late Mr. Justice P. B. Gajendragadkar, in his book *To The Best of my Memory* says and I quote "It is a magnificent treatise on Constitutional Law and can be regarded as Seervai's gift to the legal world".

His authoritative knowledge on constitutional laws and principles of fundamental rights and liberties earned him invitations:

(a) from Lord Denning, to speak on "Some Aspects of Fundamental Rights" at Grey's Inn,

(b) from Prof. de Smith to lecture on "Equality under Article 14 in relation to Backward Classes" at Emmanuel College at Cambridge,
(c) from The University of Mexico to write a monograph on Federalism in India,
(d) from Prof. T. B. Smith to address the plenary Session of the 5th Commonwealth Law Conf. at Edinburgh on "The place of Law Officers & Ministers of Justice."

But that was not all. He not only interpreted and expounded the Fundamental Rights as laid down by the Constitution of India but he lived by them and he proved this, not because there was any need for him to do so, but because of his belief in upholding the principles of law and justice, when, at the peak of his career, he resigned as the Advocate-General.

And even then, to this man of letters and law, who never sought acknowledgements, acknowledgements came: — in 1972 the Padma Vibhushan, in 1981 the Dadabhai Naoroji Award, in 1982 the Corresponding Fellowship of the British Academy in the field of law and till date he is the only Indian to be so honoured, in 1992 Hon. Fellowhip of the Asiatic Society of Bombay and in 1994 the Living Legend of Law Award by the International Bar Association.

But above all he was a family man. And here, with Mrs. Seervai's permission, I quote her own words.

"50 years ago we set out, to lighten each other's path and liven each other's journey and so he has done for 50 years, keeping me always in happy laughter". His affection and respect for his wife, who was his companion of over fifty years and a constant source of inspiration, and for his three children and six grandchildren can be likened, in the lines of Wordsworth, his favourite poet, to, and I quote "The type of the wise who soar but never roam, True to the kindred points of Heaven and Home". In his home, surrounded by all his loved ones and amidst the peace only a happy family knows, he celebrated, on 6th December 1995, his golden year of marriage and the navjote of one of his grandchildren."

As years went by, we did not see of him in the Courts as much as one would have liked to, but whenever one did, those beautiful lines from James Elroy Flecker's poem on "Old Ships", which were inscribed to him by Mr. Khandalavala, came to mind and I quote "It was so old a ship, who knows, who knows? And yet so beautiful, I watched in vain, to see the mast burst open with a rose, and the whole deck put on its leaves again".

On the 22nd of January 1996 Mr. Seervai, on account of his failing health could not attend the meeting held at the Prince of Wales Museum to mourn the demise of his friend Mr. Karl Khandalavala but he caused a Tribute to be read out by his wife Mrs. Feroza Seervai, wherein, he stated and I quote "In his death, I and others like me, have lost a dear and warm hearted friend the like of whom we will not see again." Little did one know that four days later it would be our turn to say that in the death of Mr. Seervai we have lost a dear and a warm hearted person the like of whom we will not see again.

Our heartfelt condolences go out to Mrs. Seervai, Navroz, Meher and Shirin. Having blazed a brilliant trail, the flame has died. Farewell Mr. Seervai, May you rest in eternal peace!

H. M. SEERVAI — A TRIBUTE

Justice R. S. Pathak
Former Chief Justice of India and former Judge,
International Court of Justice (The Hague)
14 March 2005

THE IMAGE WHICH I shall always possess of Homi Seervai is that of a courageous knight in shining armour who had dedicated his life to protecting the purity of the administration of justice, to the upholding of its traditional values and to promoting a consistency in the policies and direction of judicial law making. That he achieved this in great measure was due to his personal qualities. Transparently loyal to the high principles he believed in, he was driven by a strong sense of duty, emboldened by the valour of his passion and his personal convictions. There was a nobility of classical quality in all that he did, emphasized by his deep sincerity and his fidelity to the ethics of professional life.

I did not know Seervai until quite late in life. But I often heard high praise of him from my father who confirmed the popular impressions of Seervai's reputation during his association with him when Seervai was led by my father in a case in the High Court of Bombay about the year 1957. Since then, they enjoyed a regard for each other, which only increased with the years. I came to know Seervai when he appeared in the *Needle Industries Case*[1] at its earlier stage and later when he appeared in *S. P. Gupta's Case*[2]. The first involved issues of commercial law, and

1. Needle Industries (India) Ltd. v. Needle Industries Newey (India) Holding Ltd. AIR 1981 SC 1298.
2. S. P. Gupta & Ors. v. Union of India & Ors. AIR 1982 SC 149.

on a difference between my senior colleague and me, was heard thereafter by a larger Bench (of which I was not a member). The second involved serious issues of far-reaching importance of constitutional law and vitally affected the constitutional position of the Chief Justices and Judges of the High Courts and of the Chief Justice of India. It was a privilege to hear Seervai's submissions. They would have matched the highest level of legal erudition and forensic distinction witnessed anywhere in the world.

By then Seervai's reputation as a lawyer had already spread far and wide. He was well-known for his single minded devotion to the brief he accepted, for his painstaking industry, reckless of the time and effort it cost him, his fearless and undaunted advocacy, and his authoritative exposition of the principles of law. In all this, he was fastidious to the point of perfection. To every cause he believed in applying his notable forensic abilities with a sincerity of purpose which excited the admiration of all who witnessed his endeavours. Frankness and honesty marked his every utterance, a directness of speech voiced every thought. The lure of high fees and public adulation mattered not to him nor indeed the unpopularity of the cause; excellence in the discharge of professional obligation was his only standard. The Courts came to respect him with a respect given to few.

And well they might. For he was extremely jealous of protecting their public reputation, anxious to see that the stream of justice flowed unpolluted, and ensured that no deviation, which came to his knowledge, remained uncorrected. Seervai saw in the traditional norms of judicial law-making the history of an evolution which gave to the process its unique effectiveness. In matters concerning the sanctity of judicial law making, therefore, he was keenly sensitive to the quality of the ethos affecting it. For that reason, he emphasized that counsel's primary duty was to assist in the administration of justice. Likewise, he attached the utmost importance to the values of intellectual honesty, independence and impartiality in the Judge. He would admit no exception in judicial functioning. To his exacting mind, no compromise was permissible. He was aware that injustice rankled like a festering wound, and irreparably affected the reputation of the judicial institution no less than the fate of the victim.

Among his numerous contributions to the development of the law, Seervai's *Constitutional Law of India* is perhaps his most enduring achievement. This monumental work, hailed the world over, is the product of a refined scholarly mind. It occupied among the best and most productive years of his life. It is a permanent testimony of his conception of the Rule of Law in the shaping of a constitutional democracy. The role of the judicial institution has been carefully assessed, and the views of various Courts in relation to Constitutional issues brought before them have been critically weighed, and when found wanting they have not been spared. Seervai's *Constitutional Law of India* is not a mere commentary of the usual kind. It is a searching, appreciative but at times scathing, analysis of what went into the judicial dicta. From another perspective, this great work represents the personal philosophy of the author as it emerges from his treatment of the subject in its various dimensions. His dedication to this personal testament was so complete that he compelled Death to wait until he had concluded the final page of the last volume of the last Edition. The next day he was gone.

The place of Homi Seervai as lawyer, jurist and constitutionalist in the rank of the immortals will remain ever secured.

MEMORIES OF H. M. SEERVAI

The Hon'ble Lord Mackay of Clashfern, M.P.

Former Lord Chancellor of England

I FIRST MET H.M. Seervai when he came to the Commonwealth Law Conference in Edinburgh in 1977. My wife and I had the privilege of entertaining him in our home. Our children were young and he amused them greatly by making the calls of a number of different birds most realistically to them without using any aids but his fingers. They were mystified, but tried to copy his feat. Although he gave them patient tuition they did not succeed in matching his skill.

He was the speaker at a plenary session of the Conference when he spoke on the House of Lords decision in *Gouriet* and related constitutional matters. Without a single note he spoke for nearly an hour in a most eloquent, lucid and penetrating manner on these intricate subjects. Every one present realised that he was a master of Constitutional Law.

I met him from time to time after that. When my wife and I were in India in 1987 he and his very talented wife entertained us in his hospitable home. I gave a talk in Bombay, as it was called then, and he gave a generous vote of thanks in which he said he esteemed Lord Reid the greatest lawyer of the twentieth century in Britain. He added that this view was taken on the strictly intellectual level. If popular appeal and communication skills were taken into account the accolade would go to Lord Denning.

His great work *Constitutional Law of India* is a permanent memorial to his massive erudition. He held strong views on the way in which the arrangements in India were developed. Although not everyone would agree with him no one could fail to admire the cogency and courage of his position.

With his passing the legal profession lost a brilliant and illustrious member.

MY MEMORIES OF H. M. SEERVAI

Justice Sujata Manohar
Judge (Retd.), Supreme Court of India and Chief Justice (Retd.)
Bombay High Court and Kerala High Court

My first introduction to Homi Seervai was as a philosopher who retained his love for philosophy but had distinguished himself in the field of law. He was a distinguished Elphinstonian. I was a student of Elphinstone College. After winning the F.G. Selby Memorial Prize of the Bombay University in the Intermediate Arts Examination in 1952, I decided to do my graduation studies in Philosophy with Sanskrit as an optional subject. When I went to see Dr. Chubb, Professor of Philosophy at Elphinstone College, he was delighted. He asked me whether I wanted to be a philosopher. I had to tell him, much to his disappointment, that I wanted to be a lawyer. "Oh, so you want to be like Seervai," he said. I learnt later that both he and Seervai had been very distinguished students of Professor J.C.P. d'Andrade, a renowned Professor of Philosophy, much loved by his students. From the prize money, one of the books I decided to buy was Professor d'Andrade's collection of essays *Philosophy and Life*. It was in this connection that I went to meet Seervai for the first time and with much trepidation, in his chambers. My fears were unfounded. He was charming. Of course he knew my father. But he was delighted that I was going to read philosophy and wanted the book of his beloved Professor. Since then, both Homi and Feroza Seervai have taken an interest in my activities and my "pursuits". I suspect that my father allowed me to opt for Philosophy instead of Economics for my B.A. because of his example.

Later, when I was looking for a good school for my young children, I happened to meet Feroza. I told her about my disappointment with some of the so-called 'best' schools in Bombay and told her that I wanted my children to receive education in the true sense and inculcate in them a love of learning, a love of literature and a critical and independent bent of mind. She told me that Homi and she and some parents who felt the same way, had just established a new school which I might like. That is how my eldest son Aneesh joined the newly established Bombay International School, despite warnings and discouragement of almost everyone we knew. Later my two other children also joined the same school. It was one of the best decisions I made.

By the time I joined the bar in 1958, Seervai was already Advocate General of Maharashtra. He was highly respected for his immense learning, a principled approach to life and law and his total dedication to his work. He disapproved of frivolity and lax morals. His two juniors Tehmtan Andhyarujina and Atul Setalvad were not allowed by him to accept any brief against the government, irrespective of whether they were briefed on behalf of the government or not. Both of them are now outstanding senior lawyers with a fine reputation for integrity and scholarship.

Listening to his arguments was a learning experience. His deep insight into law was a result of his knowledge of the history of every law, its evolution down the ages and its present form. This understanding of law with a historic perspective was particularly evident in the case of constitutional law. But as a result, his arguments in court tended to be elaborate — which was a source of joy for the young advocates but not always welcome to the judges. He was thoroughly prepared in every matter he argued, and he never accepted conflicting assignments in different courts. Nor did he charge fees for matters in which he did not appear.

To me he epitomized what an Advocate-General should be. He was a true leader of the Bar. Apart from his legendary knowledge of constitutional law, he was also a brilliant speaker. During his seventeen years as Advocate-General, Seervai as leader of the Bar spoke at Court References to pay tributes to some outstanding lawyers at the Bar and Judges. His speech on the occasion of the death of Sir Jamshedji Kanga, one of the greatest lawyers that the Bombay High Court has produced, was special. Seervai had belonged to the distinguished chamber of Sir Jamshedji Kanga and he spoke from the heart when he said, "... the debt which we owe to him is one which can never be repaid. There is only one way in which we can try to repay it a little and that is to ask ourselves every time whether the way in which we conduct ourselves at the Bar would meet with his approval, and would be in consonance with the exacting standards which he laid down for himself."

For almost my entire career at the Bar (except the last four years) he was the Advocate-General. As leader of the Bar, the Advocate-General was also the President of the Bombay Bar Association — until Seervai resigned as Advocate-General in 1974. The Bar Association discontinued the practice and started electing its own President. When Ramrao Adik was appointed Advocate-General after Seervai, he was not made the President of the Bombay Bar Association. Seervai's resignation was a result of a dubious maneuver by the Law Minister who appointed Ramrao Adik and Ajit Mehta — two "party lawyers", as Seervai put it — as Hon. Advisors for Legal Affairs and that too without consulting the Advocate-General. Seervai rightly interpreted this move as designed to undermine his authority, and resigned. This was in September 1974. On June 5, 1975, the President of India proclaimed an emergency on the sole advice of the Prime Minister Indira Gandhi. It deeply affected Seervai and brought a sea change in his attitude. In his words, "With every week that passed, the dark pall of tyranny seemed to descend inexorably over India." *(The Emergency, Future Safeguards and the Habeas Corpus Case)*. He defended the judiciary against attacks on its independence through transfer of judges from one High Court to another without their consent if their judgments were unwelcome to the government. He fought in the Supreme Court against Justice Sheth's transfer. His book, *The Emergency, Future Safeguards and the Habeas Corpus Case: A Criticism* eloquently expresses his deep concern. The jacket of the book carries a quotation from Wordsworth:

> "Enough if something from our hands have power
> To live, and act, and serve the future hour."

But the book which has secured for Seervai an abiding place in the hall of fame is his book *Constitutional Law of India*. He gave up all other work to concentrate on the book. His deep insight into constitutional law, his sharp and critical analysis of some crucial Supreme Court judgments and his forthright displeasure at unprincipled conduct, wherever he found it, makes the book a remarkable reading. He completed its fourth edition the day before he passed away and willed that there shall be no further edition of the book. I met him at his Golden Wedding celebration at PVM Gymkhana shortly before he died.

He called me aside and said that he had almost finished the fourth edition. But this time he would not give complimentary copies to any of the judges! "For one, they can now afford to buy it" (referring to improved service conditions of judges). I will not quote the other reason.

That celebration was special. Homi and Feroza lived for each other. All important decisions in his life were made only after consultation with Feroza and with her approval. Both have the stamp of extraordinary human beings. That is why, when Feroza asked me to read something in Homi's memory at one of the monthly meetings to remember him, I chose Hardy's tribute to Ramanujan, the amazing mathematical genius.

One can only say of him what he said of Sir Jamshedji Kanga, quoting from Milton's Paradise Lost:

> "Unmoved
> Unshaken, unseduced, unterrified,
> His loyalty he kept, his love, his zeal,
> Nor number, nor example with him wrought
> To swerve from truth or change his constant mind."

H. M. SEERVAI: A MAN OF CHARACTER, COURAGE AND COMMITMENT*

Tehmtan R. Andhyarujina
Senior Counsel, Former Advocate General of Maharashtra,
Former Solicitor General of India

H. M. Seervai was a renowned lawyer and the foremost authority on constitutional law in independent India. He was the author of the leading and widely-acclaimed treatise on the constitutional law of India. He held the post of Advocate-General of Maharashtra for 17 years with great distinction. All those achievements, doubtless, made Seervai a distinguished lawyer, but it was Seervai the man, with his sterling character and conduct, that made him the great personality that he was and gave him a unique eminence which none of his peers achieved.

---

* Re-published from *Constitutional Perspectives*, Universal Law Publishing Co. Pvt. Ltd.

I had the good fortune and privilege of being Seervai's 'devil' and of assisting him in several leading cases in which he appeared. Besides, he and my father (who was also a lawyer) were life-long friends for 80 years and Seervai's family and our family were close to each other. I was, therefore, acquainted with him in a way few of his friends and admirers were.

If I were asked to identify the outstanding qualities of Seervai as a man I would say that he was a man of character, great courage, conviction and integrity. He had the courage to practise and to say the plain truth and stand up for his principles disregarding any prospect of advancement. His courage flowed from his deep and ingrained philosophical principles of morality and righteousness which he had acquired from his family upbringing and from his teachers in school and at university. He often reminded his juniors of the words of Walter Scott, "Without courage there can be no truth and without truth there can be no other virtue." For Seervai there was no antithesis between success in life and adherence to moral principles. Indeed, he believed that eventually such principles contributed to the successful achivements of what a man set his heart on.

He believed in an idealistic notion of justice which governed, and prevailed in, a seemingly ill-ordered and unjust world. Few persons would have believed that Seervai, with such a pedantic and philosophical outlook, was carved out for a successful career in the highly practical and competitive legal profession. Yet, he proved by precept and example that the heights of the profession could be reached without compromising moral character and ethical conduct.

Commitment

Seervai was a man of enormous commitment. He believed that every person must have a commitment in life with which he had to work in total sincerity, honesty and devotion. A man without a sense of commitment was like a ship without a rudder and did nothing to progress himself or society. In whatever task he engaged himself, Seervai had a sincerity of purpose and total dedication — whether it was a case in court, the writing of his book, or advocacy of a cause in which he believed. His transparent sincerity and commitment to his case was his great strength as a lawyer. He confessed that he made a poor lawyer for a cause to which he did not subscribe. There were no half measures in whatever he set out to do. Given a task, he took it up with a single-minded application of mind setting aside all other work. He was incapable of doing more than one thing at a time — whether it was a case in court or producing an article or preparing a speech.

Unlike other successful lawyers of his day, he never accepted more than one brief at a time, refusing other briefs until the one in hand had been worked out.

Seervai's exposition of law, whether in court or in his book, was sometimes too personal and lacking in proportion. He was criticised for this but the sincerity of purpose, and the vigour and fervour with which a proposition was canvassed, commanded attention; in a lesser man, this would have been rejected out of hand. Appropriately, he inscribed in his book the stirring words of Jacob Brownowski: "The personal commitment of a man to his skill, the intellectual commitment working together as one, has made the Ascent of Man."

Complementary to these qualities was his inflexible rectitude and integrity. He believed that for most people religion was the bedrock of morality and ethics. Though not outwardly religious, he had an abiding faith in his Zoroastrian religion and lived up to its tenets of *'Humata, Hukhta, Hvarshta'* i.e., good thoughts, good words and good deeds. Early in my tutelage with him he inscibed on Lord Denning's Hamlyn Law lectures on *Freedom under Law*, one of the numerous books he presented to me, these words —

Be it written or be it oral,
'Tis only Law; to be moral,
To nobly live outside the Line
Is the ideal: make it thine.

Denning and Seervai had great admiration for each other. In some respects they had similar outlooks on religion and morality. When I requested Denning, during one of his visits to Bombay, to autograph this book, he read Seervai's incription on it and told me it was typical of Seervai to inscribe it as he did.

Humble Origins

Hormasji Maneckji Seervai was born on 5th December 1906 to a middle class Parsi family in Bombay. He matriculated from the Bharda New High School, Bombay, and entered Elphinstone College, Bombay, in 1922, graduating in 1926 with a first class degree in Philosophy. He and his wife, Feroza, were students of a distinguished teacher of Logic and Philosophy, Prof. J.C.P. d'Andrade, who had become a legend in his own lifetime. Long after his college days, Seervai retained a love for philosophy and was for several years an active member of the Bombay Philosophical Society. He was appointed a lecturer in English at Elphinstone College where he also became a fellow for two years.

He did his LL.B. from the Government Law College and in 1932 joined the Chambers of the then doyen of the Original Side of the Bombay High Court, Sir Jamshedji Kanga, who was also the Advocate-General of Bombay.

Seervai had no family or other connections in the legal profession to push him in active practice. In those days it was usual for a lawyer to wait, briefless, at the Bar for several years until he made it good. At that time the Original Side of the Bombay High Court had outstanding lawyers like F. J. Coltman, Sir Jamshedji Kanga, Sir Nusserwanji Engineer, Bhulabhai Desai, Chimanlal Setalvad, V. Taraporewala and K. M. Munshi, all of whom dominated the profession. Seervai himself had to wait for nearly seven years before being recognised, but never for a moment did he doubt that he would make it good at the Bar once his ability was recognised.

Early in his professional career he showed his fearlessness when he felt that a certain senior judge of the High Court was favouring his son by running down the son's competitors. Seervai took up the cause of the Bar and demanded that the Chief Justice should move the judge from his then assignment to another, which the Chief Justice eventually did. Later, Seervai opposed the giving of a reference to the judge when he was elevated to the Supreme Court.

Older members of the Bar recall that Seervai was conspicuous in the Bar library by his ebullience and confident and emphatic pronouncements on cases and on the issues of the day. He had a remarkable self-assurance in his own opinion and judgment. He was gifted with an extraordinary memory and would recall entire passages of English prose and the poetry of Milton, Wordsworth, Keats and Tennyson with ease. He had a sure command of the English language and a quick, logical and incisive mind and a hatred for superficiality.

There was hardly any litigation in constitutional law prior to the advent of the Indian Constitution in 1950. Seervai, like the rest of lawyers at the Bombay Bar, busied himself in commercial law litigation which thrived in the city of Bombay. Strangely, he confessed that initially he had no inclination for constitutional law, a field in which he later distinguished himself. His logical mind found more attraction, he said, in the law of evidence and contract law.

Prohibition Cases

In the early 1950s, the Government of Bombay's prohibition laws came under attack in the State's High Court. In an important case,

Seervai was engaged as a junior by the Government to defend the Bombay Prohibition Act with the then Advocate-General, Mr. C. K. Daphtary. Seervai told me that Daphtary, who relished his peg of whisky every evening, had really no heart in defending the Government's stand. At a Bar function in 1950 to celebrate Republic day, Daphtary as Advocate-General is reported to have joked that a republic without a pub was only a relic! On the other hand, Seervai was a lifelong teetotaller who detested alcohol and had seen families ruined by the evil of drinking. So, defending such a cause was natural to his inclination. It fell to Seervai's lot to make the final speech in the case. He did it with great vigour and conspicuous success. The then Chief Minister of Bombay, Morarji Desai, was a moralist and fanatical believer in prohibition. Though temperamentally apart in their outlooks, Morarji Desai saw in Seervai the right defender for the Government's actions in unpopular causes like prohibition and the requisitioning of premises. Seervai was, thereafter, much sought after as Counsel for the Government in a number of cases.

In 1956 Seervai was briefed to defend the Government of Bombay's decision to ban prize competitions, which were in reality lotteries, in the case of *R.M.D. Chamarbaugwala v. State of Bombay*[1]. Seervai was unsuccessful both in the trial court and in the appeal court in Bombay which held that the ban was illegal. Undaunted, Seervai advised an appeal to the Supreme Court. The Government's appeal came up before a Constitutional Bench of the court.[2] The Government attached considerable importance to this appeal and, therefore, briefed C. K. Daphtary, who had by then become the Solicitor-General of India, with Seervai as his junior. By a stroke of good luck for Seervai, Daphtary was not prepared to argue the case when it reached hearing and it fell to Seervai to conduct the appeal. Seervai was completely prepared and only too eager to argue the case. He did it with total dedication for several days and with spectacular success. The case involved difficult and complicated questions of extra-territorial operation of State laws, interpretation of legislative entries in the Constitution, the scope of the fundamental right to carry on business in gambling, inter-state trade and commerce and the question of severability of unconstitutional statutes. Seervai was opposed by a formidable galaxy of lawyers, including M. C. Setalvad, the then Attorney-General for India, Sir Nusserwanji Engineer, N. A. Palkhivala and others. Single-handedly as

1. AIR 1956 Bom 1.
2. (1957) SCR 930: AIR 1957 SC 699.

usual, Seervai argued for the constitutionality of the ban. The Supreme Court unanimously set aside the judgments and orders of the Bombay High Court with costs throughout.

Advocate-Generalship

The post of Advocate-General of Bombay was a distinguished one. Its origins could be traced back to as early as the East India Company's times and the office had been occupied by only the leading practitioners of the Original Side Bar of Bombay. Seervai's own senior, Sir Jamshedji Kanga, had occupied it for 13 years. The Advocate-General by virtue of his office was also the leader of the Bar. When the office became vacant in 1957, Seervai was offered it and he accepted. Seervai held this office with great distinction for 17 years. During those years, he devoted himself almost exclusively to State Government work, though according to the terms of his retainer, he was free to appear for private parties in all cases except those to which the Government was a party.

The Legal Department of the Government of Bombay of those days was a highly competent one and was headed by a Remembrancer of Legal Affairs who was fit to be a High Court judge. Seervai's opinion was sought in several difficult and delicate matters in which the Government was involved. Sometimes, Ministers desired legislation or action whose legality was doubtful, merely to please their constituencies. At such times, the legal department, not being able to prevail over the Minister, turned to Seervai for his opinion. Such was his stature that his opinion casting doubts on the legality of any proposed action usually silenced the controversy and politicians and Ministers readily accepted it without demur. He was quite indifferent to the fees he received. At a time when other seniors at the Bar made handsome incomes, Seervai's income was modest. It seems ludicrous, but by the terms of his retainer the Advocate-General was not paid for any Government brief on the Original Side, unless it was recovered by way of costs, and only Rs. 150 per day per brief on the Appellate Side

Seervai was able to maintain the high stature of his constitutional office and his own position as he was not a political appointee and did not consider himself one. The makers of the Constitution, adopting the provisions relating to the Advocate-General from the Government of India Act 1935, had stressed that the Advocate-General should be a person of independence and standing and, unlike the office of Attorney-General in the United Kingdom, the Advocate-General's office should not be a political office. They stated that the Advocate-General should have no political affiliations with the Government of the day, and the person selected should have the confidence of successive Governments who would retain his appointment, irrespective of the political fortunes of the Government or Governments with which he may be associated during his tenure of office. Seervai was a law officer in that mould.

Governments came and went but Seervai did not feel it necessary to resign with the installation of a new Government nor did any new Government ask for his resignation. This was because Seervai remained above the dust and din of politics. Indeed, barring the Chief Minister and the Law Minister, he knew no Minister or political functionary. Such was his professional standing that in important consultations the Minister-in-charge came to Seervai for consultation in his Chambers. The only exception he made was in a rare case when the Chief Minister required his advice in a matter of great delicacy; on such occasions, Seervai would meet the Chief Minister in the latter's office in the Secretariat. This detachment from politicians and from the Government of the day was his strength.

In an address delivered to the 5th Commonwealth Law Conference in Edinburgh in July 1977 on 'The Place of Law Officers and the Ministers of Justice' — an address which, incidentally, was applauded by English observers as a masterpiece — Seervai gave what has been described as a "magisterial repudiation of the heresy that a Government lawyer must be committed to the philosophy of the Government which employs him."[3] He refused to defend those policies of the Government which he felt were unconscionable and against his convictions. He refused the Government's brief when it sought to ban the teaching of English in Anglo-Indian schools, believing that the policy was wrong. He did not think it right to defend the erection of a 'martyrs' memorial' in Bombay in honour of States formed on the basis of languages.

Constitutional Law of India

On the other hand, where he was not constrained by his personal convictions of inequity, no more redoubtable defender of the Government's power and privileges could be found than Seervai. In *State of Punjab v. Sodhi Sukhdev*,[4] he vigorously defended the

3. C. Kemp Davison in (1977) 22 LSS 300.
4. (1961) 2SCR 371: AIR 1961 SC 493.

Government's privilege of not disclosing documents on the ground of it being injurious to the interest of the State. In the celebrated case of *K.M. Nanavati v. State of Bombay,*[5] the Governor of Maharashtra had exercised his power of pardon to suspend the sentence of life imprisonment on the appellant, Commander Nanavati, pending the hearing of an appeal to the Supreme Court. This action was challenged in the High Court. Seervai successfully defended it before a Special Bench constituted to hear it and the Governor's action was upheld. However, the Supreme Court by a majority judgment set aside the Governor's action on the ground that it trenched on the court's power of entertaining the appeal. Seervai was convinced that the majority opinion of the Supreme Court was egregiously wrong. As he listened to the powerful dissent of Mr. Justice Kapur in that case, Seervai felt that the time had come for him to write a critical commentary on the court's decisions. For several years Seervai had felt that there was great need for a book on the Constitutional Law of India similar to the work of Dr. Wynes on the Australian Constitution. Thus was born the idea of what he later considered his life's greatest achievement — his book on the *Constitutional Law of India,* over which he laboured for 35 years to eventually produce four editions.

When Seervai began writing his book in 1961 he underestimated the task as he believed he knew most of the law to be written. It took him six years to publish the first edition. The last chapter on Amendments to the Constitution was written within a few weeks of the *Golak Nath Case.*[6] Seervai made a devastating criticism of the majority judgment of Chief Justice Subba Rao in that case which, incredibly, held that the power to amend the Constitution was an ordinary legislative power to be found in the residuary entry of the Union Legislative list and that a constitutional amendment was subject to Fundamental Rights. The Fundamental Rights could, therefore, not be amended at all. The judgment was hailed as a great libertarian achievement of the Supreme Court, but it was legally indefensible. Seervai exposed the fallacies in the judgment with withering criticism.

I consider the first edition of Seervai's book as the best of his writings. When the book was published, it was proclaimed a masterpiece. Nothing like it had been written in India before. Distinguished academicians abroad and in India hailed it. Geoffrey Wilson, reviewing the book in the *Cambridge Law Journal,* said of it "To

5. (1961) 1 SCR 497: AIR 1961 SC 112.
6. *I.C. Golak Nath v. Punjab* (1967) 2 SCR 762: AIR 1967 SC 1643.

read [the book] is like cramming years of training in the busy Chambers of an important practitioner..." Another reviewer, A. W. Bradley, writing in the *Law Quarterly Review* said "The author... is an undoubted master of Indian Constitutional Law." Professor P. K. Tripathi said that it was "one of the greatest books of the present decade."

Seervai insisted that his book would be a 'critical commentary'. He said in his preface in a Socratic dialectical way, "The cause I serve is that of a correct and coherent interpretation of our Constitution. If any of the criticisms are found to be correct, the cause is served; and if any are found to be incorrect the very process of finding out my mistakes must lead to the discovery of right reasons or better reasons than I have been able to give, and the cause is served just as well." The book contained trenchant expressions of disapproval of Supreme Court judgments, sometimes even proffering the view that a particular judgment was "productive of great public mischief and ought to be overruled". Seervai's views were often cited in judgments of the Supreme Court and in that sense his purpose was served. But a highly personal approach of Seervai was always manifest in his writing. Towards the end, particularly in the fourth edition, Seervai seemed to have crossed the legitimate limits of criticism by becoming too personal in his criticism of judges and their judgments and being polemical and harsh. These were small blemishes in the monumental achievement of a man who devoted all his energies and talents to the book's production for the better part of his professional life. For his efforts he was made a Corresponding Fellow of the British Academy, a distinction not yet conferred on any other Indian in the field of law.

Seervai believed that no one would have the competence, independence or industry which he had brought to editing the book, and that anyone who attempted the task would mar his life's work. He therefore, willed in his last testament that, after his death, no new edition should be published. As a result, the book is likely to become dated as far as the case law is concerned. Despite this, it will have an enduring value as a brilliant and lucid exposition of the basic principles of Indian constitutional and administrative law. His son, Navroz, who wrote a moving preface to the third volume of the last edition after his father's death has aptly described the epitaph of Sir Christopher Wren by his son inscribed on his tomb in St. Paul's Cathedral as applicable to Seervai's book:

'Sic monumentum requiris circumspice'
(If you would see his monument, look around).

Courage

Seervai was a man of great courage. In 1964 the High Court of Allahabad came in conflict with the Uttar Pradesh Legislative Assembly over the exercise of the latter's privileges. Two judges of the Allahabad High Court, in ignorance of the privileges of the legislature to commit for contempt, released one Keshav Singh on bail when he was summoned for contempt by a warrant of the Assembly. The Assembly thereupon resolved that the two judges and the Counsel for Keshav Singh were guilty of contempt as well and that they should be taken into custody and brought before the Assembly. In a spectacular show of solidarity the High Court sitting (or rather standing because there was no place on the dais!) as a bench of 28 judges, ordered the stay of the warrant of the Assembly. The ensuing confrontation led to a Reference by the President of India to the Supreme Court for its advisory opinion as to the correct legal position concerning legislative privileges.[7]

It was obvious that the Assembly would be at a disadvantage to justify its action before the judiciary, however sound the action may be in law. The Assembly had, therefore, to secure the services of an advocate who would fearlessly defend its actions and its privileges before the judges. The Speaker of the Assembly, Mr. M. M. Verma, had been advised that only an eminent English QC who could defend the Assembly's privileges with sound knowledge of the law and custom of Parliament, should be engaged. However, the Speaker had heard of Seervai as a fearless advocate. He and several members of the Assembly therefore, came to Bombay for consultations. I remember that meeting very well. After consulting him, the Speaker was convinced that Seervai was the right person to defend the Assembly's privileges. He requested him to accept the Assembly's brief. Seervai on his part assured the Speaker that he would not flinch from making any argument to defend the privileges of the Assembly, however unpopular it may appear to the Court. Thereafter, Seervai gave up all other work for the preparation of the case. I was briefed to appear with him. Seervai and I devoted the entire summer vacation for the preparation of an exhaustive statement of case.

Seervai kept his promise to the Speaker. He took the Court by surprise by boldly stating that by appearing for the Assembly he was not submitting its privileges for examination by the court but was only present to apprise the court of the law and custom of Parliament. If this position was not acceptable he would withdraw from the case. He

7. President's Reference No. 1 of 1964 (1965) 1 SCR 413: AIR 1965 SC 745.

maintained that a general warrant issued by the Assembly was not examinable for its cause by any court.

Of all the cases in which Seervai appeared, I consider Seervai's performance in that case to be the most masterful and brilliant of his career. At one stage, in an electrifying moment full of tension, Justice J. C. Shah asked what would be the position if the Court quashed the Legislature's warrant and ordered the release of a person who was arrested by the Legislature for its contempt. Seervai boldly replied that as the Court's order was a nullity it would have to be ignored.

Attorney-Generalship

In 1971 Seervai was offered the post of Attorney-General for India. He turned down the offer because he believed he would be able to make a greater contribution by working on successive editions of his book. Declining the offer with thanks, he wrote in his own hand to the Law Minister: "It seems to me that my best contribution to Constitutional and Administrative law in our country does not lie in my arguing Constitutional cases before the Supreme Court and before various High Courts — exciting and financially remunerative as such arguments can be. The best contribution that I can make is to embody in the successive editions of my book the result of much reflection and careful and patient analysis of judicial interpretation of the Constitution." I cannot think of any other lawyer declining such a high office for the sake of a commitment to expounding and correcting the law.

The *Fundamental Rights Case*

In an assertion of its plenary power to amend the Constitution and to reverse the *Golak Nath* judgment, Parliament enacted the 24th and 25th Amendments to the Constitution. The Government of India's strategy was that, when these amendments were challenged in the Supreme Court (as they inevitably would be), the correctness of the *Golak Nath* decision would necessarily have to be decided. Such a challenge was not long in coming. When it came — in *Kesavananda Bharati v. State of Kerala*[8] — the Supreme Court constituted the largest ever bench of 13 judges to consider it. The then Law Minister, Mr. H. R. Gokhale, and the Minister for Steel and Mines, Mr. Mohan Kumaramangalam, both well-known lawyers, were entrusted by the Prime Minister, Mrs. Indira Gandhi, with the task of effectively defending the two Acts and reasserting Parliament's supremacy. They both believed that Seervai

8. (1973) Supp. SCR 1: AIR 1973 SC 1461.

who had written in the first edition of his book that the *Golak Nath* judgment was "clearly wrong and productive of the greatest public mischief and should be overruled at the earliest opportunity," would be the best lawyer to expound Parliament's case in court and not the then Attorney-General for India, Mr. Niren De, who, though an able lawyer, had unfortunately been on the losing side for Government in successive important cases such as *Golak Nath*, the *Bank Nationalisation Case*[9] and the *Privy Purses Case.*[10]

Seervai accepted the brief only on the condition that he would open the case on behalf of the Respondents. Seervai rather naïvely believed that, as the State of Kerala was the first Respondent and the Union of India the second Respondent, Government of India should ask the State of Kerala to brief him and he would have the first strike. Accordingly, Seervai was briefed for the State of Kerala.

When the case was called out, there was perceptible tension between Niren De and Seervai as Niren De believed that it was his right as the Attorney-General for lead the defence. Both sat on the first row of Counsel for the Respondents, Niren De by right occupying the first place as Attorney-General and Seervai beside him but each not conversing with the other.

Nani Palkhivala opened the case for the Petitioners, and argued for over three weeks. As the differences between Seervai and Niren De became known, this was exploited by the Petitioners' side, who frequently referred to the different approaches of the Union of India and the State of Kerala in their statements of case. Seervai turned to the Law Minister and said that he would walk out if the impasse was not resolved. Matters would have taken an ugly turn if the problem was not resolved before the Respondents were called upon to reply. However, behind the scenes, the Prime Minister was able to persuade Niren De to relent. I had become quite friendly with Niren De during the hearing of the case. One day he called me and said that he understood that Seervai was very keen to open the case. He said Seervai should be assured that he would have the first opportunity but the method of doing that should be left to him. I communicated the message to Seervai who said he would trust Niren De. I arranged a tea party in the chambers of Fali Nariman, who was then the Additional Solicitor-General of India. Both Seervai and De became quite friendly and the next day, to the discomfiture of the Petitioners, they presented a united front. When Palkhivala ended his arguments, Niren

9. *R. C. Cooper* v. *Union of India* (1970) 3 SCR 530: AIR 1970 SC 564.

10. *Madhav Rao Scindia* v. *Union of India* (1971) 3 SCR 9: AIR 1971 SC 530.

De rose to tell the court that as he had an important international legal conference to attend, he should be excused and would request his learned friend, Seervai, to open the Respondents' case.

Seervai began the Government's case by exposing the fallacies in the *Golak Nath* judgment. This was not too difficult as no one on the Petitioners' side seriously defended it. The new challenge, on the suggestion by Chief Justice S.M. Sikri, was based on there being implied limitations on the amending power rather than on the express limitations in the Constitution, such as Fundamental Rights. Seervai, though full of the subject, was not properly organised in his preparation for a case of this magnitude. He should have had the help of several lawyers to research the case, as well as clerical and other staff for logistical support. The presentation of this case required massive typing of extracts from books, journals and law reports as photocopying was not developed at that time. Consequently, Seervai was severely handicapped in his presentation. Though his arguments at times were brilliant, they lacked the consistency and smooth flow from topic to topic in the organised way which the case required. This exasperated some of the judges. By the time Seervai could address a reply on the most important topic of implied limitations, the time allotted to him by the Chief Justice was over. On the other hand, Niren De had prepared his case well in advance with extensive volumes of documents. Niren De's performance was, I must say, superior as he was more organised and better prepared.

At the conclusion of a five-month trial marked by obvious dissensions amongst judges which became evident in Court at times, and much bitterness between the rival sides, a summary of the views of the majority of 7 judges was given by the Chief Justice. One of the conclusions was — "Article 368 does not enable Parliament to alter the basic structure or framework of the Constitution." Four of 13 judges refused to sign the summary as they believed that it was not for the Chief Justice and judges to summarise the effect of several judgments. It was very doubtful whether the several judgments of 7 judges which held that the power of amendment was limited for differing reasons led to this conclusion. Seervai himself maintained that a summary signed by 9 judges had no legal effect and was not the law declared under Article 141 of the Constitution. But the excesses during the 1975-77 Emergency, and the reality of actual abuses of the amending power by, for example, the introduction of Article 329A to validate Mrs. Indira Gandhi's election, made Seervai change his view and in later editions of his book he subscribed to the view that the doctrine of the basic structure was the only one which supplied an answer to the abuse of the amending power.

Resignation as Advocate-General

In 1974 Seervai came in conflict with the Law Minister of Maharashtra who wanted to dislodge him from the office of Advocate-General, but could not do it openly. His position as Advocate-General was, therefore, sought to be undermined collaterally by a number of steps taken by the Minister. Rather than submit to this, Seervai resigned. Seervai went to the press indicting the Law Minister. In an unseemly controversy, the latter retaliated with much economy of truth, ironically accusing Seervai, of all things, of having amassed large amounts by way of fees over several years! So much for gratitude by the State for a law officer who had devoted all his time and energy to loyally serve the Government for 17 years! Despite this unfortunate ending of an exceptionally successful tenure as an Advocate-General, Seervai carried no bitterness towards the Government. Almost twenty years later, I sought his views about accepting the same office when it was offered to me. To my great surprise, he heartily encouraged me to accept it saying that the Government needed an able non-political lawyer to advise it, but he cautioned me that I should not give any oral advice but always insist on giving my advice in writing.

Independence of the Judiciary

In June 1975 Mrs. Indira Gandhi suddenly declared a national state of emergency in the country after the Supreme Court had declined to fully stay her disqualification as a Member of Parliament following a successful challenge to her election on grounds of corrupt practices. Surprisingly, Seervai initially believed that it was about time that some stern measures were taken to control the Opposition, which had started a campaign of destabilisation and disobedience of laws and obstruction of meetings of State legislatures. But as the brutal suppression of freedom of speech and other civil liberties and the incarceration of hundreds of persons under preventive detention laws came to be known, and Seervai's own friends and family members vehemently criticised them, he changed his views and became a strong critic of the Emergency. He did not take part in any public opposition to the Emergency, but when 16 judges were punitively transferred from one High Court to another for their fearless judgments in civil liberties cases with a view to terrorising other judges into submission, Seervai took up the cause in a petition which challenged such transfers in the Gujarat High Court. He stationed himself in Ahmedabad for the case for several weeks and, with typical devotion to the cause, argued that the Government's power to transfer a judge was not unlimited as the

Government had claimed and that the transfers were a *mala fide* exercise of power. The Gujarat High Court[11] held that the transfer of Justice S.H. Sheth, the petitioner in the case, was invalid because there was no consultation between the President and the Chief Justice of India, but it rejected the principal argument of Seervai that a transfer of a judge could only be made with the judge's consent.

The Government of India carried the case in an appeal to the Supreme Court.[12] The appeal was heard after the Emergency had been lifted. In the Supreme Court, the new Government conceded that there had been no justification for transferring Justice Sheth from the Gujarat High Court and agreed to transfer him back to that High Court. Though the petition would, in the circumstances, have had to be withdrawn, Seervai insisted that the Supreme Court should lay down the law on the transfer of judges. To his chagrin, the majority of the judges held that the consent of a judge was not required for his transfer. Nevertheless, Seervai made a significant contribution to the independence of the judiciary as the Supreme Court's judgment held that there was no unfettered right of the Government to transfer a judge and it was proved that the mass transfer of 16 judges was an attempt to terrorise independent judges, the like of which would never be repeated in future.

In 1981 the Government of India issued a circular requiring the consent of High Court judges at the time of their appointment for future transfer to another High Court at the discretion of the Government. The legal fraternity saw this as an act undermining the independence of the judiciary and challenged it in the Supreme Court of India. This challenge led to a host of far-reaching questions concerning the independence of the higher judiciary, particularly the meaning of 'consultation' between the Chief Justice and the President of India in the appointment of judges as provided for in Articles 124 and 217 of the Constitution, the power to transfer judges, and the confirmation of 'additional' judges as permanent judges.

Seervai led the principal arguments in that marathon case which occupied the Court for several months. The judgment in the case, *S.P. Gupta v. Union of India*,[13] held that the Government had the primacy in the appointment of High Court judges and the Chief Justice was only required to be consulted. It gave absolute power to the Government to reject the advice of the Chief Justice. This was a great disappointment to

11. *Union of India* v. *Sankalchand* (1976) 17 Guj. L. R. 1017.

12. (1978) 1 SCR 423: AIR 1977 SC 2328.

13. AIR 1982 SC 149: (1982) 2 SCR 365: (1981) Supp. SCC 87.

the Bar. The judgment was seen as a self-inflicted wound by the Supreme Court.

After the *Judges Case*, except for rare appearances in court, Seervai devoted himself almost exclusively to writing of the 3rd and 4th editions of his book. In between, he made a foray into constitutional history and wrote a monograph entitled *Partition of India: Legend and Reality* — a historical account of the transfer of power from the British to Indian nationalists.[14] Seervai drew heavily from the 12 volumes of Professor Nicholas Mansergh's monumental work, *The Transfer of Power, 1942-47*.[15] I doubt if any scholar has read these massive volumes with such thoroughness as Seervai did for his historical account. In the 3rd edition of his book on constitutional law, Seervai included this monograph as Chapter 1. Seervai demolished many popular myths and was critical of several nationalist leaders for their part in the partition of India. This required considerable courage. He was particularly severe on Lord Mountbatten's suppression of Lord Radcliff's Punjab Award and his hurry in bringing forward the date of partition, which cost the lives of tens of thousands in the riots which followed that event. Seervai wrote that history would judge these days as the infamy of Mountbatten. He also took up the cause of civil liberties as the President of the Bombay unit of the Peoples' Union for Civil Liberties and often spoke on public platforms in that cause.

Family Man and Loyal Friend

No account of Seervai would be complete without mentioning Seervai's love and devotion to his family and loyalty to his friends. Seervai was first and last a family man and drew his inner strength and inspiration from his family. Even in his busiest days, he would set aside time to chat and play with his children and help them with their studies. In his wife, Feroza, he had a companion of equal grit and determination who identified herself with everything Seervai believed and acted on in his life. It would be difficult to find a couple so totally matched to each other.

He hated disruption in his family life. In 1956 he declined the offer of a judgeship in the High Court, as that ran the risk of him being transferred out of Bombay. He declined to be a judge of the Supreme Court as it would involve keeping two households, in Bombay and Delhi.

14. Bombay: Emenem Publications, 1989.
15. London: HMSO, 1970.

He had no inclination to befriend people merely because they were influential or important, but for his old friends he had a touching loyalty and devotion regardless of their condition or status in life. Till the end of his life he and Feroza would visit my old father of 92 years out of devotion and friendship for him. Even when my father failed to respond to their conversation, they would keep the conversation going, promising to come the following week at the same time.

On 25 January 1996 Seervai, at the age of 89, wrote the last lines of the third volume of his last edition. The next day, he quietly laid down his life whilst he was watching one of his favourite films on video. It appeared as if he had only pulled on to accomplish his life's mission.

Tributes poured in from every corner following his death. A Full Court of the Bombay High Court assembled in the Central Hall of the High Court, the scene of many of his battles and triumphs, to pay tributes to a lawyer who had brought fame and distinction to it. The Supreme Court of India likewise paid its tribute in a Full Court reference. *The Times of India* carried a tribute to him entitled 'A beacon light is extinguished'. His friend Lord Denning wrote to me, "He was a great personality and one of the most learned I have met."

With his death an era in the legal world in India had come to a close. In the end, one cannot help feeling that there was something heroic about him. With his unfailing courage, his moral fibre, a deep and sincere commitment to any undertaking, and his natural talents, he had fought and secured for himself a leading position amongst his fellow men. Lawyers of great prowess have existed and no doubt will continue to thrive in India, but few will carve out a niche for all times as Seervai has done by the sheer force of his character, courage and commitment.

H. M. SEERVAI — IN RETROSPECT*

Tehmtan R. Andhyarujina
Senior counsel, former Advocate-General of Maharashtra
Former Solicitor General of India

THOUGH NOT AN ELPHINSTONIAN, in an indirect way Elphinstone College providentially played a part in my life. My association with Homi

* Re-published from *The Elphinstonian*.

Seervai came about because of his lifetime friendship with my father who was his contemporary in the Elphinstone College, and later at the Bar. For over 75 years my father and Seervai remained close and steadfast friends. There was something noble and touching in that friendship which came to an end only when both died within a year of each other, Seervai first at the age of 89 and my father a year later at the age of 93.

My father was born in an humble Parsi priest's family in Udwada. As a boy he was faced with considerable financial constraints and social backwardness but he educated himself with the help of scholarships and by residing with a poor relative in Bombay. He joined the Bharda High School in Bombay and after matriculation he joined the Elphinstone College. Seervai came from a middle class Parsi family in Bombay with a Western outlook. He and my father first met in the Bharda High School. Though my father was in many respects a contrast to Seervai, and held different views on contemporary politics, Seervai took to my father because he sympathised with the efforts of a struggling village youth who wanted to overcome his handicaps by the dint of hard work.

Later when I was associated with Seervai as his junior I came to know of many instances of Seervai's kindness and help to young persons who were struggling in life against adversity. Behind Seervai's seemingly elitist and haughty appearance was a very kind and loving disposition which revealed itself in his actions but never in lip sympathy.

On my father's part it was an admiration for Seervai's intellectual gifts of mind which attracted him to him. With his powerful memory, his ready recitation of English prose and poetry, his faultless English pronunciation and diction and command over the English language and his academic distinctions, Seervai was a model to emulate for him. Over the years Seervai became a friend of our family. Well after he had made a name for himself at the Bombay Bar, in his bachelor days he would spend whole Sundays in our home. As children, I and my sisters looked upon him with a kind of awe as he appeared to be such a superior person expressing strong irrefutable opinions. Yet he was full of fun and humour, and would joke and play with us. Many years later when I became his junior he would tell his little son Navroz that when I was a child of his age he had held me in his arms and thrown me up in the air. Navroz would mischievously ask him whether he continued to do that, and Seervai would relate his son's prattle to us with great glee.

Amongst his many endearing traits was his love for children. He had a favourite gimmick for attracting little children by imitating a bird by putting two fingers on his lips and making funny bird noises coming from his throat. It never failed to engross children. Once when he did that to a wonderstruck child, the child demanded that the birdie should be brought out.

When I passed out from the Law College, he felt he owed it to his great friendship with my father to invite me to his Chamber as his "devil". He had only recently been appointed the Advocate-General of Bombay. In his letter of invitation he warned me that there were no quick rewards in his chambers but there was always a good future for a junior in the Bar if he worked hard and that Government was in need of good lawyers. He knew that I would have no income for a long time. He therefore paid me a small but generous stipend of Rs. 160 every month for several years. I remained his junior for seventeen years appearing with him in several leading cases. If I have achieved anything in the profession it is because of Seervai's innate kindness and encouragement to me in those years.

He himself had to wait for several years before he made good at the Bombay Bar. However, there was not the slightest doubt in his mind from the very beginning that sooner or later his abilities would be recognised. People who knew him in his junior days spoke of his ebullience and his readiness to express his views emphatically and loudly in the Bar Library.

While he waited he saw lawyers of lesser merit forging ahead in the profession because of their connections. That did not bother him. He observed the quick ways of success which others adopted, but shunned them. Some at the Bar derided him as a philosopher and an academic. He did not mind that, he said. What he did mind was that they believed he was so innocent that he was not aware of the ways of the men of the world.

He brought to bear to a practical and highly mercenary, and at times an unprincipled legal profession, a moral eminence. The conspicuous traits of his personality were his transparent sincerity, commitment to his work, an indomitable courage to stand up and fight for the principles he believed in, and an inflexible rectitude in life.

He was totally sincere in his words and actions. He never knew the gentle art of flattery or dissembling. He was completely dedicated and committed to whatever work he undertook. For 17 long years he was the Advocate-General for the State of Bombay, later Maharashtra. No Advocate-General served the State so faithfully as Seervai did. In all his years as Advocate-General he appeared as a lawyer for private parties only in 4 or 5 cases though he had the liberty to appear in private cases.

At a time when his colleagues at the Bar were earning huge amounts, Seervai confined himself to a few cases each year and to a modest income and he was indifferent to monetary rewards in the profession. It is almost hard to believe today that the Advocate-General at that time was not paid at all for appearing for the State on the Original Side of the High Court, and was paid only Rs. 150/- per day for an appearance on the Appellate Side. For several years between 1971 to 1974 he stationed himself in New Delhi to appear for the State of Maharashtra in the Krishna Water Disputes Tribunal returning over the weekends to his home and family in Bombay. He dominated the proceedings of that Tribunal, and the substantial allocation of the waters of the river Krishna to Maharashtra by the Tribunal was due largely to his efforts. The people of the State of Maharashtra owe a debt of gratitude in perpetuity to this selfless man.

In the cases he appeared in, no effort was spared for their preparation. He would work in his High Court Chamber No. 24 on the first floor, which had accommodated so many earlier Advocate-Generals of the past, even on holidays and on Sundays. Until a case in hand was over, his mind would be completely engrossed in it — "gyrate over it" as he used to say — and he would refuse all other work during that time. He never took two briefs at the same time believing it was unfair to the client. Appropriately the man of commitment wrote on the title page of his monumental book on Constitutional Law the words of the scientific writer Bronowski: "The personal commitment of a man to his skill, the intellectual commitment and the emotional commitment working together as one, has made the Ascent of Man."

His advocacy was typical of his character. It was direct, blunt and never obsequious. He spurned what other lawyers lauded as "court craft" and was never known to mislead the court. He had the rare courage to stand up and tell the judge how egregiously wrong he was. In his long English tail coat of an English law officer, he presented a commanding figure. He looked every bit an English barrister of old, so much so that some of his colleagues addressed him till the end of his days as "Serjeant" — referring to the English title for certain designated Barristers.

His most brilliant performance was in the *Parliamentary Privileges Case* in the Supreme Court in 1964. He was selected to plead the case of the legislature in what essentially became a contest between the legislature and the judiciary because it was believed that only a man of his courage would be able to tell the judges that they did not have the powers which they claimed over the privileges of the legislature.

I remember how, in an electrifying moment full of tension in Court, he told the judges of the Supreme Court that their order was liable to be disregarded if they exceeded their jurisdiction. What a contrast to the feeble and pusillanimous advocacy of today's lawyers. He often reminded us "Without courage there can be no truth and without truth there can be no other virtue". Earlier he appeared for the State of Bombay to defend its prohibition policies. That came naturally and convincingly to him as he had a lifelong hatred for liquor and knew of its evils on family life.

In 1961 he decided to write his book on the Constitutional Law of India. When he conceived of the idea I think he underestimated the labour involved in it. Single handedly for over six years he put in hard and unremitting labour in it. When it was published in 1967 it was a masterly analysis of the Constitution and a critique of the case law. I consider the first edition of his book to be the best of his work. For the first time it analysed the Indian Constitution and exposed many popular myths on Constitutional theories. His treatment of the Supreme Court's decision in the *Golak Nath Case,* which was popularly hailed as a great charter of liberty, was full of fire and brimstone and exposed the judicial excesses in that decision. For more that 30 years he laboured over its four editions. The book was acclaimed as the most authoritative and valuable contribution to the subject of Indian Constitutional Law. It earned him the distinction of being elected a Fellow of the British Academy. Seervai himself considered the book to be his greatest achievement. in his illustrious career as a lawyer. Over the years the book became the overpowering mission in his life, side-tracking his forensic work as a lawyer.

In 1971 he declined Government of India's offer of the Attorney-Generalship for India because he believed he would make a greater contribution by working on successive editions of his book. Declining the offer with thanks he wrote to the Law Minister "It seems to me that my best contribution to Constitutional and Administrative law in our country does not lie in my arguing Constitutional cases before the Supreme Court and before various High Courts — exciting and financially remunerative as such arguments can be. The best contribution that I can make is to embody in the successive edition of my book the result of much reflection and careful and patient analysis of judicial interpretation of the Constitution". No lawyer in the world must have declined such a high office for his intellectual and emotional commitment to his work.

Twice he declined the honour of a Supreme Court judgeship, as he hated a disruption of his family life and home in Bombay. Seervai was intensely devoted to his family. However hard he worked in the day time in his chamber, he laid aside and forgot the burdens of office and litigation in his home. However burdened he was with his work, he set aside some of his time at home for his children and would read aloud to them the best of English literature and prose. He dedicated his book to his family with the moving words, "This book is dedicated to the memory of my father and mother the spirit of whose teachings animates its pages and to Feroza, Meher, Shirin and Navroz who willingly gave up their claim to the time which would have been theirs, in order that this book may be written". A Supreme Court judge who visited his home in Bombay told me that he could not help noticing the atmosphere of a happy family in his house. For Seervai this was the most gratifying compliment which could be paid to him and his family.

When Seervai died on 26 January, 1996 a void was created in the Bar. Though not an active practitioner at the age of 89, he had been the moral force in the profession for over fifty years. With him an era in the legal world of India ended. In a recent letter to me the doyen of English judges and lawyers, Lord Denning said of Seervai "He was a great personality and one of the most learned I have met".

When one of the tallest lawyers in the Bombay Bar, Invariarty died, his junior the great Sir Jamshedji Kanga, the then Advocate-General and Seervai's own senior recited Walter Scott's famous lines on the death of Pitt in a reference to Invariarty in the High Court. When Sir Jamshedji Kanga died, it fell to the lot of Seervai, the Advocate-General, in a full court reference to recite the same lines in a moving reference on the death of his revered senior. When Seervai died I recalled those lines in a tribute to him.

> Now is the stately column broke
> The beacon light is quench'd in smoke;
> The trumpet's silver voice is still
> The warden silent on the hill.

H. M. SEERVAI

Atul M. Setalvad

Senior Counsel

WHEN I WAS ASKED TO contribute a memoir of Mr. H. M. Seervai for *The Elphinstonian* I agreed to do so with reluctance as I was fully aware of my limitations and knew that I could not possibly do justice to such a man, a man with enormous interests, a man who was one of India's most outstanding lawyers, and a very distinguished scholar and Advocate-General.

H.M. Seervai, to first mention a bare outline of his very rich life, studied at the Elphinstone College where he was a student who participated in several extra-curricular activities, in particular the Covernton League. He then joined the Bar and was in the chamber of Sir Jamshedji Kanga, one of the greatest lawyers Bombay has produced; he soon distinguished himself at the Bar, becoming known for his thorough and meticulous preparation, and his absolute fairness; he soon started representing the State of Bombay and became the Advocate-General of Bombay. He held that post, titled Advocate-General of Maharashtra after 1960, till 1974. He had always been interested in philosophy, and found time, week after week, to participate in the meetings of the Bombay Philosophical Society. Similarly, he found, indeed, made, time to write the leading commentary on the Constitution of India. He was, however, a devoted family man and however busy he was, he always went for an evening walk with his wife Feroza, and read every evening to his children, Meher, Shirin and Navroz.

What I have said still does not cover everything about this man with such a rich and variegated life; he was widely read; he took a keen interest in current affairs; he was generous and interested in several charities; and however full his day, he could always find time to discuss a personal problem with a friend or give professional advice to a colleague at the Bar.

I was associated with him when I joined his chamber in 1958 as his junior; he was already the Advocate-General. In those days the person appointed as the Advocate-General was the leading advocate at the Bar, and Bombay was then, as now, the leading High Court in India. Seervai was already a pre-eminent lawyer and I was a raw junior. Yet, from the very day I met him, he talked with me as an equal. He loved to talk and the subjects could be wide-ranging: law, of course; literature; current affairs; with people knowledgeable on the subject (I was not) music; almost anything else. Within a few months of my joining him my respect for him as a lawyer grew and grew as I slowly became competent to judge his greatness; my respect for his integrity increased as I saw instance after instance of his devotion to the truth and his refusal to conceal a fact or avoid an awkward statement. Most of all, like every one who got to know him, I became fond of him for he was one of the most lovable men I knew. Fortunately, it was mutual! And it was not confined to me. My wife, and later, my children, became as fond of him as he was of them.

I was in Seervai's chamber for nearly 15 years, before I shifted to my own chambers. During that period, we met almost every day; chatted in the morning before Court; sat together for lunch; had tea and biscuits; and left together in the evening. What did I learn? Of course, I learnt a lot of law, much about advocacy, about the very high standards of ethics and integrity which ought to be observed at the Bar. What I experienced, and hope I have learnt, is his generosity: his readiness to give credit in open Court for some trivial or small point that I may have suggested; with typical generosity, he never referred to the far more numerous instances when my suggestion was quite irrelevant.

He was a formidable advocate but a truly outstanding lawyer. An advocate is admired for his style, his presentation, his persuasiveness. Seervai was very successful as he was thorough in his preparation and with his deep knowledge and phenomenal memory, could cope instantly with any question from the Bench. There were others at the Bar who, as advocates, were superior; one whose name immediately strikes me is C. K. Daphtary, who was so famous that juniors flocked to hear him. What made Seervai unique was his profound knowledge of the law. He became known for his study of Constitutional law but he was an expert in almost all branches of Civil Law: Charities, Trusts, Contracts, Company Law, Banking.

Seervai had a large opinion practice. This is a field different in many ways from appearing in Court and, perhaps, little known to lay persons. Clients want to be advised of the correct position in law, at times to know where they stand, more often, before they do certain things. They approach a lawyer who they know will devote enough time to analyse the problem in all its facets. Most of all, they want a lawyer who will give the correct opinion, not an opinion which will please clients. This is important: when a lawyer argues in Court, he makes submissions for the Court to accept; whilst no good lawyer will make a submission which he knows to be contrary to law, he is, after all projecting a stateable point of view, it being the responsibility of the judge to decide. When, however, a lawyer gives an opinion, he is expressing what he believes the law to be, and no lawyer ought to give an opinion unless he is convinced that it is correct. This is where integrity comes in and Seervai with his knowledge of the law, willingness to work long hours and very high standard of integrity made an outstanding opinion lawyer.

His reputation in Bombay, however, was really built up because he maintained these standards of integrity when he appeared for the Government, initially as private Counsel and later, as Advocate-General. On countless occasions, he refused to defend illegal, arbitrary or even unjust Government orders. If he came across such cases, he fearlessly expressed his opinion in writing, and his advice was accepted. He became, also, a great source of comfort to the honest civil servant. I remember a case when the then Chief Minister wanted to transfer valuable land at Tardeo earmarked for the B.E.S.T. to private developers. The officers concerned brought this proposal to Seervai's notice; he promptly despatched a note; and the suggestion died. This was not the only such instance.

By 1974, he had become an institution; Chief Ministers and Ministers came and went; he had always been there. And no Chief Minister or Minister had the courage to act contrary to his advice.

The law, Seervai always maintained, was a profession, not a trade. And he always maintained the traditions of a profession. A professional owes a duty to himself to maintain certain standards. He refused to argue an unsustainable point of law; he always marked very modest fees in spite of being told that the client was rich or the stakes were high.

He decided to write on the Indian Constitution. The result was a masterpiece, now in its fourth edition, and running into three massive volumes. He devoted to this work many years of his life, and even gave up a very lucrative practice to do so. His interests in the field led him to make a study of the eventful years of 1946-47, and he was so incensed about what he saw as a distortion of the truth in the popular accounts of the period that he incorporated in his book a long Chapter on the Transfer of Power in India which expresses a wholly different point of view.

All his life, he was fond of literature, particularly poetry. But his tastes were truly catholic. He had read Conan Doyle and Wodehouse, and every book written by Churchill. He maintained that Gandhiji's Autobiography was a masterpiece of English writing. In casual conversation he often related an apposite quotation from "Bertie" or "Holmes" or "Winnie". And, there were quite a few occasions when during the course of arguments in Court in a heavy Constitutional Law matter there was a long quotation from Wordsworth.

He was devoted to his family and children; indeed, he loved all children, and would spend minutes with a child playing with it.

He was always proud to have been a student of the Elphinstone College, regarding it as a great college, and for many many years took a very active interest in its affairs and was a Trustee of its Endowment Fund. The Elphinstone College has produced many great men and women; Seervai was certainly one of them.

HOMI SEERVAI — A PERSONAL TRIBUTE

Soli J. Sorabjee
Senior Counsel, Former Attorney-General for India

No single expression or sentence can do justice to the many splendoured personality of Homi Seervai. He was post-independent India's greatest jurist. Seervai's claim to fame truly rests on his monumental work, *Constitutional Law of India,* which in the words of Lord Bingham "has an assured place among the great legal treatises of the world".

For Seervai this work was his mission in life. He spent months in its preparation: checking all the cases himself, re-drafting the text several times and ensuring there were no errors in printing. He was so totally absorbed in this mission that if you happened to meet him during that period you could be sure of an erudite dissertation on some article of the Constitution and how the Supreme Court had made a mess of the Constitution by some of its recent judgments.

The first time I set eyes on Homi Seervai was in 1946 at a meeting of the Bombay Philosophical Society. He and his wife Feroza were engaged in an animated discussion with other members. The next occasion was in 1950 in the Bombay High Court which was considering the constitutionality of the Bombay Prohibition Act. The Government team was led by C. K. Daphtary and Seervai was the junior counsel in the case. Somehow it fell to his lot to give the final reply. Thanks to his forceful advocacy he persuaded a hostile court to hold in the Government's favour on some points.

I first came to know Seervai in June 1953 when I joined the great Jamshedji Kanga's chambers, the nursery of many eminent lawyers. At that time there were two rising stars on the legal firmament, Homi Seervai and Nani Palkhivala. Seervai's thorough preparation, powerful personality and mastery of the English language made him an irresistible opponent. Yet he was kind to juniors who opposed him in Court and gave them generous guidance and encouragement.

Seervai frequently appeared for the Government. Of his several brilliant forensic performances the *RMDC Case* in the Supreme Court can rate as the finest. He was rightly proud of his success and there was hardly any case in which he appeared in which reference was not made to that judgment, one of the endearing idiosyncrasies of this genius.

On 1st July 1957 he assumed office as the Advocate-General of Bombay, an office which he held for 17 years with great distinction and dignity. He added lustre to the office.

Of Seervai's many qualities courage was the most outstanding. In his treatise on the Constitutional Law of India he severely and somewhat harshly criticised some judgments of the Supreme Court without caring for the consequences. He was fearless. He complained to Chief Justice Chagla about what he perceived was judicial misbehaviour by senior Justice N.H. Bhagwati in the Bombay High Court and also opposed the proposed reference to the judge on his elevation to the Supreme Court. Years later he came down heavily on his son, a sitting judge of the Supreme Court, Justice P. N. Bhagwati, for his fulsome letter to Mrs. Indira Gandhi after her landslide victory in the 1980 elections and which was reproduced in his *Constitutional Law of India*. Soon thereafter he appeared in the famous Judges case, *[S.P. Gupta]* before a seven judge bench presided over by Justice P. N. Bhagwati, who treated him with unfailing courtesy. Unfortunately the judgment went against Seervai and thereafter Justice Bhagwati was beyond redemption. Seervai had strong likes and dislikes.

Seervai and I often appeared on opposite sides. Sparks did occasionally fly in court. In the *Hall's Wine Case* in the Bombay High Court, Seervai, a teetotaller, demolished our stand that Hall's Wine was not liquor but a nutritious product outside the mischief of the Bombay Prohibition Act. Considerable heat was generated during the hearing of the celebrated *Keshavanand Bharati Case* in the Supreme Court when Seervai derided our arguments about the basic structure of the Constitution. Although firm in his beliefs, Seervai was not obdurate. He was willing to learn by experience and change his views in the light of subsequent events as he did in accepting in his *magnum opus* the correctness of the Supreme Court decision in *Keshavanand Bharati*. Seervai initially believed that stern measures ought to be taken to control the opposition forces, which had in 1974 started in his perception a campaign of destabilisation and disobedience of laws. When the excesses committed during the spurious 1975 June emergency became known, he became its trenchant critic.

I was associated with him during the hearing of the Judges Case [*S. P. Gupta*] in the Supreme Court. The hearing of the case, with intermittent breaks, lasted for nearly four weeks. That was the last time I had the pleasure of working closely with Seervai: Long conferences in the evening, settling frequently revised submissions in the morning, exchanging case law, and discussing strategy was a stimulating experience. During his free time in the evening he would sometimes come home and enjoy the L.Ps. which had recitations of his favourite poems and prose pieces. Palgrave's Golden Treasury was our mutual favourite. He particularly enjoyed Claire Bloom's recitation of Keats' Ode to the Nightingale.

Justice Frankfurter's advice to a young man who wanted to join the legal profession was that the best way to prepare for the law is to come to the study of the law as a well-read person and by cultivation of the imaginative faculties by reading poetry and listening to great music. Seervai did not need any such advice. His mind was well stocked with literature and philosophy, his twin loves, apart from the law. He also enjoyed good music. Although Seervai's first love was philosophy his knowledge of literature was immense and his memory was phenomenal. He could recite from memory passage after passage from Grey's Elegy or the sonnets of Shakespeare.

Seervai practised law in a grand manner, not as a tradesman operating on the basis of demand and supply. He would have been shocked by the savage fees charged by some senior advocates incommensurate with the work and effort involved in the preparation and presentation of the case. Greed was alien to his nature. His professional career, his principles and ethical practices remind us about the nobility of the legal profession. He belonged to a generation which cherished the ideals of truth, goodness and beauty and approximated them in his daily life.

When Seervai joined the Bar the waiting period was long. He declined offers of lucrative jobs following his mother's advice to continue in the profession and to "be not afraid because short-cuts and compromises are not open to you". Seervai acted on that sound advice throughout his life. He made no compromises, took no short-cuts.

It was indeed a good fortune to be in the intimate circle of Seervai's friends. In a sense he endorsed Madame D'Epinay's sentiment in her letter to Rousseau that "We should love our friends as true lovers of art love pictures; they keep their eyes fixed on the good points and do not notice the others". His affection and loyalty for his friends was boundless. He regularly visited his old and dear friend, the late Rustom Andhyarujina, and especially during periods of illness. When I was

Attorney General in 1989-90 I informally consulted him on certain vexed issues. He gave his advice freely and without at any time breaching my confidence. I shall always be indebted to him for that and many other anonymous acts of kindness.

No account of Seervai's life can be complete without mention of his wife Feroza with whom he discussed and whose advice he sought on every subject under the sun, including the ill effects of consumption of mayonnaise after reading about the subject in the Encyclopedia Britannica. If marriages are made in heaven, theirs was one of them. I have yet to come across a couple so understanding, so loving, so devoted as Homi and Feroza. Daughter Meher recounts that they would stop to embrace and kiss as they took a walk in that delightful and unique hill station, Matheran. Many a romance has bloomed in Matheran as I can personally testify.

The last time I met him was on their 50th golden wedding function in Bombay in December 1995. I was happy to hear his comments on my critique of the Supreme Court judgment in *Bommai's Case* which dealt with the parameters and extent of judicial review regarding imposition of President's Rule in the States. "That's all very well. But remember, Sorab..." that's what he called me. For some unfathomable reason he did not refer to me as Soli but Sorab.

His was indeed a life which constantly reminds us that by following his principles and example we too can make our lives sublime.

LAST OF THE SERJEANTS*

Fali S. Nariman

Senior Counsel, Member of Rajya Sabha,
Former Additional Solicitor-General of India

IN 1929, THE YEAR THAT I was born, H.M. Seervai was enrolled as an Advocate. When I joined the great Chamber of Sir Jamshedji Kanga in 1951 — one-year-old-at-the-Bar — Seervai was already a regular senior — leagues ahead of me in age, wisdom, and experience.

---

* Khurshedji Bhabha, my own immediate Senior in Bombay, affectionately addressed Homi Seervai — always and to the end — as SERJEANT; not "Sergeant" as in the army, but as in "Serjeant-at-Law": formerly, the highest order of Counsel at the English Bar.

Kanga's Chambers were located on the ground floor of the High Court Building — it was a small chamber, no more than 30 ft x 15 ft — but it was a Chamber of All Talents. Murzban Mistree had a table close to that of Sir Jamshedji; next came Rustom Kolah, and then Homi Seervai (all had large tables); then sitting opposite were Jal Vimadalal, Nani Palkhivala and Khurshedji Bhabha — their small tables were almost stuck into the wall on the other side, each with only one extra chair at the side for the Solicitor or client! The juniors — and there were many — just fluttered around: it was a crowded Chamber. Justice N.H.C. Coyajee once told me that he was surprised how nobody had tripped and broken a leg in Kanga's Chamber! But it had an atmosphere — best described by Seervai himself when speaking in the Central Court on March 24, 1969, in a deeply moving tribute to his leader. This is what he said about the Chamber and its head:

> "It was an extraordinary atmosphere. If you did not want to work or wanted to chat, or gossip — about the share bazaar or about current gossip — you were free to do so. But if you were willing to work he was extremely generous. He acknowledged both to the solicitor and to the Court the debt which he owed to his juniors. The long years of waiting at the Bar would have been unendurable but for his nature which radiated vitality and charm. *In his room there was always sunshine.* He delighted in the success of his juniors, though he modestly put it down to his chamber being a lucky chamber. But they knew better. For to them he was both an example and an inspiration, unspoiled by success, modest and unassuming in manner, retaining, inspite of all his great powers, the simplicity and candour of a child."[1]

It is the sunshine in Kanga's Chambers that we all fondly remember.

When Seervai was appointed Advocate-General in 1957 he moved into the Advocate-General's Chamber on the first floor of the High Court building and remained there for seventeen long years. As Advocate-General he was brilliant — but he was also a very fair opponent. At that time it was customary that in all land acquisition references in the High Court — where the quantum of compensation awarded for lands acquired by the State was finally determined — the Advocate-General should represent the State. And as Advocate-General he would not yield a rupee more from public coffers than what the evidence justified; at the same time if he found that an opposite party (an individual client) was poorly represented he would go out of his

1. Vol. 71 (1969) Bombay Law Report (Journal Section) pages 25-27.

way to suggest enhancing the compensation already awarded if he felt that this was the just and proper thing to do.

I knew him and admired his qualities of head and heart — at a distance. We got to know each other really well — man to man — only years later when circumstances pitted us together for a full hour every day for forty-five days, in New Delhi during the hearing of the *Keshvanand Bharati Case.* He was still Advocate-General of Maharashtra and was specially appointed at the request of the Union Government to represent the State of Kerala, along with the then Attorney-General for India, Niren De. I had shifted to Delhi in 1972 on my appointment as Additional Solicitor General of India and had a Chamber all to myself in the Supreme Court building. I could not appear for either side in the great case — because I had previously appeared for the petitioners in *Golak Nath* — a decision of a Bench of 11 Judges which was being reconsidered by the larger Bench of 13 Judges.

At my request Seervai lunched with me in my Chamber every single day during the hearing: my wife Bapsi made it a point to send something special each day. And since Seervai always wore his heart on his sleeve and never minced words, I was fortunate enough to get a blow-by-blow description of the proceedings in the *Fundamental Rights Case.* And more importantly, I really got to know the great man.

I believe the greatest disservice the Government of Maharashtra did to itself was when it made it impossible for Seervai to continue as its Chief Law Officer. Maharashtra never had a more illustrious Advocate-General. He gave to his client — the Government — unstinted attention and valued advice and his name soon became a household word amongst Advocates-General, and members of the Bar throughout the country. Lord Elwyn Jones, once Attorney-General in the United Kingdom, was described as the "bull-dog of the Crown". Seervai was the "bull-dog" of the Government of Maharashtra for nearly two decades — guarding it with erudition, fine advocacy and high integrity.

Whilst he was Advocate-General and even after he demitted the office — in fact for a continuous period during the last 35 years of his life — he was occupied with his Magnum Opus, and successive editions of it — he always referred to it reverently as THE BOOK. It was his showpiece to posterity — to the young lawyers who had never seen him in Court. I have heard people criticize his commentary in editions subsequent to the first — it has been said that he needlessly lambasted judgments and Judges of the highest court: some of this criticism is justified. As he himself confessed in the Preface to the very first edition (which his talented son Navroz quoted again in his preface to the 3rd Volume of the 4th edition), Seervai was deeply conscious of the charge that his criticisms may be mistaken — but then as he put it "to refuse to criticize for fear of being mistaken is to abandon criticism altogether"! And there is always a risk (as David Pannick has said) that in the absence of criticism the Judge will be drowned in veneration and self-satisfaction.

I have known Justices of the Supreme Court anxiously turn over the pages of his later editions to see what Seervai had to say about their judgments: not a bad thing for Judges to be conscious of their *shortcomings* and to be constantly reminded of them by India's leading constitutional historian.

In that delightful book *Miscellany-at-Law* Sir Robert Megarry recalls an incident going back to the year 1882, the time of the opening of the Royal Courts of Justice by Queen Victoria: a meeting was called by the Lord Chancellor (Lord Selbourne) to consider a draft of the proposed address to the Queen. The draft contained the words: "Your Majesty's Judges are deeply sensible of their own many shortcomings...": Selbourne thought there could be no objection to obsequious language — certainly not for one's Queen! But Jessel (Sir George Jessel, Master of the Rolls) thought differently. He strongly objected, saying "I am not conscious of *many shortcomings;* if I were I should not be fit to be on the Bench". After some wrangling as to the terms of the address, amity was restored — only after Lord Justice Bowen suggested a compromise. He said: "Instead of saying that we are "deeply sensible of our own many shortcomings" why not say that *"we are deeply sensible of the many shortcomings of each other"!*

Let me confess that I have been a beneficiary of Seervai's criticism of Supreme Court judgments: because he reserved fifteen closely printed pages of his 3rd edition to a sharp and biting critique of the judgment in the *Escorts Case:* a case which I argued and won in the High Court, and argued and lost in the Supreme Court. I have benefited by many parts of the great BOOK and have frequently consulted it. But let me say that nothing pleased me more than those fifteen printed pages in which Seervai roundly chastised dear old Justice Chinnappa Reddy for his judgment in the case. When Hari Nanda of Escorts was writing his life's story I sought and obtained for him Seervai's permission to reproduce these pages, in his autobiography. Old Hari, bless his soul, was tickled pink when I sent him copies of those fifteen pages — "a Daniel come to judgment", he said to me, and added: "Fali, we have been vindicated".

Do harsh words about judges and their judgments *have* to be used? Well, not always — perhaps only occasionally: because of what that great economist Lord Keynes used to say: "Words have sometimes to be harsh since they represent an assault on the thoughts of the unthinking". It shakes people up — and it is good for the soul to shake up some people some of the time!

Seervai had a prodigious memory, for ever quoting lines of verse or prose without referring to any text. He was particularly fond of the works of Sir Walter Scott. It is in Walter Scott's novel "Guy Mannering" that there is a description of the home of a Scots lawyer (Counsellor Pleydell). Guy Mannering is shown into the lawyer's study whose walls are lined with the best edition of the best authors and a collection of the classics: "These are the tools of my trade" says Pleydell. "A lawyer without history or literature is a mechanic, a mere working mason; if he possesses knowledge of these he may venture to call himself an architect".

Seervai was an "architect" — an architect amongst (far too many) masons. His speeches as Advocate-General were a rich treat for us all, full of literary allusions and quotes from memory, on the not infrequent occasions when the members of the Bar (on the Original and Appellate Sides) assembled to welcome and/or to bid farewell to Judges. Looking back I think it was a gracious tradition — you will find these most entertaining and enlightening speeches reported in the Journal sections of the Bombay Law Reporter. Alas, we have fallen on dull mundane days: gone is the Bombay Law Reporter, and gone too the old tradition of welcoming the new judge in and honouring the old judge out.

On *truth*, Seervai would not compromise — nor on courage. In that great work of John Morley *(On Compromise)* the inscription at the beginning (a quote from the logician Richard Whately) reads as follows:

> "It makes all the difference in the world whether we put Truth in the first place or in the second place."

Seervai always put truth in the first place — even when it hurt. Quite early in his long career at the Bar — long before he became Advocate-General, long before he was famous, or even well-known, he was told that a Judge of the High Court had done a great wrong to his own junior and to several other juniors: he checked the facts and found them to be correct: the truth had to be exposed. So he walked up to Chief Justice Chagla and told him the facts, and said that if the Judge continued to sit on the Original side he would not shirk from taking all appropriate steps necessary to bring the Judge to book, including if necessary, to move Parliament for his impeachment! Chagla knew that young Seervai was not only truthful, but fearless: by an administrative order (passed by the Chief Justice) the particular judge was directed to sit on the Appellate Side; which he continued to do till he remained a Judge of the Bombay High Court. When Seervai approached Chief Justice Chagla and unburdened himself about the Judge in question, Sir Jamshedji, who came to hear of it — tearfully from the Judge himself — chided Seervai about this one evening when he returned from Court to Chambers. Unflinching, Seervai said he could not compromise on this; he had thought over the matter and made up his mind and if his action displeased Sir Jamshedji he was even prepared to leave the Chambers. Leave Kanga's Chambers? "Oh no, no," said the noble soul. "You are entitled to do what you think is right — there is no question of you leaving the Chamber." So Seervai remained in Kanga's Chambers; it was the particular Judge who no longer remained on the Original Side.

On March 24, 1969, in an obituary reference to condole the passing away of Kanga, the Advocate-General of Maharashtra quoted a few lines from Milton's *Paradise Lost*; which were appropriate words apt to describe his own leader's sixty odd years at the Bar:

> "Unmoved,
> Unshaken, unseduced, unterrified,
> His loyalty he kept, his love, his zeal,
> Nor number, nor example with him wrought
> To swerve from truth or change his constant mind."

These same lines would form a fitting epitaph to Seervai's own illustrious career. Truly, he was the last of the Serjeants: when they make great men, they break the mould.

H. M. SEERVAI — RANDOM MEMORIES AND RECOLLECTIONS

Anil B. Divan
Senior Counsel

I. First Thoughts

WHEN FEROZA INVITED ME in February 2004 to contribute my memories and recollections to a book to commemorate Seervai — a celebration of his life — I felt honoured and thrilled.

The Indian oral tradition down from the 'Vedas' is of 'Shruti' and 'Smriti' — what one has heard and what one remembers. My recollections about Seervai are an amalgam of memories, recollections and events heard and believed. Some will be of interest to the general reader and many to the brotherhood of lawyers. They have passed into the collective memories of my contemporaries and seniors at the bar and form a rich heritage of traditions and timeless ideals. Many of them are worth preserving for posterity. We must rejuvenate and reinvent ourselves in the legal profession by learning the lessons from the inspiring messages which emerge. They are a treasurehouse of many battles which Seervai fought and won, of victories celebrated and defeats borne with fortitude and a philosophical smile.

It was during the Emergency in the latter half of 1975 that I received a telephone call in the morning at my Bombay residence. "This is Seervai speaking — Divan, I believe you are going to argue for some of the detenus who have been preventively detained in the Supreme Court regarding the maintainability of a Habeas Corpus petition. I have some points which I would like to discuss with you."

A meeting was arranged. So my wife Smita and I met Seervai and Feroza at the P.V.M. Gymkhana one evening. We were entertained to tea and snacks and we had a fruitful discussion. He particularly stressed that the doctrine of *ultra vires* was independent of fundamental rights and referred to the famous case of *Eshugbayi Eleko* [(1931) AC 662 at 670] followed by our Supreme Court in many cases where Lord Atkin said:

> "In accordance with British jurisprudence no member of the executive can interfere with the liberty or property of a British subject except on the condition that he can support the legality of his action before a Court of Justice. And it is the tradition of British justice that judges should not shrink from deciding such issues in the face of the Executive."

He also drew my attention to the right of self-defence both under the Indian Penal Code and the Law of Torts against an illegal attack on personal liberty. Notwithstanding the Presidential order suspending fundamental rights, Seervai's view was clear that a Habeas Corpus petition was maintainable.

Initially it was widely known that Seervai's stance on the Emergency of 1975 was ambiguous. He had just resigned as Advocate-General of Maharashtra in 1974. He was an outspoken critic of various decisions of the Supreme Court including the *Golak Nath Case*, the *Bank Nationalization*

Case and the *Kesavananda Bharati Case* (the *Fundamental Rights Case*), but his perception of the Emergency and its excesses gradually changed. It hardened after the Habeas Corpus judgment *(ADM Jabalpur v. Shiv Kant Shukla* — AIR 1976 SC 1207) delivered on 28th April 1976 and the punitive transfers of independent judges with a view to overawe them. In fact he successfully fought, pro-bono, the petition of Sankalchand Sheth, (a High Court Judge transferred from Gujarat to Andhra Pradesh against his wishes) before a full Bench of the Gujarat High Court [(1976) 17 Gujarat Law Reporter 1017].

In 1978, Seervai wrote the most severe condemnation of the majority judgments in the *Habeas Corpus Case* in words worth recalling:

> "The four judgments were delivered in the darkest hour of India's history after independence and they made that darkness complete... Ordinary men and women could understand Satan saying "Evil be thou my good" but they were bewildered and perplexed to be told by four learned judges of the Supreme Court that in substance, the founding fathers had written into the Emergency provisions of our Constitution "Lawlessness be thou our law"."

This strong criticism from a lawyer who argued for the Government in the *Fundamental Rights Case* which led to the supersession of three seniormost judges was remarkable. How Seervai gradually changed his opinion on the doctrine of the un-amendable basic structure of the Constitution as laid down in the *Fundamental Rights Case* will be recalled by me a little later.

II. A Knight in Shining Armour

When I joined the Bar and started practicing in January 1952 I joined the chambers of M. L. Maneksha, Bar at Law. Maneksha was a great lawyer and a distinguished advocate but above all he was known for his strict ethical standards and his impeccable integrity and etiquette. Later, I discovered that Seervai was Maneksha's first pupil while studying for the Original Side Advocate's Examination. On passing the examination, he joined the chambers of J. B. Kanga.

Even before I joined the Bar I had heard about Seervai through my uncle B. J. Divan who was practicing on the Original Side of the Bombay High Court. Seervai was an examiner for the Original Side Examinations which was a very tough examination and many candidates took it in parts but Seervai passed in one shot several outstanding students namely R. J. Joshi (later his junior), R. M. Kantawala, (later Chief Justice of Bombay) and B. J. Divan (later Chief Justice of Gujarat). Seervai affectionately bonded with them in the

Bar library and acted as friend, philosopher and guide. They were appreciative of Seervai's encouragement to them in their early briefless and disheartening days and always turned to him for advice.

Seervai was an indefatigable fighter in causes which he believed in, particularly when he was convinced of unethical conduct compounded by injustice. He would pick up the gauntlet and would tenaciously pursue the cause unafraid of personal consequences. He was the Warrior Prince of the Bombay Bar, a knight in the shining armour of the law. I would like to recount a few of these battles.

Before I joined the Bar, Seervai took up cudgels on behalf of his junior ("Devil" as per the idiom at the Bombay Bar) the late R. J. Joshi. A senior judge sitting on the original side whose son was also practicing made remarks on several occasions disparaging of Joshi and other junior advocates in open court: remarks which were perceived by Solicitors to be to the disadvantage of those juniors and which would indirectly benefit the judge's son. Seervai meticulously collected the material and walked up to Chief Justice Chagla with his complaint. Suddenly, overnight Chagla in an unprecedented move transferred the judge to the Appellate Side from the Original Side. The concerned Judge (later elevated to the Supreme Court) was a liberal and fearless judge who was a champion of citizen's rights and who would stand up to Government but his filial feelings clouded his judgment.

The Bombay City Civil Court Bench has contributed many distinguished judges to the High Courts and the Supreme Court. The Court was established in 1948 and many bright young members of the Bar were attracted to go on the City Civil Court Bench and rise with seniority to become Principal Judges with an opportunity to be elevated to the High Court. The Principal Judge of the Court was normally selected on seniority basis in that court. Justice J. M. Shelat was one such example who became Chief Justice of Gujarat and later a Judge of the Supreme Court.

Three outstanding senior judges in the City Civil Court namely B. J. Divan, V. D. Tulzapurkar and J.R Vimadalal were overlooked and a favourite was appointed as Principal Judge from the Districts with the concurrence of Chief Justice Chainani. The three judges threatened to resign but were advised by Seervai, then the Advocate-General, to hold their hands as he was taking up the issue. With matchless courage and supported by the Bar, Seervai campaigned with the Government and consequently the decision was reversed and the injustice remedied. He came in confrontation with Chief Justice Chainani who was the first service judge appointed as Chief Justice in the Bombay High Court. It required extraordinary courage to lobby with the Government against the views of the sitting Chief Justice. Seervai was willing to take up the cause which he found just, disregarding personal consequences to his own career. Later B. J. Divan became Chief Justice of Gujarat but during the Emergency was punitively transferred to Andhra Pradesh as Chief Justice; V. D. Tulzapurkar was elevated to the High Court and later to the Supreme Court and proved to be one of the most fearless, outspoken and courageous judges to stand up to the Government. J. R. Vimadalal, because of his liberal judgments in preventive detention matters during the Emergency was punitively transferred to Andhra Pradesh even though he had a very short time before retirement.

The Supreme Court was slated to hear a case involving discriminatory compensation being given — more for normal land acquisitions but less for Housing Schemes. The question was whether such laws fell foul of Article 14. In some cases in Bombay, solatium was denied by law. A member of the Bombay Bar, Naval Gamadia was heir to a large piece of land with a small bungalow on the Gamadia Hill Estate which was under acquisition. [This piece of land has been now completely developed and a huge commercial complex called "Heera Panna" stands just opposite Haji Ali in Bombay.] Gamadia found that Chief Justice Gajendragadkar was presiding over the Bench. He happened to be a member of a Cooperative Housing Society which would benefit if the laws were valid. Thus there was a pecuniary angle as far as the Chief Justice was concerned. Seervai, devoting considerable time and energy prepared a note on the law of disqualification of a judge for pecuniary bias, to help Gamadia, so that an objection could be taken. Such an objection was unprecedented and most of the counsel appearing were unwilling to offend a strong Chief Justice like Gajendragadkar by raising such an objection. However one of the fearless doyens of the Supreme Court Bar, Purshotam Trikamdas raised the objection. Gajendragadkar initially was taken aback and appeared hesitant to recuse himself. However C. K. Daphtary, then Attorney-General, who was appearing for the state, in his usual inimitable style said that no party should have even a feeling of possible bias in the highest court in the land and it would be wise not to participate. Gajendragadkar had no option but to opt out of the Bench and ultimately Justice K. Subba Rao presided and the petitioners succeeded in invalidating the discriminatory laws. (AIR 1965 SC 1017 — *Vajravelu Mudaliar v. Special Deputy Collector* and AIR 1965 SC 1096 — *N. B. Jeejeebhoy v. Assistant Collector*).

(Seervai refers to this case in *Constitutional Law* 4th Edn. Vol. II page 1736 footnote 77)

In the early fifties *ad-valorem* court fees were sought to be imposed on the Original Side Suits in Bombay. Young Advocates were apprehensive that this additional burden on the litigants would mean that junior briefs from solicitors would dry up and they would have no future at the Bar. Some of them wanted the dual system of solicitor and counsel to be abolished so that advocates could file their appearances on the original side. Seervai and K. T. Desai at great personal cost in terms of time, energy and work went from table to table in the Bar Library persuading young counsel like me that the dual system had great virtues. They also worked out a scheme by which advocates in good practice would voluntarily designate themselves as seniors and would desist from accepting a brief unless briefed with a junior counsel. This was at a time when the distinction between Senior Advocates and Advocates introduced by the Advocates Act 1961 was not in operation. As a result the Resolution moved to recommend abolition of the dual system in the Bar Association was defeated and the dual system remained current for many years. Many of us were beneficiaries of that continuation. One does not know who would have made good or even continued at the Bar if the dual system had been abolished.

The Centenary of the Bombay High Court was to be celebrated in 1962. P. B. Vachha a senior and leading member of the Bar and a master of the English language was requested by Chief Justice Chainani to write a history of the Bombay High Court on that occasion. Vachha stipulated that he should have a free hand to express his views and comments. However when the manuscript reached the High Court, objections were raised to some of the views expressed. A via-media was arrived at that in the beginning of the book it should be mentioned that:

> "The opinions expressed in this book represent the opinions of the writers and the statements of fact made therein have been made by the writers on their own responsibility".

The book would be published by the highest officer of the Court namely the Prothonotary in his capacity as the Secretary of the Centenary Celebrations Committee. However one objection remained, which Vachha was not willing to delete i.e. his postscript to the second Tilak trial in Chapter XV (See Vachha *Famous Judges, Lawyers and Cases in Bombay* Preface page v and vi and pages 264 to 271).

At the end of the second Tilak trial for sedition Bal Gangadhar Tilak spoke his famous words:

"All that I wish to say is that, in spite of the verdict of the jury, I still maintain that I am innocent. There are higher powers that rule the destinies of men and nations; and I think it may be the will of Providence that the cause I represent may be benefited more by my suffering than by my pen and tongue."

Tilak was sentenced by the judge to six years' transportation and a fine of Rs. 1000. This trial took place in 1909. These words of Tilak are now inscribed on a marble tablet fixed outside the Central court where he was tried. Vachha in his postscript was critical of the speech of Chief Justice Chagla on that occasion and made his comments in the postscript. He said among other things:

"The Chief Justice's speech was admirably patriotic or patriotically admirable; but legally and judicially inexplicable and indefensible and was delivered from a wrong platform". (Vachha page 270).

Vachha was not willing to remove this postscript. As a result Vachha writes in his Preface:

"...the High Court was of the opinion that it would not be proper to include the postscript in a Commemorative Volume published at the time of the centenary. I was thus faced with the alternative of either withdrawing the postscript from my history or withdrawing my history from the High Court; and the latter course appeared to me to be the obvious path of duty."

It was at this juncture that under the leadership of Seervai, then Advocate-General, a Committee was formed to publish Vachha's history including the postscript. The Committee consisted, among others, of K. M. Munshi, G. N. Joshi, A. G. Mulgaonkar, Murzaban Mistree, Porus Mehta, S. Baptista, N. A. Palkhivala, R. D. Chadha and Atul Setalvad. Again Seervai through his leadership made possible the publication of Vachha's invaluable history, written in a delightful epigrammatic style, for posterity. Seervai was a great admirer of Chief Justice Chagla but he thought he had a higher duty to the freedom of speech and expression. He believed in that famous quotation attributed to Voltaire "I may disapprove of what you say, but I will defend to the death your right to say it."

III. Kesavananda Bharati — Emergency — Seervai's Changed Response

Nani Palkhivala commenced his arguments on 31st Oct. 1972 in the *Kesavananda Bharati Case (Fundamental Rights Case)* (AIR 1973 SC 1461). I was briefed on behalf of the sugar factories of Maharashtra and was supporting and assisting Nani Palkhivala for the petitioners and was throughout present at the hearings. The arguments concluded on 23rd March 1973 and the judgment was delivered on 24th April 1973.

On the next date three seniormost judges of the Supreme Court namely, J. M. Shelat, K. S. Hegde and A. N. Grover were superseded and A. N. Ray was appointed Chief Justice of India. This was the first major assault on the independence of the judiciary and led to countrywide protests.

Seervai was then Advocate-General of Maharashtra and had represented the State of Kerala in the *Fundamental Rights Case.* Seervai's position was non-committal and ambiguous at the time of the supersession. He continued to be Advocate-General till his resignation in 1974. He had firm views that the *Golak Nath Case* was wrongly decided and that the Supreme Court had erred in propounding the doctrine of basic structure in the *Fundamental Rights Case.* This doctrine fettered and restricted the amending power of Parliament. But all this changed gradually but decisively as the excesses of the Emergency snowballed and the extreme contentions in *Indira Gandhi's Election Case* (*Indira Gandhi v. Raj Narain* AIR 1975 SC 2299) were argued. Seervai's outraged conscience found expression in his later comments on the judgment in the *Habeas Corpus Case* which have already been mentioned above. His considered views on the basic structure doctrine are now clarified in Seervai *Constitutional Law of India* (3rd Edn.) Vol. II at pages 2686 and 2692. To quote:

> "We can now answer the question: does the doctrine of the basic structure provide a correct interpretation of Article 368 ? It is clear from our discussion that it appears to be the only doctrine which supplies an answer to the question." (Page 2686 para 30.71).
>
> "Coming to the second answer, our discussion has shown that the consequences of rejecting the doctrine of the basic structure would be so grave, and so opposed to the objectives of the Constitution, that the consequence of uncertainty would be insignificant by comparison. This is all the more so because the Kesavananda doctrine has neither prevented an amendment of the Constitution in the public interest nor the enactment of socio-economic laws..." (Para 30.77 at page 2692).

This 180 degree turn in Seervai's views was because of several reasons. First, in the *Fundamental Rights Case* the amending power and its width was discussed in the light and context of property rights. Secondly, in the *Indira Gandhi Election Case* the widest amendment power was claimed even to subvert the democratic basis of our polity and interdict and override the judicial power by a constitutional amendment attempting to decide a case in favour of a candidate who was disqualified for corrupt practice. But apart from this the abuse of powers during the Emergency, namely, preventive detention without trial of Opposition Leaders and other activists, rushing through far-reaching constitutional amendments in a rump Parliament, the complete muzzling of the Press, the ill treatment of detenus, Press censorship of court judgments which were against the Government and attacks on judicial independence must have decisively influenced Seervai's thinking.

Seervai's arguments, which I heard in the *Fundamental Rights Case* could not be ranked as one of his best performances. There must have been several reasons but a couple of them can be identified. First, Seervai had made it a condition with the then Law Minister H. R. Gokhale that he would only accept the brief provided he would have the first word and lead arguments for the respondent Government. In other words he would precede the arguments of the Attorney-General, Niren De. Thus there was continuous tension in the Respondents' team. Everyone knew about this and so did the Attorney-General. Every effort must have been made by the Attorney-General to overturn this decision till the last moment. If the Attorney-General had started the arguments, Seervai would have definitely returned the brief and disassociated himself from the case. This dissension was only publicly resolved at the conclusion of Palkhivala's argument when the turn of the respondents came and the Attorney-General requested Seervai to start, on the ground that he had other, international commitments.

This internal conflict between the Attorney-General, Niren De and the Advocate-General, Seervai must have been heightened by the fact (then unknown to us on the petitioners' side) that Seervai had been offered the office of Attorney-General by H.R. Gokhale, which he had declined in September 1971.

Secondly, the principal reason for forming a bench of 13 judges was to test the correctness of the *Golak Nath* decision which had held that fundamental rights could not be amended and to test the validity of Constitutional Amendments made to overcome that judgment. Seervai's preparation therefore was mainly directed to this issue. However Chief Justice Sikri guided the arguments in the case to another question which became central namely, inherent or implied limitations on the amending power of Parliament. This was a much wider issue on which the respondents may not have had sufficient time to focus and prepare.

Seervai's performance and arguments, though impeccable, were not one of his outstanding performances. It is difficult to speculate the reasons but some of them I have outlined above.

Part of the inside story, before the judgments in the *Fundamental Rights Case* has now been unravelled and is worth recalling.

Justice Jaganmohan Reddy's (a member of the Bench in the *Fundamental Rights Case*) remarks in his autobiography *The Judiciary I Served* (page 230):

"Gokhale brought Seervai who only accepted on condition that he would begin on behalf of the respondents and Niren De would come after him. Ray and I however, protested. We said the Attorney-General had precedence and he should begin and pointed out that the Chief Justice, Shelat and Hegde in the *Bank Nationalization Case* had said that this reversal of order could not be allowed. In any case Chief Justice Sikri later said it is for both Seervai and De to settle the issue and if De permitted Seervai could start first. This, of course, was right but evidently by then at the instance of Gokhale, De was asked to give way to Seervai. I understand on authentic information that De had gone to the Prime Minister and complained. She asked him to come and see her again and when he did she told him that there was nothing she could do because she was dependent on the advice of the legal members of her cabinet. De quietly lumped this insult and later tried to make a virtue of it."

Some of the other observations of Justice Jaganmohan Reddy are worth recording:

"Seervai was most courteous and his court manners were unexceptionable except when it came to views held by the Court being contrary to the views expressed by him in his book on the Constitution." (page 230).

"There were clear indications that the Government while awaiting the decision knew what the decision would be before it was delivered and had already made up its mind to supersede three Judges to make Ray J. Chief Justice." (page 242).

Justice Reddy narrates how at a dinner prior to the delivery of the judgment (not noticing that Justice Reddy and his wife were within hearing distance) Kumaramangalam and Ray J. conversed :

"When Ray and his wife came near the door Mohan Kumaramangalam shook hands with Ray and said 'Congratulations Next Week'. Ray held Mohan's hand, gave a smile while bending his head to one side to show his appreciation or thanks ... In the morning when we met on our walk I asked Ray, 'what was Mohan congratulating you for?' He said, 'I don't know, perhaps it is because we will be delivering our judgment next week'. I said, 'why congratulate you alone, I am part of the bench too.' He said he did not know." (page 243).

Justice Jaganmohan Reddy further remarks :

"There was one occasion when Dwivedi made a startling proposal to Palkhivala. He said if he (Palkhivala) agreed to property rights being taken away he (Dwivedi) would get Parliament to declare that other Fundamental Rights would not be taken away. Palkhivala replied: 'Have I referred so far at any time to property rights? I was dealing with implied limitations and natural rights, etc'." (page 227).

IV. A Final Word

In December 2000, Feroza Seervai presented me with a collection of Essays, Speeches, Letters and Tributes edited by her called *The Seervai Legacy*. I gathered from her article that the word "Seervai" comes from 'sher-vai' which means 'like a lion'. Seervai came from a long line of master builders of the Mazagaon Docks in Bombay who were noted for inflexible integrity and moral courage.

On reflection, I realized what I owed to Seervai. Seervai never passed any work to me and I was only briefed independently in a very few matters with him. Nor did I work closely with him. But the high standards of integrity, ethics, fairness, and fearlessness which he set at the bar had an immense effect on many of us. He was an icon worth emulating if one could stay the course and was not bewitched by prizes which politicians could offer. In that sense I consider myself a beneficiary of the "Seervai Legacy".

In my reply to Feroza for her kindness in presenting me the *Seervai Legacy* I replied on December 22nd 2000. I reproduce below portions of my letter.

"Seervai's words and example have inspired many of us at the Bombay Bar. In my formative years at the Bar, Motilal Setalvad as Attorney-General and Homi Seervai as Advocate-General were two shining examples of independent fearless advocates who had reached the top of the profession without indulging in unethical practices and without fawning on politicians and developing rapport with the powers that be. Unfortunately, it is a different world now."

"It was a revelation to me that Seervai is derived from 'Sher-vai' 'like a lion.' Homi was undoubtedly a lion at the Bar, but he was more, he was a role model for the young and rising advocate."

"It is a sad commentary on our leaders that after 17 years of his distinguished tenure as Advocate-General, he received no word of appreciation from the Government. I am reminded of what M. C. Setalvad has written in his autobiography, *My Life* about a similar experience when he demitted office as the first Attorney-General. He was treated similarly by the then Prime Minister

Nehru. In contrast he mentions the courtesy and appreciation shown to him by a letter written by Sir Roger Lumley then Governor of Bombay when Motilal resigned as Advocate-General of Bombay as a result of the freedom struggle. So Seervai was in good company."

"Seervai's views on the duties of a Law Officer be it Advocate-General or Attorney-General are refreshing. He regarded the duty of a Law Officer to represent the public interest and acting independently of the Government. Current practices in India, are now more tailored to the practices of what Seervai has referred to as Mr. Worldlywiseman and Mr. Facingbothways."

"It was a wise decision on your part to have published this Collection even though it is only a part of the Seervai Legacy. As you have said in your introduction, the book recalls the man and the mind. And what a man!"

The above extracts from my letter encapsulate my small tribute to a great lawyer, an incomparable builder like his forefathers who contributed immeasurably to legal learning and ethics but above all who displayed indomitable courage to fight for his beliefs and convictions ignoring all consequences to his personal fortunes.

Surely, one would like to think of him as the Warrior Prince of the Bombay Bar, a Knight in the shining armour of the law.

SOME REMINISCENCES

Ashok H. Desai

Senior Advocate, Former Solicitor-General of India

I HAVE VIVID MEMORY of one of my earliest meetings with Seervai. He was the Advocate-General of Maharashtra and I called on him at his chambers in the High Court. The Advocate-General's chambers were then located in a huge and historical room. The walls were covered by very tall cupboards which required ladders for retrieving the books on the top shelves. And there was Seervai engrossed in reading a book which looked too small in size to be a respectable law book. He mentioned that he was reading the funeral speech of Pericles immortalised in the History of the Peloponnesian war by Thucydides. When he saw that I was not unfamiliar with it, he started to read aloud excerpts from the speech including the famous passage to the effect:

"For the whole earth is the sepulchre of great men. They are not remembered merely by the inscription on the columns of their native land.

Better than all inscriptions are the memories in the hearts and minds of all men which continue for generations."

Here are some memories of Seervai:

I worked closely with Seervai in the series of cases on conditions of detention. Earlier, in *A.D.M. Jabalpur,* the Supreme Court had been persuaded to hold that an Indian citizen had no right of life and liberty once Article 21 was suspended during an emergency. Now the only hope was to ensure that the detenus received decent treatment in jail. Virtually, every High Court in India has recognized that any detenu would be entitled to basic facilities like reading material, visiting rights and medical attendance. The fair amount of case law was founded on an observation of Chief Justice Shah that preventive detention was qualitatively different from punitive detention and that the constraints laid on a detenu under preventive detention should be the minimum consistent with the requirement to ensure that he remains in detention. But we had not reckoned with the Bench of Ray C. J., Beg J. and Jaswant Singh J. After Seervai elaborated the distinction between preventive detention and punitive detention, Justice Beg made the rather unguarded observation, "Mr. Seervai, you have been submitting at length on preventive detention as against punitive detention. I do not quite understand what is all this difference. After all, detention is detention." He had not reckoned with Seervai who lowered his voice and reproved the judge, "My Lord, there is a clear difference between preventive detention and punitive detention even though it may not be always apparent. For instance, there is a time when it is day and there is a time when it is night. In between there is dawn and, later, dusk when it is difficult to insist at a particular point whether it is day or night. But only a strange mind would discern no difference between day and night." Judicial silence followed. But the Government appeals were duly allowed. Justice Beg enthusiastically gave a concurring judgment containing a curious malapropism "We are all aware of the dictum of Justice Holmes that 'law is not logic'."

Seervai would be very candid in Court. Not for him the customary appreciation of the Bar for the ability of the judge before whom they are arguing. Once he was in full flow of argument before a Division Bench presided over by Justice Tarkunde. One issue that arose during the discussion was about the income of lawyers as compared to what was earned by judges. Tarkunde casually mentioned to Seervai "Do you not think, Mr. Advocate-General, that Judges would earn much more if they continued at the bar?" The response of almost any lawyer would have been to agree promptly and suggest that the judge had made a remarkable sacrifice in responding to the call of public service and accepting the judgeship. But not Seervai! He paused and lowered his head and characteristically brought the tips of his fingers together. In the ensuing silence, one could feel that he was going down the list of all the judges and working out who would earn more and who would earn less by a transit to the Bench. At the end of a few minutes, he raised his head and said: "My Lords, I have reflected on the subject. While some of your Lordships would have earned more, many would not." The poor judges were left to speculate to which of the two categories they belonged.

One of the most endearing things about Seervai was his love of literature which he readily shared with others. He introduced me to what has now become a favourite anthology, viz. *Other Men's Flowers* compiled by Field Marshal Wavell. To my surprise, I learnt from him that this volume of about 400 pages represented poems which Wavell knew by heart. I particularly remember Seervai citing to great effect the following lines when the State of Bombay was divided and many lawyers and judges who were a part of the Bombay High Court shifted to the High Court of Gujarat at Ahmedabad in 1960. He said:

> "From the lone sheiling of the misty highland
> Mountains divide us, and the waste of seas –
> Yet still the blood is strong, the heart is Highland,
> And even in dreams we behold the Hebrides."

Some observers felt that Seervai sometimes made submissions which were too detailed for the case. But they overlooked his high standard of advocacy. Firstly, he would confine himself to appearing in only one court at a time. Once when Mr. Asoke Sen, a formidable but very mobile lawyer, complimented Seervai on his arguments in a Court, Seervai's candid response was "You are right. But then you see one does not hop across from one court to another." Further, when Seervai took a matter, the case was dealt with with utmost thoroughness. He attributed to his opponent his own level of excellence and tried to meet the arguments by preparing on every point that could possibly be raised against him. In 99% of the cases, the opponent was unlikely to touch the points. The analysis of various judgments in his great work *Constitutional Law of India* reflects a remarkable dissection of the arguments of the Judge by breaking down each statement into various parts and exposing the inconsistencies when he found them.

Seervai was so single-minded that in working with him one was reminded of the concentration of Arjuna. It is said that during an archery test, the Pandavas were asked to aim at a bird. Their preceptor, Dronacharya asked the various brothers what they could see. One announced that he could see the tree; the other that he could see the branch; the third that he could see the bird. But Arjuna, the greatest of the archers, could only see the eye of the bird. And Seervai was generous with his time. While arguing Antulay's case when I was faced with the problem of admissibility of documents in a writ petition, I troubled Seervai in the morning and had a small discussion on the telephone. The afternoon found me in the middle of an argument. As the Court rose for lunch, I looked forward to a little respite. But there I found Seervai himself entering the court room. Seervai was not wearing his robes and had carried two relevant authorities all the way across the Oval out of sheer kindness to explain his response. In his crisp voice he said "Let's hop across to the chambers and I shall resolve your problem". I was greatly touched when I realised that he had devoted himself to the problem for two hours just to help the submissions of a colleague. His guidance was readily available even when I moved to Delhi as Law Officer for the Union.

Seervai practised what he preached. When in Delhi on State work, he was conscious that any money spent by an Advocate-General was money spent by the State. I recall that when he came to Delhi to the Ashoka Hotel, he would insist on staying in a room which had no balcony because a room with balcony would cost fractionally a little more. Even though you were appearing for a Five-Star client, he would not want to stay in a Five-Star hotel. In the *Judges' Case*, the Bombay Bar had requested him and other colleagues to appear for them. Seervai was the leader of the team and he had made it clear that since the Bar was paying for the lawyers and sending them to Delhi, no lawyer should send his clothes to the hotel laundry or telephone from Delhi. So, all the lawyers carried their laundry bags every weekend to Bombay. As his juniors, we all knew that when you went with him to the hotel dining room, you would have to ensure that you did not order Champagne and Caviar but had to stay content with a moderate dish.

In our journey through life it is of a few that we can assert that it was a privilege to know them. Seervai was one such. Seervai would surely approve if I end with the words of Milton from *Paradise Lost* that he used to describe his leader, Sir Jamshedji Kanga:

Unmoved,
Unshaken, unseduced, unterrified,
His loyalty he kept, his love, his zeal,
Nor number, nor example with him wrought
To swerve from truth or change his constant mind.

MY RECOLLECTIONS OF HOMI SEERVAI

Venkat Iyer
Barrister, Professor of Law, University of Ulster,
and Editor, *The Commonwealth Lawyer*

MY CONTRIBUTION to this volume is, I am afraid, going to be pretty anaemic in comparison to the other sparkling recollections that adorn its pages. This is because I cannot, alas, claim any personal familiarity with Homi Seervai, having never had the good fortune of interacting closely with this extraordinary man. Why then did I agree to write? Largely because I could not bear the thought of turning down an invitation so charmingly extended by Feroza, whose abiding love and dedication for her late husband animate this book as they did her previous labour of love, *The Seervai Legacy*. That, and of course the high regard in which I have held Hormasji over the years.

Like many Indians of my generation, I grew up admiring Homi Seervai as one of the towering giants of legal scholarship. As a student in high school I used to follow the great legal debates of the day (more out of interest, I might add, than with any special talent for absorbing the finer points involved in them), and I was immediately struck by the clarity and the passion with which Hormasji used to contribute to those debates. His spirited attacks on the Supreme Court for its rulings in, among other cases, *R.C. Cooper* v. *Union of India (The Bank Nationalization Case)*[1] and *Golak Nath* v. *State of Punjab*,[2] showed erudition of a high order and a truly remarkable capacity for incisive analysis which I found irresistible. As it happens, I couldn't have disagreed more with his views — my own position on those controversies was much closer to that held by the likes of Nani Palkhivala and Minoo Masani — but that did not alter my opinion of Hormasji as an outstanding legal mind of his day.

1. (1970) 3 SCR 530.
2. (1967) 2 SCR 762.

Later, while at law college, I had occasion to watch Hormasji in action as an advocate during my frequent visits to the Bombay High Court, and I must say I was a tad disappointed. True, he was meticulous in the way he presented his case, scrupulously fair to his opponents, extremely clear-headed in his analysis of the facts and law, and completely dedicated to the brief in hand, but what was missing was that flamboyance which to my young and impressionable mind — a mind which, like those of many aspiring lawyers before and since, had been fed on a copious diet of legal fiction — was an indispensable attribute of every successful advocate. (Mercifully, it didn't take me very long to be rid of that idiotic view; and a few years later, when I began observing proceedings in the English courts where the highly measured and understated style of their barristers stood out, I couldn't help feeling how misguided I had been in even entertaining the idea that great advocacy had anything to do with a flashy style.)

My first personal contact with Hormasji came under rather peculiar circumstances. As a student, I used to dabble in journalism and one of the publications to which I contributed fairly regularly in those days was the Bombay-based monthly magazine, *Debonair* — a magazine which had the dubious distinction of being dubbed the Indian clone of *Playboy*. Incredible as it may seem for a journal of that reputation, *Debonair* carried some serious, even high-minded, journalism, and attracted a smattering of respectable writers. Its then editor, Vinod Mehta (who later went on to edit a succession of newspapers and now presides over *Outlook* magazine), commissioned me to do an article explaining the implications of the 42nd Amendment to the Constitution of India, an amendment which, it may be remembered, sought to bring about some extremely radical changes to the constitutional framework and which was being steamrolled through Parliament by the highly impatient emergency regime headed by Indira Gandhi.

Wanting to seek as wide a range of opinion as possible for a box item which was to accompany my article, I rang Hormasji with some trepidation, half-expecting him to bang the phone down the moment he heard the word *"Debonair"*. To my great surprise, he was remarkably civil and invited me for a chat in his chambers a day or two later. When I called at the appointed hour, he could not have been kinder. Putting aside the work he was engaged in, he proffered his views on the subject of my article — and on the emergency and related issues more generally — at great length. What is more, unlike many of my other interviewees, he did not insist on seeing a transcript of the interview prior to publication and was willing to trust me to reflect his views accurately in the ensuing article. I was pleased as punch.

A few years later, when I had been in practice at the Bombay Bar for a while, I had occasion to experience his kindness again. I had been instructed in a case involving oppressive behaviour by the telephone department (a not uncommon phenomenon in those days), and was arguing the matter before a Judge who had been known to have a chip on his shoulder. Shortly after I had commenced my arguments it became clear not only that the Judge was far from favourably disposed towards my client, but that he had decided to treat me with utmost discourtesy and rudeness. Unbeknown to me, Hormasji had come to know about the difficult time I had been having before this Judge, and, to my pleasant surprise, he sent word through mutual friends at the Bar that, if I was agreeable, he would be willing to accompany me to the Chief Justice to apprise him of the Judge's behaviour which Hormasji thought was quite inappropriate. Although I did not, in the event, take up this kind offer (the case had, shortly thereafter, been decided in my client's favour despite the hostility of the Judge), I was deeply touched by Hormasji's expression of concern.

The years immediately following the declaration of the 1975 emergency brought out the best in Homi Seervai's character. Not only did he show great courage in opposing the outrageous assaults on civil liberties which accompanied the emergency, but, more significantly, he also acknowledged that his earlier belief in Parliament's unlimited powers of constitutional amendment was wrong. His subsequent endorsement of the "basic structure" doctrine, enunciated in *Kesavananda* — a doctrine which he had found little merit in previously — showed that he was big enough to learn from experience and was far from dogmatic.

Hormasji's courage was also reflected in his willingness to publicly criticise those in positions of authority, including judges, where their conduct fell short of the standards expected of them. His magisterial work, *Constitutional Law of India,* is littered with examples of such criticism. That it did not make him popular hardly needs stating: I have heard even some of his friends argue that, by being so trenchant and so forthright in his views, he contributed to a diminution in the worth of his scholarly analysis. I am not so sure. In a country where sycophancy and genuflection before the "great and the good" has often led to self-serving rationalisations and shoddy work being unquestioningly accepted, the need for someone to shine a critical torch from time to time can hardly be denied. I am therefore inclined to give Hormasji the benefit of the doubt in this regard, because I believe that, vigorous and spirited though his criticisms often were, he was usually careful to keep within the bounds of propriety. To take but one example, while writing about Justice Krishna Iyer's highly controversial judgment in *Akhil Bharatiya Soshit Karmachari Sangh v. Union of India*,[3] he had this to say:

> The judgment is a strange mixture of sermon, prophecy and platform rhetoric; of thinly disguised contempt for those who take a different view from his own, of discourteous remarks on Counsel's arguments which ran counter to his own views, accompanied by the recurrent theme song of strong moral indignation at the unjust and inhuman treatment to which the depressed classes were subjected for centuries and their sad plight even today. *After much reflection, the present writer had decided that he cannot, with propriety, deal with the judgment as it might be dealt with outside a textbook.* Therefore, the reader must decide for himself what he thinks of the tone, the temper, the approach and the reasoning of Krishna Iyer J.'s judgment.[4]

Not exactly the approach, I would have thought, of someone who sets out to launch a gratuitous personal attack of the kind that Hormasji was sometimes accused of doing! I would argue that, on the contrary, he had, through his fearless and occasionally biting criticisms, struck telling blows against the incomprehensible drivel and obfuscating jargon that was often dressed up as pearls of wisdom and legal learning.

Homi Seervai's tireless, self-denying, life-long labours on his *magnum opus* were testament to his love for perfection — a quality that has shone through all his work and which has been commented upon time and again by those who knew him intimately. I was flattered to learn from his publisher that, although he had decided at one point to be very selective in sending out review copies of the *Constitutional Law of India* (if I remember right, he only wanted such copies to be despatched to journals based outside India), he had, apparently, agreed to make an exception in my case and to allow me to review the book in *Freedom First*, the journal which I had the privilege of editing in the 1980s.

My last recollection of Hormasji also concerns one of his books, albeit the lesser-known but well-researched *Partition of India: Legend and Reality*. This book had been published by a fledgling Bombay-based firm in a rather unattractive format, and had consequently not enjoyed the visibility that it deserved. Although I cannot remember who broached the subject with me — it certainly wasn't Hormasji — I was asked to explore the possibility of having the book reprinted and/or

3. (1981) 2 SCR 185.
4. *Constitutional Law of India*, 3rd ed., vol. 1, p. 443 (italics added).

marketed by a publisher in England in the late-1980s, which I readily agreed to do. I tried to interest a number of British publishers, but without success. Most of the people I approached were impressed by the quality of Hormasji's writing, but thought that there was not a big enough market for the book in the United Kingdom. I was sorry that this piece of scholarship could not enjoy the wide circulation that it so clearly deserved.*

For all my regrets about not having got to know Hormasji well, I did have one consolation, though, which I shall cherish for a long time to come. A few years after his passing, Feroza and Navroz Seervai did me the honour of asking me to edit a volume of essays in his honour and memory. This was an invitation which I was only too pleased to accept. The book, entitled *Constitutional Perspectives,* was published in 2001,[5] and I thoroughly enjoyed putting it together. It is testimony to the high regard and affection in which Homi Seervai had been held by his friends and admirers, in India and outside, that I had little difficulty in attracting contributions to that volume. I am convinced that this book of recollections, compiled so lovingly by Feroza, will also serve to keep the memory of this noble son of India alive for many years to come.

THE LAST OF THE MOHICANS

Rohinton F. Nariman
Senior Counsel

Homi Seervai was an extraordinary human being; so extraordinary that even as a young man, his contemporaries referred to him as "Serjeant". (Incidentally, the expression "Serjeant" is referral to an advocate of yester-year, who practised mostly in the Chancery Courts in England.) I have had the great privilege of being able to see uncle Homi at very close quarters, for his son Navroz is almost like a brother to me — even though we were in different schools, we grew up together, playing games at the P.V.M. Gymkhana.

As soon as I completed my I.S.C. Exam, I moved to Delhi from Bombay as a 16-year old boy with my parents. Very early in my having

* The book will be published for the world market, by Oxford University Press, in June 2005.

5. Universal Law Publishing Co., New Delhi.

settled in Delhi, I recall an incident which is so touching that it bears upon the greatness of heart of Seervai. My parents were away for a week-end, and I was left to my own devices in a sprawling government bungalow in New Delhi, which was all the more forbidding to a 16-year old youth, given the contrast between a small flat in which I had always lived in Bombay and the noise and chaos of the Bombay streets, which invariably floated up to the flat. Here, all of a sudden, everything was gigantic and silent — the silence of the grave, to a young boy who was left alone in this huge bungalow. By about 7 p.m. on that Sunday evening, I had had enough. I knew that Seervai was at that time engaged as a Counsel in the biggest ever decision handed down by our Supreme Court — in the land mark judgment of *Keshavananda Bharati.* I picked up the telephone, and made bold to phone up Seervai in his room at the Ashoka Hotel. As soon as I introduced myself, I called him over for dinner that very evening. There was a long pause. The first question he asked me after that long pause was, "Where are your parents?" I explained that they were out of town. After another long pause, he readily agreed to come for dinner, and asked me to pick him up from Ashoka Hotel at 8 p.m. sharp. I did so — he was already waiting for me. I remember his talking to me of many things at my level, having dinner with me and then being dropped back. I later realised that Seervai would never have accepted a dinner invitation from anybody else on earth, as he was steeped in preparing his argument for the next day.

While he was involved in *Keshavanand Bharati's Case,* Seervai came every afternoon to lunch with my father in his chamber in the Supreme Court, for my father was the Additional Solicitor-General of India at that time. Even though I was a mere school boy, I remember the tremendous impact of Seervai's opening in reply to Palkhivala's argument in *Keshavanand Bharati's Case.* I had already had a preview of what he was going to say, at lunch time, and recall, even though I did not understand much of what he said then, that without touching his papers, he spoke to the 13 judges hearing the case, who heard him in pin drop silence. He was a powerful advocate who stated his point boldly and fearlessly and had the advantage of having a phenomenal memory from which he could pull out the facts and the law laid down in almost any judgment of the Privy Council dealing with the Canadian and Australian Constitutions and the Government of India Act, 1935.

He served with great distinction as Advocate-General of Maharashtra for 17 long years until differences between him and the then Law Minister, Mr. A. R. Antulay became such that he had to resign. I recall an amusing incident where Antulay was walking down the Supreme Court corridor a few years after Seervai's resignation and extended a hand to greet Seervai. Seervai looked at Antulay, as if he could not believe his eyes, put both his hands behind his back, and said in a voice audible to all, "I do not wish to have anything to do with blackguards like you." This incident more than anything else demonstrates how utterly straight forward and completely devoid of guile Seervai was. The great Shankaracharya had said that if a grown up man is like a child in his innocence, only then would he break the bonds of being reincarnated. Seervai fitted this description perfectly — he was child like in his simplicity, frankness and above all honesty. He was not at all a man of the world.

A few examples of this, which I have been privy to come to my mind. Seervai was one of 12 Parsis who was honoured by the Bombay Parsi Panchayat by being given a 'Mān Patra'. This was done at a large function on the CCI lawns, where each of the recipients of the Mān Patra had to give a speech. Seervai began giving his speech and suddenly, mid sentence, said "please put out that light — you are blinding me — I have just had a cataract operation." The offending light was immediately put out and Seervai carried on mid sentence — as if nothing untoward had occurred. On another occasion, when Navroz and I joined him for dinner at his favourite hotel Claridges, in Delhi, he asked for two separate bills and signed his own bill and took out cash and paid for Navroz and myself. I was also reliably told that even though he may have stayed in Delhi week after week, he always brought his laundry back to Bombay so that the client would not have to bear this additional expense.

Another incident which I have been informed about would perhaps give the best insight into his noble character. A Bombay Solicitor went to Seervai for an opinion in a complicated case. Seervai held long conferences and called the Solicitor and the client about 6 or 7 times. After the opinion was delivered, when Seervai's bill was given to the Solicitor, the Solicitor expressed shock at the paltry amount that he had charged. He went straight to Seervai and told him to increase the amount charged, as what was charged would not reflect the amount of work Seervai had put in. Seervai's answer was remarkable. He told the Solicitor that the client had come for his opinion on the assumption that Seervai knew the law. It took Seervai 6 or 7 long conferences and a lot of reading by himself in between those conferences, to best acquaint himself with the law. It was, Seervai said, for Seervai's knowledge of the law and not for his ignorance of it, that the client had come to him. Therefore, the fees charged, (which were abysmally low), were fully justified on this count.

By the time I had joined the profession in 1979, Seervai had stopped active practice and was concentrating on his *magnum opus* — *Constitutional Law of India*. However, it was my good fortune, that I was briefed with him in a Writ Petition on behalf of some police constables. Seervai held 3 conferences with me and I recall his being extremely thorough, painstaking and patient. He was also very kindly to whoever came for conference with him. The person was put at ease immediately and the conference proceeded at a leisurely pace. Unfortunately, when the matter was actually argued in the Court, I had to go to Delhi and therefore missed Seervai arguing it.

One other personal incident comes to my mind. Seervai was a person who strongly believed that alcohol was evil — it did mankind no good and only produced depression. However, Navroz and I, after we were 18 used to share a drink together in Navroz's bed room. One evening we decided to have our drinks in the hall. As we began drinking, Seervai came and joined us. Even though he realised what was being done, not once did he say anything — and the self control that he exercised on that occasion was remarkable. I was reliably informed that many years later, after a trip to the UK, he even brought Navroz at his request, a bottle of liquor as a present.

On their Golden Anniversary, there was a big party on the P.V.M. Gymkhana lawns. Seervai was seated on a high chair looking like a minor Prophet from the old Testament. People had lined up to wish him. As soon as he caught sight of me, he politely asked all the persons who had lined up to greet him to please wait. He then turned to me and said that I was to ensure that no body touched his book after his death, not even his beloved son Navroz. Only after he was satisfied that I had fully understood what he said, was I allowed to go. I am told that what he said to me orally became a part of his 'Will'. At that time, I wondered why he wanted his entire life's work to perish with him, but after some time I have come to the realisation that he was right. His book involved a labour of love, which took one over several continents and required both vast knowledge and time. Assuming that another practising lawyer could acquire this vast knowledge, it is most unlikely that he would devote the time necessary to write another edition of this monumental treatise. Upon sober reflection therefore, and also taking into account the fact that the style in which the book is written is also highly personalised, I feel he made the right decision even though I am very sorry to see such a great book becoming dated. The Colossus of Rhodes was one of the ancient wonders of the World. It lasted a mere 50 or 60 years until destroyed by an earthquake. The ***Colossus Homi Seervai*** lived to the ripe old age of 90 and will never be forgotten — atleast not until there exists the legal fraternity in India who are to live by, uphold and defend India's great Constitution.

SEERVAI — AS I KNEW HIM

Mr. Shantilal Shah
Advocate

IT WAS A GREAT PLEASURE, and the happiest moments of my life and of my memory to have worked with one of our great humanists and a Jurist of International Repute.

In 1973-74 two organisations were formed, Citizens for Democracy and People's Union for Civil Liberties.

In 1975 emergency was imposed and there was an all-pervading feeling that even Courts could not interfere with any executive order or orders.

In those days, Judges of almost all High Courts raised their heads and started setting aside executive orders. My friend Justice Sankalchand Sheth of the Gujarat High Court was one of them. The executive, with the assistance of the Supreme Court, started transferring the unwanted Judges with a view to control them. Justice S.H. Sheth, along with Justice Divan and one more Judge from Gujarat, was transferred to the Andhra Pradesh High Court.

Justice Sheth wanted to challenge this order. He had two great constitutional lawyers in mind. Seervai was one of them. He telephoned me and asked my opinion. I quoted some of the arguments from the Judgment of Hon'ble Supreme Court while granting stay in Indira Gandhi Election Appeal, and the observations of Seervai in his books and articles on the point. Justice Sheth came to Bombay. It was June 1975, and Seervai was on holiday at Pune with his family. I and Justice Sheth discussed with other friends and having decided to take the assistance of Seervai, we took an appointment to meet at Pune.

We were to reach Pune at 6 but it was a day of very heavy rains, and we reached Pune at mid-night. Till then Seervai with his family was waiting for us. They gave us a warm welcome and expressed sympathy for our travelling so long in such uncertain weather. Justice Sheth and Seervai discussed the law and Seervai expressed the view that it was not within the powers of the executive to transfer Judges. He had, prior to that time, drafted a Petition for another Judge (of the Bombay High Court) who was also a victim of the transfer policy. A copy of that Draft was handed over to Justice Sheth and we left at about 3 a.m. The whole family waited for us and gave us a send off. This is Seervai, the man, the lover of democracy and the Judiciary. He said "The day the Judiciary will be controlled, that will destroy one of the strongest pillars of democracy, and liberty will vanish."

Justice Sheth filed the Petition in the Gujarat High Court. Seervai stayed at Ahmedabad for more than three weeks to argue the petition. The Order of Transfer was declared void and without jurisdiction and set aside.

We then arranged a Meeting at Bombay (to felicitate both Justice Sheth and Seervai) in a hotel at Marine Drive. M. C. Chagla, an equally eminent lawyer, a Great Judge and a greater humanitarian, presided. This is what M. C. Chagla said about Seervai.

"Mr. Seervai is not only a great Constitutional Lawyer, but a man of great integrity, conviction and action. I had the pleasure to hear him as Advocate-General of Bombay, and if any one would come forward to save the judiciary, it would be Seervai." All speakers spoke very highly about him. He proved them right by appearing in the Supreme Court, in what is known as *The Judges' Case.* The hall of the hotel was packed to capacity and the Spirit and value of liberty were seen.

We have in Bombay State two organisations, Citizens for Democracy, of which Justice Nathwani was the first President and I and Mr. M. A. Rane were Secretaries. Subsequently M. C. Chagla became President. The other organisation was People's Union for Civil Liberties, of which Ex-Chief Justice J.C. Shah was the first President and Justice Chagla followed him. Thereafter Seervai was elected President, Justice Nathwani, Dr. Aloo Dastur, Dr. Usha Mehta and myself were Vice-Presidents. Thus for seven long years I was closely associated with Seervai as a member of People's Union for Civil Liberties, or as Vice-President. In almost all the meetings, we had free and fair discussion. Even on issues on which Seervai had contrary views, we always took decisions, by consent. This only proves how fexible this great Jurist was.

His last but not the least great contribution was in the case known as *The Judges' Case* in the Supreme Court. When he returned to Bombay from Delhi, we gave him a hero's welcome. Mrinal Gore, Shanti Patel, G. G. Parikh, D. S. Parikh, Cooper and many people garlanded him, and a felicitation meeting was arranged.

During this period of seven years I and others experienced his politeness, his affection, and his feelings for fellow members. He was fearless and firm. In spite of difference of age, experience and knowledge, he gave love and affection to us like a head of family. He would inquire as to the cause of our cold or weak health. He showed such personal concern.

It was a great pleasure to hear him across the tea table. He had great love for literature and would recite poems and quote great works of the 19th and 20th Centuries, literature of both the East and West.

The world has not only lost one of the greatest humanitarians but a constitutional wizard.

When I went to invite Seervai for my daughter's wedding, he said his health would not permit him to attend, but his wife would surely come, and in fact she did so and graced the occasion.

In the passing away of Seervai we have lost an action-oriented personality, which is a rare quality and most needed in these days.

In short we can say that Seervai lived life:

> "Life is real. Life is earnest. The grave is not its goal.
> Dust thou art, to dust returnest, is not spoken of the soul."

He has left "Footprints on the sands of Time."

RECOLLECTIONS BY FAMILY FRIENDS

HOMI SEERVAI — AS I KNEW HIM*

Sheryar K. Ookerjee
Former Head, Dept. of Philosophy, Wilson College

"As Homi Seervai would have said" is a remark that is often on the lips of those who knew him. It is sometimes said to lend support to a point of view, but more often simply out of affection for a person whose character and personality had made an indelible impression on all those who had come in touch with him.

I first saw Homi Seervai fifty-five years ago. He was chairing a public debate at the Government Law College, Bombay. I can see him vividly, a man of slight and slender build and sharp features, making his chairman's remarks in clipped, incisive accents. A young woman who had invited me to the meeting asked me, at the end, what I thought of the speakers and I replied that they were quite competent. "And the chairman?" she asked, "wasn't he brilliant?" I agreed. Only a few months later this young woman announced that she was engaged to Mr. Seervai. Feroza Lalkaka was two years ahead of me in Wilson College, Bombay. Soon afterwards I met Homi when he came to the college to fetch Feroza after a lecture of J.C.P. d'Andrade's. That was the beginning of a close and enduring friendship.

This friendship took deeper root some years later when d'Andrade was nearing his end. He had been a senior lecturer in philosophy at Bombay's prestigious Elphinstone College, and was generally regarded as one of the most eminent teachers of the subject. Homi had been his

* Re-published from *Constitutional Perspectives,* Universal Law Publishing Co. Pvt. Ltd.

student and d'Andrade used to say that Homi's success at the Bar had shown how a study of philosophy helped to develop the mind. In July 1949, I learnt from Dr. Borges of the Tata Memorial Hospital that d'Andrade had a recurrence of the cancer for which he had undergone surgery a year earlier and that he had only a couple of months to live. I immediately passed on this information to the Seervais. Feroza and Homi appeared at the hospital next morning and, from that day onwards, they visited d'Andrade at the hospital and then at his home almost every evening until he died on 5 September.

Intellect and Humanity

For me, a raw and recently appointed lecturer, these evenings made up an unforgettable experience. It was fascinating, evening after evening, to listen to a dialogue, sometimes serious, sometimes sparkling with wit and wisdom, carried on between d'Andrade, Homi and two other friends, both educationists. All of us, including d'Andrade, knew that he had not long to live, but that did not interfere with the richness of the conversation or the warmth of fellowship. It was during these evenings that I came to realise the quality of Homi's intellect and of his humanity. In spite of being a busy lawyer, he set aside so many hours to be with his teacher. His feelings are well recorded in his tribute in *Philosophy and Life,* a collection of d'Andrade's talks and papers posthumously published by the Bombay Philosophical Society and of which Homi was one of the editors.

Homi was an early member of this society which was founded in 1941 by d'Andrade and John McKenzie, the then Principal of Wilson College. There is little doubt that it was, to a great extent, due to d'Andrade's presence that the meetings were well attended by teachers and students of philosophy. Therefore, following his death there was a marked fall in attendance. It is then that Homi and Feroza came to the rescue. Homi took it upon himself as a kind of commitment not only to attend all the meetings (about twelve in a year) but also to persuade and bring with him a number of other persons. Once again the society bloomed. He read several papers before the society. I particularly recall one on Plato's *Republic* and another on Justice. Around 1958 Homi was elected President of the Society and it was during his presidentship that the then famous Oxford philosopher, Professor A. J. Ayer, addressed the society.

It was Homi who, as one of the editors, undertook the task of seeing *Philosophy and Life* through the press. This brought me even closer to the Seervai family. During 1951 Feroza and I would spend afternoon after afternoon in their flat overlooking the large playground of the Oval, and we would put together the material that was to be sent to the press, later correct the galley proofs and, finally, the page proofs that came pouring in. A routine was established. After completing our job we would go to fetch Homi at the High Court, he would come down precisely at 7.15, we would then drive to the seafront at Marine Drive and walk for precisely forty-five minutes before returning home. So completely immersed was Homi in his profession that he would relate to us in considerable detail what had happened in court that day, how the judge talked too much instead of just listening (as a good judge should) and what were the arguments and counter-arguments that were bandied about. I must confess that sometimes I found this talk a bit too technical to follow but I was chary of admitting this lest I tarnish the glowing image Homi had of me as a young man learned in the law as well as being a teacher of philosophy! He had, in fact, generously offered to take me in his Chambers as one of his 'devils'.

Optimistic Outlook

Apart from legal matters, these walks gave me an insight into the man's nature, ideas and beliefs, his generally confident and optimistic outlook on life, and the depth of his feelings and concern for others. People used to say to me in those days that they found Mr. Seervai somewhat forbidding in manner and stern in looks, particularly as he addressed the court or walked the corridors with his flowing black gown and wearing the regalia of the Advocate-General's office. But if he flashed a smile at you, you realised that behind that austere exterior was a very human person, sociable and kind, happy in the company of friends and always ready to help if they had a problem. Not only ready but even anxious to help and, in fact, mildly annoyed if, out of consideration for his time, they did not come to him for assistance. "Why didn't you come to me?" he would say, "all sorts of people come to me."

Many were the occasions when he gave his well-considered advice on legal matters, routine matters for lawyers but to which he gave special individual attention whenever they concerned his friends. Thus, he carefully examined the 'agreement for sale' of my old flat and asked me to get the latest edition of the Co-operative Societies Act, which he studied in order to guide me about obtaining the 'no-objection certificate' which was needed to enter my new flat. Both Feroza and Homi went considerably out of their way to help my wife and me in a personal matter at a crucial stage of our lives. Keen as

Homi was that I should join his chambers and practise law, he appreciated my decision to take up teaching, which he stoutly defended against my parents' ambition to see me make a reputation at the Bar. Many years later, when I applied for a government scholarship and asked him for a testimonial, Homi immediately wrote out a very generous one. Again, after some fifteen years, I applied for a post-doctoral research fellowship; when Homi came to know of it he, on his own, offered to give me a fresh testimonial and told me to submit his name, if required, as my referee. It should not, however, be concluded that he was ready to dish out testimonials for the asking, for when a close relative of mine whom Homi had met quite a number of times asked him for a testimonial, he refused to give it on the ground that he did not know the person well enough for the purpose. Homi always acknowledged and appreciated the work of others. If he thought well of a paper read at the Bombay Philosophical Society, he would go up to the speaker and tell him it was 'top-class' (a favourite expression of his). Indeed, I think he was at times too generous in his praise. If, on the other hand, a talk or a paper did not come up to his expectations, he would soon cease to take any interest in it. He was, to some extent, a 'first impressions' man; the first impressions counted for much and if you happened to make a favourable impression on him to start with, he would be staunchly loyal to you. He was generous in acknowledging a service done to him, however, insignificant it might be. He once sought my confirmation, as a teacher of logic, for a fallacy he had detected in a judgment he was examining when writing the third edition of his magnum opus, *Constitutional Law of India*. I did nothing more than say that he was right, but my name appeared in the volume among the people who were thanked.

Brilliant Speaker

Homi's cross-examination of witnesses was reputed to be devastating. I saw him in action only once in the 1950s in a case that ran for twelve consecutive days. It involved a man who had filed a suit for damages against one of Bombay's major public institutions which, he alleged, had treated him unjustly. Homi knew the man well and had high regard for him. He, therefore, appeared for him without charging a fee. Apart from the fact that he was completely convinced about the merits of the case, Homi's compassion was aroused because he was a man of moderate means and had a large family to support. The case had evoked considerable interest because it was a David and Goliath match; the courtroom used to be packed to overflowing every day. The defendant institution was represented by a well-known and highly respected person who stepped into the box with a show of arrogance and self-confidence. Seervai's performance was brilliant. With a meticulously prepared case, he launched an attack in which the cutting edge of his questioning was sharpened with sarcasm and ethical fervour. His voice could be distinctly heard in the corridor outside the courtroom. After three days of battering, the witness was escorted by his friends out of the room in a visibly shattered condition. Following an earnest plea from the judge, a settlement was eventually reached out of court, which was unfortunate because, had the case been fought to the end, some heads would surely have rolled.

It was in a very different voice that Homi addressed a large gathering at the cemetery following d'Andrade's death. Asked to speak at short notice, the words came from the heart. When I told him later that it was a very moving and finely uttered tribute, he just said, "How could it be otherwise when one was looking on that beloved face for the last time?"

Homi used to say that with some people he would be 'monumentally silent,' but I never found this to be the case. He could always hit upon some suitable topic which allowed him to display his vast erudition and incredible powers of memory. Quotations were always within easy recall. The famous couplet from one of his favourite authors is surely appropriate here:

and still they gazed and still the wonder grew
that one small head should carry all it knew.

Only once have I known Homi stumped for words. The Seervais and my wife and I were holidaying at the Cecil Hotel in Matheran, a beautiful resort some seventy miles from Bombay. One day a fellow lawyer called on the Seervais. Homi made one of his standard moves, "So how do you amuse yourselves in this place?" "We go for walks, we read", said the fellow lawyer. "What do you read?" was Homi's next question. "We have some books," was the enlightening answer. That line having proved a dead end, Homi tried another gambit. "Come", he said rising, "I'll show you round our rooms." "We have seen them in the past." Homi gave up.

Avid Reader

Homi was always genuinely interested in knowing how his friends spent their leisure hours and, more particularly, what they had been reading. His own reading, in addition to the law, was extensive. In spite of his heavy work, he read literature and history and occasionally even made time to read some philosophy, which was, of course, his subject for his B.A. and M.A. degrees. While he admired and was considerably influenced by the British Idealists, Bradley and Bosanquet, his favourite, I think, was Aristotle.

In literature, his favourites were Shakespeare, Goldsmith, Boswell on Johnson, and Churchill. Every new book on Churchill was soon to be seen in his library. He admired Thackeray's *Esmond* and loved Trollope.

Feroza and he had read *Barchester Towers* aloud to each other many times. He found Meredith's style too tortuous for pleasant reading. Conan Doyle and Wodehouse were a staple diet. He could not empathise with Virginia Woolf, which is surprising in one who was so sensitive to the magic of words. Strange too in a man who read so much poetry that he did not seem to respond too keenly to the beauty of Nature.

Whether in his reading or on the screen or in life, the slightest exhibition of violence or obscenity revolted Homi. He was no film buff, but he was ready to see a good film and particularly enjoyed *My Fair Lady,* Leslie Howard's *Scarlet Pimpernel,* Jose Ferrer's *Cyrano, All This and Heaven Too, Portrait of Jennie,* and *The Scent of a Woman.*

Initially he did not care much for music, but as the children grew up and got bitten by the music bug, Homi also began to give the bug a fair chance and although, I think, he was never severely bitten, he did grow to like the great standard works and used to attend concerts with the family.

Family Man

But it was his children who afforded him the greatest joy. He was charming with all little children. My wife once wrote to me from Poona, 'Dear Homi made a queer sound by putting his mouth on his hand and blowing, and vowed it was the call of some bird, I forget which. What a child he is at heart! With children he is really the merriest of companions!' I mentioned earlier how Feroza and I used to fetch him at the High Court in the evenings. As he got into the car, the first thing he would invariably ask was, 'Well, how is Mehloo?' (meaning his daughter, Meher, then about five), and Feroza would invariably reply, 'Jolly'. Only after he was satisfied that Mehloo was well and jolly would he turn and greet me. After our usual walk, he would reach home at exactly 8 o'clock to be with the child for some time before her bed-time.

He would read to her or tell her stories or entertain her in diverse ways. I once saw him wearing a home-made paper cap to impersonate a fictional character. In the early days, till his children grew up, he did not accept dinner invitations because they cut into his time with the little ones. When someone expressed surprise that he left even a Menuhin concert without waiting for the encores, he said, "That's because you don't know what a bright-eyed little person was waiting for me at home." There was another ritual to be performed without fail and that was to buy three small slabs of Cadbury's milk chocolate before going home. When the children fell ill, he was a 'ministering angel', making them comfortable, ensuring that they took their medicines regularly, reading to them and keeping up their spirits in various ways. The practice of reading aloud to them was continued, I think, even into their teens.

I must mention one particular occasion. We were returning after a holiday at Matheran, which is at a height of some 2,500 feet above sea level. From there to Neral down in the plains we rode in a narrow-gauge train. We were four adults and three children in a small compartment for a journey which took an hour and a half. As the train wound its way, serpent-like, around the folds of the great mountain, the sun would sometimes peep in through one window of the carriage and sometimes through another. Every time its hot rays happened to fall on his other daughter, Shirin, then aged seven, or his son, Navroz, then aged four, Homi would jump up from his seat and pull down the wooden shutters and then, as the train took a different turn, push them up again. My wife and I were amazed at this concern and that too with an aching back which he had hurt in a fall a few days earlier.

Strong Views

Homi held strong and definite views on many subjects and never hesitated to express them strongly. He was particularly hostile to liquor.

As Advocate-General of Maharashtra he defended the state's prohibition policy not only as a legally permissible action but with total conviction as to its necessity. Homi once heard a doctor recommending a little brandy as a 'stimulant' to a patient who felt rather low. He immediately corrected the doctor with "It is *not* a stimulant; it is a *depressant*." To fight the Government's prohibition case he had made a thorough study of the nature and effects of alcohol.

Naturally, no liquor was served at the Seervai lunches or dinners. When occasionally I succumbed to Navroz's offer of a wee peg, Homi regarded the lapse with obvious disapproval but restrained tolerance. Indeed, restraint and control were major elements in Homi's character. I have never known him to lose his temper or self-control. He would show impatience or irritation, but never temper. He would make a cutting remark or rejoinder. 'Bizarre' was an oft-used expression of disapproval.

I had once visited him when, unknown to me, he had just received the news of the death of a dear friend of his. He did not seem his usual cheerful self, but he did not tell me what had happened. He just took down a book from the shelf and read to me a moving passage from it. When their second child died soon after birth, Feroza and Homi showed remarkable restraint. Homi sat with me and narrated, very quietly, all that had happened and then, referring to some visitors who had continued sitting for a long time, he said, "I wish people would realise that sometimes one wants to be alone."

Homi was forthright and never minced words. Some people did not react favourably to this but at least they knew where they stood with him. There was no hypocrisy in the man. The following incident is illustrative. A certain Minister of the State of Maharashtra had conducted himself very offensively at a meeting when the office of the Advocate-General was a subject of discussion. Homi was present at the meeting. Some months later, the said Minister telephoned Homi and the following dialogue ensued:

Minister: "I am Mr. … , Minister for …"

Seervai: "Yes"

Minister: "How are you, Mr. Seervai?"

Seervai: "I am well."

Minister: "I am Mr … "

Seervai: "Yes, you told me; and you asked me how I was and I said I was well".

Minister: "Mr. Seervai, I would like you to write an article for a journal my wife is publishing …"

Seervai: "After the part that you played at the meeting that day, I have decided to have nothing to do with anything you might be remotely connected with. Goodbye."

Discipline and Attention to Detail

Homi was an extremely methodical and disciplined person, very particular about punctuality. There was a time for the daily evening walk, a time for meals and a time for going to bed. The self-imposed rule, while the children were young, of not going out to dinner was later relaxed, but the host would be requested to serve dinner early. Once I was a little late for lunch at the Seervais'. I made some lame excuse about my watch having let me down. Homi asked me how I set it, and, upon my saying that I set it by the municipal siren every morning, he promptly advised me to set it always by the BBC signals. On another occasion, I was to read a paper at the Bombay Philosophical Society and I had given Homi a copy of my paper in advance. Again I was a little late in arriving for the meeting and was surprised to see that Homi had already begun to read the paper on my behalf.

Even little things did not escape his attention. His choices were the result of careful deliberation. At the hotel at Matheran, for example, he would select one set of room for the summer and another set, just opposite, for the winter months because of the position of the sun. He advised my wife not to wear shorts with a panther-skin pattern on them in case some sportsmen might be around with a gun!

Homi was basically a simple person, unostentatious in dress and behaviour. He was not arrogant, but like a true Aristotelian, he took pride in his abilities, his work and in being a virtuous man. In spite of his position as Advocate-General and his erudition, he was never aloof. He always greeted you with a big disarming smile and never tried to hustle you away because he was busy. One morning I went to his chambers just to return a book of his. Seeing that he had a heap of files and papers in front of him, I gave him the book and was about to beat a hasty retreat. He would have none of it. He made me sit down, ordered tea, and for twenty minutes explained what he was working on. He was one of those lucky ones whose work is their pleasure.

Tea was undoubtedly his favourite drink. Many were the occasions when, after a philosophical lecture, he took some of us to a restaurant across the road for tea and buttered toast. His tastes in food, as in most things, were simple. He avoided anything spicy or exotic. I believe he never went to a Chinese restaurant. His usual recreation, apart from reading and, latterly watching television selectively, was to walk on Marine Drive or at Apollo Bunder or around the garden near the new Council Hall. He carried a large torch and a walking stick, not to help him in walking but to ward off "cats and dogs and other such creatures". He was no animal lover; he was, in fact, rather scared of them. When Meher expressed a desire to keep a dog, she had to be satisfied instead with a very tiny turtle.

Homi held strict moral views and principles. He despised any hint of dishonesty or 'crookiness' in anybody and had a withering way of asking, "Do you mean to say?" He was scrupulously particular about not making use, for private interests, of his official status. Once when, on returning from a holiday, he found that a railway compartment was reserved for him as the Advocate-General, he was extremely annoyed with the person who had done it. In giving me the testimonial I have referred to, he did not use his official letterhead because the testimonial was not given in his official capacity. The several honours which he received sat easily on his shoulders; in no way did he keep reminding people that he had been awarded the Padma Vibhushan, and never attached it or allowed anyone to attach it before his name.

Friendly Disposition

Homi had a sunny and friendly disposition. He had a balanced outlook on life and faced it with a reasonable optimism, developed probably and to a large extent from his study of philosophy and his continued interest in the subject. He was not attracted to the 'transcendental' philosophy of India. He liked people and enjoyed the company of his friends, he was gracious towards his many admirers and he was very loyal to his close friends and relations. For many years, even after his work greatly multiplied, he used to go to the Chambers of a college friend and fellow counsel, have a cup of tea with him and then proceed to his own Chambers.

If you happened to find a place next to Homi at a party or a dinner, there was never any fear of awkward silences, for with child-like zest he would tell you about what at that point of time interested or absorbed him, be it the case he was fighting or the book he was reading. Or he would inquire about your problems, if he knew you had any, and give you his considered advice. Like Burke, whom he admired, he could talk on many themes (for in his profession, he would say, one had to know something about a variety of subjects) and you would be struck by the breadth of his knowledge. If you were at his home, he would delightedly display the books recently acquired during his periodic visits to the Strand Book Stall, Bombay. If you presented him with a book, he wanted you to inscribe it and if he gave you a book, he always inscribed it suitably in his carefully moulded hand.

As a public speaker Homi displayed immense self-confidence and poise. His preparation was extremely thorough, whether he addressed a court, lectured to the general public, opened a school building or replied on being felicitated on his eightieth birthday. The speeches were timed almost to the last minute. His was not a flamboyant, oratorical style; he depended on well-marshalled points and arguments expressed in appropriately chosen words spoken in a loud, clear and high-pitched voice. His manner of speaking, in public speech or private conversation, was (to quote a friend) "sharp as a razor's edge".

As I sit writing this piece, I can see Homi in many different roles. I can see him standing in full court, head held high, holding his notes in his left hand while stressing a point with the help of his right, delivering lethal blows to his adversary's arguments; I can see him sitting and having tea with Feroza on the lawns of Princess Victoria Mary Gymkhana; I can see him springing up at a philosophical meeting to answer a question; but what comes to mind most readily is a very pleasing picture of Homi at home of an evening in casual Parsi dress and completely relaxed, with his wife and grandchildren around him, stretching out his hand to shake yours in a firm grip and welcoming you with a huge smile straight from the heart.

H. M. SEERVAI

Gillian Tindall
Writer

Dear Feroza,

A BRIEF NOTE IN response to your appeal for recollections of Homi — not that I think I ever actually called him Homi to his face, since he was for me a rather intimidatingly distinguished old person! In fact one of my clearest memories is of first meeting him, in your company of course, I think in the pleasant small club you used, called something like the Princess May Club — nice sandwiches on a green lawn with buildings around. I, having been suitably informed by Foy Nissen, said to him: "I hear you're rather a grand lawyer." "Mmm, nyuph," he said, giving me a knowing lawyer's look, "Moderately grand." I was amused and charmed, because his accent, his diction, his whole style reminded me of a beloved grandfather of mine, who also had a distinguished career (in the Indian Civil Service and afterwards in the Treasury where he finished up with a knighthood. He had in fact wanted to be a barrister, but he lacked the private family money which, in the England of those days, was almost indispensable to a young man setting out on such a career). The two men must indeed have had a very similar style of education: my grandfather was at Winchester public school and then took a double first at Oxford. The difference was that actually my grandfather was a full generation earlier. He was born in 1866, whereas Homi, of 1906, was really of the same generation of my father born in 1910 and still alive and doing reasonably well. But under the British Raj, and for a long time after I think, the traditions of the kind of British education Homi received became fixed in India in something of a time-warp, an unchanging standard, a Latin-and-Greek-influenced way of speaking and reasoning, that are now recalled, nostalgically, by a dwindling number of people.

Of course Homi's integrity and power of reasoning, that his education helped to reinforce, were essentially his own. I remember both Foy, and Rustom Choksi, telling me how honourably Homi had behaved during the bad days of Mrs. Gandhi's Emergency.

I also recall how attached he was to you and what a happy, successful marriage you two busy people appeared to have, by any standards — eastern or western.

HOMI SEERVAI

Persis P. Kothawala
Environmental activist

Dear Feroza,

I ALWAYS REMEMBER Homi's ability to be one with the children. I recall my Cyrus dashing off at the P.V.M. to hear "Homi Uncle's birdie songs".

My last recollection of Homi was shortly before his demise, — we were having an Oval Trust meeting in your dining room. I recall that Rafiq Dada was there — in the midst of serious discussions as to how to proceed in our matter, little Riyad came in to show off his clothes before going to a birthday party. The transformation in Homi was unforgettable. The immediate putting aside of weighty matters to pay close attention to Riyad — to admire his clothes — to tell him to enjoy his party — and within a few minutes, the child went away happy with his brief but satisfying moments with his Grandpa — and before we knew it — we were back in the midst of protecting the Oval from encroachments! This is a memory I treasure — the ability to be both learned and loving at the same time. You and Homi indeed were blessed with great familial happiness.

Editor's Note

A famous 15th Century figure of the Florentine Renaissance is described in a book of that name by Vincent Cronin (1967 Collins) in a similar incident, which is very interesting in this context, and I cite it here. Cosimo de Medici had contributed to the adornment of the city on an unsurpassed scale. Here he is, an elderly man, with ambassadors from Lucca:

"The audience was held in his own house, according to custom, and during discussions a small child, his grandson, came up to him with some oatsticks and a little knife for Cosimo to make him a whistle. *Cosimo signified that the discussion was adjourned, devoted himself to the child and made the whistle, telling him then to run away and play. The ambassadors were somewhat offended.* 'Sir Cosimo, we are surprised at your behaviour. We have come to you on behalf of our commune to treat of grave matters and you desert us for a child.' With a laugh Cosimo flung his arms round their shoulders. 'My brothers and lords, are you not fathers too? Don't you love your children and grandchildren? You are surprised that I should have made that whistle; it's as well that you didn't ask me to play it. Because I would have done that too'."

In the Preface to the last volume of the 4th edition of Constitutional Law of India, which was posthumously published, our son Navroz, referring to our grandchildren, wrote "No amount of work would permit him to turn them away. And so, in the midst of a dictation critically examining a Supreme Court judgment, a nursery rhyme would be recited or a story read and re-read. The grandchildren satisfied, would depart; the dictation would continue."

HOMI SEERVAI

Shashi N. Thakar
Educationist

Dear Mrs. Feroza Seervai,

I AM TOO SMALL and an ordinary person to write about the late Mr. Homi Seervai. But when you rang up inviting me to attend his first death anniversary I could'nt resist the temptation to put down on paper the impact he made on my mind.

I wonder if you remember that first I met Mr. Homi Seervai and you as the parents of my student, Shirin, in the Bombay International School.

As a college student I had heard of Mr. Homi Seervai, as the 'giant' of Indian Constitutional law and read his writings that came across our way with great awe and admiration. Our Professors used to say "whatever Mr. Seervai does not know about constitutional law is not worth knowing."

One day Shirin suggested that she would not go back home unless I promised to go with her and see her father. I was thrilled. Little did little Shirin know that she was opening a door to me which I had thought would always remain distant and closed. I was going to meet a man about whom I had heard much as a young girl.

When I met Mr. Seervai I was struck by his clarity of thought, not only about politics and the constitution, but about things like 'how we should carry water when we take children for trips and outings!'

I was an ardent, almost a blind, follower of Gandhiji when I met Mr. Seervai. But I went home that day accepting that the history of India can paint different pictures for different persons.

I had met you earlier, several times as an active member of the BIS but I had never met Mr. Seervai.

When I met Mr. Seervai I realized that the small and frail figure of Mr. Seervai held fearless convictions and fiery eloquence. I definitely carried home that day much clearer ideas — much clearer than any layman is expected to — on several points in the constitution.

I met Mr. Seervai after that on five or six occasions along with my father and it was a pleasure to listen to him talk with authority on many topics including 'how alcohol is bad for the human body and how rural work often fizzles out to nothing but just a day's outing from a dirty city to a dirty village.'

We, Thakars, will always cherish with great fondness and admiration the 'lively' moments spent with him, with you and your family.

HOMI SEERVAI*

Homai J. Shroff
Former Principal of Elphinstone College

I AM GRATEFUL TO the Editor of *The Elphinstonian* for giving me the opportunity to pay a tribute to the memory of Mr. H. M. Seervai. The

* Republished from *The Elphinstonian*

two distinguished lawyers, Mr. Atul M. Setalvad and Mr. Tehmtan R. Andhyarujina, whom she has also requested to write are beyond comparison better qualified than me to give an appreciation of his legal acumen, his outstanding brilliance as a lawyer and his monumental work on the Constitution of India.

What I can try to do in this personal tribute is to record his association with the Elphinstone College during the years when I was privileged to come in close contact with him — from the 'seventies till the time of his death in January 1996.

One of the most heartening things about the Elphinstone College ethos is that a large number of its distinguished alumni cherish affection for the College throughout their lives and are ever ready to respond to the call of the College for help.

Of these Mr. H. M. Seervai was the most outstanding in his devotion and loyalty; indeed, in this matter the example he set was one that people far less eminent or busy would feel embarrassed not to emulate.

Any achievement of the College gave Mr. Seervai joy; if anything untoward happened, it distressed him. Of course he was never a person to sit back and remain distressed; he went all out to see that something was done, and matters were rectified in the best possible way.

At such times his preoccupation with his important legal work, the pressing need he felt to complete the writing of his authoritative books, or his health was not allowed to stand in the way.

He served without demur as a trustee of the Endowment Fund of the College for over thirty years, till a year before his death; this in spite of protests from his family, which rightly felt that he should shake off the burden.

During the whole year of the 125th Anniversary Celebrations of the College in 1981-82, when he was already 75 years old and still committed to fighting zealously for the variety of political, social and legal causes in which he believed passionately, he ungrudgingly spared time and energy for the College.

Heading the College as Principal at the time, I could not have managed either the celebrations or many other vexing problems with half as much assurance, without his imaginative ideas, his clarity of mind and prescience, his meticulous attention to detail and his unfailing courtesy. His leadership could not but inspire others to do far more than they would otherwise have done. Of course any appeal from him was enough for even non-Elphinstonians to rally round and contribute generously to the fund-raising drive for the celebrations.

As a person, H. M. Seervai was certainly not less admirable than as a legal luminary. Indeed it was his character and personality that made him such a shining example for the legal profession. Brilliant and nimble and flourishing lawyers there are a plenty; but, let us hope, that at least a few lawyers are left who can stand some comparison with a man of such a sterling character, total honesty and unflinching adherence to principles and values.

To strike a personal note, what drew my admiration was his optimism, even his buoyancy, at his advanced age. When things looked grim, as they indeed often did during the latter years of his life, in the political, social and ethical life of the country, the courts, the college, on some occasions one let fall murmurs of pessimism or frustration. And he would fix one with his eye and say: "Yes! ... However I am an optimist."

But Mr. Seervai was not an optimist because he chose to bury his head in the sand. His perception of the world was clear-eyed and unsparing. The optimism derived from his belief that by an unwavering fight against wrongs and injustice, it was ultimately always possible to set things right. He had fought for lost causes and turned them into triumphant forces so often, that it was second nature to him to take on one more challenge — and succeed once again.

Though Mr. Seervai was a student of philosophy and the law during his years in College, his extensive knowledge of English literature and his infectious enjoyment of it could put professors of English to shame.

His attachment to his family was another facet of his character that struck those who knew him. He used to remark that even during the years when he was making his way up as a lawyer, unlike other 'busy' lawyers, he would come home early in the evening to be at home with his children. Reading aloud from books with his family, was an experience which gave him great pleasure.

The Elphinstone College owes a deep debt of gratitude to H. M. Seervai; I hope it will not fail to perpetuate his memory in a way which in some small measure will inspire future students to live by his ideals.

Men like H. M. Seervai, whether they die at ninety or hundred, may be said to have died prematurely. The world needs their kind.

RECOLLECTIONS BY THE FAMILY

H. M. SEERVAI

His Personal Life

Feroza H. Seervai

H. M. SEERVAI HAS BEEN known personally to some, and to many more as a lawyer, thinker, lover of literature, author and Advocate-General. He has also been known as a philosopher who lived according to his philosophy and as a man actively concerned with public causes for which he gave his professional time, donated and raised funds. His personal life was private and known to but few.

Few persons have as lovely private lives as public. Seervai's integrity of character being complete and entire, he had excellences which glowed equally in private and in public.

Seervai must be seen wholly. Friends have written of him as they knew him. Our children also have written of him from a son's, a daughter's point of view; here you will see Seervai in the words of an old woman who had fifty remarkably happy years with him.

They were years of close comradeship, friendship full of laughter, of complete freedom of thought and action, of gentle and passionate love, of incessant recitation of poetry and prose and of talking, talking, talking, of walking for pleasure, and also of silent togetherness, of reading books aloud to each other, of a deeply shared parenthood. He would, however, miss me, whenever I spent too much time with our children and away from him. Our neighbour wondered that a couple married over 40 years, had so much to talk about with each other.

Seervai was 38 when we met. I was 21. Our marriage could be fixed only if my parents approved, he said. "They would naturally be concerned for your welfare" he added. My impulsive and impetuous nature was then, as always, offset by his temperament, calm, controlled, considerate, temper never lost. All our lives I was excitable, and full of angers. Homi maintained calm, Homi reasoned. On the few occasions when my words were too ill-considered, he may exclaim involuntarily, the next moment, apologise (although in my view, he did not need to apologise, for it was I who unwittingly said what was provoking).

Seervai's Family and Childhood

Homi often spoke to me of his ancestors and of his childhood. His ancestors were distinguished: The Wadias on his mother's side, were renowned Master Builders. Ships wrought by them were acknowledged to be superior to those built abroad. On his father's side they were KOTWALS and pillars of the community in Navsari. One ancestor arrived from Persia hundreds of years ago, when Zoroastrians under persecution left Pars in Iran and came to India. He was Dastur Naryosang Dhaval. By his pre-eminence he earned a place in the galaxy of revered ancients and heroes, whose names, since centuries, are still recited in the religious ceremonies of the Zoroastrians.

Homi's paternal grandfather was awarded by the royal ruler of the Baroda Court whom he served, a silver anklet to do him honour. Ancestors of his mother were awarded medals, lands, silver rulers, ivory. All were marked for their high personal integrity. The Wadias are an integral part of India's maritime history.

Homi had a happy childhood. Although his father's agency for the sale and distribution of sewing machines, Home and Company at Parsi Bazar Street was a modest one, and his mother was not a wealthy woman, she had skills which made a little go a long way. Her husband acknowledged that he had been supremely happy with her. Homi's family lived at Parsi Bazar Street. To build the house where they came to live, the first Master Builder, Lowji Wadia, had received from the East India Company, his employers, a loan of Rs. 1000. This is recorded as follows: "The Board, taking into consideration the merit of the petitioner — we have none other of his profession equally skilled — unanimously agreed to it and granted Rs. 1000, returnable within 7 or 8 years" (see Public Department Diaries, Vol. XV, pg. 81).

The two-storied house was built during 1742-43 and Lowji brought to it, his family from Surat. Fifty years later, to accommodate the expanded family, two stories were added. However, on 4th February 1933, this house at No. 6, Parsi Bazar Street was destroyed by fire. But some years earlier, Homi, his parents and his brother had already moved from the house. Even so, Homi's mother was the person to whom all the family looked for help of every kind.

Homi's parents and Homi and Nusserwan lived for some years in that house of the Wadias, seventy strong, opposite W. and A. Graham and Co. When Hirjibhai Merwanji, Homi's grandfather, the tenth and last of the shipwrights, retired (having served the East India Company and the British Government), on the abolition of the Indian Navy, he lived in that house and was there until his death in 1885, aged 68. In 1863, four Wadias were serving in the docks. Of them, two were asked to retire voluntarily, because of retrenchment.

Homi's mother was born in 1864. At first, for five years after retirement, Hirjibhai was with his brother's firm Dosabhoy Merwanji and Co., which had extensive relations with England and America. From 1868 to 1885, he was with A. and W. Graham and Co.

In the Wadia house there was a vast kitchen, where Parsi cooks daily provided meals to 75 persons, all family members and some staff.

Homi's father had his own firm dealing in Singer sewing machines. It was known as M.N. Home and Co., at 21, Elphinstone Circle. The family's new residence (upto 1927) was at Shastri Building, 15-A Elphinstone Circle. From the top floor windows of this house near the Town Hall, they looked out to sea over the docks.

In 1927, Homi took the tenancy of a large flat at Cozy Building, Gowalia Tank. He paid the rent, as only he of the family of three could do so. Maneckji had died in 1920.

Meherbai had declined marriage with a wealthy cousin and risked the displeasure of her aunt. At 39 she was an unmarried woman, for she would marry only for love. Homi felt contempt for anyone who married for money.

Homi's father, Maneckji Nusserwanji Seervai was a 39-year old widower when he married Meher Hirjibhai Wadia, also 39. Their first son, Nusserwan, was born in January 1905 and Homi in December 1906, when his parents were aged 42 years. There was a teen-aged daughter by Maneckji's first marriage, who died when Homi was four years old.

As an infant, Homi had a large head with deep-set bright eyes, and a small body. At 8 months he stood up and took steps, not letting his hand be held, saying in Gujarati "HATHE JATHE", which means, "by myself". It is rare but true. We have two studio photographs, one of Homi and one of Nusserwan. I imagine their date would be 1910. Each child is dressed in sailor suit, thigh hugging shorts for the elder, large ill-fitting skirt for the younger. Homi insisted on holding a spade. He turned out to be a man who did spade work, produced great and memorable writing, laboured hard at briefs and at his Book, dressed simply, did not care for fashionable attire.

A sweet, innocent face looks out of the photograph with naturally falling curly hair, which earned Homi his mother's soubriquet of "little basket of curls" (BAAL-NI-TOPLI). Homi loved this photo. For several years I had lost it. He frequently asked me to look for it. I could not find it. He was resigned to the loss, although he complained, about carelessness, without berating me. About a year before Homi's death, I came upon it, unseeking. It was a joy to see his delight at the recovery of this photograph.

And Nusserwan? Quite the little man of the world, although aged only 6. I see a smart, posed attitude, the boy standing with a short cane under one arm, short straight hair plastered down, face handsome, almost self-conscious. Nusserwan grew fond of fashionable three-piece suits from the best tailors, rings on almost every finger, a cane, a chiroot, and an affected walk. He too worked hard, though: at painting, at securing clients for insurance, at his veterinary practice. Financial rewards were small.

We have a magnificent oil portrait of Maneckji's father Nusserwanji, by the famous artist, M. F. Pithawalla, painted in April 1896. Over 80 years old, there he sits, erect and imposing, staff in hand, dressed in high Rajasthani fashion, with brocaded shawl and PAGHDI and around his left ankle, a heavy silver anklet, his feet resting on tiger skin. His face is distinguished, with a thick heavy white beard parted at the cleft of the chin and a magnificent turned up moustache. Significantly, although not prominently painted, there are rings on several fingers. The rings are not noticeable. Our dear friend Dr. Phiroze Masani, a scholar of Parsi history, on first seeing Nusserwanji's portrait, went straight to PARSI PRAKAR a publication about Parsi events and personalities. It contained a description of the modes of dress and ornaments of Nusserwanji, including his habit of wearing rings. It was this description that sent us back to the portrait to find the rings. We said to each other, "This explains Nusserwan's addiction to rings". And to think that the grandsons had never seen grandfather and his rings in person!

As for the heavy silver anklet, which was an honour awarded by the Ruler of the State of Baroda to his loyal RAJVAID (doctor), Homi used to say that the national award given to him, (Padma Vibhushan, 1972) corresponded to the award of the silver anklet made to his grandfather. (The gold anklet was reserved for royal personages).

Homi often told me that his grandfather used to go on horse back on his medical rounds. This accounted for his erect bearing in old age, as seen in the portrait by Pithawalla.

Something else Homi used to tell me. His grandfather had a predeliction for spending hours by the river, saying prayers, while patients waited. He was admonished by Homi's great-grandfather Bachaji, who told him sternly to make a choice between the service of man by attending to his patients, or the service of God by day-long prayer! Homi's grandfather chose to serve God by serving man!!

The innocent look on Homi's face at age 4, was surely a sign of natural temperament and character. At 7, Homi was interviewed by Jalbhai Bharda for admission to the Bharda New High School. He was an educationist who introduced modern methods. In order to test Homi's counting skill or ability, Mr. Bharda asked him: "There are 7 buttons on your jacket. Were you to lose two, how many would remain?" Swift and sure, Homi answered "Father's business is not doing well. We are told to be careful with what we have. I would not lose any buttons."

Homi was destined to lose his childhood early. Maneckji died in 1920, Homi was barely 14. The next year would be his last year at school. He was required to take a good deal of responsibility for his father's business, far beyond his years. Childish things had to be things of the past. Shouldering responsibility, if it meant the passing of childhood, yet did not mean the passing of innocence.

And later, much later, beyond the age of innocence, and all his life, Homi retained a temperament which turned him from bawdy stories, borderline jokes, banal gossip. People learnt to check themselves as he froze such talk with a stern and unflickering eye. He declined to have a holiday at a certain hotel, because his friends there organised games he did not like because they were bawdy. Seervai frequented that part of the Bar Library where bawdy stories were not being told.

When we used to read together, he and I, I read out the questionable joke with a laugh. Homi's face would be unsmiling, if not stern. So too, when we told a lie to a very old man (with whom at times one could do nothing without lies) Homi would not join. He remained disapproving.

Euphemisms were lost on Homi. Once we were at a Parsi wedding, where, due to Government regulations, liquor could be served and consumed in an area not open to public view. Being a teetotaller Homi never went to the bar. A euphemism used for visiting the bar was "to go tie the *KUSHTI*." An acquaintance came up to Homi some years ago, and asked him "Aren't you going in to tie the *KUSHTI*?" Homi hadn't a clue as to what was indicated, and said quite simply "There's no need to." I told him he was being invited to visit the bar.

However, Homi enjoyed the joke of our son's violin-teacher, Adrian d'Mello, about the bar. A man returning home late told his wife he had been to see his doctor. "What did he diagnose?" She asked. "Syncopation", he replied. She sought the meaning, and found "an irregular leap from bar to bar"!

While Maneckji was alive, cycling, swimming, a little something at Mongini's — regular outings for the boys, with father. Cricket by the sea, at the Oval, where men played chaupat with excitement and loud dispute. The sea lapped the boundaries of the Oval, in which Homi played. In later days, and now, where the sea used to be, stands the house in which Homi and I made our home in 1949, and where he died in 1996.

In the home, reading the *Shahnama* in Gujarati, other Gujarati literature, books from J. N. Petit Institute, where at 13 Homi was enrolled in the Library. Although Homi neither visited nor borrowed books from there for decades before he died, he turned down every suggestion of mine, to resign his membership since he did not use it. Homi's mother was a faster and keener reader. "Her memory was better than mine", Homi told me. Mother and son were voracious readers.

Violin lessons for Nusserwan, French with father, for Homi. Also for the boys, a turn or two at the sewing machine, in order to lessen their mother's burden.

At the age of 10 and 8, both boys were placed in a fire-temple for a month's apprenticeship for priesthood; stoical living, unpalatable food except sweet *MALIDO*, made with wheat flour. The enchanting photograph of the two ordained priests aged 8 and 10 years, in full priestly regalia, holding the symbolic *GURZ*, shows Homi's cheeks round and chubby, following that month of what he called "digusting" *MALIDO*.

In order to qualify (and to be word-perfect at the *NAVAR* and *MARTAB* ceremonies in the presence of an audience), Homi and Nusserwan committed to memory hundreds of verses in Zend Avasta, the language of the Zoroastrian scriptures. It is believed by many that Homi's excellent memory, which remained almost faultless till death at the age of 89, was the result of this training and practice. But the fact remains that Homi's mother had a superior memory, and that her brother Dhunju's memory was unsurpassed. Homi had the same memory genes as his mother and uncle. Dhunjibhai Wadia was the assistant Registrar of the University of Bombay. Before anyone else arrived at the office, he had disposed of the early morning mail. Years after a student graduated, Dhunjibhai could reproduce his marks from memory.

In 1945 when Homi introduced me to Dhunjibhai, telling him that Nani Moos was my uncle, at once Dhunjibhai told me where and on what date (40 years earlier) my uncle and aunt were married. I asked whether he had known one of them and had been present at the wedding. He said "No. I had read the press announcement. I remember it."

He could tell you from memory cricket scores of ages past. He corrected from memory, information published in the TIMES (London) or in a cricket Magazine, and received an acknowledgement that he was right. Homi likewise sent corrections to editors of books. At the University, after Dhunjibhai's retirement, three card index cabinets were installed to contain the information that he had carried in his memory! Once someone said to Sir Jamshedji Kanga, the most formidable Advocate at the Bombay High Court, second only to Invararity, that Dhunjibhai Wadia's memory was like his. Sir Jamshedji answered: "Certainly not. Dhunjibhai had a better memory."

Dhunjibhai was inordinately shy. So, in their youth were his nephews and my husband. Homi's school reports uniformly stated "His teachers speak very well of him. He is a good steady boy." His rank ranged from 2nd to 11th in the exam., 3rd to 13th in the daily marks. The Medical Inspector stated (1920) that his "mental capacity is very good", "physical stature average", nutrition "medium".

Homi was always raising his hand to answer questions, Nusserwan and Homi were always ready to declaim prose and poetry, and debating was a highlight of school days.

The teachers who made lessons exciting were remembered by Homi for ever, and so too, the ones whose behaviour shut him up like a clam: the one who wanted him and Nusserwan to take tuitions, the one who once ridiculed Homi, so that he took no further interest in grammar — regretting all his life that his hold on grammar was weak. However, his vocabulary was vast and varied and gave him fluency in speech and writing.

In the early twenties, the University of Bombay had an age-limit on admission. Homi was an "under- age" matriculate in 1922, and eager to join Elphinstone College. His father had died two years earlier. The sooner Homi graduated, the sooner he would be in a position to start earning, to support his mother and his brother and himself. The family income was small.

All three of them were trustees for Maneckji's Trust, which included a VAJIFA in the suburbs, with a small income. There were small investments whose income according to Maneckji's Will was receivable by Meherbai, later by their sons; and there were legacies for their wives, if any, and the capital was to go ultimately to their children, after the son's demise. In 1973 our legacies were given to me and to Nusserwan's widow. At the same time, Homi promptly made a "Deed of Release", releasing his own inheritance to our children. They were persuaded to make individual settlements in their turn. To be provident, Homi regarded as part of living.

I have a copy of Homi's letter dated 7.11.1931, the paper almost falling apart when handled. Homi had a good grounding in Gujarati at school. The school reports of the early school period are headed "Std. 1 to 4 Gujarati". In classes 5 to 7, English was the medium of instruction. His 1919 School Report states "Highest marks in English, in the class". While Homi retained a strong hold of the mother-tongue and could translate from Gujarati to English at sight, even in Court, substituting, supplementing, or improving the official translator's translation, (perhaps because he had a better hold on English); yet, — *writing* Gujarati was not easy for him. If he had to send a letter in Gujarati, I was the one to write it, at his dictation. My hold on the language *per se* and my fluency in reading it, was less than his. I have his letter in English which is obviously in reply to one written in Gujarati. Homi cites a sentence from it, in Gujarati script. I reproduce his letter because it gives some idea of their financial affairs in 1931.

"My dear Maneckbai,

I read Mr. Desai's letter to my mother, and since Mr. Desai has made rather offensive remarks about my mother, I shall ask permission to reply to them. I hope you'll take no offence at my replying to him in plain terms, for the reply which I make is to his letter alone.

(1) *My mother has never written any letter to Mr. Desai which would suggest in the slightest degree that Mr. Manecksha is making any profit out of the VAJIFA.*

(2) *Nor has she ever written a letter which could offend Mr. Manecksha, for she always wrote to Mr. Meherwanji (Desai) that Mr. Manecksha was a pretty busy man, having much work of his own and could not be expected to attend continually to our work.*

(3) *Far from my mother supposing the VAJIFA to be a gold mine, she is so tired of managing it that she has made up her mind to sell off her*

investment in the mortgage at the price offered by the Mehervaids, and was going to write to give you and Pestonji the first preference when Pestonji should have returned from his tour.

(4) *If she had to write to Mr. Meherwanji Desai now and again to do all he could to collect the arrears, it is because the income belongs to the trust which my father has created and it is the plain duty of the trustees to use all reasonable means to collect money which is outstanding. You will recollect that when my father was alive and the income was his own absolute property, he was content to receive Rs. 72 every three years.*

(5) *Mr. Manecksha writes (here Gujarati follows): "this time an expense of Rs. 32.8 as. is written in the account, which I have purposely included." I don't quite understand what the underlined words mean, but if they are intended to be a sort of protest against my mother's letter to Mr. Meherwanji Desai, they are unfortunate. For, as I pointed out to my mother, the money spent on item one (17/8/-) and item three (Rs. 5/-) were spent to obtain information which we did not want and could not possibly use. For there was no dispute about the fact that we had paid the increased assessment, nor that the grand total would come to a very big sum. The only important question was, ask whether the increased revenue was a personal debt to be recovered every three years, or a mortgage debt which could be recovered for the whole term, and for that the lawyer's opinion was all that was required.*

You will see from the above explanation that my mother had done nothing to offend Mr. Manecksha, and she asks me to write that if nevertheless she has unconsciously offended him, she is sorry to have caused him any pain. Etc."

It is plain to see the need for Homi to start earning for the family at the earliest. The earlier he completed studies and got his degrees and professional qualifications, the better.

What a happy home Homi grew up in, I am able to tell in his own words from his letter to me before our marriage:

"I was brought up in a home of singular happiness and love. I have never seen my parents quarrel, and a little before my father died he told his friends that he never had a happier life than my mother made for him. Both of them taught me to put my heart in things which really mattered in life — and not on fashion or pomp or power. My mother and I thought alike — all that is good in me is hers and I believe that she was a finer and more capable person than myself. But we thought alike. I completed a sentence which she had begun and she did the same to what I had half said.

"She could have married wealth and position — she offended an aunt who loved her, by rejecting her son — but she preferred to wait and marry a man

she loved. She married my father when she was 39: he had a small salary but she had nimble hands, great capacity for work and one of the kindest hearts, and on a small income she made a home of amazing happiness. People thought she was worth 2 lacs, when she wasn't worth 20 thousand. ***You see now that it is natural for her son to have contempt for men who marry for money; and equally natural to love friends who married the women they loved and try to make them happy."*** (emphasis added)

If Homi lived, it was a triumph of reason over sentiment: Meherbai, his mother had readily and instantly agreed to being separated from her newborn son for six weeks, on being told that due to inexplicable (viral?) infection in the ward, only those babies were surviving who were tended elsewhere, away from their mothers. Many a mother who refused to be separated, lost her infant in that time, at the Masina Hospital, where the "lying in" time was then a routine six weeks.

Did Meherbai and her son lose out on bonding? Forty-two, and separated at birth for six weeks from her newborn, she yet had so deep, so unswerving a love from Homi, so great and single-minded an attachment and devotion, that few women have a comparable lifelong bond with their children.

Grown to manhood, Homi took a reasoned decision: while Meherbai lived, he would not marry. He considered that in the event that she and his wife (if he had one), had strong differences, he would inevitably make one or the other unhappy. He would not contemplate such an eventuality.

When Homi was an examiner of LL.B. papers, and he and his mother were on holiday at Matheran, he saw to it that after a trip to Bombay for work, he got back to her even at 10 p.m., what though it meant being rolled up the hill by rickshaw in the dark on that risky journey.

NEVER in his life did his attention to professional duty mean neglect of family duty.

Bachelor, Advocate, Friend

"Tell Nanimama, I have engaged Seervai, Advocate, for the Ruby Lodge matter." My uncle's nephew, Dr. Dady Banaji, then Court Receiver, who looked after a property at Pali Hill for my uncle and aunt Moos, was on the 'phone. He collected the rent, paid the Municipal bills, the Government ground rents, saw to the repairs and waterproofing. A dispute arose with the Government or the Municipality, because of a covered passage-way between the house and the out-house used as a kitchen and staff-quarters, which passage the authorities wanted removed. They increased the levies. In our home,

Seervai's name began to be heard. He handled the case successfully. His advocacy and his uprightness were discussed. The words of praise and appreciation fell on my ears. I never saw Seervai, but I heard his name. I was a school-girl.

"Tell Behramji (my father) we have succeeded in our tax-appeal. Sir Jamshedji's junior, Seervai argued it." I was still a school-girl, and father's Solicitor cousin, B. H. Vakil, was giving the message. The Income Tax Department was demanding additional tax from my father on the income enjoyed by his minor children, income that came from a settlement he had made in our favour. Seervai handled the appeal, and his name was again heard in our home. I never saw him.

I was not even a teen-ager when Seervai's name came up in conversation between my sister, thirteen years my senior and a college-girl, and her friend Homai, with their professor, J.C.P. d'Andrade who was a regular visitor in our home. His niece Vera was my class-mate, and a frequent week-end visitor from boarding-school. Seervai's intellectual attainments, his scholarship, his debating skills, his fearless and upright conduct were talked about, and the twelve-year old school-girls listened.

"Tell Porus his brother-in-law's matter has been completed. He can now leave Bombay without worry. Seervai handled it well." The message came to my sister from Dorabji Patel, a Solicitor. The matter pertained to some business deals of her friend (later husband) Porus Mehta's relation.

I heard too, about the famous *Telephone Case* in the High Court, that brought wide recognition of Seervai's arguments in Court, about his persistent, fearless and unflinching stand, and his success.

Then, in the forties, after my family had left our old home and were living in Mon Repos, the military authorities de-requisitioned the old house which had been our home and had been subsequently used by the military authorities for an officers' Mess. There had been much damage done by rough usage, and my uncle and aunt, the owners, had to get compensation. There were hearings before the Collector of Bombay. Gregson, Batley & King, Architects, were the expert witnesses. Seervai argued the matter, and secured an appropriate compensation.

After my sister's marriage (1941), I began to hear more and more about Seervai, who was my brother-in-law's closest college friend. All the members of his family, Porus's mother, sisters, nieces, nephew, knew Seervai closely, and admired him, were fond of him, in regular touch with him. Still I did not see Seervai.

Seervai saw me at the wedding of my sister and Porus Mehta, on 2nd February, 1941. The guests at the wedding were many, and no one introduced us, no one pointed out Seervai to me. I could not guess which man was Seervai. He had heard of me from the Mehtas, he spotted me, but he was not the man to accost a girl he did not know and who did not know him. I would certainly have accosted him, given half an opportunity, for I never hesitated. Even though Seervai was the only man, the only person, of whom I had an awe, from hearing of his intellect, his austerity, his sternness, I was at 17, equal to introducing myself to a man more than 16 years older and sustaining an animated conversation with him, one to one. But the evening passed. I dined with some uninteresting stranger. Seervai dined alone among strangers, and left. I felt sad that still I had not seen him.

The Mehta family used to be guests of Seervai at a cinema and a restaurant, on a Saturday or Sunday, once or twice a month. On other Sundays, there were other families Seervai entertained. I felt aggrieved at not being asked, for Seervai knew how often I was at the Mehtas' home. He had heard about me.

On a day when one of them, for whom a ticket had been taken by Seervai, dropped out, one of the Mehtas asked me to go along instead. I absolutely declined, but I wept copiously on the train between Churchgate and Bandra. And still I had not seen him. He had heard about me. I had heard about him.

Came the day when Seervai asked my sister to invite me on his behalf. The film had Charlie Chaplin in THE GREAT DICTATOR. My loud laughter resounded in the Cinema, unladylike. No one told me it was unladylike, and had I been told, it would have made no difference.

From the Empire Cinema, we all went to the Soda Fountain at the Excelsior Cinema.

I saw Seervai. Curly hair parted in the centre (not a becoming parting, I thought), sharp, bright, deep-set eyes, round gold-rimmed glasses, dark jacket and white drill trousers, jolly among friends, not severe and not austere, making jokes, talking, offering cold drinks and refreshments. I had my first taste of Coca Cola and disliked it. No one sat silent, I least of all. I had my first taste of Seervai, and I loved it. We were now acquaintances. Four years later, I was Seervai's "dear acquaintance", the phrase he borrowed from Mary Webb, whose novel *Precious Bane* gripped his imagination all his life, as did the phrase. The heroine Prudence Sarn, is the beloved of an itinerant village weaver, who saves a bear that is baited, and his life is saved from the fangs of the dog he takes on as an alternative amusement for the boorish men deprived of their sport. Prudence Sarn plunges a knife into the dog and kills it. Prudence commences the book with the words "I am an old woman". And here am I, writing about my beloved, when I am an old woman, as he always said I would!

Four years passed, Seervai went his way and I went mine. For him, the Courts, reading, correcting University exam papers, a newly acquired radio, and B.B.C. broadcasts. On Sundays, visits with his brilliant cousins D. J. Wadia, and H. H. Wadia, and their sister Dinoo and her family, and the family of Dorabji Patel. In the suburbs, the Andhyarujinas, the Mehtas, the Bhatts. Fun and games with the children of these families, putting a fractious infant to sleep, cradled in his gentle rocking arms, giving the slightly older children rides on his head, telling stories, jolly times. With their parents, stimulating talk, sage advice, when called for.

And time spent with other friends, Prof. d'Andrade, other men of brilliance with intellectual and literary interests. There were other numerous friends from the Bar as well. Rustom Andhyarujina never tired of describing to me, their long walks, and the very animated discussions they had as they walked, "the cynosure of all eyes," he said.

At Seervai's home, there was only his elder brother, Nusserwan. On birthdays, at the New Year, they went to a cinema together. For the rest, each went his way. Homi told me later, how simplified was their housekeeping: a part-time cleaning-man, locked boxes affixed on the wall outside the front door, for the milk to be left, for the dinner to be left in a DABBA. And as for the expenses, each brother put into the kitty an equal amount at the beginning of the month. When that got over, Homi put in more, and more, and more. No questions asked. His brother managed the house. They had no telephone, no radio (till the war years), no entertaining at home. Homi's very close friends visited.

He eluded the married state.

As for me, ballet, philosophy, arguments, books, music, debating, dramatics, daily trips by suburban train, cycling, visits to my sister's home, holidays with aunts and cousins, Matheran, Poona, and letter-writing. No time for thoughts of marriage.

Homi was the "q.b." *par excellence.* (His phrase for qualified bachelor).

I was the qualified spinster. My friend Zubi once said to me, or wrote, "you could not flirt, even if you wanted to. You wouldn't know how." Not that I didn't spend many hours with men students at College, arguing, arguing, arguing. Nothing further from flirting can be imagined, albeit other students wondered about my long conversations with men. And none, except my four particular friends, girls in my class, called me by my first name. Someone once addressed me by name, only to have me turn sharply on him, with "Miss Lalkaka, if you please." Of the men I talked with most, Nissim Ezekiel became a renowned poet; Sheryar Ookerjee, a renowned professor of philosophy, music critic and performer on the piano and organ, and a sketch artist making fine sketches from nature; and Dorab Patel, Chief Justice in Pakistan.

I can recall no more than three specific meetings between Seervai and me, between 1941 and 1945. One was at my cousin's engagement to Hilla, my sister's niece. There was a party at the Mehta home. Homi remembered all his life, the few words that were spoken between us, and often recalled them. On arrival, dressed as usual in white drill trousers and dark jacket, he asked my sister, "Is the little philosopher come?" I was busy rushing around, serving cake. He remembered my saying to him "Have more, there's plenty where it comes from." Abstemious as ever, he took no second helping. I asked him to visit our home at Mon Repos, adding that I had learnt to drive, and would bring around my father's car for him to the Bandra Station. But he never visited us.

The second time was hardly a meeting at all. I was on the wide central stair of Wilson College. Prof. d'Andrade's Adult Education Class held on the first floor, had got over. At the bottom of the stair stood Seervai and his friend Manibhai Prataprai, who had to see someone at the College. Miss Lalkaka was duly introduced and directions were asked to get to the relevant class-room or office room, or whatever the appointed place was. Seervai's memory of that briefest of brief encounters was of "a statuesque woman descending", and of my helping them find the room. Had Seervai been an artist, that is the way he would have painted me. Some years later, after our engagement, Mr. Prataprai sent Homi his good wishes, and recalled that he had met me once at Wilson College, and remembered me as a statuesque figure! Such are people's impressions. They are in the eye of the beholder. I myself have the impression that I was too heavy, fat, to be statuesque.

In 1944, I obtained my bachelor's degree in Philosophy, and was appointed at Wilson College, a Fellow for the year 1944-45, while working on a thesis for M.A., on the subject "The Right to Revolt." I also began corresponding with colleges in Cambridge and London, with a view to joining one of them in September, 1945.

For me, at this time intellectual stimulus came largely from endless discussions with my sister's husband who made my mind grow when I was 17 to 21 years old. My sister and Seervai said later that Seervai had influenced my brother-in-law's thinking, so that my thinking was *indirectly* influenced by Seervai: we met without knowing it — in the realms of the mind. And both Seervai and Mehta, and my sister as well, had been influenced at Elphinstone College, by Prof. d'Andrade, long before I myself came under the Professor's spell, for they were thirteen to sixteen years my senior.

From college days, Porus Mehta and Seervai had been great friends for 20 years. How great, appears from the following abstract from Mehta's letter in 1940: "I need not say much about what is obvious, that our long and devoted friendship can in no sense be affected by either of us getting married, but on the contrary I shall need your comradeship more than ever …

"As you know, a true friend is irreplaceable even by a true wife, and your friendship fills a need that nothing else and no one else can fill and that for me it is a tower of strength as well as of sweet refuge and pleasure abiding."

Seervai's strongest and longest (nearly 80 years) friendship started in school and even after Seervai's death at the age of 89, his older friend could not be informed, for his family feared he could not sustain such a break. Till his own death at 93, he believed Seervai to be alive and abroad. This friend was Rustom B. Andhyarujina. His son Tehmtan, who joined Seervai's chambers, is our close friend, and continues the family friendship.

It was Seervai's loyalty, affectionate nature, intellectual gifts, outgoing, talkative and helpful spirit that made him a much appreciated friend and confidant to very many people.

Some of his college-day friendships lasted and were mutually enjoyed till death intervened, and sometimes, as in the case of Homi J. Bhabha, till Bhabha no longer had time to spare from his work as a famous atomic scientist, or like Yusuf Meherally immersed in his life as a nationalist activist, who died in his forties.

From Seervai's college days, there were people whose friendship we both enjoyed till it ended with death. Notable among these was Prof. J.C.P. d'Andrade, B. P. Sett (Sethna), Karl Khandalavala, the Parpia brothers, Dr. Ruzbeh Mehta (who survives Seervai). Among those whom Seervai came to know in the world of law, some he regularly visited till the end, notable among them being Sir Jamshedji Kanga, P. B. Vachha (and later his son, Rustam), Homi Banaji, Mahmud

Parpia and his wife Kamalini, R. J. Joshi, and his wife Sharda, J. B. Wadia and his wife Piloo, J. B. Dubash, Sorab Vimadalal, Jal Vimadalal and K. S. Savaksha.

Among the Solicitors, till the end, Dorab Patel and J. P. Thacker remained closest to Seervai.

Among the judges, with whom he was close but did not socialise while on the Bench, he was closest to M. C. Chagla, P. B. Gajendragadkar, V. D. Tulzapurkar and M. S. Pendse (after their retirement).

Among his relatives, his close friends till the end, were D. J. Wadia, (Asst. Registrar of the University), Solicitor Dorab Patel, Dinoo and Rattanji Wadia and their sons, Adi, Homi and Dorab.

Among the academics, notably there were Miss Sulabha Panandikar, whose last post was Director of Education, Dr. G. N. Lawande and Dr. Sheryar Ookerjee, Professors of Philosophy, who were stalwarts (with Prof. d'Andrade and Miss Panandikar) of the Bombay Philosophical Society. While they remained in India, there were also from the same Society, Principals Dr. John Mckenzie, Dr. James Kellock, Dr. H. J. Taylor.

Overseas, Seervai's particular friends till the end, were Lord Denning, M. R., the Lord Chancellor, Lord Mackay, Prof. C. J. Hamson, Prof. S. A. de Smith, Vice-Chancellor of Cambridge University Sir David Williams, Prof. Sir T. B. Smith and Prof. A. W. Bradley. They kept up a correspondence for many years.

There were friends from the Peoples Union for Civil Liberties, particularly and notably Yogesh Kamdar.

From Bombay International School, a particular friend till the end was N. G. Thakar, one of its successive Principals.

From among those in Government service, there were Bobby Dalal, R.L.A., Dhurandhar and Lad in the Legal Dept., and Purviz N. Damry, who became Deputy Governor of the Reserve Bank and finally joined the International Monetary Fund.

Among my college friends and their families, to whom Homi was also close, are Dolly Masani and her husband Dr. Phiroze (our family doctor), and Sheryar and Amy Ookerjee.

There were many other good friends, but I have mentioned only those who were closest. In 1986, our son married. His father-in-law Lachman Daswaney, who pre-deceased Homi, became a friend, when Homi was 79, and many evenings we spent with him at his famous jeweller's shop, Rai and Co. and at his home, specially after he became ill.

None of Homi's friendships were casual, although there were so many friends. Homi cared for them, and over many years the friendships gave mutual pleasure. Of what might be called "party friends", we had none, for we were not party-going people. In fifty years, we may not have attended two hundred dinners.

I must add here, that although his friends were persons who shared intellectual and literary interests with us, yet, Homi was not above friendly converse with very simple people. Whether they took in all that he said, or not, he had the courtesy and kindness to converse with them the same as with anyone else, with concentrated attention.

Husband and Father

Frequently Seervai was urged to write an autobiography. His response was that he did not intend to indulge in "anecdotage". It is a pity, because he spoke of his varied experiences in private and in public life, which delighted the hearer, so interesting and rich they were. If written, and published, they would have been of great general interest.

My husband was a man of immense moral authority for he never "preached" what he did not practice. Our children were, as others were, deeply impressed by this fact. He was also an extremely optimistic person. During the last seven months of his life, he and his family and friends were aware that his life may suddenly end, by reason of a diagnosis that he had an aneurism of the aorta. But no gloom dampened our bright and happy home, nor did he stop work for a day, on *Constitutional Law of India*. He worked the harder, for he said, "If I die, who will finish my book?" He finished it one day before he died.

To pessimists afraid to take bold action, he said, "If one is to be afraid of one's own shadow, it were better to be dead." He was cautious by nature, but never without courage, never without good cheer, never hesitant to act as reason led. His was the philosophy of Dickens's Mark Tapley: "What is the use of being cheerful when things are going right? One must be cheerful when they go wrong." From his early years of brieflessness for almost ten years, he practised this philosophy.

If his was a successful life, in every sense of the term, it was in great measure due to his simple living: simple and abstinent eating habits, total abstention from alcohol, regular exercise and regular times in day to day life, his simple joys and pastimes and his high expectations of the capacities of women.

Homi never regarded women in a dismissive or flippant way, but considered them as entirely the equal of men. He once wrote to me, after a description of the high capacities and generosities of a cousin of his, who practised medicine in poor areas of Iran, suffering privations, "You will understand why I like and expect women to be capable as well as kind. I was brought up by three women, my mother and two cousins, who had both capacity and kindliness."

Consequent upon his attitude towards women in general, I was a beneficiary in particular: unless he ever thought my stand wrong, he was invariably and unhesitatingly supportive of me, in all circumstances.

Morarji Desai, as Chief Minister of Bombay, appointed Homi to be the Advocate-General in 1957. Homi had not met him, for he did not meet Ministers, unless officially requested.

Four days after Homi took office, there was a Reception (4th July, 1957), at which I introduced them, for I used to meet Ministers in the course of my voluntary social work, and knew the Chief Minister, with whom I had sharp differences.

Immediately Morarji said to Homi, "Last year your wife gave me a threat." Immediately Homi responded, "I quite agreed with the view she took." I wonder how many a man supports his wife in such circumstances.

As for gambling, he said that he only took two gambles, and both succeeded: he gambled on his choice of profession and on his choice of marriage partner. In 1945, he wrote to me: "I gave myself a 5% chance of marrying, for not a dog would sniff at a briefless barrister, not a beggar would ask his alms."

In 1945 his income had barely risen to Rs. 2000. He told a couple of intimate friends, that if he really cared for someone, he would not hesitate to marry. He told them he sought a girl of intelligence, with brilliant eyes. Later he wrote to me," When they see you, they will say I was a prophet."

My husband's indifference to culinary excellence was a blessing to me for I took little interest in the kitchen. He would not eat exotic or spicy food. He did not bother, if I met his query about the menu with the answer that I did not know. I could do this because our cook (who has been in our service since 1957) knew exactly what to serve up. Extremely simple food was manna to Homi and he would always voice appreciation of it.

In his bachelor days, he used to prepare desserts and his oven cooked cheese toast was in constant demand with our children, whom he humoured by preparing it in an elaborate ceremony.

At Connemara Hotel in Madras, he instructed the staff on how the best buttered toast must be prepared, and at the time of our large functions (weddings, navjotes) one caterer would rather discuss the menu with Homi than with me, saying: "Mr. Seervai understands."

Equally simple was his taste in clothes. He had no suits, till he was 38. Only at our marriage, with the suiting material he received from my parents, did he order a suit. Unlike his grandfather the RAJVAID and unlike his brother Nusserwan, he wore no rings, except at our wedding, when he felt that the gift received from my parents should be worn.

He declined other gifts. Of dowry there was no question at any time, in our family, neither at our marriage nor at the marriage of our children.

There were for us no "traditional" nor religious observances, except the **ASHIRWAD** ceremony, as we never thought of substituting it with a civil marriage. At our wedding, my clothes were not traditional white, nor did I wear jewelry. No sort of superstition intervened. The glass bangles Homi's old relative insisted on my wearing, broke accidentally within minutes of the marriage ceremony; and my horoscope (got made by my father's mother in Ahmedabad) said I would be a very young widow ! Our marriage lasted fifty happy years!!

We remained inseparable. Homi referred to books as seductions and his love for books and for his wife and family remained supremely important to him. Except in his bachelor days, Homi never went on holiday without the family and after our children were grown up, never without me.

When he returned home from some meeting or official gathering where I was not with him or when in the years after a fracture in 1986 he would come home for lunch and rest, he always crossed the threshold with the words "Where's Ferozee?" In the evening we always came home together.

Homi's frolics with our children and grandchildren and with many small children at our home or our club, have been written about by our children. He adjusted himself to others' needs and he never considered his own needs first. During one holiday at Mahabaleshwar when our eldest child was an infant, and Homi had a dislocation of his arm which he himself set, it so happened that all of us fell ill — myself with asthma, the child with whooping cough, and the maidservant with a scorpion bite. Homi took over tending to Meher and me, without a word of complaint, and as cheerful as ever, albeit the circumstances, and was considerate and solicitous of the maidservant.

During childhood illnesses, it was Homi who, with exemplary patience and cheerfulness tended to the sick child as my temperament was impatient and easily disconcerted. He would put aside the next day's brief, do what needed doing, put brandy ice packs on the child's stomach, soothe and caress the child and then return to his brief, stinting only his sleep. He always had the good fortune to fall asleep quickly, to sleep soundly and awake refreshed, ready for energetic action. But when teenaged children came home late, he remained sleepless till their return.

In 1957 our son fell critically ill, having lung surgery at 5 weeks old. When he was brought home from hospital, I fell ill and was compulsorily separated, being segregated in the home upstairs, of Dr. and Dolly Masani. The infant's only diet was mother's milk, which was temporarily stopped, "formula" milk being substituted, two hourly. He had to be prevented from crying, for fear of new aircysts blowing up in the lung and then bursting.

Homi would have none of the suggestion of engaging a wet nurse, as human milk on demand was considered the only appropriate nourishment. He took over, at least at night, although the pressure of work was heavy in Court, he having been just then given a Government retainer (three months later he became Advocate-General), and end-of-term professional demands were heavy.

Having taken over, he devised a method of supplying instant formula milk, freshly prepared: Keep ready boiling water in a thermos flask, keep dissolved formula powder ready in semi-frozen condition, when the baby demands a feed, pour out the two together. Presto, milk at required temperature is ready in a moment.

At night, Homi himself bottle fed the ailing baby every two hours, during intervals from heavy legal work, when there was a brief to study or prepare.

How did he manage it? He slept very little during the crucial week. If Homi believed that women could do what men could, he also believed that men could do what women could. And he unhesitatingly practised what he believed. It was my husband's overwhelming love, his patience, his optimism and cheerfulness and his stamina that saw the family through that hectic week of immense emotional tension and untold anxiety.

As for Homi's ability to handle a tiny baby, I recall 1946, when Meher newly born, came home on the eleventh day. From day one, Homi handled her expertly and rocked her in his arms, saying "You would have thought I had done nothing else all my life." He had had some practice with the Andhyarujina and Bhatt children, in his bachelor days.

Exemplary patient himself when ill, exemplary in caring for patients, exemplary husband and father, who could easily adjust to others' needs not considering his own needs, a man who could be all that, remained a bachelor till he was 38.

I never went for a gynaecological consultation, that Homi did not accompany me. At Meher's birth, in the hospital, Homi gave me a bottle of perfume with the label "Bien Aimée" (well beloved).

Homi was happy only with his family around him. He did not accept dinner invitations. We rarely had people over to dinner at home, or at my club. Homi never joined a club. Neither wine nor liquor was ever served — we did not keep any. Yet, brandy came into the house — for medicinal use — honey with a dash of brandy was a specific for a heavy cold and cough, and Homi himself applied ice and brandy packs to the children to bring down high fever.

After he took office as Advocate-General, it was expected that he should attend the dinners of the Bar Association, he being ex-officio President. It was one of the duties Homi never shirked. Our son was 3 years old, seated in his high chair for dinner when Homi was about to leave for a Bar Dinner. It was customary for him to see the children and kiss them before bed. Navroz, on seeing Homi dressed up in dinner jacket and bow tie, said "It is not daddy who is going for dinner. It is the Advocate-General."

Homi did his best to miss the dinners at Raj Bhavan, where he and I were invited on formal occasions. But at the Republic Day and Independence Day functions, he would be present in the evening, leaving early so as to be home for our children's dinner time.

Our children were put to sleep before 9 o'clock. What games, what dramatic scenarios, what singing of songs, what laughter preceded it! As often as not, the youngest child would be put to sleep by Homi, with a lullaby, or stroking of the forehead, or the telling of a story, usually made up by him.

In extant correspondence with the children, are to be found mentioned, the imaginary characters of those tales invented by Homi. Wingoosh would come to close the eyes of the sleepy heads, or to pull their toes one by one. And there would sometimes be the imaginary character of Bomanbai (who was supposed to have been his erstwhile wife) and six children with the funny names of Adar, Fakira, Ooker, Coli, Asi and Sukli.

There have been many children including our children's cousin and friends, who would cluster round Homi on the arms of his large easy chair, touching his shoulder, and on an adjoining chair, singly or in groups, to look at pictures and hear stories read. It started with Meher aged two and continued with our other children, with visiting children, and lastly with our grandchildren, when Homi was old. It gave immense pleasure to him and to them. For Meher, it went on till she had good literature read to her when she was a college student, a medical student, and to Navroz as he grew up as well. Shirin opted out. This chair now belongs to our youngest grandchildren.

Homi was a person with whom no child felt a stranger. He enjoyed amusing them. His "birdie whistle" is remembered by umpteen children and their parents, and Lord Mackay mentioned it in a letter he wrote to me, and in his Recollection of Homi.

Our children were free to speak their minds. They never had an anxiety that truth would be put down, if it seemed impertinent or was inconvenient. They were always consulted in matters affecting the home and family. On one occasion, when a consensus was not reached, my husband said "In this matter, we will abide by what Feroza says — she is the lady of the house." Our eleven year old son, arms akimbo, retorted: "She is not the lady of the house, she is the volcano of the house." My quick hot temper was undeniable. Homi responded quick as lighting. "I quite agree with you: like Mount Fujiama, she is eternally beautiful." For so I was to his eye of affection! and so, with integrity intact, he did not put down a statement of truth, knowing that I too would not deny my volcanic temperament, and at the same time he was supportive of me.

Last Days

At the end of his life, Homi had trouble with his legs and with his skin. It did not make him irritable or demanding of my time. "You are free as a bird" he would say. It was most unwillingly and as a last recourse that he would ask me to assist him into or out of his deep chair. Or into or out of his bath, or assist him sometimes when walking. He regarded the few minutes needed to help him, as a restriction on my freedom. So little I did for him and he would say "You have done so much for me." All through his life he would call me from Chambers, "just to hear your voice" he would say.

I continue to marvel at his self-reliance and his self discipline till the end, at age 89. Till shortly before he died, he continued to be in Chambers by 9 a.m., carrying in a basket, his hot tea and milk, and flowers. By 9.15 a.m. work commenced, undisturbed by the screaming of children who had their break, in two neighbouring schools. Before work came tea, Homi himself washing up the cups and saucers, arranging new flowers or freshening the old ones already there on his desk. His peons arrived at 10. In the end, for some months he called his secretary to the house and steadily dictated his book, till the very end, only making a concession by having a break for afternoon sleep. Morning and afternoon, he woke to the sound of an alarm clock.

In the evening, Homi's impelling desire to meet our son the moment Navroz set foot in the house, was effectively reigned. Calmly he waited in our room, waiting eagerly, but patiently, quietly, knowing that Navroz would come to us in his own time, with lively talk about his family and about the Courts, about cases, about lawyers and matters of law, about books (many of which he presented to Homi or brought him from the British Council), about literature, politics, economics, health, biography.

Above all, Homi's unfailing adherence to moral values and reasoned principles, and his compassion while adhering to them, abided in all matters big or small.

Homi and I did not believe in life after death, in rebirth. Nor do I now. In what he thought, and said and wrote, recited and remembered and gave, in all he did, in all he was, we had a part. In this sense he is present still. There is no other presence. The stuff of a being, his flavour and essence can no more be held than a sunbeam. But I long to preserve something of Homi, for myself and for others.

Homi's was a long and lovely life. Its early hardships he overcame, its sorrows he transcended, its simple joys and pleasures he enjoyed, and shared, and said that Providence was kind to him. Providence, which he thought of as the beneficent care of nature. Life's tasks he performed with a self-discipline which made them easy if not always agreeable and the pleasant duties of daily living were to him like breathing in and breathing out. The unpleasant duties he never shirked, and repeated laughingly, the poet's line, "They took their medicine as it came."

When my husband used to be in Delhi for arguing cases, he wrote to me and to our children, with amazing frequency and regularity — at least one letter daily, sometimes two in the day. Once, when I wrote to him to skip writing when he was pressed for time, working, as he did 10 to 14 hours a day, this was his reply: "I must be very hard pressed indeed, if I cannot write to you." In addition, he booked a phone call ensuring that his call was at an appropriate hour, seeing to the children's early bed time, so he could talk to them.

On now re-reading his host of letters, I find that even the short ones tell of his train journey, (for years, because of my anxiety, he did not fly), of the people he met, of what conversation they had, of what time he reached the hotel, of his room. "The first thing I have done on coming to this room is to write this letter to you...." (11 PM 28.1.73) He wrote about the arguments urged in court, how they went down, how hopeful was the result; of what book he was reading, of what film he went to and the commencement and ending of each letter was loaded with terms of endearment.

Among the lines I learnt first from Homi were A.E. Houseman's, with his own optimistic variation substituting 'happiness' for the word 'trouble' where it occurred, with my name in the last line.

The thoughts of others
Were light and fleeting,
Of lovers' meeting
Or luck or fame.
But mine were of *happiness*
And mine were steady
So I was ready
When *Ferozee* came,

In conclusion, I reproduce the poem I wrote some years after he died, (at a poetry workshop in Letchworth, U.K.)

Twenty-sixth of January

A frost came in the night and stole my world.
All day you had been at last
Free from your Book, the work of your life
Had ended, the last sentence done,
The unwanted paper torn and thrown away.

You told me once again,
Life with you has been sweet, Ferozee.
We talked of that August evening
Fifty years before, when we
Climbed the mango orchard on the hill.

You gave me in a little box, your mother's jewels,
To tell me we were now engaged
And to fix our wedding day.
I almost cracked your ribs
With the intensity of my embrace.

You agreed to come home to tell my mother.
With zest you shared the impromptu meal
My mother offered, and straightaway she knew,
A man who relished such simple fare
Would love her girl without demands.

And so you did.

In fifty years not a day
When you didn't say
Ferozee, what lovely eyes you have,
What a lovely face, what lovely hair.
But age had spotted my face and robbed the
Sparkle of eye and hair.

It is to the eye of affection, I said as always,
I remain your girl of twenty-two,
For beauty is in your eye though not in me.
You pressed my hand, you kissed my cheek,
And then you went away.

Suddenly your breathing changed,
You gasped for air. Your dear heart failed
In the grip of the seed that grew and grew
Before my eyes into the frosty face of death
Before we could any future breathe.

To complete the picture, I am reproducing several lines which I heard from my husband for fifty years, to tell me of his love. They are beautiful lines, and worth repeating, both for their own worth and to show how Homi loved to express his feelings, which he did almost daily.

"Yes, Yours, my love, is the right human face
I in my mind had waited for this long,
Seeing the false and searching for the true,
Then found you as a traveller finds a place
Of welcome suddenly amid the wrong
Valleys and rocks and twisting roads,
But you,
What shall I call you? A fountain in a waste,
A well of water in a country dry,
Or anything that's honest and good, an eye
That makes the whole world bright. Your
Open heart,
Simple with giving, gives the primal deed,
The first good world, the blossom,
The blowing seed,
The hearth, the steadfast land,
The wandering sea,
Not beautiful or rare in every part,
But like yourself, as they were meant to be."

"So sweet love seemed that summer morn
When first we kissed beside the thorn
So strangely sweet, it is not strange
We thought that love would never change.
But I can tell, let truth be told
Love will change in growing old.

Tho day by day is nought to see
So delicate his motions be,
Till in the end, 'twill come to pass
Quite to forget what once he was,
Nor even in fancy to recall the pleasure
That once was all in all.

That little stream that sweet we found
So deep in summer floods is drowned
I wonder, bathed in joy complete
How love so young could be so sweet."

"So they loved as love in twain
Had the essence but in one
Two distincts, division none
Distance there in love was slain."

"Thyself away art present still with me,
For thou no further than my thoughts cans't move,
And I am with them, and they with thee."

"Conversing with thee, I forget all time,
All seasons and their change. All seem alike".

"Thought leapt out to wed with thought,
Ere thought could wed itself with speech."

"Fair as a star when only one is shining in the sky."

Repeating Pierre Curie's words to Marie
"If one of us dies, 'tho one live like a body without a soul,
work must go on."

RECOLLECTIONS OF MY FATHER

Meher J. Pocha

When I was asked to write about my father for this festschrift, I was delighted that my family had nominated me for this task. Memories of my father are never far away and I saw myself filling page after page with anecdotes and experiences, but putting them down on paper has proved rather difficult. My father was a very private man, despite his high profile in the legal profession. With one or two notable exceptions, he did not like sharing our family life with others; he enjoyed and treasured our little jokes and sayings, which meant a lot to us but which were incomprehensible to the uninitiated. I found I was editing myself as I selected what I would write but that seemed to take away much of his charm as a loved and respected father.

Memories with blurred edges come to me as I write — memories of me running down hills with him in Simla, crunching autumn leaves; my later embarrassment as we walked in Matheran and my parents stopped to embrace or kiss; my father patiently letting me rub soapy water into his 'bad' shoulder to make it better; walks on Marine Drive talking of all sorts of things and listening to him reciting poetry till we were joined by his friend, Mr. J. R. Vimadalal,[1] after which the conversation usually turned to law and to various cases, old and new. He loved telling of how he hurried to the hospital when I was born and how expertly he held me, without any previous experience or training! He loved setting up elaborate surprises and special treats. He would dress up in strange outfits to amuse us but quickly take them off if, as sometimes happened, the younger ones got nervous.

Love of Family, Friends and Simple Pleasures

Work and family were the two most important aspects of his life. We were always aware of his dedication to his work but never got the feeling that it took precedence over the needs of his family. He had an unvarying, regular routine, from waking at six every morning and turning on the World Service of the BBC on his antiquated but treasured radio, to his daily exercises and leaving punctually for work, his evening walk with my mother, and his bedtime. Without hesitation,

1. Who later became a Judge of the Bombay High Court.

however, he would alter this routine if any of us needed it. My sister Shirin, my brother Navroz and I always felt we could interrupt his work to ask for help with homework or advice on a presentation, or speech for a debate. He would put aside whatever he was doing, give us his full attention, look up references, make suggestions and then sit up late or wake early to complete the task. We were always aware of his complete absorption in his legal briefs, his careful preparation and attention to detail. Yet, he often commented somewhat critically on people who were too perfectionist and said, "Don't let the best be the enemy of the good."

My father was happiest when he was at home with the whole family – his children and then his grandchildren. His happy family life gave him greater joy and fulfilment than his success in the legal profession. He was offered the post of Attorney-General and of Judge in the Supreme Court but he refused them both largely because it would have meant moving to Delhi and disrupting our education and our social circle in Bombay. He did not enjoy travelling to other parts of India for cases in other courts, and was not at all happy about having to spend a long time in Delhi for a case involving the Krishna River Waters dispute. He came home almost every weekend, to be with his family.

Though my father did not enjoy parties and big celebrations, he had a number of close and valued friends and loved to be with them. He visited them if they were ill or infirm, and tried to find ways of cheering them or offering more practical help. They, in turn, valued his friendship and esteem. As he grew older he would sometimes monopolise one or two guests, talking of things that were important to him — law and literature — but assuming, usually wrongly, that the listener shared his knowledge of important cases and treasured books. My mother sometimes said, "I think it's time to rescue that poor man/ lady from your father" but often I found, to my surprise, that they didn't necessarily want to be "rescued"!

There was a significant age gap between my father and mother, but they had many interests and enthusiasms in common. Their love for each other was palpable; they always spoke to and of each other with affection and supported each other in many ways. My father would often phone home to ask my mother some trivial question or give a superfluous reminder. She sometimes said to us afterwards, "Couldn't it have waited?" but we pointed out it was simply because he wanted a reason to hear her voice. A family friend who lived in one of the buildings along the route of their daily walk once said, "I always see them talking to each other animatedly. After more than 40 years of marriage, that's quite amazing, isn't it?" A favourite story was of my father's first visit to my maternal grandparents' home. There was a simple meal, which he ate with enjoyment. My grandmother is said to have commented that anyone who could eat spinach like that would look after her daughter well. "And she was right," he would say.

Indeed, he always liked simple food and did not like anything spicy. If the cook had been over-enthusiastic with chillies or chilli powder, he would say, "It's okay — I'll have an omelette." He was delighted to hear the famous chef Escoffier say that excessive spice masked the true flavour of food and that once your tongue was burned by the first mouthful you couldn't taste the flavour anyway, which echoed my father's own view. He loved ice-cream. Our cook made a very rich ice-cream, loaded with pistachios and almonds, which he particularly enjoyed. "Better make it pistachio and almond ice-cream, or the servants will worry about my financial situation," he'd joke.

He had a gentle and wholesome sense of humour and would often make up elaborate jokes to amuse us. He frowned on ribald humour and sexual innuendo and somehow people avoided them in his company. He loved to make us laugh and his (and my mother's) hearty laughter led the way. He loved children and they seemed drawn to him. One of his ways of amusing small children was to say, "Do you want to hear the birdie?" and make a chirping noise, finger to lips. He loved to tell of one little girl who said, "Take it out and show it to me." "I can't do that," he said, "it's in my throat." Undaunted, she said, "Then cut your throat and get it out." When my parents were sitting chatting on the lawns of the Princess Victoria Mary Gymkhana, a little group of small children would come along to join them and my father would keep them amused for half an hour or more, to the surprise and delight of their parents.

He had a generally philosophical outlook on life. However, he was a very practical man and he tended to be a bit dismissive of people who were 'given to deep questioning to endless dole'. He would say, "Your mother preaches psychology but I practise it." He had a favourite quote about a man who said, "When I was younger, I had six theories of education. I had no children. Now I have six children but no theories of education." He was not dismissive of our sometimes half-baked theories and arguments but would discuss them patiently. My brother recollects heated arguments when he ended up shouting at our father, who would say, "Right" and then walk quietly away. When my brother had calmed down, he would come back and talk quietly to him again. We all had arguments with our father about coming home late from parties or other outings. We regarded it as blackmail that our father would be up, reading or writing on the sofa when we got home in the early hours. When we said we thought he was being unreasonable, he would say, "I'm sorry, I'm made that way and I'm too old to change. I can't sleep till you get back but it's better if I get some work or reading done rather than lie tossing and turning in bed. You come home whenever you like." This applied as much to Navroz as to Shirin and me. We were all expected to be home in time for a family meal at eight o'clock. I found this irksome, as most of my friends had to be home only by nine, but in our case this rule was almost inflexible. In turn, I go to great lengths to accommodate my children's programmes so that we can all eat together and I can see why it was so important to him to have us all around him.

Generosity, Courage and Integrity

My father often reminded us that money was not plentiful when he was growing up. He took great pleasure in helping others, particularly talented students who were struggling to pay their fees. The employees at his Chambers often 'borrowed' money, which ended up as a gift. Once Shirin and I were working in his Chambers when we heard one of them asking for a loan. "No," said father firmly, "You have already had more than one loan" and he continued writing. Later, I said, "Well done, Dad, you really took a tough line with him — it was great the way you carried on writing while he was standing there." "Why did he carry on standing?" asked Shirin. "I was writing him a cheque," said father, just a little sheepishly.

He believed that money should be enjoyed but often said, "Money should be your servant, not your master." He was perhaps unusual in paying his income tax dues in full, but tried to put money into tax-free investments as a legal and legitimate way of keeping the tax burden down. He was very proud of having studied the options and put together a little booklet which was useful to others. He was unimpressed by wealth and conspicuous consumption, judging people on what he saw as their merits. He made a point of treating the poor and humble with particular consideration and respect, and was loved and respected by all our servants. He could not always hide his negative view of certain individuals and it showed through, despite his attempt to be uniformly courteous. Someone once said that his *"saibji"* (hello and goodbye) could be as sharp as a surgeon's knife. I think most people accepted that he was guided in all things by his sense of justice and about doing the right thing, as he saw it, so that whether they liked or disliked him, agreed or disagreed with him, they always respected him.

I do not remember my father shouting (except to draw someone's attention). It was evident when he was annoyed or displeased but he usually managed to remain calm. His favourite attributes were moderation in all things and a sense of proportion. He believed it was wrong to lose his temper in court. "I am often sorely tried," he would say, "but I am representing someone else and it would be wrong to show my annoyance and jeopardise the case." He loved telling us of successful cases. "One of the reasons for my success as a cross-examiner is that I look a fool but I am not one," he would say (we quickly assured him that he did not look a fool!). He would tell us how he would ask simple, open questions until the witness felt this was going to be really easy, then strike with a telling question that got the result he wanted. Somehow, I got the impression my father believed that the purpose of the legal process was to arrive at the truth and that, as an advocate, his role was to assist in this. Though I realise this is probably an unusual view, I know my father put it into practice and it has made me feel much more comfortable when I go to court, in the course of my work as a paediatrician, than is justified by the workings of our adversarial legal system.

When I was a medical student, one of the lecturers asked me if I was related to H. M. Seervai. On hearing he was my father, he said, "He is a wonderful man." He then went on to say that my father had once appeared for the State Government against him, but found that he was innocent of the charges, and said so. The charges were dropped. I remember feeling pleased; he thought my father was wonderful but I didn't think there was anything special in my father's actions.

This approach led my father to be deeply hurt and angry if he felt colleagues who should know better, behaved, as he saw it, badly. He regarded it as deplorable for anyone to be dishonest in their argument of a case but, if the individual was a friend, it became a matter of serious misconduct. This applied to matters outside the law courts and, as his family, we sometimes felt the way he dropped relatively close friends for this sort of failing was a little extreme. It often took years to bring about a reconciliation. He used to say that his good opinion, when lost, was difficult, if not impossible, to regain, but once there had been a reconciliation, it was as if there had never been a rift.

Perhaps his requirement that all around him should meet his high ethical standards could be regarded as a failing, especially when linked to his inability to accept that not everyone could meet them. He himself was always prepared to stand up for truth and justice as he saw it. In this he was fully supported by my mother and we were encouraged to give our comments and opinions. I realise now that immense courage was needed to speak out against powerful people and Government departments. Even today I can feel the atmosphere of outrage and determination that hung over our home if a letter was being drafted or some action planned in response to bad behaviour, injustice or dishonesty. I must have absorbed some of this and write some letters of this type myself and encourage others to do so!

My father's resignation as Advocate-General, a post he loved and had made uniquely his own, was on a matter of principle. He enjoyed being Advocate-General and delighted in the Advocate-General's Chambers — a large, bright, airy room with wood panelling surrounded by bookcases. The bookcases had been double-stacked when he took over but an upper bookcase fell and injured a man who was cleaning them, so all the loose upper bookcases were removed and the panelling exposed. This was decorated with pictures — paintings and family photographs. On Sunday mornings he often went to his Chambers to work, and in the run-up to our exams Shirin, Navroz and I went along with him, to work undisturbed till lunch time, except for a tea break. He loved tea and took a flask of tea to his Chamber everyday — a special design, which allowed the milk to be stored separately. He would comment on the quality of tea offered to him and when the tea at the restaurant in Hatfield House met with his approval, I knew it could be regarded as a really successful trip.

He was always punctual. Repeated unpunctuality in anyone annoyed him greatly. However absorbed he was in a legal matter, he had the discipline to put it aside if he had an appointment to keep, including his daily appointment to go for a walk with my mother. If we were late arriving independently at a theatre or cinema, he would be impatient and restless till we got there. "You cut it very fine," he would say, with disapproval.

When involved in any case, my father absorbed himself in it completely, reading around the subject so that he was technically well informed. My brother recollects that as a school child he saw father read Lancelot Hogben's *Mathematics for the Million* and standard textbooks on Physics for the River Waters dispute. Years later, a senior Government engineer told Navroz of our father's complete mastery of the technical aspects of the case. He was proud of his mastery of the principles of nutrition for the *Hall's Wine* case, which allowed him to cross-examine, and demolish the evidence of, a well-known nutritionist. This degree of preparation for each matter, whatever its relative importance, meant that he would not take on more work than he could deal with to his own high standards. He also insisted on never spending more on accommodation and expenses, just because a client was paying, than he would be prepared to spend if he were paying for it himself.

Influences

He had a deep affection for Elphinstone College. He would sometimes say, only partly seriously, "If someone has studied at Elphinstone College I assume they are sensible. If they have studied elsewhere, it has to be proved." He was a Trustee of the College for almost forty years, up to the time of his death. He played a role in the centenary celebrations and, for the 125th anniversary, he also helped raise a substantial sum of money. In recognition of his active role, he was guest of honour at both celebrations. It was at Elphinstone College that he first met J.C.P. d'Andrade, Professor of Philosophy, an inspirational teacher who also taught my mother some years later. My father did his B.A. and M.A. in Philosophy guided and inspired by Professor d'Andrade, whose portrait had an important place in our home.

Of the people who influenced my father greatly, he would regard his mother, Meherbai, Professor d'Andrade and Sir Jamshedji Kanga, in whose Chambers he began his legal career, as the three most important. He always spoke of his mother with great affection. He would say, "I have a high regard for women, having been brought up by a remarkable woman." He loved to share with us a book made by her, with beautiful embroidery, and her wedding ring to show us how small and dainty her hands were. His father died while he was still a child and his mother brought him and his brother up in relatively difficult financial circumstances, but in an environment enriched by affection, and love of learning. Though they had very different temperaments and interests, my father and uncle were fond of each other, but one could sense some irritation from time to time on the part of my father. He also spoke of his cousin, Hirjibhai Wadia with respect and gratitude for offering him financial support when he needed it, for instance when he wanted to start his career at the Bar.

My father did not particularly care for foreign travel. He loved England and enjoyed the few visits he made here, but he felt the world came to him through radio (and, later, television), reading and visitors. He listened constantly to the BBC World Service. He often spoke of hearing Sir Winston Churchill's speeches live on the radio during the war years. He greatly admired Churchill and knew many of his speeches from memory.

Love of Literature

Shakespeare was special for my father and I know much of his plays from hearing him recite Shakespearean speeches from memory. Understandably Portia, with her speech on the quality of Mercy, was a particular favourite. I memorised Richard Ill's speech, "Now is the winter of our discontent..." without realising it — he recited it so often! Among other authors whose works were read and re-read many times were Dickens, Trollope, Scott, Jane Austen, Goldsmith, Johnson, Butler, George Elliott and P. G. Wodehouse. He loved the novels of Thackeray, and often said that, though it was unfashionable to like Kipling, he did. In a talk he gave about Kipling, he reminded the audience that people often quoted the lines, "Oh East is East and West is West, And never the twain shall meet" but most of them forgot the next lines — "But there is neither East nor West, Country nor class nor birth, When two brave men stand face to face, Though they come from the ends of the earth." He also enjoyed reading to us Alexandre Dumas' stories of *The Three Musketeers*. He could be moved to tears by a sad or tender passage and, when reading aloud, this might be heard as a slight pause and clearing of the throat.

As children we absorbed poetry and literature from our father without being fully aware of it. I can still recite poems or bits of prose, triggered by a word of recollection. I get the same patient, or not so patient, tolerance from my children that I sometimes accorded my father when I was a teenager, wishing that my parents were more like everyone else's — not serious, and learned and well-known! When my friends came to visit, my father would sometimes make an effort to 'draw them out', as he put it. On one occasion, he was rather upset that I had left him on his own with a group of friends who had dropped in to discuss arrangements for a party. After a while he came to find me. "I'm very sorry if I upset your friends," he said, "I tried them on Art, I tried them on Literature, then, because the exam results have been out recently, I asked them how they'd done." "Oh, Dad!" I said, "All but one of them has failed." "Yes," he said, "I know now! Nobody had told me about it, so at first I thought they were joking. Please tell them I wouldn't have asked if I had known ..." Often, the harder he tried with my friends, the more they retreated into silence or monosyllabic replies. I think Shirin's and Navroz's friends got on with him somewhat better.

Enthusiasm and Optimism

He loved knowledge for its own sake. He delighted in learning something new or finding out a new aspect of things already known. Two favourite programmes were Kenneth Clarke's *Civilisation* and Bronowski's *Ascent of Man*. He read and re-read the books based on these programmes. He always thought things through for himself and did not readily accept the established view. Though he had strongly held views — we sometimes accused him of unreasonable prejudices — he was prepared to change them if he had the evidence to do so. His flexibility, when this was necessary, contributed to his effectiveness as a lawyer.

Having listened to the BBC World Service for years, my father was slow to get into television. I think both my parents thought television was relatively frivolous. Once they had acquired a television, however, my father loved watching the news and even changed his bedtime to take in the 10 o'clock news. He quickly built up a list of favourite programmes. When we were visiting Bombay, my mother would suggest he ought to spend time with us rather than watch some of these programmes. He would ask us, especially our children, if we liked a particular programme. If we said we did, he'd say, "See, Ferozee, they like it too" and we'd all settle down to watch. Inspector Morse was a great favourite and meal times were re-organised so that we could watch — my father, my son and I. My parents had built up a collection of favourite films on video and again my father would try and interest us in watching them. It was lovely to see such enjoyment and enthusiasm for this new toy in a man of 89.

At our last visit — he died about ten days after we returned to England — he also spoke with enthusiasm about inventions he had seen on *Tomorrow's World*. He wanted to finish the Preface to the fourth edition of his book on Constitutional Law and was planning a second edition of his book on the Partition of India. Always optimistic and forward-looking, he never lost faith in India to resolve her problems and in the world to move in the right direction. Once, when I was grumbling about the state of things, he said, "Wait, I'll read you something." He then read out a piece bemoaning the decline of civilisation, the laxity of society, the wildness of the young who no longer respected their elders and so on. "Well?" I said with some irritation. "Well," he said, "it's from Thucydides, around 400 BC, and here we are, so things can't be all that bad!" However bleak a situation, he always faced it with fortitude and optimism, seeking, and often finding, some positive aspect or some way of relieving it.

There was a regular ritual of reading aloud before we went to bed; not just when we were little and shared his delight in books like *Winnie the Pooh* and the poems of A.A. Milne, but later, when we graduated to Dickens, Sherlock Holmes, P.G. Wodehouse, Thackeray and Trollope. Special favourites like the *Just So Stories, The Cloister and the Hearth,* the *Jeeves* and *Mulliner* stories and *Precious Bane* were often repeated. If I remember rightly, my sister Shirin chose not to join us after a while and there was no pressure on her to do so. As children we took it all for granted and as we grew older, we felt we were humouring him in his many enthusiasms.

A Happy and Fulfilled Life

Shirin, Navroz and I were privileged to grow up in a home full of love, light and laughter, respected as individuals and taught by example. Good sense, integrity, honesty and decent human values formed the basis of our parents' lives and overflowed into ours. If we sometimes found it a burden to be expected always to be rational, logical and sensible, it was a small price to pay. Our father died suddenly, without a preceding illness, while watching the video of a favourite film, *Cromwell*. The day before, he had finished dictating the last case for an addendum to the fourth edition of his book, that had absorbed so many years of his life, and he had celebrated his Golden Wedding a short time earlier. These had been two important goals. He died with plans for the future and still full of enthusiasm and optimism. Mixed with my sadness at his death was thankfulness for the way he had died and the sustaining thought that he had lived a full, fulfilled and happy life. I must end with a quotation, but it is hard to choose one. Navroz has suggested two which our father loved:

unmoved
Unshaken, unseduced, unterrified,
His loyalty he kept, his love, his zeal,
Nor number, nor example with him wrought
To swerve from truth, or change his constant mind.

– Milton

and, Johnson's lines, as my father had adapted them when writing of his admired teacher, Professor d'Andrade:

His virtues walked their ample round
Nor made a pause, nor left a void,
And sure the eternal master found
His shining talents well employed.

A SON REMEMBERS HIS FATHER*

Navroz H. Seervai

MY FATHER LIVED A COMPLETE LIFE, devoting his time and energy in equal measure to law, literature, his family, his friends. If one had to single out one quality and characteristic of the man, amongst many, one would have to speak of his absolute or inflexible honesty and integrity. For him, Truth was sacred and he never swerved from the path of Truth and Righteousness. Apart from this what comes to mind was his affection and kindness for all; his courteousness to even the most humble person; his courage in fighting causes, but never through improper means. He despised the glib phrase "The ends justify the means". He used to say "Once you swerve from the path of truth, you are on the slippery slope." It was with justifiable pride that he said that in over 50 years of active practice, he never once shouted in Court, or lost his temper in Court. But his voice was dominating and could be heard in other court-rooms. Iron will power and control saw to his not losing his temper, although once in a while he would say "I was terribly provoked, but I kept my temper in Court."

He used to quote, with a shaking voice and tears in his eyes, the lines of Walter Scott "Without courage, there cannot be truth and without truth there can be no other virtue."

My earliest memories of father are of playing with him as a small child, either at home or in his chamber — chamber No. 24 on the first floor of the High Court. It was one of his rare qualities, that he somehow found time for his family — however busy he was. I never once heard him tell my mother, or my sisters, or me "Later, I'm busy just now." One incident, to highlight this, sticks out in my mind. It

* Written for himself and not for publication. Several years later he has agreed to its publication, at my request. Ed.

was 1973. My sister was in Inter Arts. Dad was in the midst of *Keshavananda Bharti*. He used to be in Delhi through the week and in Bombay at the weekends. One morning I happened to wake up around 3.30 a.m. and to my amazement I found dad reclining on the living-room sofa with a book in hand and paper and pen next to him. On questioning him I discovered he was reading *"Deductive Logic"* by Joseph. (It was his own copy from the 1920s). He said "Shilliboo (his petname for Shirin) is having some problems with the subject, so I'm helping her. She'll be coming to the Chamber at 10 a.m., so I must be ready for her."

To him poetry and literature were amongst the most precious things in life. My aunt Freny Mehta once told me, that he had told her, that through the 10 lean years at the Bar, he sustained himself by learning up poems by heart and by absorbing himself in poetry and literature. He said the same in his talk at PEN on POETRY AND LIFE. When I once asked him about this, he said "Yes, I used to try and learn atleast a couple of poems a week. It kept me going when there was precious little, or no work." He knew by heart hundreds of poems. And each was recited with body, mind and soul. Scott, Milton, Tennyson, Browning, Blake, Keats, Shelly, Fielding, Byron, Johnson, the list is endless. But his dearest poet was Wordsworth. A special look suffused his face when he recited Wordsworth's great sonnets and other poems. Be it "Daffodils" or "Upon Westminster Bridge" or "On the Extinction of the Venetian Republic" or "1812" or any of the other great poems, long or short, he would recite the lines with great feeling and with perfect diction. It was as if the poem, the poet and he were merged into one. It is no coincidence that in the first two editions of his book on the Constitution and in his book *Partition of India* he put, on the title page these lines of Wordsworth: "We shall exult if they who rule the land Be men who hold its many blessings dear, Wise, upright, valiant; not a servile band, Who are to judge of dangers which they fear; And honour which they do not understand." And in his book on the Emergency, these lines, also of Wordsworth: "Enough if something from our hands have power to live, and act and serve the future hour."

Apart from these greats, Shakespeare held a very special place in his heart. Be it the Sonnets or the great lines in the plays, he knew them by heart. Henry V at Agincourt; Hamlet's great soliloquies; Macbeth's soliloquy before murdering Duncan, Portia on the Quality of Mercy ... the list is endless.

But this was not all. Dickens, Trollope, Scott, Jane Austen, Goldsmith, Johnson, Meredith, Fielding, Samuel Butler, George Elliot and hundreds of others had been read and re-read, and, as he would say, re-re-read. Entire passages from *Pickwick Papers* or *Pride & Prejudice* or *Esmond* or *Precious Bane* were known to him.

His love of knowledge manifested itself in his deep affection for Elphinstone College. He participated in the College's Centenary and its 125th Anniversary. On the latter occasion, through his personal efforts, the College collected Rs. 7.5 lakhs. He was its Trustee for almost 40 years — until his death.

It was at Elphinstone College that he first met J.C.P. d'Andrade — his professor of Philosophy. It was because of him that he did his B.A. and M.A. in Philosophy. Apart from his mother Meherbai, the greatest influence on father in his early years, was d'Andrade. If there were three persons whom he revered they were his mother, Prof. d'Andrade and Sir Jamshedji Kanga. A life-long student of Philosophy, he did his B.A. with Philosophy and his M.A. by his Thesis on *God and Existence.* He voraciously read the great philosophers: Plato, Aristotle, Spinoza, Kant, Hegel, Bradley to mention only a few. He loved to quote Aristotle on Plato: "Plato is great, but Truth is greater". He studied philosophy and he lived his philosophy. His quote of Plato on Socrates was also often repeated to us: "Of all the men of his time, he was the wisest, the justest and the best".

His knowledge of English history and politics was profound. Once in 1973 when on our first trip to U.K. he and I were at Pitt's Cottage, and some lines were inscribed over the fire place, to the amazement of the English guide, English tourists and others, dad said: "Oh Scott — But what a pity that the next few lines were not inscribed." And in his mellifluous voice he recited the lines "Now is the stately column broke; The beacon light is quenched in smoke ..." and he completed the last stanza. One tourist said "Are you a professor of history or literature at Oxford or Cambridge?" Dad laughed and said "No, no, no! I'm a lawyer from India, but these lines are so famous, everyone knows them." Of course, nobody but he knew them in the whole group!

On a celebration for 4th July, at the U.S. Consulate in Bombay, Dad amazed the Vice Consul by reciting Abraham Lincoln's Second Inaugural Address. And then rattled off the Gettysburg address. At home he said "The silly chap didn't even know that Lincoln had made one of his greatest speeches at his Second Inaugural." And I said, "But dad, everyone isn't steeped in history and prose like you." "But surely an American should know of Lincoln's great speeches", he retorted, with just a hint of irritation.

We children owe it to dad that we know so much poetry and prose and so many speeches by heart. We would hear him recite a poem repeatedly and learn it over a period of time. My daughter Shanoor learnt her first poem in the same manner from my dad.

If he was familiar with the life and times of Cromwell, Pitt the Elder, Pitt the Younger, Chatham, Bright, Fox, Peel, Gladstone and Disraeli, his knowledge of, and familiarity with, the life of Churchill, was in a class of its own. Apart from having read almost every book by Churchill, he had read dozens of books on Churchill. He was proud of the fact that he had heard almost all of Churchill's great war-time speeches live, on the BBC. To him a visit to Chartwell & Blenheim Palace (in 1973) was both a pilgrimage and a source of intense pleasure. If the tourists at Pitt's Cottage were surprised at his knowledge of Pitt and of Sir Walter Scott, those at Chartwell were amazed. He virtually took over from the guide. It was hilarious — H.M.S. with his little group and the guide with her little group! At Blenheim, knowledge of Churchill was complemented by knowledge of the 1st Duke of Marlborough and his war campaigns and his great victories, including at Blenheim.

Father was above all else a perfectionist. He took infinite pains to achieve his exacting self-imposed standards. As a school child I remember dad reading Lancelot Hogbein's *Mathematics For The Millions* and several standard books on physics, for the Krishna River Water dispute. Eric Saldanha, a top engineer with the Maharashtra State Government told me years later, of dad's absolute mastery of the technical aspects of the case. In the Court fees case, since Government did not provide facts and figures, dad obtained 2 passes to the Legislative Assembly from his old friend Bobby Dalal, former RLA, and we spent 3 days pouring over the Budget books to get at all the relevant figures. At that time he was 74 or 75.

No case, howsoever small or unimportant it may be, passed through his hands, without the facts being thoroughly mastered and the law thoroughly researched. This I learnt, amongst others, from Atul Setalvad. Once as a very raw junior, I complimented Atul on having dug out all the relevant law for a writ petition — at the admission stage. He looked askance at me and said : "What are you congratulating me for ? It's nothing more than what your father did for every matter of his. We have only learnt from him."

But over and above the law, his books, his poetry, was his family. His love and affection were overwhelming and all consuming. As adolescents it sometimes proved irksome and we would rebel. He would let us blow off steam, berate him, sometimes even shout at him and then without raising his voice, he would calmly say: "You are right, but I'm made that way, and I'm too old to change. I can't help my anxiety when you all come home late at night. So I will stay up, but please do come home as late as you like."

He was never happier than with his family and in the last decade or so, he revelled in the company of his grandchildren. His love for children manifested itself and flowed over for his grandchildren. I believe that he considered his happy family life as being of infinitely greater value than success at the Bar, the success of his books and the honours and awards bestowed upon him. For this did he refuse judgeship of the Supreme Court in 1956. Had he accepted, he would have had a tenure of 15 years — 5½ as Chief Justice. For this and for his Book did he refuse Attorney-Generalship in 1971 for he did not want to disrupt his family life in Bombay and felt that the move to Delhi would inevitably disrupt the family life.

But it was not only his family upon which he lavished his love and affection. He was a devoted and loyal friend. Many of his friends were of over 50 years' standing. He visited them when they got old (Manekshaw, P. B. Vaccha) or when they were ill (Prof. d'Andrade, Porus Mehta, J. C. Bhatt, Rasesh Bhatt). In the last few years he repeatedly visited and met Jehangir Dubash, Sorab Vimadalal or Rustomjee Andhyarujina who was a friend for well over 75 years, the friendship going back to school days. Churchill said of his dear friend F.E.Smith that he did not need a statue or memorial to remember him, for his greatest memorial was that he would live in the hearts of men. My father loved these lines. I believe they equally apply to him.

How to sum up his life and what he stood for? It can only be in the poetry or prose he loved. He was fond of so many and quoted them appropriately as the occasion demanded. These were some of his favourite lines:

"Without courage, there cannot be truth, and without truth there can be no other virtue." (Sir Walter Scott).

"Heaven doth with us as we with torches do, Not light them for themselves;" (Shakespeare — Measure For Measure)

"In our heart of hearts believing
Victory crowns the just;
And that braggarts must
Surely bite the dust;
Press we to the field ungrieving,
In our heart of hearts believing
Victory crowns the just." (Thomas Hardy)

"The woods are lovely, dark and deep
But I have promises to keep;
And miles to go before I sleep
And miles to go before I sleep." (Frost)

But two sets of lines, I believe, sum him up better than most. The first are the magnificent lines of Milton

"unmoved
Unshaken, unseduced, unterrified,
His loyalty he kept, his love, his zeal,
Nor number, nor example with him wrought
To swerve from truth, or change his constant mind."

In a recollection written by him in 1950 under extreme emotional pressure, on the death of Prof. d'Andrade, my father chose these lines to describe his beloved professor. He wrote:

"But the words which seem most applicable to him are the words which were written about a humble man by a man with a very great heart:

"His virtues walked their ample round
Nor made a pause, nor left a void,
And sure the Eternal Master found
His shining talents well employed."

My father substituted 'ample' for 'narrow' and 'shining' for 'single'. I truly believe that if my father had had to choose some lines to sum it all up, he would have chosen these favourite lines of Johnson.

GRANDFATHER

Jehangir P. Madon

HORMASJI MANECKJI SEERVAI. H.M. Seervai. Homi Seervai. These names all refer to the same man, but I knew him simply as Grandpa. I was the first grandchild that Grandpa got to know, since Cyrus and Shirin, who are both older than me, lived in England and visited Bombay every two years. As a child, I remember spending time at my grandparents' house, and I remember some of the flat before it was converted to accommodate both my grandparents and my uncle. Though the flat changed, my grandfather never did. He always spent time with my sister and me, and any other children that wanted to spend time with him. My earliest memories involve eating at the dining table, and using the dessert cutlery to eat since the regular cutlery was too big for me to handle. At first I used to sit at the head of the table with one of my parents, but as I got older, I used to sit next to Grandpa and eat with him. He would always tell us to eat in moderation, and to save a little room for dessert. Often, dessert was a piece of Cadbury's chocolate, which was given to us in the 'magic' room. The 'magic' room was his bedroom, but it was always magical to me. Before having his afternoon siesta, Grandpa would always tell me the story of the three little pigs and the big, bad wolf. It is not a version that one can find in a bookstore, but was modified to include family members that I knew. The story never ended with the wolf failing to blow down the 3rd pig's house, but instead it ended with my father and me watching the sunrise. Grandpa knew how to tell a story to entertain a young child, and the same story was magical every time it was retold.

Tea time was always fun for me, since it was the only meal I remember my grandfather eating outside of Shiv Shanti Bhuvan. We would often spend the early evening at the Princess Victoria Mary Gymkhana (PVM Gym) where a cup of tea and a plate of buttered toast were standard. Sometimes my sister and I had chips instead of the toast, but my grandfather never changed his menu. He would then watch us as we played on the swings, the slide, and the seesaw. We would then go back to their flat for dinner, which was promptly served at the same time every day, with only one exception. When Inspector Morse was shown on Star TV, the dinner schedule was rearranged to allow him to watch the two-hour episode uninterrupted. I was there for one such dinner, and the entire family, including Meher and Cyrus, who were visiting from England, sat in the living room to watch Inspector Morse. I will never forget meal times with my grandfather, and it was always more fun when the whole family was present.

Grandpa would never raise his voice in anger, and only shouted at me once. He had had eye surgery, and had lost peripheral vision in one eye (I think it was the left). On one occasion, after returning from the PVM Gym, I decided to run into the flat. My grandfather was in front of me, and I cut him off in the corridor. He shouted out of fright, because he did not see me coming. I was scared, since I had never heard him shout and did not know what to do. He realized that I did not know what I had done wrong, and calmly explained to me that he could not see out of the side of his eye and had not seen me coming. I became aware of this, and I was very careful when I was in his blind spot. Grandpa had some problems with his legs, and had gone in for some surgery. I remember when he returned and had to walk using a walker, before going onto the stick that I remember him by. When I was older, he would walk using the stick in one hand and holding onto my arm with his other hand. I had always thought of my grandfather as a frail man, but his grip ranks among the firmest I have encountered to date. I was always nervous when he held onto my hand to steady himself, because I did not want to be the cause of a fall. My fears were put to rest, as there was never a mishap when I helped him get back into the building.

Books. Shiv Shanti Bhuvan was full of them. Both Grandma and Grandpa used to read to us when we were younger, and continued to read to us even into our teen years. My favourite book was the book of Japanese stories that my Grandfather used to read to us after lunch or dinner, and we loved listening to him speak. The stories were never the same when I read them myself. When I was older, Grandpa used to talk to me on subjects that were more serious, like Winston Churchill, and I felt guilty every time he did so. I was unable to concentrate for the entire discussion, and would often start daydreaming about the material that he had just spoken about and miss what he was saying. I would then suddenly realize that I was daydreaming, and would return back into the present. I do not know if Grandpa knew about my daydreams, but he never showed any signs of such knowledge. I still remember part of what he said on his visit to a museum related to Churchill in England.

Grandpa loved poetry, and could recite many poems from memory flawlessly. I do not remember his poetry as much as his songs that he would sing to us. He would sing "It's a long way to Tiparary" and "All I want" from "My Fair Lady." I still remember those songs whenever I see "My Fair Lady," or hear the soundtrack from that movie. When I had to choose a poem to recite in the 9th grade, I chose "Upon Westminster Bridge" by Wordsworth, because Grandma told me that it was one of his favourites. I had liked it when I first read it in the 7th grade, and I knew that this poem was for me. I still remember it to this day, and am proud of that fact. I may not know as many poems as Grandpa did, but one has to start somewhere.

Homi Seervai represents many different things to different people, but I will forever know him as Grandpa. I have read and heard stories about him and what he has done, but it has not changed my views of him. When someone wanted a book inscribed by him, he acted as if he was in the presence of a great hero. I knew him well, and his demeanour changed completely in Grandpa's presence. I feel that if I knew all I do about Grandpa today, when I was a child, I would not have acted any differently. He never acted like the former Advocate-General of Maharashtra, and did not live in his past glories. I have learned a lot from Homi Seervai, but the lesson I have taken to heart the most is to remember that no matter how great the accomplishments are in one's life, one must remember who one is. That is what I have taken as Grandpa's legacy to me.

TWO CONDOLENCE LETTERS

Shanoor S. Forbes

1-2-1996

Dearest Meher,

SAROSH, SIMONIL, RESHAD and myself condole with you all and send you our sympathy on the sudden but peaceful death of dear Homi. I'm really glad we spoke on the phone in the relatively first moments of the raw grief you must have been feeling, particularly being so far away from home, and I now write to you to share my own sense of loss over his death. Even though he had reached the grand old age of ninety and one did expect that this would happen sooner or later, when the final parting actually comes one is always faced with a sense of shock and dismay and grief, and the passing away of a parent is particularly heart-wrenching, and Homi was such an 'alive' person. What a mind! And how fearless of other people's opinions in the face of "Right". Very, very few people can be so brave in heart. (I know I can't!).

Meher, you must feel such a sense of loss and emptiness right now, for I know how close a bond was yours and your dad's. So many memories come back to me of when we were children and grew up together in each other's homes, and how whenever I was at S.S.B. which was a lot of the time, we used to eat together at the dining table with Homi's lively conversation and anecdotes and lines of poetry being recited, which made meal times such a 'family' affair. Also whenever I stayed overnight, I remember after dinner the ritual of going into his airconditioned cosy bedroom and us being read to by him. He loved his hours spent with his immediate family and I always felt happy at never being excluded from these intimate family rituals and 'togetherness' which always made my hours at S.S.B. so rich and happy. Also, I know though your dad admired and adored his Feroza, Meher, Nauji and Shirin almost to the exclusion of all else, and guarded the moments of privacy with his family so zealously, he was always very warm and generous with the "intrusion" of all of Feroza's family being constantly in and out of S.S.B. — I recollect coming over regularly after school and lunching and spending many hours with you all. My mum, being so attached to Feroza, used to likewise spend many hours of the afternoons at S.S.B. too. Mehra-masi, though sleeping at Dolly's upstairs, was always downstairs. Thus your parents had open house, and their warmth and generosity and feel of strong family ties still bond us all together and particularly praiseworthy in a man like Homi, who guarded his time with his family so zealously, to be on the other hand so understanding and warm and generous with Feroza's family members.

I have always, from childhood, been aware of the very close tie between Feroza and Homi, and in fact, their marriage has been a role-model for me in my own marriage! The words of Khalil Gibran come to mind when I think of your parents' union over fifty years. I quote:

"Then Almitra spoke again on marriage and said 'You live together, and together you shall be for evermore. You shall be together when the white wings of Death alter your days. Aye, you shall be together even in the silent memory of the Soul. But let there be spaces in your togetherness. And let the wings of the herons dance between you. Love one another, but make not a bond of love. Let it rather be a moving sea between the shores of your souls. Fill each other's cup but drink not from one cup. Give one another of your bread but eat not from the same loaf. Sing and dance together and be joyous, but let each of you be alone. Even as the strings of a lute are alone though they quiver with the same music. Give your hearts, but not into each other's keeping. For only the hand of life can contain your hearts. And stand together yet not too near together. For the pillars of the temple stand apart. And the oak tree and the cypress grow not in each other's shadow'."

Now I do believe that the union of Feroza and Homi embodies these beautiful lines of the Poet Gibran, and their coupling in such perfect compatibility and the spirit of give and take has been a source of inspiration to us all.

The other thing I was always impressed with and absorbed from my association with Homi over the years was his strong sense of discipline. Indeed he was disciplined in life and disciplined in death. It is very fortunate to be able to have not only a good life but also a good death. And I feel certain that it was Homi's strength of character and his enourmous courage that enabled him to have both. And the most important of all, it is your mother's utmost and unswerving devotion that eased his path throughout his life. Another simple rule I learned from him by way of his example are in the words of H. Denkar. "When things go wrong, in time of trouble, the best medicine is to do what you are obligated to do". And this I feel was the essence of the fine man that he was.

Another observation I always used to make was his capacity to draw out the best in anyone working under him, be they his juniors, devils, peons, secretaries, chaffeurs or house servants. He was always considerate and courteous to them and extremely generous and most of them grew old in his service, giving him years of their devotion and loyalty and getting it in return from him.

I wish you could have been there at the full court reference in his honour at the High Court. It was such an uplifting experience, and a great honour to have all the judges and 'be-gowned' attorneys standing throughout and speaking about Homi's achievements and strength of truth and character. One could feel his vibrant presence in that court whilst this was going on and I imagined in my mind's eye, his striding the corridors and court rooms in his legal robes, and advising and chatting with colleagues and friends and arguing with a fiery zeal in the very room we were sitting in. It was impressive and moving and a fitting adieu to a man who loved his work so much in that court and who made such a difference to the legal profession and who stood out a man apart from his more mundane fellowmen. I salute your father and feel proud to have been his niece.

All my love,
Shanoor

12-2-1996

My dearest Nauji,

JUST LAST NIGHT I got the opportunity to read your little note to me and your piece written in the first depths of anguish and grief after your dearest father's death, and it moved me greatly. I have always been aware of how much you loved and admired him, and how much he adored you. You were the polished apple of his eye! And you have been a good son to him. You will always be able to warm yourself with that comforting thought.

I well remember showing Homi, one day when I was at your house, my own thoughts penned immediately after my dad's death and he quietly took the paper into his bedroom whilst I was sitting with Feroza outside, read it through, and coming up to me started quoting these lines, "I like not only to be loved but to be told that I am loved. I am not sure if you are of the same kind. But the realm of silence is large enough beyond the grave. This is the world of light and speech, and I shall take leave to tell you that you are very dear". Nauji, in one fell swoop with this quotation of Elliot's he'd summed up my intense cry of pain in my letter to my dead father. I had not been able, ever, to tell him how much I loved him when he was alive. Of course he knew, by my actions and the close bond I had with him. But to my everlasting regret I could never verbalise this. In some strange way, Homi's gently speaking out these beautiful lines comforted me. They also taught me a lesson I shall never forget. I will never make the same mistake again with my mother and others dear to me.

By a strange coincidence your mother (who has been one of .the strongest influences in my life from very young days) had sent me a copy only three weeks ago, of her piece written when Homi was well and alive and immediately on reading it I remember thinking, "How wonderful that Feroza has written this whilst H is alive and can get so much pleasure from this loving tribute of her love for him, rather than after he goes — and wouldn't then be able to read it!" He died soon after. She can now take so much comfort and delight from the fact that she made his life so joyous and fulfilled and meaningful in every way. (And he her's of course). We have all, in one way or another been touched and warmed by the fire of their love and devotion to each other.

I recall Sarosh so often saying over the past so many years that "it's most amazing that Feroza and specially Homi, are such powerful and towering personalities, and yet none of their children shrink in their shadow. They have been allowed, nay encouraged, to grow and spread their wings and become successful in their own selves." He has admired this quality in you all greatly.

I know you must feel bereft and will miss your father horribly, but you have been so lucky in having had such a warm and loving bond and such a happy and content upbringing over such a long stretch of time. You gave him much, much happiness and specially so, I'd say, because he was lucky you returned home rather than lived abroad, and took up the same beloved profession as his, and then married and settled at S.S.B., and gave him the gift of grandchildren in very close proximity. He was so, so fortunate in that he was superb and famed in his profession as well as family. — "So we live again in our children and because of them can never entirely die... and there lies immortality".

You have been very dear to me, right from when you were born, and I hope my sharing this with you helps in a little way to ease your present pain and hurt.

Lots of love,

Shanoor

SEERVAI'S ARTICLES, PAPERS, MEMORANDA

JUSTICE*

THOUGH MY DAYS are spent in the law Courts, "legal justice" is not the theme of my paper today. The problem of justice is primarily an ethical and a metaphysical problem: it formed the central theme of Plato's *Republic,* and in the *Niohomachean Ethics* it called forth a masterly analysis from Aristotle to which subsequent thought has added little.

A philosophical discussion of justice is particularly necessary at a time when the cry is loud for "social justice", and when that cry is heard side by side with the cry of pessimism according to which the injustice of man to man is nothing compared to the injustice which resides in the scheme of things.

Now the demand for social justice has its legitimate side, but some of the popular assumptions about "social justice" are unfounded and are bound to lead to disappointment and disillusionment. For instance, it seems to be assumed that perfect justice would reign in this world if all men could be made equal, though a little reflection would show that the only place where all men are equal is the grave — where justice and injustice are of small moment. These false assumptions are also at the root of current pessimism which finds its vindication in the obvious inequalities of life. Let me set out this feeling of injustice in the words of a writer of genius who was himself an optimist: "We talk of life as a journey, but how variously is that journey performed! There are some who come forth girt and shod and mantled to walk on velvet lawns and smooth terraces where every gale is arrested and every beam is

---

*A paper read before the Bombay Philosophical Society on February 22, 1952. [See: 54 BLR 33]

tempered. There are others who walk on the Alpine paths of life against driving misery and through stormy sorrows over sharp afflictions, walk with bare feet, and naked breast, jaded, mangled and chilled."

You see then that our discussion requires us to answer questions which come home to all of us.

Now in speaking of justice it is hardly necessary to point out that we do not ordinarily speak of a man as being just or unjust to himself. We say that he is just or unjust to others and they to him. In other words justice requires a plurality of persons or a society.

Our views of justice and injustice take their colour from the legalistic aspect of justice which looks upon each one of us as a unit having "rights" capable of protection and enforcement. But the question we have to consider is whether this aspect, however necessary and desirable, expresses the real nature of human beings. Are we solid, independent and mutually exclusive atoms, each of which has ascertained or ascertainable claims against others? If we are, then the non-enforcement or non-satisfaction of these claims would be unjust. When the question is asked "Is it just that the sins of the parents should be visited upon the children?" we are thinking of the child as a unit having certain claims. One of these claims is that evil should not befall it which it has done nothing to deserve. In other words it is unjust that a person should suffer evil which he has done nothing to deserve. If this were true, we should equally say, in the same context, that when good befalls a person which that person has done nothing to deserve, it is unjust. But we never do. We are not shocked and surprised when a child of gifted parents inherits their gifts — we are surprised when it does not.

We must then retrace our steps and see whether the assumption which has led to this inconsistent result is well founded. And we see that it is not. The finite self has its content from the society and the world in which it lives. No doubt the self acts on the world and society just as they act on it; but the greatest self has to act in a world of other wills and chance circumstance. The finite self is born not into the welfare state of popular imagination where there are "fair shares" for all, but in a world of hazard and hardship, where the shares are, from the very nature of an organic whole, unequal, and where chance plays a great part. Any one of us may be run over and killed by the negligence or stupidity of a driver. Or we may be blown up while travelling in a train by the malignity of a terrorist, and so on. But these and other hazards and hardships are the stuff of which finite selves are made, and the greatness or smallness of a self lies in the manner in which these hazards and hardships are faced. And it may be noted that very often, if the choice were given to us, we would reject the discipline of circumstance which would make us more worthy. You remember the cry which preceded the Crucifixion: "O MY FATHER, if it be possible let this cup pass from me"; but the cup did not pass and the drinking of it marked the triumph of the human spirit. In our own times we have seen how a nation achieved its "finest hour" when in a situation which seemed hopeless it faced every terror and every hardship and triumphed over them all. In our ordinary moments we may wish for a simple and easy life, but when we are most true to ourselves we know that our desire is not for tasks equal to our capacities but for capacities equal to our tasks. The brilliant student is not one who finds answers to elementary questions but one who confronts difficult problems of art, or knowledge or practice and either finds a solution or brings the solution nearer. And in all contests we wish to have foemen worthy of our steel.

Again, justice, considered as the enforcement of rights, is concerned primarily with material standards, and material standards are inadequate when we are considering spiritual values. Let me give an example. A man aged 35 is run over by the negligence of a bus driver. The man was earning Rs. 1,000 a month; his health was good and he leaves behind him a wife and three young children. The justice which we do in the case is to award damages to the family of the dead man, and we measure the loss to the family by reference to the income it has lost. Since the man had a good income and fair chances of earning it for a long time, substantial damages would be awarded against the owner of the bus. But all the spiritual factors in the situation are left out. No question is asked whether he was a loving husband and father or a wicked and cruel one. No question is asked whether the light and warmth of a home have gone out with him, or whether they have come back now that he is dead. These things are left out not because they are of no value but because the good things are of incalculable value and the evil things are measureless in their pain.

You see, then, that the legalistic conception of justice fails because men are not isolated units, but members of an organic whole, or, if you prefer that phraseology, because men belong to a world of spiritual membership, and because material standards are inapplicable to spiritual goods. And one further point must be noticed in this connection. When you speak of being just to a man do you mean just to him during his life? But what is his life? Take a man like Shakespeare. What was his real life? Was it only that which palpitated in his body or does it include that portion of it, which still palpitates in our own? And what is the justice we are supposed to do to Shakespeare: to load him, and his descendants, with riches and titles or make his wonderful art and wisdom our own?

Yes, you may reply, all this shows that there is inequality in the world, and chance, and hazard; but why should there be? If the question means: Can you tell us why reality is what it is? the answer must be that all thinking presupposes that things are rooted in reality and reality cannot be explained, as it were, from the outside. But if the question means: does our experience give us a clue to understanding the world as we have described it? the answer is "Yes, it does." Take things which are most valuable in life — which seem almost independent of time and change — such as art or knowledge and you find that they exhibit not a dead uniformity but the complex unity of an organic whole. Music does not consist of the monotonous repetition of one note, nor literature of one word. Various elements combine to make a whole, and some must, of necessity, be more important than others. Hamlet without the Prince of Denmark would cease to be a tragedy — leave out the grave digger and the tragedy stands, though robbed of a necessary element of its beauty. And the characteristic of an organic whole is that a part out of the whole is very different from the part within the whole. Let a great poet describe what I mean. In "Abt Vogler" Browning makes the musician say of music:–

> "And I know not if, save in this,
> such gift be allowed to man.
> That out of three sounds he frame,
> not a fourth sound, but a star.
> Consider it well: each tone of our
> scale in itself is nought;
> It is everywhere in the world –
> loud, soft, and all is said:
> Give it to me to use! I mix it with
> two in my thought;
> And, there! Ye have heard and seen:
> consider and bow the head."

In other words, sounds loud and soft exist everywhere in nature but they do not make music. It requires a composer of genius to bring them together and musicians of genius to play them if the music is to delight the heart and ear.

You will have noticed that society as an organic whole differs in one very important particular from an organic whole like a piece of music.

The music is a finished product: it does not change, neither do its parts. Society is changing all the time and so do the members who compose it. It is this characteristic of society as an organic whole which has set the problem to every philosopher as to how a just society should be organized. But I will revert to this topic a little later in this paper.

I have spent some time in discussing the metaphysical implications of the world in which we live because popular slogans like "equality" as a synonym for justice are doing incalculable harm to the social fabric and are affecting the administration of justice itself. There is no such thing as democratic education or democratic justice. Education as a training of the mind is directed to training the mind at its best and society suffers when in the name of democracy and social justice you aim at anything less than the best and more so, when you aim at that which is second rate. So also with the administration of justice. There is no scope for democracy in the administration of justice. In the highest Courts you want the ablest lawyers of high character to be Judges, and you want a system which will give you lawyers of high capacity and character. England has secured both these requirements and the Bench and the Bar in England are one of her chief glories. Under the English example we in India were seeking to build up such a system and had partly succeeded. But mistaken notions of equality have led to a denial of a difference of function — as between those who prepare cases and those who argue them; or difference of qualification for different kinds of legal work. And this is happening at a time when, for the first time, our Courts are made the guardians of our Constitution! This is not the place to pursue this subject further but let the Attorney General for India describe the result. He said:

> "It is, I think, generally felt that our standards both in respect of efficiency as well as ideals have of late deteriorated. It is said that the practitioner of today on an average lacks the thoroughness, the skill and even the integrity of his counterpart of ten or twenty years ago. This decline in the efficiency of the Bar is said to be reflected in the deterioration in the calibre of the Bench."

I believe that the Attorney General is not a metaphysician, otherwise he would have traced this decline to the mistaken application of the notion of equality and democracy to a sphere where they are inapplicable.

You will say that so far I have tried to show what justice is not, and you might wonder whether I propose to deny justice altogether. I do not; and I will now proceed to deal with the positive aspect of justice. Aristotle has noticed that the word justice has a wider and a narrower meaning. In the wider sense, justice is complete virtue:

"It is complete because he who possesses it can exercise his virtue not only in himself but towards his neighbour also; for many men can exercise virtue in their own affairs but not in their relations to their neighbour."

But this is not the sense in which we generally speak of justice. We prefer to speak of a just man in this wider sense as a good man or a virtuous man.

In the narrower sense of the word, justice is concerned with a part of virtue. Aristotle divides justice in the narrower sense into two classes which we may call distributory and rectificatory. Distributory justice is concerned with the distribution of honour or money or other things which fall to be divided. Rectificatory justice plays a rectifying part in transactions between man and man.

Taking distributory justice first, the unjust man is one who takes too much good for himself and leaves too little for another, and correspondingly suffers too little evil leaving others to suffer more than their share. In other words injustice lies in making unfair gain or in unfairly avoiding proportionate loss. If the distribution is to be made by one person among others, that person is unjust when he makes the distribution to secure an advantage for himself.

However the practical difficulty in determining what is just in the distribution of goods lies in determining the principle on which goods are to be distributed. Let me suppose that you have Rs. 30,000 to distribute between your 3 children on your death. What does justice require you to do? You may say that the principle of relationship is so decisive of the case that irrespective of any other consideration you will distribute the money equally. Or you may say that you will distribute the money having regard to the needs of your children giving most where it is most needed and least where it is least needed. Or you may say that you will distribute the money according as the children have behaved well or ill with you. In the abstract it is difficult to say which of these courses you must follow. In practice, for most of us, the matter would be decided by doing what is usually done in the society in which we live, in the belief that what is usually done is likely to cause the least resentment and feeling of injustice. But this consideration cannot be pressed too far because what is generally done may be unjust as in the grossly inadequate provision so far made for daughters as opposed to sons.

These considerations apply in full force to rectificatory justice which covers the whole field of the law of contract, trust and civil wrongs. The Judge who administers rectificatory justice has to see to it that if a contract is broken damages are awarded, if trust property is misappropriated the loss is made good and so on. A great and just Judge is one who perceives the principles applicable to particular cases and who resolutely sees to it that the right principles prevail. In order to do justice it is not enough that a Judge acts according to the best of his lights — his lights must be luminous and he must take pains to keep them luminous. An honest Judge, who lacks wisdom and knowledge, might do the most unjust things, but popular language and opinion calls him an ignorant or incompetent Judge and not an unjust Judge. That term is reserved for a Judge who allows his judgment to be influenced by motives of personal gain either directly, as when he takes bribes, or indirectly, as when he shows favours.

I now revert to the question how a just State is to be organised. Plato's basic conception of a just State is fundamentally right — he rightly treats the State as an organic whole. A just State is one in which each citizen fills his proper station and discharges the duties of that station. Plato's detailed application of the principle is, however, open to question. You know how he divides the citizens into three classes: the wise men or philosophers are to be rulers or guardians of the State; spirited and brave men are to be warriors ready to defend the State, and the rest are to be traders or labourers each doing his job within the law. If Plato's classes do not degenerate into castes it is because he recognizes that merit entitles a person to be promoted to a higher class and demerit requires that he should be degraded by being put in a lower class.

This division is based on his analysis of man's nature as consisting of appetites, spirit and reason. Reason directs both spirit and appetite and therefore corresponds to the rulers; spirit is on the side of reason and controls appetites and corresponds to the warriors, and appetites are subject to the control of reason and spirit and are represented by tradesmen and labourers. This analysis though it contains important elements of truth does not do justice to man's nature because the nature of man is not divided into distinct parts each having a distinct and separate function. This error has been further aggravated by Plato's conception of division of labour. Plato rightly regards the State as an organism — but he goes for his prototype to the human body. The eyes see but do not hear; the ears hear but do not see. The end, or excellence of the eye is sight and not hearing; the end or excellence of the ear is hearing and not sight. Therefore, Plato argues, the end or excellence of a shoemaker is to be a good shoemaker and not a warrior or philosopher. But this analysis fails to be completely true because whereas the organs of the human body have a fixed function, a human being has manifold functions, and each one of us has capacities and infirmities which education, time and circumstance are bringing to light every moment. In the words of an ancient historian there are men who were judged fit for the highest office only until they attained and held it. There are others whose fitness for an office was not recognized till they actually held it.

But if Plato did not go all the way in giving us the ideal Republic which could also be real, Thucydides has drawn an ideal state which Plato would have approved, and which the most modern exposition of democracy has not bettered. The funeral speech of Pericles should be read as a whole: but let me give you two or three passages which portray a just State:

> "Our constitution is named a democracy because it is in the hands not of the few but of the many. But our laws secure equal justice for all in their private disputes and our public opinion welcomes and honours talent in every branch of achievement, not for any sectional reason but on grounds of excellence alone. And as we give free play to all in our public life, so we carry the same spirit in our daily relations with one another... We acknowledge the restraint of reverence; we are obedient to whomsoever is set in authority, and to the laws, more especially those which offer protection to the oppressed and those unwritten ordinances whose transgressions bring admitted shame."

> "We are lovers of beauty without extravagance and lovers of wisdom without unmanliness, wealth to us is not mere material for vainglory but an opportunity for achievament; and poverty we think it no disgrace to acknowledge but a real degradation to make no effort to overcome... we decide or debate, carefully and in person, all matters of policy, holding, not that words and deeds go ill together, but that acts are foredoomed to failure when undertaken undiscussed."

> "Let us draw strength...from the spectacle of our great city's life as we have it before us day by day, falling in love with her as we see her, and remembering that all this greatness she owes to men with the fighter's daring, the wise man's understanding of his duty and the good man's self discipline in its performance...the whole earth is the sepulchre of famous men; and their story is not graven only on stone over their native earth, but lives on far away, without visible symbol, woven into the stuff of other men's lives."

Here lies the organization of a just State: a public opinion which welcomes and honours talent for its excellence, a people full of reverence, obedient to laws and to the moral code which it is a disgrace to break. A State which combines thought and action, wisdom and beauty; a State not puffed up by wealth but using it for general well-being; a State founded, as Plato would have it founded, "on the fighter's daring, the wise man's understanding of his duty and the good man's self discipline in its performance."

I should like to touch upon a few questions relating to social justice and a just State with special reference to India. It is well to recognize that the love for justice is rare — what most people desire is injustice which favours them. An examiner who is unapproachable, a man who distributes patronage on merit, are not popular. It requires a high social and political tradition to make people love justice.

However, a State or society cannot be just if its members are given to fatalism and inaction. We have seen that man's life is subject to hazard and hardship; but that is no reason why human effort and foresight should not provide against them. If the sins of the parents will be visited on the children, we are not absolved from trying to make the parents better and see that the children suffer less. Winston Churchill saw a restaurant blown up during the Blitz: he saw its owners stand dazed and tearful in front of what was once their home and business. He did not say "Kismet" and pass on. He promptly asked the Chancellor of the Exchequer to put into operation a great national scheme of compulsory war damage insurance with a direction to pay 80 per cent of the claim at once. Here was social justice born out of a man's kindliness and vision.

We in the East are said to be a spiritual people scorning worldly goods. The distinction between the material and the spiritual is clear enough, but it should not be forgotten that there is no absolute opposition between what is spiritual and what is material. A house as a structure of cement and steel is a material thing; considered as an investment it may still be a material thing; but when it becomes a home it is not merely a thing of steel and cement but of wonder and desire, the centre of a man's affections and hopes. Or take books. A man who buys books for show is after material possessions; but the man who buys them that they may be his friends and companions through life is surely after spiritual possessions. The philosophical insight and practical wisdom of Aristotle perceived this connection and he set it down that a moderate amount of worldly goods is necessary for a happy life. Asceticism for its own sake is a barren creed. In India we profess respect for an ascetic mode of life and to that it is now fashionable to add a belief in equality between men which does not exist. These beliefs with their illogical application in the civil and political administration are doing much to retard a just society. The strange belief that there is considerable merit in a minister working for a pittance when a civil servant is paid twice or thrice the salary of the minister is a case in point. Or again take the position of teachers and professors. We are not tired of maintaining that education is the foundation of a good democracy; that teaching is a spiritual mission. And yet we pay teachers less than we pay millhands, with this difference that if teachers threaten a strike we face the prospect calmly: if millhands threaten a strike we hasten to appoint tribunals to settle the dispute.

Is it not time that we tried to learn the lessons of political philosophy and of our past history? If you multiply things which divide men you make justice more difficult. Leaders of opinion in India of an earlier day thought of India as a unitary State with a common language for all official work, and as a medium of instruction; with common laws and a well-paid, efficient and incorrupt administrative, judicial and educational service. They thought that it should be possible for an educated Indian to follow a profession anywhere in India. They provided common bonds which would make "people welcome talent not for sectional reasons but for excellence alone." We have seen all that work undone. We have a federation and not a unitary government, widely divergent laws in the provinces, a promised common language which is not to be the medium of instruction; fragmentation of States on a linguistic and therefore racial and sectional basis; a poorly paid civil, educational and judicial service with its attendant train of inefficiency and corruption. Before long an educated Indian from Bombay will be unable to practise a profession in Madras or Bengal or share in the intellectual life of those provinces. If these policies continue, a just State must remain a dream — we can only have its pale and ghostlike shadow.

A just State then requires *(a)* common bonds between the citizens *(b)* a proper appreciation of material rewards for honest work and a realization that material goods may subserve spiritual ends *(c)* an incorrupt and efficient administration, civil and judicial *(d)* and a proper reconciliation of the theory of political equality with the fact of natural inequality. The last point requires further discussion.

If you told a soldier that he was as important as the Chief of the General Staff I have little doubt that he would say that you were "pulling his leg," unless he felt that you did not know what you were talking about. The political equality of the soldier and the Chief of Staff only means that a well governed State requires that certain rights should belong to all citizens as citizens and as human beings irrespective of the position they occupy. But there the equality ends, and the differences of natural and acquired gifts and the differences arising from stations assert themselves and must assert themselves. In times of peace the chances of a soldier rising to be a general or field marshal are negligible, because the station he fills does not give opportunities for the exhibition of his talents for strategy and command even if he should have them. In times of war the situation is changed: his qualities find scope for their exercise and a corporal may end by being a marshal of the realm. But it is important to note that only few people can be at the head of the army at any particular time, or at the head of any organization. Except on a theory, people feel no sense of injustice that some should do more important work than others. The sense of injustice arises, if those who are charged with doing the less important work were in fact better fitted to do the more important work and were left out and when conditions do not exist in which a man filling a particular station can show that he is fit for higher things. Reverting to my example of the soldier, a well organized army should provide opportunities for a soldier to pursue military studies; it will provide courses in strategy and tactics and if a private should show that he possesses gifts above his station the next promotion should be his. It must, however, be realized that the business of the State must go on, and while an attempt must be made to find the best man for the job the best man may not be the best absolutely. If a choice is to be made now, it must be limited to people now available, and it does not help to say that had the choice to be made earlier or later a better man would have been available.

I believe, I have touched upon most of the points I wanted to consider in connection with a just State and I will only add what you know too well:

> "Scarce thousand years suffice to build a State
> An hour may lay it in the dust."

THE JUDGES' CASE AND THE SUPREME COURT*

ON DECEMBER 30, 1981, the Supreme Court handed down seven judgments running into 1,500 pages, dismissing the petitions which had been filed in the Supreme Court by lawyers from all over India and from various states of India. On that very day, Mr. Shiv Shankar, the Law Minister, hailed it as a New Year gift. Had he read the judgments, or to use his metaphor, looked into the gift box, he would have turned

* (Based on a speech delivered to the Rotary Club, Bombay.)

away in stunned silence from what he saw. I am delighted to think that poetic justice has been done to him for this wonderful gift; for on January 15, he ceased to be the Law Minister.

Now you will appreciate that if judgments running into 1,500 pages have to be read, all that I can say today is to give you a broad outline of some of the most important features of the judgments. Detailed discussion will have to await another occasion.

When petitions are dismissed, people will say, well, it is a pity; here are the lawyers from Bombay who filed the petition — here are four lawyers who have spent three months of their time free of charge, fighting for the cause, here is the Bombay Bar which collected Rs. 1,35,000 to meet the bare out-of-pocket expenses of travel to and back from Delhi and for staying in a hotel. Surely, it is a sad end to a great endeavour.

But I am here to tell you that we have substantially won and the Law Minister has substantially lost. First of all, what were we fighting for? We were fighting in the first instance for the independence of the Judiciary and, in the second, only a shade less important, for the freedom of the press; for without an independent Judiciary, the freedom of the press must come to naught. You have not far to seek. In an epoch-making article, brilliantly written with his usual care and with a liveliness of style, an editor in *The Indian Express* exposed the misdeeds of the Chief Minister of Maharashtra. That article ought to have swept him out of power.

But nothing happened. It required a brave and independent judge like Justice Pratap, who admitted the petition, and a brave and independent judge like Justice Lentin, who, in language of sobriety, which befits a judge, carefully analysed the evidence and found that the charges brought against the Chief Minister were well founded. It was that judgment which swept him out of power. So, an independent judiciary is necessary to preserve the freedom of the press, and the freedom of the press is necessary to lend moral support to the judiciary, against the ill-conceived attacks which are made against it from time to time by people who do not like public misdeeds to be publicly exposed.

Locus Standi

Whenever the government does a wrong thing, let us say, selling land at a gross under-value, and a public spirited citizen goes to the court, the government has two weapons: the first is to tell the court, as it was told in the case of Mr. Piloo Mody, who exposed the Backbay Scheme — How are you concerned? Supposing the government has gone completely wrong, supposing it has sold valuable property at an under-value, who are you to question it? That is called *locus standi*, and the first objection is "*no locus standi*". Well, Justice Gandhi, a fearless judge, held that land in Backbay was sold at a gross under-value by the *mala fide* action of the Chief Minister and two other ministers. He passed an order which secured for the State of Maharashtra one crore of rupees a year for 99 years at least. So, that was the benefit of a person going to the court out of public spirit and to right a public wrong. So, lawyers from Bombay, from Allahabad, from Delhi, from Patna and from Madras filed petitions challenging the circular letter of the Law Minister dated March 18, 1981, and his appointment of judges for short periods of time — three months, six months — and his claim that he could drop a judge at will and appoint another in his place. Not the Attorney-General, but the counsel for the Law Minister for about three days strenuously argued that we were, as it were, fussing busybodies who had no right to approach the Supreme Court. By a unanimous judgment of the Supreme Court, *locus standi* was conceded, and it has been extended to the widest extent possible. Any public spirited citizen, who goes to the court in good faith to vindicate public rights is, as a matter of public law, entitled to be heard and he cannot be turned away. This judgment would have delighted the heart of Lord Denning who is doing his best to widen *locus standi* in England. So, if we had done nothing more than strike off this weapon from the hands of the government, we would have rendered a service to the country which will endure. Any public spirited citizen can now expose public misdeeds provided he does it honestly.

Privilege

The second weapon in the hands of the government is the cloak of concealment or secrecy: correspondence carried on in secret, damaging things said in that correspondence, cannot be disclosed. Why? Because, it is said, these documents are "privileged" from disclosure, which means that you cannot prove your case by reference to them. By a majority of six to one — Justice Fazal Ali being that one — the Supreme Court held that the plea of privilege cannot be raised, that public interest in the administration of justice must be balanced against the interest of the government, and they ordered disclosure of those documents. Stripped of that cloak, what was left were the sorry figures of the Chief Justice of the Delhi High Court and the Law Minister. But Justice Fazal Ali was very angry and he used words derogatory to his colleagues and insulting to the advocates who appeared before him. I quote:

"Carried away by the stormy and emotional debate of the lawyers appearing for the petitioners and their egotistic slogan that independence of the judiciary was in danger this court ought not to have broken the age old solid and sacrosanct tradition of privilege which caused serious injury to public interest."

I will show my respect for the judiciary and for its independence by not repelling an insult by an insult even stronger. I will only say this: the violence of his language is the measure of our victory. So, if we had done nothing except secure the widest *locus standi* and if we had done nothing except strip the mask of fraud and deceit, we would have served the country well, because we were fighting for broad principles of public law, and in both these matters we have completely succeeded.

But you may say, after all, you did go to fight for judicial independence, you were fighting for the judges and have you anything to show for it? The answer is, yes. First of all, consider, what were the claims made by the Law Minister in respect of additional judges? He said that the Government had absolute power to drop an additional judge after his term was over, and to appoint anybody else in his place. He contended that judges could be appointed for short periods of time — three months, six months, or such other shorter periods as less than two years — and he said that all these powers could not be reviewed by the court. An additional judge had no right to be reappointed. Every single one of these arbitrary claims has been rejected by the Supreme Court. It has held that an additional judge cannot be appointed for a period of less than two years having regard to the state of arrears in various high courts which, it was thought, could not be removed even in 10 years as a matter of conservative estimate. They held that though an additional judge could not automatically be reappointed as an additional judge or appointed a permanent judge, he had a right to be considered for reappointment before he was dropped. He could not be dropped without a full consultation by the President of India — and let me make it clear that all this talk of high dignitary, the President of India, means in law, the Government of India, which means the Council of Ministers. The President of India must consult the Chief Justice of the High Court, the Governor of the state and the Chief Justice of India. The consultation must be full; nothing must be withheld; nothing concealed. If after that it was thought fit to drop a judge and an order was passed, the order would be scrutinised. If it was passed for irrelevant considerations, if it was passed *mala fide,* the court would strike it down. And the Supreme Court is quite clear on one vital point: nothing done by a judge in the discharge of his duties, whether he was quick or slow, brilliant or second rate, could be the ground for dropping him. So, as far as additional judges are concerned, if we have not won 100 per cent, well, we have won 90 per cent, and what I am going to tell you next will show that we built better than we knew.

For when the Law Minister embarked on his rash adventure of challenging the bar and the bench, he did not realise an unexpected consequence. When our Constitution was first enacted and came into force in 1950, there was no provision for the appointment of additional judges. That provision was introduced later, six years later, by an amendment in 1956. Therefore, from 1950 to 1956 only permanent judges could be appointed. For, a relevant article of the Constitution provides that every high court shall have a chief justice and such other judges as the President may, from time to time, deem necessary to appoint. Though discretionary in form, the article confers a power coupled with a duty to exercise it, whenever occasion requires, and the Supreme Court held that the appointment of permanent judges is the rule and the appointment of additional judges, the exception. During the past 25 years, a mistaken practice had grown up, for which both the executive and the judiciary must share responsibility, of appointing judges as additional in the first instance, and then confirming them as permanent judges. This was shown to be clearly wrong, contrary to the provisions of the Constitution, and the Supreme Court held that it was the duty of the President to keep the permanent strength of the judges of the high courts under review from time to time and to increase that strength. The unexpected consequence of applying this finding to the present situation is, that since the combined strength of permanent and additional judges is unequal to disposing of current arrears, all additional judges, or almost all, must be made permanent, and many more permanent judges must be appointed. On this point, Justice Venkataramiah issued a *mandamus* to the Union of India to make a realistic assessment within a reasonable time, and to appoint permanent judges. The other judges said, well, there is some difficulty but in view of the statement made on behalf of the Government that they were going to consider the position in the light of the situation which had been disclosed, we do not pass such an order. But on one thing the Supreme Court was clear. You cannot appoint an additional judge, if there is a vacancy in the strength of permanent judges. Are these small gains which we have secured? The judges are not at the mercy of the Law Minister. The Government has not the arbitrary power to deal with them. The whole structure of the judiciary will suffer a change, because once you make judges permanent, the grotesque theory that a reputation for dishonesty is enough to disqualify a judge, no matter how honest he may be in fact, will disappear. So much for additional judges.

The next point which calls for attention is the dropping of judges at will, and Justice Kumar of the Delhi High Court was dropped, and Justice Vohra of the Delhi High Court, who had delivered a judgment in the *Kissa Kursi Ka Case* committing the son of the Prime Minister to prison, was dropped. Well, the defence of the Government was that they had no right, and you see that has been rejected. Now, Justice Kumar's case raised a question of privilege — and a strong attempt was made to conceal the documents, or to put it differently, not to disclose the documents to the court. The documents were ordered to be disclosed. In the light of the documents a very strong argument was put forward by my learned friend Mr. Garg who appeared for Justice Kumar — and I ought to tell you as a happy feature of the case that all the counsel appearing in this case against the Government worked as a team and in complete unanimity, each helping the other, each aiding the other — Mr. Garg made a strong case which according to him was that there was a conspiracy between the Chief Justice of the Delhi High Court and the Law Minister. In a tempestuous judicial outburst, on the third day, the court said: "We will not go into this question". This has been recorded by Justice Tulzapurkar and it is known to me personally. It is an unfortunate feature of this case that three judges, having stopped Mr. Garg from arguing the question of conspiracy said that there was no foundation for it. One judge has asked what motive could there be, what advantage could there be for the Chief Justice to enter into a conspiracy? Well, members of the bar were not born only yesterday, and they know what things are happening, and if an answer was wanted, the motive could be that he may not be transferred from Delhi or that he may be elevated to a higher court. But whether it was so or not, an inquiry was forbidden and it is not right to draw conclusions after you have stopped the inquiry.

No Consultation

Now, three judges have held that the consultation which was required by law had not taken place in the case of Mr. Kumar, because the Chief Justice of the Delhi High Court wrote a letter dated May 7, 1981, to the Law Minister giving details and particulars and asking the Law Minister to keep it secret from the Chief Justice of India. The three judges held that there was no full consultation, because the most material document was not supplied by the Law Minister to the Chief

Justice of India. The other four judges held that there was full consultation. The contents of the letter had already been communicated to the Chief Justice in a personal discussion. I propose to subject the evidence to a close scrutiny on another occassion. I will only say that it does seem absurd that the Chief Justice of a High Court should wish to conceal from the Chief Justice of India facts which he had already told the Chief Justice of India. One would expect him to say in his letter to the Law Minister that "My dear Law Minister, I am giving the particulars you want, but I have already mentioned them to the Chief Justice of India". That could not be, because the reason which he gave for concealing the letter from the Chief Justice of India was that he wanted to maintain good relations with the Chief Justice of India. I wish to put on record my considered view, which I am glad to say is shared by a large number of people who heard the arguments, that the finding of fact by the majority is perverse. But what about the Chief Justice of the Delhi High Court? I do not have to use words of my own. I will state what Justice Desai has to say about the Chief Justice of the Delhi High Court. This is what he says:

"Before I conclude, I would like to record my disapproval of the request made by the Chief Justice of the Delhi High Court to the Law Minister for not showing the letter dated May 7, 1981 to the Chief Justice of India. If independence of the judiciary is likely to be threatened, it may or may not emanate from the executive or from some outside agency, but it would be corroded by the action of the members of the judiciary itself, by internal corrosion and if proof for this were needed, it is demonstrably supplied by a very improper request made by the Chief Justice of the Delhi High Court to the Law Minister not to show the letter dated May 7, 1981, to the Chief Justice of India. I am unable to conceive a situation where in the correspondence, assertions, statements, expression of doubts concerning a high judicial functionary like a judge of the High Court can be made by the Chief Justice of a High Court which he is not willing to show to the Chief Justice of India. I am not implying any hierarchy. I put them on a par and accord status and dignity to the high offices occupied by both. They may differ. Healthy differences are the life-blood of honest opinion. But it is unthinkable, albeit wholly improper for a Chief Justice of a High Court to write to the Law Minister something which he is not prepared to show to the Chief Justice of India. This conduct, if allowed to pass uncensured, would give rise to such fissiparous tendencies which would wholly undermine the independence of the judiciary.

"I also feel that the way in which the Chief Justice of the Delhi High Court has dealt with the case of Shri O. N. Vohra leaves much to be desired. The Chief Justice of the Delhi High Court seems to be completely unaware of his duty and obligation while recommending or refusing to recommend a colleague for extension. He holds no position superior to a high court judge functioning in his court. He is only first among equals, enjoying the status not on merit but on accident of seniority. He is not supposed to sit in judgment over the decisions of his colleagues. Where does he get this authority passes comprehension. Mr. O. N. Vohra took a dignified stand and did not participate in this squabble, undignified as the whole episode appears to be. Had he come and participated, may be the Chief Justice of the Delhi High Court would have found his position so untenable that there would have emanated a strong censure about the method and manner of his dealing with his colleagues. These may appear to be strong words, but they still fail to express my feelings adequately. I say no more."

CJ Responsible

Well, it was this Chief Justice who was responsible for Justice Kumar's dismissal in substance, or his non-appointment as a matter of form. It is a remarkable feature of this judgment that although all these severe strictures have been passed against the Chief Justice of the Delhi High Court, not a word has been said about the Law Minister who was a party to this concealment. His fault was greater: it was the duty of the Law Minister to send all material to the Chief Justice of India and it was his imperative duty to tell the Chief Justice of the Delhi High Court that he would receive no communication from him which was to be kept secret from the Chief Justice of India. So, it is not right to describe the Chief Justice of the Delhi High Court in the terms in which Justice Desai has rightly described him, and yet leave the Law Minister, like Mary's little lamb, completely "white as snow". But there is one thing more: Justice Kumar was not given an inkling of the charges which were made against him and we said to the court that surely, if a criminal is entitled to fairplay, and if the humblest government servant is entitled to fairplay, and fairplay is not accorded to him, the court will strike down the order; surely, the judge of a high court cannot be in a worse position. Justice Desai has dealt with that issue. He has expressed concern, and let me quote what he said:

"....Fairplay in action demands that they (allegations against judges) should first be brought to the notice of the colleague.... But to make assertions in secret and confidential letters without giving the slightest indication to the colleague and then to shrink back to the extent of not permitting the same to be shown to the *pater familias* in the judiciary (the Chief Justice of India) scales the height of impropriety. Let the past be buried and bygones be bygones, but in future, a conduct and approach commensurate with the high office held by the Chief Justice of the High Court must inform his action. Fairplay in action is the watchword of the judiciary and if it is extended to all others, a colleague in the High Court should not be at a comparative disadvantage."

Did the judge realise what he was saying? He said Justice Kumar has not received fairplay. Fairplay is essential. But forget it; let Mr. Kumar be buried. Do it in the future. This attitude can be aptly summed up by the statement in *Alice in Wonderland:* "Jam yesterday, jam tomorrow, no jam today". In my submission, having regard to the Supreme Court judgments, the moment a conclusion was reached that fairplay was denied to Justice Kumar, the order ought to have been struck down. That briefly is the case for Justice Kumar. The evidence would require to be scrutinised with some care and I have not the time today. But I do wish to say that Justice Kumar, when he reads the seven judgments will have the feeling that there has been a miscarriage of justice and justice has not been done to him. I do not know the rights and wrongs of the charges against Mr. Kumar, but no charge can be held as proved until an inquiry, however elementary, and some opportunity of defence, however small, is given to meet a charge; and to think that an illegal immigrant from India who has not the right to enter England, who has no right to stay in England, should be held entitled by the Lord Chief Justice to fairplay, and if fairplay is not shown, the order should be struck down; it does strike me as odd, that what is conceded to an illegal immigrant should be denied to a high court judge.

Now let me come to the circular letter. We said that the circular letter is coercive in its effect on additional judges. It seeks to obtain their consent to an indefinite uncertain appointment, and that advantage would accrue to judges who gave their consent and that disadvantage would accrue to the judges who did not give their consent. Now instead of talking in purely legal language let me give you a homely image. Let me assume that my neighbour, like one of the characters in Sherlock Holmes, is in the habit of keeping reptiles as pets, and his particular fancy is for poisonous snakes. They harass me by floating in and out of my house. But if I wish to protect myself against the reptile, what shall I do? Two ways are open. I can kill the reptile or I can engage a snake-catcher and have its fangs, that is, poisonous teeth, removed. In either event, I have protected myself. That is exactly what has happened in this case. The three judges who have held the circular letter void, have killed the snake, and the other judges — at least two of them, and that is enough for my purpose — Justice Bhagwati and Justice Desai have removed the fangs, so that the judges are protected in either way. Let me quote two small passages from the judgments of Justice Bhagwati and Justice Desai which will prove my point. Says Justice Bhagwati:

> "The circular letter is a document without any legal force and does not by itself of its own force, create or alter any legal relationship, or arrangement, or produce any legal consequences at all."

In substance, in law the letter is a piece of waste paper, which its author may frame carefully, and look at from time to time, as having produced results disastrous to himself. Justice Desai is more explicit when he says:

> "I am not impressed by the submission of the Attorney-General that one who gives consent may have advantage over one who does not. I do not see any remote advantage, and if any such advantage is given and if a charge of victimisation is made out by the judge not giving consent, the arm of judicial review is strong enough to rectify the executive error."

Sanction of Truth

So, have we not won all that we fought for? Three judges say, it is violative of law and we strike it down. The other judges say, it is completely harmless, it can do you no harm; but if under its pretence harm is done to you then you will be fully protected by the court.

I will tell you one thing which I have held all my life and which 52 years' practice at the bar has not shaken — my faith that the sanction of truth is that it holds together and the sanction against falsehood is that it falls apart; the sanction against vice is that it breaks down and the sanction for virtue is that it stands together. When I was appearing for a professor in a libel action when he was being persecuted by the university, and when during some dark days, because the matter was adjourned and he was without a job, and he felt distressed I recited certain lines which comforted him. I will repeat them here, for they represent the spirit in which we fought:

> "In our heart of hearts believing
> Victory crowns the just,
> And that braggarts must
> Surely bite the dust,
> Press we to the field ungrieving,
> In our heart of hearts believing
> Victory crowns the just."

PARLIAMENT AND THE CONSTITUTION

Article published in *The Indian Express* on 19-5-1980

ON MAY 9, 1980, the Supreme Court handed down four judgments holding that the Land Ceiling Acts of Andhra Pradesh, Uttar Pradesh, West Bengal and Haryana were valid. However, as to the Land Ceiling Act of Maharashtra, Chief Justice Chandrachud while holding the Act valid, passed an order observing that reasons for the order would be given later.

The Chief Justice's order dealt with constitutional questions of the greatest importance for the welfare and happiness of our people, and, naturally, it has been the subject of public interest, comment and criticism. However, the absence of reasons has left the lay reader of newspapers with the question — "What is it all about?"

Reading the Chief Justice's order, I can answer that question, because I have done so in *"The Constitutional Law of India"* 2nd Ed, Volumes 2 and 3. A technical discussion would be out of place in this article, but the story can be simply told.

The Chief Justice's order is obviously based on what is popularly called the *Fundamental Rights Case* in which the Supreme Court held by a majority of seven to six that Parliament's power to amend our Constitution under Article 368 did not extend to damaging or destroying the basic structure of our Constitution. This decision was followed, and applied by five Judges of the Supreme Court in Mrs. Gandhi's election appeal.

After that appeal was heard, but before the judgments were delivered, the Attorney-General applied that a larger Bench should be constituted to reconsider the decision in the *Fundamental Rights Case*. The application was granted, and a Bench of 13 judges was constituted for that purpose.

However, after hearing arguments for two days, the Bench was dissolved, which would suggest that the Bench was not in favour of reconsidering the *Fundamental Rights Case*.

This history of the second Bench of 13 judges answers the current suggestion that Government might ask for a larger Bench to reconsider the matter. For such reconsideration would mean a second attempt to ask for a reconsideration of the *Fundamental Rights Case*.

If 13 judges of the Supreme Court were not prepared to reconsider the matter, in 1976, there is still less reason to think that a larger Bench would be prepared to do so in 1980. And in my opinion such reconsideration would be wholly unjustified.

I hold that the doctrine of the basic structure is correct, and there are sound legal reasons for saying so. But the following popular account is sufficiently accurate for the present purpose.

A constitution which does not provide for its amendment does not provide for its survival. But it does not follow from this that the power of amendment should be unlimited.

We know that it can be said of our Constitution that it was conceived in liberty and was dedicated to equality. It was to be a free democratic constitution, because in the end government was not in the hands of the few, but of the many.

Having been framed for a country with many races, languages, religions and cultures it guaranteed to all the people freedom of religion, faith and worship, and it conferred on minorities educational and cultural rights. These fundamental rights preserve the unity and integrity of India, for few things promote disunity more than religious persecution and an attempt to suppress the language and culture of minorities.

In conferring the power of amending the Constitution, was a power conferred to convert a free democratic Constitution into a dictatorship, in which freedom of thought and expression, and freedom of religion were suppressed, equality disregarded, and abuse of power unchecked by an independent judiciary? If the answer is "No", then what are the limits on the amending power?

In the *Fundamental Rights Case* the limits were drawn, at the basic structure of the Constitution, and fundamental rights, free elections, an independent judiciary, judicial review and the federal structure are certainly parts of the basic structure.

In the *Fundamental Rights Case,* the minority of judges looked upon the fears expressed by the petitioners of an unlimited power of amendment as unreal. After Mrs. Gandhi's election appeal it was not possible to say so. And the Emergency showed that the fears had come true, and Article 368 (Amendment of the Constitution) was itself amended during the Emergency to put any amendment of the Constitution beyond judicial challenge, and extensive amendments of the Constitution were made during the Emergency which "institutionalised" the Emergency.

Mr. Justice Fazal Ali summed up the Emergency thus: "(i) that grave Emergency was clamped on the whole country, (ii) that civil liberties were withdrawn to a great extent, (iii) that important fundamental rights were suspended, (iv) that strict censorship on the press was placed, (v) that judicial powers were to a large extent crippled." Actual abuse of the amending power made all talk of "fear of abuse" unreal.

Chief Justice Chandrachud's order rightly strikes down Clauses (4) and (5) which were added to Article 368. Clause (5) asserts that there shall be no limitation on the power of Parliament to amend the Constitution. This was clearly contrary to the *Fundamental Rights Case*, and the Chief Justice struck it down.

Clause (4) which provided that no amendment shall be called in question in any court for any reason was held void, and for the same reason. It is also void on the further ground that it is in conflict with the special majorities in each House prescribed by Clause (2). If an "amendment" is passed without such majorities, it is not an amendment at all and the court must strike it down.

But, it may be asked, by putting any limitation on the amending power are you not affecting the supremacy of the Parliament of a sovereign country? There are several answers. Mr. Palkhivala, in his argument in the *Fundamental Rights Case*, rightly pointed out that there must be some limitation, otherwise a party in power having made amendments to secure its power, might repeal Article 368 and substitute a new Article 368 providing that "this Constitution shall not be amended."

An unlimited power of amendment, which can lead to the destruction of the amending power itself must be rejected as absurd. We must, therefore, imply a limitation on the amending power by saying that the amending power must not be damaged or destroyed. But if the amending power is looked upon as a basic feature which cannot be damaged or destroyed, it must be irrational not to imply a similar limitation on Parliament's power not to damage or destroy other basic features of the Constitution.

Secondly, the history of Canada and Australia shows that states can be sovereign states without having an unlimited power of amendment. In 1931 the British Government drafted the Statute of Westminster giving power to the two dominions to pass laws which were in conflict with laws passed by the British Parliament. This would have given the Parliaments of Canada and Australia unlimited power to amend the British North America Act, and the Commonwealth of Australia Act respectively.

But the Parliament of Canada, and the state legislatures of the provinces, and the Parliament of Australia and the legislatures of the states asked the British Government to exclude their Constitution Acts from the freedom to pass laws contrary to the laws passed by the British Parliament. Consequently, the two constitutions were excluded.

In other words, two sovereign states which were offered unlimited power of amendment declined the offer, for such unlimited power of amendment would have destroyed their federations.

In 1931 Canada had an insignificant power of amending its Constitution. In 1964, the British Parliament considerably enlarged the power, but, as Professor Sawer said in *Modern Federalism,* the British Parliament "reserved from each amendment the basic features of the federal distribution of (legislative) competence".

The concept of the "basic features" of a constitution is not the invention of the judges of our Supreme Court. A distinguished writer on federalism had used the expression in 1909 to describe the limitation on the power of the Canadian Parliament to amend its Constitution.

Finally, as Mr. Mohan Kumaramangalam pointed out: "Under a written Constitution, there can be no question of any 'absolute sovereignty'. Parliament's sovereignty is limited by the following: (1) fundamental rights, (2) conformity with the provisions of the Constitution, (3) the division of powers between State legislatures and the Parliament."

If Parliament's sovereignty was deliberately limited in order to secure a free government and a free and open democratic society, and to provide checks against abuse of power, then the objection that by limiting the power of amendment, the sovereignty of Parliament is limited does not survive, because as we have seen, Parliament is not supreme and sovereign.

On the contrary, to claim unlimited power of amendment for Parliament would be to enable Parliament to convert its limited sovereignty into an absolute sovereignty, and the history of the framing of our Constitution, the objectives proclaimed in the Preamble and embodied in our Constitution, show that no such transformation was intended by the exercise of the amending power.

This is all the more so when it is remembered that the Constitution is for a country with racial, linguistic and religious minorities, and for states in different stages of culture and development.

The Chief Justice's order dealt with Article 31B and Schedule IX which had been introduced in our Constitution by the First Amendment. In the *Fundamental Rights Case* a majority of judges held that the amendment was valid, and the numerous Acts included in Schedule IX could not be challenged for violation of fundamental rights.

However, the Chief Justice said that any Act, included in Schedule IX after the judgments in the *Fundamental Rights Case* on April 24, 1973, would not get the protection of Article 3IB, and could be struck down if the Act violated the basic structure of the Constitution.

This is clearly right. For if Parliament itself respects the structure of the Constitution, Parliament cannot amend Schedule IX of the Constitution to protect a law which violated the basic structure of the Constitution. What Parliament cannot do directly, it cannot do indirectly.

In the *Fundamental Rights Case,* a majority of the judges held that the newly added Article 31C, excluding the conclusive Declaration Clause, was valid. Article 31C enabled the state to make laws to implement the directive principles of state policy in Article 39 (b) and protected such laws from challenge for violation of the fundamental rights conferred by Articles 14 (equality), 19 (the seven freedoms), and 31 (acquisition of property).

Article 39 (b) and (c) provided that the state shall direct its policy toward securing that the ownership and control of the material resources of the community are so distributed as to subserve the common good, and that the operation of the economic system does not result in the concentration of wealth and means of production to the common detriment.

This protection given to laws implementing these two directives of state policy, was extended by the 42nd Amendment to laws implementing any directive of state policy. This would, in effect, enable Parliament and State legislatures to wipe out Articles 14, 19 and 31 which are clearly part of the basic structure. Consequently, the Chief Justice's order held the changes made in Article 31C void.

There is a popular belief that fundamental rights are selfish individual rights, and directives of state policy subserve social ends. This belief is unwarranted.

The objectives of our Constitution, as recited in its Preamble, are mostly realised by fundamental rights. Liberty of thought, expression, belief, faith and worship are secured by Article 19(1)(a) and by Articles 25 and 26 (freedom of religion). Equality of status and opportunity is secured by Articles 14, 15 and 16. The unity and integrity of India is secured by Articles 19(1) (d), (e) and (g), and by Articles 29 and 30 (cultural and educational rights).

Rights can only be enjoyed by individuals, but they are conferred on individuals to serve broad national and social goals of a free democratic society. Hence the primacy given to fundamental rights in our Constitution.

DUTY OF CENTRAL AND STATE GOVERNMENTS

[In the matter of "the Supremo"]

The letter printed here was drafted by Seervai at the request of citizens, on the subject of the 1993 riots in Mumbai and the duty of the Central and State Governments. It was signed by many.

As a citizen and as a lawyer, Seervai was active in exposing Bal Thackeray. J.B. D'souza (ex-IAS) and Dilip Thakore had filed a Writ Petition. The Petition filed in the Bombay High Court was drawn up by Seervai. It was dismissed.

In January 1995 **Communalism Combat** *published Seervai's detailed Opinion on the dismissal.*

I want to draw attention to the commitment by "the people of Maharashtra" published in a booklet, GUIDING PRINCIPLES OF MAHARASHTRA STATE [May 1960, Director of Publicity]. A speech was made by the Chief Minister, Y. B. Chavan on 5th January, 1960 at Sangli, when the State of Maharashtra was formed.

Y. B. Chavan said "We, the people of Maharashtra are committed to strive for the achievement of ideals on which our Prime Minister has laid so much stress. This is the meaning of the unveiling of the statue of our Prime Minister. In front of the Prime Minister's statue stands that of the Father of the Nation, Mahatma Gandhi. Both the guru and his devout pupil are standing before us, and we swear in their presence that we shall put their precepts into practice."

The same booklet has published the solemn statement of Government Policy, made on the floor of the Bombay Legislative Assembly as follows: **"The cosmopolitan character of Bombay City will be preserved."**

Thirty years later, Shiv Sena leaders viciously propagated the opposite views in language undreamed of when "we the people" gave their pledges.

29 January 1993

To
The Governor of Maharashtra,
Raj Bhavan,
Bombay.

Subject: **The recent riots in Bombay and the duty of the Central and State Governments.**

Sir,

We, some of the citizens of Maharashtra, desire to bring to your attention the following facts which are vital to the happiness and well-being of the people of Maharashtra. We write to you as the head of our State, because our founding fathers provided that every Governor of a State shall swear or solemnly affirm : "I, ... will to the best of my ability, preserve, protect and defend the Constitution and the law, and that I will devote myself to the service and well-being of the people of (name of the State)."

The recent riots in Bombay city, and the trail of death and destruction which they left behind has caused in members of the Muslim, the Hindu, and other communities a sense of fear, insecurity and hopelessness for themselves, their loved ones, their properties and their business, professions and the like.

The grisly part played by the Shiv Sena in the riots in Bombay is a matter of common knowledge. That part has been openly admitted by its "supremo", Mr. Bal Thackeray in the interview which he gave to "TIME" International published in January 1993. The following extracts from that interview have been copied from "TIME" International of January 1993, by *The Afternoon* of 21 January, 1993:

No compromise with Muslims — "KICK THEM OUT"

The latest "TIME" carries an interview with Mr. Bal Thackeray, the Shiv Sena chief. Titled "Kick Them Out", and conducted by Anita Pratap, it reads:

■ Why is Shiv Sena attacking Muslims?

❑ Muslims started the riots, and my boys are retaliating. Do you expect Hindus to turn the other cheek? I want to teach Muslims a lesson. Our fortitude has gone too far.

■ Why are you so angry with the Muslims?

❑ They are not prepared to accept the rules of this land. They don't want to accept birth control. They want to implement their Shari'a (Islamic law) in my motherland. Yes, this is the Hindus' motherland.

■ But Muslims are fleeing Bombay.

❑ If they are going, let them go. If they are not going, kick them out. If Pakistan feels Muslims in India are being harassed, let it, please, take this lot back.
■ Is this a stepping-stone toward a Hindu nation?
❑ We don't need stepping-stones. This is a Hindu *rashtra* (nation).
■ What will be the position of Muslims in your Hindu *rashtra*?
❑ They will not be happy unless they behave like good citizens.
■ Indian Muslims are beginning to feel like Jews in Nazi Germany.
❑ Have they behaved like the Jews in Nazi Germany? If so, there is nothing wrong if they are treated as Jews were in Germany.
■ These riots have damaged India's image abroad. Don't you care?
❑ I don't care two hoots for international image.
■ Are your men extorting protection money from civilians?
❑ Yes, we want money. The CIA is not giving us funds.
■ Does it depend on you alone to bring peace to Bombay?
❑ Yes, I am the person fighting for justice. (The mob) are under my control.
■ Have you decided to stop now?
❑ Yes. How long can you continue, and for what? I hope the Muslims have understood the lesson well.
■ Is your party named after Lord Shiva (the Hindu god who opens his third eye to destroy) or Shivaji (the medieval Hindu warrior king of the Bombay region)?
❑ In politics it's Shivaji, in religion it's Shiva. The third eye is now opening.

Courtesy: **City,** Thursday, 21, 1993

The *MID-DAY* and other dailies also published the above extracts.

It will be seen that Mr. Thackeray's interview violates our Constitution and the law in the grossest manner : he asserts that India is a Hindu nation; that Muslims should be kicked out of India; he admits that his "boys" retaliated and took part in the riots; and he admits to extorting "protection money" from people.

Later, Mr. Thackeray has claimed that words had been either put in his mouth or twisted out of context by the interviewer and the publishers of "TIME" International. In effect Ms. Anita Pratap, a seasoned journalist, who had interviewed Mr. Thackeray has said in her account of the interview that Mr. Thackeray's denial was false. In her account of the interview published in *The Afternoon* of January 24, 1993 she further explained that the whole interview took 45 minutes and had it been reported fully it would have occupied 10 pages of *The Afternoon* of January 21, 1993 where certain extracts were reprinted verbatim, except that the words "birth control" were substituted for "family planning" which words would be unfamiliar to Western readers. Mr. Thackeray has asked Government to read the full tape. Ms. Pratap has stated that the full tape would support her completely. A copy of Ms. Pratap's full explanation in *The Afternoon* of January 24, 1993 is set out below.

Govt. investigating Thackeray interview
By A Staff Reporter

The state and central government are understood to be investigating into the Shiv Sena chief, Mr. Bal Thackeray's indiscreet and offensive interview appearing in this week's Time international and reproduced in national dailies. There are possibilities of arresting him for inciting violence and damaging the credentials of an entire community.

Mr. Thackeray has claimed that words have been either put in his mouth or twisted out of context by the interviewer and the publishers of the magazine. He has said that his reference was only to those Muslims who had come from Pakistan and Bangladesh, and the local Muslims who were supporting them, and he wanted them to be kicked out as any patriotic Indian would.

The interview was taped, and Mr. Thackeray has asked the government "to get hold of the original interview tape and listen to it publicly".

Our New Delhi correspondent yesterday contacted Ms. Anita Pratap, the Time correspondent, who had flown to Bombay last week to cover the riots and interview Mr. Thackeray. Ms. Pratap, a seasoned journalist, said: "It is all there on record... on tape".

She said: "The entire interview was of 45 minutes on tape, and, had we carried the whole thing, it would have used up at least ten pages of Time, so we carried excerpts. And the excerpts, as per the policy of the magazine, were entire sentences pulled out of the text of the interview and carried verbatim". The only word changed was family planning'; since western, readers would not be familiar with that phrase, it was changed to 'birth control'.

As for Mr. Thackeray's claim that he was referring to Pakistanis and Bangladeshis, she pointed out that all the questions in the interview were about Muslims in India, and, only once towards the very fag end of the interview, did he mention Bangladeshi Muslims. That was the one and only instance."

She said: "Throughout the interview, I repeatedly asked him how he expected Pakistan or any other Islamic Republic to take in 100 million people and he replied that they were not his responsibility either. For veracity of the interview, she says that it could be checked with their photographer, Bob Nicholsberg, who was present throughout the interview, and another Bombay-based journalist.

"But what could be better proof than that the whole interview is on record .... on tape! I asked Bal Thackeray if he would prefer talking to me off the record, but he refused, saying very emphatically that he had nothing to hide 'I am very bold'.

"In the interview, he was very consistent in his hatred of Muslims in general, his fascination with Hitler.... he gave me the impression that he was not speaking merely to create an effect, he knew what he was saying and made no bones about it."

It was said in *The Afternoon* of January 24, 1993 that the Central and State Governments were inquiring into Mr. Bal Thackeray's interview. A 45-minute tape recording should not take long to hear, or to transcribe. If Ms. Pratap's account is proved correct, the Centre and the State Governments should take speedy and stern action against Mr. Bal Thackeray.

We are advised that Mr. Bal Thackeray's interview discloses a number of offenses under the Indian Penal Code, namely:

Promoting enmity between different groups on grounds of religion, race, place of birth, residence, language etc., and doing acts prejudicial to maintenance of harmony

Sec. 153A. (1) Whoever — (a) by words, either spoken or written, or by signs or by visible representations or otherwise, promotes, or attempts to promote, on grounds of religion, race, place of birth, residence, language, caste, or community or any other ground whatsoever, disharmony or feelings of enmity, hatred, or ill-will between different religious, racial, language or regional groups or castes or communities, or (b) commits any act which is prejudicial to the maintenance of harmony between different religious, racial or language or regional groups or castes or communities and which disturbs or is likely to disturb the public tranquility, shall be punished with imprisonment which may extend to three years, or with fine, or with both.

We are advised that Sinha C. J. delivering the Judgment of a Constitution Bench of the Supreme Court in *Kedar Nath* vs. *State of Bihar* A.I.R. 1962 S.C. 955 at p. 970 has observed:

"It is manifest that each one of the constituent elements of the offence under s. 505 has reference to, and a direct effect on, the security of the State or public order. Hence these provisions would not exceed the bounds of reasonable restrictions on the right of freedom of speech and expression. It is clear, therefore, that clause (2) of Art. 19 clearly saves the section from the vice of unconstitutionality."

The right of freedom of speech and expression which includes the freedom of the press guaranteed to every citizen of India is not absolute, but is subject to reasonable restrictions on the right conferred by Article 19(1)(a) in the interest of the security of the State, public order, and an incitement to an offence.

The admission in Mr. Thackeray's interview that he has authorised, incited and/or abetted the taking of "protection money" to swell the funds of the Shiv Sena constitutes an offence of extortion under Sections 383 and 384 of the Indian Penal Code. These sections run :

Extortion

Sec. 383. Whoever intentionally puts any person in fear of any injury to that person, or to any other, and thereby dishonestly induces the person so put in fear to deliver to any person any property or valuable security or anything signed or sealed which may be converted into a valuable security, commits "extortion".

Punishment for extortion

Sec. 384. Whoever commits extortion shall be punished with imprisonment of either description for a term which may extend to three years, or with fine, or with both.

As Head of our State, in case of emergency, (and the recent riots which still keep simmering on, have created an emergency), the Governor of the State has wide powers to secure that his Chief Minister and his Council of Ministers do their duty and take every available step to restore normalcy in the shortest possible period of time. Members of the Hindu, the Muslim and all other communities have lost confidence in the ability of the Government to govern. And the question has been asked whether it is the Government or Mr. Bal Thackeray and his fanatical followers, who are governing Bombay. No Government at the Centre or in the State can tolerate a "State within a State" without abdicating its authority. Public confidence cannot be restored by repeated statements of good intentions and good will, or by laudable attempts to help the injured, the homeless, and the deprived people. Nor is the confidence restored by appointing an eminent judge of the Bombay High Court as a one-man Commission of Inquiry to inquire into the causes of the riots and to suggest remedies to prevent their recurrence in the future. The Report of the Commission is to be presented within six months which is a long period, but experience of previous Commissions of Inquiry shows that in a matter of this magnitude, it may take years and not months for the Commission to submit its Report.

We may add that the prosecution of Mr. Bal Thackeray under the sections of the Indian Penal Code which have been mentioned earlier should not prevent his immediate detention under the TADA or other similar legislation in force in Bombay, in order to prevent further mischief by Mr. Bal Thackeray during legal proceedings.

LAW'S DELAYS AND REMEDIES

This address was delivered by Seervai to a public meeting of the Peoples' Union for Civil Liberties, at the University Convocation Hall on 30th January, 1986. Although aged 79 years, he spoke without a note, and what is published here, is an unrevised transcript of what was tape recorded.

Mr. Chairman, Hon'ble Judges, Ladies and Gentlemen:

When in December I agreed to talk on this subject, I did not realize that it would have the topicality which it has today, for on 12th January, the *Times of India* published an article by the Chief Justice of India under the heading "The Judicial System is on the verge of collapse". It was accompanied by a cartoon; which the Chief Justice will have enjoyed as much as we have all done. I wonder whether you noticed the vulture in the cartoon; it would make an interesting parlour game to guess who the vulture was, ready to strip the flesh from the corpse of justice.

But long before this article appeared, I had realized the importance of dealing with arrears in the disposal of cases. For the first time, in the Third Edition of my book, I dealt with the working of the Supreme Court with particular reference to the arrears in the Supreme Court and in the High Courts. I did so because the fierce light which has been turned on the Supreme Court because of its judgments in the *Habeas Corpus Case* and in the *Judges' Case* might make people forget the excellent work which it has been doing for years. Secondly, failure to remedy avoidable delay in the disposal of cases in the Supreme Court and in the High Courts must bring the administration of justice into disrepute. And finally, Governments, particularly the Government of India, find in accumulating arrears in the Courts, a stick to beat the Courts and denigrate them, although, as will presently appear, the Government of India is more responsible than anybody else for delays in the disposal of cases. I believe that if Government, judges, advocates and litigants all co-operate, delay in the disposal of cases can be wiped out, or, at any rate, greatly reduced.

Under our Constitution, a duty is cast upon the President of India — which means the Government of India — to appoint a sufficient number of judges to the High Courts from time to time as the Government may deem necessary. Mr. Justice Venkataramiah rightly pointed out that this discretionary power is coupled with a duty to exercise it, by keeping the number of judges under review from time to time. He raised the whole level of the debate in the *Judges' Case* when he drew the conclusion that under our Constitution, the appointment of permanent judges to the High Courts was the rule, and the appointment of additional judges was the exception, because, as originally enacted, the Constitution provided only for the appointment of permanent judges.

The Government of India is responsible for accumulating arrears in Courts because of its failure to appoint an adequate number of judges in the High Courts. Mr. Justice Venkataramiah showed that out of a sanctioned strength of 405 judges, (permanent and additional), the number actually appointed was 320, that is, 85 judges less. Further, the Government of India admitted before the Supreme Court that in addition to the sanctioned strength it was necessary to appoint 150 more judges to dispose of current institutions of suits and proceedings. In other words, the High Courts were short of 255 judges. Having regard to the undisputed fact that the arrears would continue in the future, Mr. Justice Venkataramiah gave a carefully worded *mandamus* directing Government to make the necessary appointments and to appoint additional judges to be permanent judges subject to the limitation laid down in the judgment. The six other judges did nothing in this matter, and Mr. Justice Bhagwati talked of the law of diminishing returns, a strange expression to use in this context, for the law of diminishing returns is a concept in economics. For example, if a 40 per cent tax raises a revenue of 1 crore of rupees, 80 per cent tax will not raise 2 crores of rupees, but a substantially lesser amount. But it will yield more than 1 crore of rupees.

Assuming that the increased number of judges will not be able to adhere to the norm of 860 main matters disposed of by each judge — an assumption for which I see no warrant — even so, about 2,20,000 main matters would be disposed of per year, thereby greatly reducing arrears.

Secondly, the Government of India has failed in its duty to substantially increase the salaries of the judges of the High Courts and the Supreme Court. On 3lst December, 1949 the salary of the Chief Justice of the Federal Court was Rs. 7,000 per month, of the judges of the Federal Court was Rs. 5,500 per month, the salaries of the Chief Justices of the High Courts (except of the High Court of Calcutta where it was a little higher) was Rs. 5,000 per month and of the judges of the High Courts was Rs. 4,000 per month. Mark that in 1939 the cost of living index was 100 and in December 1949, was nearly 400. There was, therefore, no justification for reducing the salaries; in fact, salaries required to be increased. However, the salaries were reduced, the Chief Justice of India and the Judges of the Supreme Court got a salary of Rs. 5,000 and Rs. 4,000 respectively, with rent-free residence. The Chief Justices of the High Courts, and the Judges of the High Courts got a salary of Rs. 4,000 and Rs. 3,500 per month respectively. Why this happened is not intelligible. Having regard to the doctrine propounded by Mahatma Gandhi that no public official should earn more than Rs. 500 per month, the judges of the Federal Court, who were automatically to become judges of the Supreme Court, suggested that a provision should be made that the salaries of the Chief Justice and the judges of the Supreme Court should be *not less* than that mentioned in the Schedule, as had been provided in the case of the Chief Justices and Judges of the High Courts. By what process, the words "not less than" disappeared from the Constitution is not known. I asked Munshi, who referred me to Mr. Shiva Rao, but Mr. Shiva Rao could give me no explanation. The reduction of salaries appears to have been based on the ground that if the President of India was to get a salary of Rs. 5,500 a month, the Chief Justice of India could not be given a salary exceeding Rs. 5,000. However, in the Constitution, the salary of the President was fixed at Rs. 10,000 but by a curious amnesia, which at times afflicted members of the Constituent Assembly, they forgot to increase judicial salaries!

During the *Judges' Case* I submitted a Note on Judges' salaries *amicus curiae*, because the question of salaries was not directly in issue. I pointed out that with the fall in the value of the Rupee, if judicial salaries were not increased by increasing the allowances, a serious constitutional question would arise, affecting the independence of the judiciary, because that independence cannot be affected by the simple process of gradually reducing judicial emoluments.

I put it to the Court in this way: Judges of the High Court remained automatically judges of the High Court under the Constitution, unless they resigned before the Constitution came into force. Supposing that in 1950 they had been offered a salary of Rs. 1,020 per month, is there any doubt that there would have been mass resignations? And yet that is the amount which we are paying to High Court judges in 1981.

Thereafter, allowances of judges have been increased, but this has not resulted in the salaries being even doubled. In 1954 Judges of the Court of King's Bench were getting a salary of £5,000 per annum. In 1981 they were getting a salary of about £55,000. In a speech which he made, Mr. Justice Tulzapurkar has carefully set out the increase in judicial salaries in various countries, and he said that if judicial salaries were not substantially increased in India in order to attract suitable persons, judges would have to be appointed who fell below the average. It seems to me that if a small agricultural country like Mauritius can increase judicial salaries 6 times over a period of time, there is no reason why we in India cannot substantially increase judicial salaries. The Government of India which constantly complains of accumulating arrears should proceed to increase the salaries substantially because a first-class judge can dispose of cases with a speed and sureness of touch which are clearly beyond a second-class judge. We cannot afford the luxury of an ill-paid judiciary; and the greatest sufferer from such a judiciary is the State itself, although we all suffer from such a judiciary.

Having pointed out the two important causes of delay in the disposal of cases for which the Government of India is solely responsible, let me point out a cause of delay for which State Governments are responsible. Today the State is the biggest litigant and it is responsible for repeated adjournments on the ground that instructions had not been received by Counsel, from Government. Courts normally give more time to Government for filing returns or pleadings than would be given to others, because of the way in which Government functions : materials relating to a matter may be found in a number of departments — the Finance Department, the Law Department, the Department for Urban Development and the like. These materials would have to be collected and sent to Counsel. But once such extra time has been given, there is no justification for granting adjournments; **and once adjournments are firmly refused**, the nonsense of not receiving instructions would disappear. The delays caused by the Government of India are even greater. In a matter in which Counsel appearing respectively for the Government of India and for the opposite party, as well as the judge were all agreed that a settlement proposed to the Government was pre-eminently reasonable, no answer could be obtained from the Government in Delhi, for one year!

Now let me turn to judges, for all of us — Government, judges, advocates and litigants — are responsible for delays. The problem of the much-talking judge confronts us and ceaseless interruptions during arguments waste time. Realizing this, judges in the Supreme Court now use the formula "I ask myself the question...." This reminds me of the story of a member of Parliament who said "And Mr. Speaker, I ask myself the question ...." when another member said, "And a damned dull answer you'll get." Now, it wastes time. It wastes time because a carefully prepared argument is blown to bits. If it is in the High Court, some Counsel take the view, let the judge go from error to error — we'll destroy him in the Supreme Court or the Court of Appeal. I do not take that view. My view is that it is your duty to put before the judge every argument which is relevant and which can reasonably be put before him. If he decides against you, well, that's his business. So this is a great source of waste of time.

And I suggested not an unpractical remedy, but what actually exists in the Royal Courts of Justice in London, that the total proceedings should be tape recorded. You see immediately the great advantage of the proceedings being tape recorded. The judge knows that everything he says will be taken down, and the odds and ends of absurd observations which judges sometimes make will disappear. Counsel knows that what he is saying is being tape recorded. And that prevents another great evil for which Counsel are responsible : a total disregard of the obligation to the Court to state the truth. Statements are made which are false, and which are known to be false. There is no way of bringing such Counsel to book. It's word against word. In England, a member of Parliament, a Queen's Counsel, made a statement to a judge that his opponent was willing that the Court should adjourn the matter for four hours if the Court agreed. The matter was adjourned for four hours. That statement was found to be false. The Bar Council of England held a disciplinary inquiry, and suspended him from practice for six months. There was no appeal. In India, to the knowledge of judges, — they complain of it to you in private — certain Counsel are past masters in the art of what can only be bluntly described as lying; but those judges do nothing about it. So once Counsel's arguments are tape recorded, any aggrieved person can take the matter before the Bar Council for disciplinary action. And there is no question of word against word — "he said this", "I didn't say that", "I have no recollections". There it is, recorded on the tape. And, secondly, I think, as Mr. Justice Gajendragadkar has said in his Autobiography, that this is not a matter for emotion. Kindliness is all right. But I think it is within the power of the judge to put an end to this, without offence and without violent speech. The judge can say to Counsel : Mr. X you have made three statements; each one of them is untrue. If a fourth statement is made which is untrue, we will not accept any statement from you unless you prove it. And we will record that fact in our judgment. So, kindliness to Counsel, unwillingness to do your duty which is unpleasant, results in the litigant suffering. For the lie has the advantage over the truth, and it takes considerable time to show that the statement is a lie. This has happened within my knowledge, and in my presence. And the judges who are here — some of them — will bear testimony to what I am saying.

Thirdly, tape recording will stop all argument as to what was argued in a case and what was not argued. This is because every attempt I have made — and I have made it persistently for 5, 6, 7 years — to get the arguments in a case reported in the Law Reports, as is reported in the official Reports in England, in the United States, in Canada and in Australia has failed. So in the absence of a report of Counsel's arguments by independent Counsel, you don't know what was argued and what was decided. For example, unfortunately for Mr. Justice Gajendragadkar in one case, he said that such and such a point did not arise in an earlier case and was presumably not argued and presumably not decided. Well, unfortunately for him, the one in a thousand case of Counsel's arguments being reported turned up. The Supreme Court Reports showed that the point was argued — argued strenuously. It was carefully formulated by Mr. Justice Venkatarama Aiyar and carefully decided as that judge was in the habit of doing. So all this dispute as to what was argued and what was decided disappears if the proceedings are tape recorded. And this upto a point remedies the failure to report Counsel's arguments in reported judgments. However, it is pre-eminently desirable that independent Advocates, properly qualified, should sit down in Court and record arguments, which would include the interruptions made by judges, relevant or irrelevant. And if it is interruption to which Counsel has replied, the Counsel's reply must be reported, so that whoever reads the reported judgment will know what was argued and what was decided. Mr. Motilal Setalvad in his Preface to *Mulla's Transfer of Property Act* thought it necessary to say, by quoting Sir Fredrick Pollock, that unless you know what was argued and, therefore, what was decided, the value of the judgment is practically nil.

Now all that I have said is on one part of the procedure. There is another part of the procedure, and I see that Chief Justice Bhagwati has tried to grapple with it, namely, that judges ask you to give notes of your arguments. Brief notes, brief having regard to the nature and complexity of the subject matter before the Court. It passes my understanding how if Counsel cannot prepare a Statement of the Case, they can prepare something which is very much more difficult, namely, prepare a written argument, for most people whose minds are confused are unwilling to commit themselves on paper to specific propositions — Counsel want to "play it by ear". Now the most sinister feature of the system which I have severely criticised in my book is this : You prepare a careful note of arguments, say, 25 or 30 pages, setting out the points, the authorities and the principles which should govern the decision. The other side puts in a skimpy 5 or 7 page "Reply". Naturally, when you open the appeal you deal with the 5 or 6 points which have been made in the Respondent's Reply. When it comes to the Respondent's arguments in Court, his Counsel argues 8 or 9 points not contained in this written "Reply". And when you want to get up and reply to those 8 or 9 points, the answer is : "Sorry, but there is no time. Go to Bombay and send a written reply". I can think of few things more sinister and more unfair than this procedure, of which I am personally aware. The only way of preventing this abuse is to refuse permission to argue points not raised in the Note of arguments. Or if you permit arguments on points not raised, then give an opportunity to the other side to reply orally to the points which ought to have been raised but were not raised. So it seems to me that these various methods produce delay. Who is going to sit down in Bombay and prepare a written reply? Must you return work in the High Court? Which Advocate of the Supreme Court — who hardly remains in Court, is going to sit down in his Chamber for four to five days? They hop from Court to Court : so when people talk of "realism" and "practicality", they forget that practicality does not mean pandering to the wrong doing of Counsel.

Now the present Practice Note issued by the Judges of the Supreme Court goes some way to meet this evil and this delay. It seems to me that if a new practice was to be started by the judges, the Practice Note must be carefully drafted, and the Note shows grave defects of drafting, and many lacunae in the provisions. First, the Note says that if you expect the case to go on for more than five hours, you should file a written brief of your arguments which should not, as far as possible, exceed 30 to 35 pages, 15 days before the date fixed for hearing. Within 10 days the other party is to reply by a written brief. If he does not file his written reply the matter is to be adjourned. Why? Surely, Counsel have to make their arrangements whether they practice in the Supreme Court or come from other States. I see learned friends here who are almost always on the wing: One day in Bombay; on Tuesday, Wednesday, Thursday, Friday afternoon in Delhi, ready to attend a dinner on Friday night in Bombay. That is the programme. How do we arrange that? Further, there is no provision for a reply. In an oral argument, at present, the Appellant opens, the Respondent replies and the Appellant is entitled to reply generally and particularly to fresh authorities cited. There is no provision in the Practice Note on this point. The next thing is, will the judges give an assurance to Counsel that they can assume that when the matter reaches hearing the written brief will have been read? The House of Lords has given similar assurances as to what they will read in connection with a Statement of the Case. Because if you ask for written briefs and limit oral argument to 5, 10 or 15 hours then how do you propose to deal with this right of reply? Now I think the idea of written briefs is adopted from the practice of the Supreme Court of the United States, where written briefs are filed and judges give the derisory period of half an hour to each side for oral arguments. The difficulty in India is that we look at another country without looking at the circumstances under which the practice has arisen there. Judges of the Supreme Court in the United States sit in Court only for 2 weeks out of 4. The remaining two weeks are occupied in studying written briefs. And in that they have the assistance of a brilliant graduate from one of the great universities though it has been found that such assistance is liable to grave abuse. A Supreme Court judge said that he had been approached by a person to ask the Judge's assistant to looks after that person's case! The assistant can do that simply by omitting an important decision and nobody can say that he had done so dishonestly. But that decision may be crucial. Now our Supreme Court sits every day from Monday to Friday, and it is not merely a Constitutional Court, and even if it were, having regard to our fundamental rights under Article 32 and Article 226 it would still be overwhelmed with matters carried to it by the aggrieved parties as a matter of right. In my view, the experiment in the Practice Note may be worth trying, but I am inclined to think that the quailty of judgments, already not very high, will visibly go down. Because it is one thing to hear an argument and make your own note of it, and quite another thing to say to yourself, "I'll read the argument later on." And the Bombay High Court has set the right example. Chief Justice Chagla has said that, except in two cases, during all the years he was there he has delivered judgments off the reel. I have been reading his Autobiography as you might guess. I have also been reading Justice Gajendragadkar's Autobiography. And he says that in the High Court in 10 years he had hardly reserved ten judgments : Surely, if in the Court of Appeal in important complicated cases a judge can deliver a judgment off the reel, or at most after 2, 3 or 4 days, why cannot a judge of the Supreme Court do likewise? All this new practice has become necessary because any person going from Bombay to the Supreme Court, who was accustomed to the old regime, is told, "Forget all that. Forget it. Unless you go on repeating things you can never win." In fact, in a big case, a Counsel said with candour, "My Lords, I have argued this point *ad nauseum*": was it not the duty of judges to stop a point being argued *ad nauseum?* I remember that before Mr. Justice Blagden a very senior Counsel repeated an argument a second time. The judge said quietly : "Nothing is to be gained by repetition!" Chagla said of Motilal Setalvad that he did not repeat himself, thus paying the judges the compliment that they had understood his argument. So the experiment may be worth trying.

But there are a few snags in it. First you give an estimate of the time you'll take : namely, more than 5 hours. Will the judges tell you after reading the written brief, "Well, in this case we'll give you 7 hours", or do you frame your argument for 5 hours and then the Court tells you, we'll give you 2 hours more? Secondly, what about the ceaseless interruptions from the Bench? — "I am thinking aloud"; "have you checked up American Cases?" "Is not some light to be derived from Japan or Timbuctoo?" Now, is the time taken up by these interruptions to be excluded from the time allotted to Counsel, or is it to be included? And the most serious thing of all — an institution which has developed in India, but which cannot possibly develop in England, namely, what I call the "Judicial Conference". You argue a point. The judges feel it in their bone that your argument is all wrong. They do not wait patiently to see you deploy your argument, or to hear the other side's reply. They hold a judicial conference *in Court*. In Bombay, in a case under the Press Act in respect of a book *"Gandhi Hatia An'e Ami"* — a book written by the brother of Nathuram Godse justifying the brother's assassination of Mahatma Gandhi, I was arguing before a Bench of three judges. On one day, as the Court sat for the usual 5 hours, the aggregate time which I got was half an hour. The Advocate on Record instructing me said that he was amazed at my patience. I said, well, I do not see what is to be gained by creating scenes in Court. And at the end of 4½ hours of private discussion, the judges did not say what they had been discussing. Now take a very big coal mining case before the Supreme Court. The judges asked Mr. Sinha, who was appearing for the State of Bihar, "How long will you take tomorrow morning?" He replied: "1 hour." All the 7 judges came to Court at 10.30, they held a conference which lasted till 12 noon. I am against any discretion being given to judges to fix the time for oral arguments for the simple reason that the treatment of Counsel must be evenhanded. You can't tell one Counsel: "Stop in an hour" and his opponent says: "Yes, I'll finish in an hour and a half", and then let him talk for five hours! Discretion is desirable to meet exceptional, and not ordinary circumstances.**

And this brings me to another point gravely prejudicial to the fair administration of justice — the extensive entertainment of judges by Counsel. Nobody can believe that the Counsel who does not entertain judges will get the same even handed justice as the Counsel who does such entertaining. We used to say that these things cannot happen in Bombay. Mr. Justice Gajendragadkar, in his Autobiography, had said so to his brother judges in Delhi, and he refused to attend such entertainments. The editorial note says, with decorum, that things have changed. But they have not merely changed. They have changed to a shocking extent. A Counsel thinks fit to entertain about 400 people in a fashionable hotel where the charge could not have been less than Rs. 100 per head — to say nothing of "drinks" supplied in a room privately and clandestinely. A number of judges are present, high officers in the Secretariat are present, businessmen are present. For what does a man spend Rs. 40,000 to Rs. 50,000 in honour of a newly appointed Chief Justice, if not to put him under obligation and expecting a return? In this particular case, on his appointment the Chief Justice had been entertained by every single association connected with the administration of justice in Bombay. It seems to me that apart from this, "discretion" in judicial matters would result in allowing such a Counsel to talk — "well, there is much in what you say, therefore, we'll do this, we'll do that", thus bringing justice into disrepute.

This now brings me to Counsel, because they are guilty of contributory delay. First of all the proper course for Counsel who cannot attend to two matters at the same time is to return one of the briefs, unless there are two Counsel and he has an assurance from the second Counsel that he will attend if the first Counsel is absent. Ask yourself the question, if you were the client, would you like your Counsel to hop off to another Court? Now this is permitted to be done by another practice which is a great source of delay — the granting of adjournments for the so called convenience of Counsel. It is true that Counsel do require accommodation, and in fixing a case, and a particularly important case, you can ask Counsel, "Does such and such

** **Editor's Note:** I have been told that on being asked by the Court how long the case would take, C. K. Daphtary in his inimitable way replied: "I will take one hour, my learned friend, two hours, the case will take ten hours."

date suit you?" Once you have fixed that date, the fact that a Counsel cannot come to Court that day is irrelevant. In fact this evil of adjournments was so great, that the Legislature intervened. The Civil Procedure Code was amended, and the amendment provided that an adjournment shall not be granted except for a sufficient cause and it was *not* a sufficient cause that Counsel was engaged in another Court. It was *not* a sufficient cause that Counsel was ill, if there was sufficient time for him to return the brief so that another Counsel could be ready to argue the matter. If a witness is not present when he ought to be, the Court is empowered to proceed in his absence. The Supreme Court has by reckless grant of adjournments defeated the intention of the Legislature, and again created the impression that only certain Counsel should be briefed. It is my belief, and it is confirmed by no less a person than Chief Justice Chagla, that well prepared juniors argue much better than ill prepared seniors. I was arguing a case before him, and I read a reported judgment and said that eminent Counsel had argued the case on either side, to get the agreeably pleasant reply from the Chief Justice, "That doesn't matter; frequently junior Counsel argue much better, they having more time to prepare." At present, you have the spectacle of Senior Counsel telling the Supreme Court: "My Lords, there are three points." He propounds the first point; he propounds the second point. Then a clerk comes behind him and whispers something. The Senior Advocate says: "My Lords that is all." "But what about the third point?" ask the judges. "No My Lords, that's all." Is that worthy of our profession? And are we out merely to make money, charge extortionate fees and then not appear at the last moment? So, I think standards of the Bar require to be raised. And judges have it in their power by a little firmness, by a little discipline to see that they are raised, So that is another great source of delay: a reckless grant of adjournments. At one time I had obtained Chagla's express authority, before he died, as to whether I could say in his name that he looked upon adjournments as one of the greatest sources of delay. He said,"Yes, you can do so." Now that does not mean that no adjournments are to be granted: if a Counsel is suddenly ill, if he has lost his wife or son, if he has been held up by Airports being suddenly closed, an adjournment must be granted. So, a firm rule of refusing adjournments does not negative the exercise of reasonable discretion, where any ordinary man would say: "Adjournment should be granted." If a man's father has died you don't expect him to come and argue, and in fact no Court should, though a particularly wicked judge of the Bombay High Court told a Senior Counsel's junior: "How are we concerned if your Senior's son has died?" Adjournments should be refused in the Supreme Court, should be refused in the High Courts, for you have the extraordinary phenomenon that no case of a Senior Counsel can be fixed in the Delhi High Court either on a Monday or on a Friday because those Counsel are busy in the Lawyer's Paradise: the hearing of Special Leave Applications in the Supreme Court. This source of delay must be eliminated.

Now, as regards the function of a Court and the way in which cases come to it. The Supreme Court has been endowed with the power, which the Privy Council enjoyed as the advisor of the Sovereign, to grant leave to appeal in criminal matters even in cases where no appeal was permitted by statute or by law. The Privy Council consistently refused to grant leave unless there was a grave miscarriage of justice, namely, unless a judgment was founded on an irregularity of procedure, or a misunderstanding of the law so that it shook the foundations of justice. Mr. Justice Venkatarama Aiyar — in my opinion the greatest judge whom the Supreme Court has had — laid down the same principle. But now we have strange notions: a judge feels "The judgment is a little unjust. Let's grant leave." It does not occur to those judges that the Supreme Court has not been made an ordinary Court of Appeal in criminal matters. Where two Courts have concurred, then, to say that some injustice should be righted is to forget that you are doing infinitely greater injustice to the whole body of litigants because you are cluttering up the Supreme Court with useless appeals. So, this is another source of delay.

Now I come to the most important source of delay: The failure of the judges of the Supreme Court to realize what the judicial function consists of. You hear long lectures on psychology, sociology, dynamism, values of the Constitution, which the judges must protect. There, say some judges, are old fashioned judges, poor mutts who don't really know the law; they do not even know the social conditions of today. And therefore we have the present division of the Supreme Court into cliques and factions, each side abusing the other, some with dignity, some without. And it leads to total judicial indiscipline making the administration of justice a gamble. Chief Justice Gajendragadkar said in a judgment, that for a judge to disregard the plain requirement of the law because he thinks it unjust, is to convert a litigation into a gamble — a reproach from which a Court should be free. I'll read to you the observations quoted by Lord Roskill in the first Denning Memorial Lecture, from a speech of Lord Bridge of Harwich. He is one of the Law Lords and a very able person:

"The ideal at which the court should aim is to produce a result such as in any given situation both parties seeking legal advice as to their rights and obligations can expect the same clear and confident answer from their advisors and neither will be tempted to embark on long and expensive litigation in the belief that victory depends upon winning the sympathy of the court. This ideal may never be fully attainable but we shall certainly never even approximate to it unless we strive to follow clear and consistent principles and steadfastly refuse to be blown off course by the supposed merits of individual cases."

Now, what is the function of a judge? I'll take it under our Constitution. What do you call the "values" of the Constitution? Broadly speaking, we are a liberal democracy. We regard certain rights as so fundamental that even a law can't touch them. We want the dignity of the Individual. But we have given to Parliament, and to State Legislatures, certain exclusive legislative powers, and to Parliament and to State Legislatures concurrent legislative powers. Whatever the views of a judge may be — you may believe that private enterprise is desirable — when a case comes before a judge, of nationalization of private enterprise, all that you have to ask is, first, "Has the legislature got the legislative power?" "Yes." Secondly: "Does the law violate any fundamental right?" "No." Then whatever your sense of values, that sense is completely irrelevant. Your duty is to uphold the law, nationalizing an industry. Again, you believe in public ownership. A law privatizing a public enterprise — and the portents in India today are not very remote — such privatizing has taken place in the United States and in the United Kingdom on an extensive scale. Well, you may believe that privatization is wrong, but you must ask the same questions: "Is it within legislative power?" "Yes." "Does it violate fundamental rights?" "No." The law must be upheld. Then where is the difference regarding values, between judges? What is the justification for one judge saying, "Oh, I am a very advanced thinker, we must take account of social changes." Nobody says no. No judge is unaware that there is an acute shortage of accommodation in all great cities in India. And when a question arose whether a flat could be sold in execution, judges took judicial notice of this acute shortage and held that a flat could be sold in execution. We know for a fact that money lenders have been oppressive and usurious. Their loans and securities were wiped out for a limited period by a law passed by the Maharashtra Legislature. The Supreme Court upheld the law. So it does not mean that the law stands still. But it does mean that the judge ought not to read his own private philosophy into our Constitution. And I have given a quotation in my book, I have not brought it here — in the 50 pages of my book dealing with the working of the Supreme Court, and those interested will find that quotation there. Mr. Justice Desai of the Supreme Court said: "Political packing of the Supreme Court is shocking; value packing is all right." But "value" is an abstract noun. You can't pack values. You can only pack a Court by people who believe in certain values. And why are the political values of Mrs. Gandhi not values and why can't she pack the Court? So, the moment you reflect a little, all packing of a Court as the dictionary meaning of "packing" shows, is wicked and wrong.

Now once you remove the source of delay, the complete absence of judicial discipline and the complete unpredictability of the Supreme Court, which leads to endless litigation, the delay would disappear. Let me give an example. *Five judgments* of the Supreme Court had held that the distinction between a tax and a fee is that in a fee there must be a *quid pro quo*, a return for services rendered; a tax is for raising general revenues — five judgments, the last but one of them by a Bench of 7 judges which was reaffirmed later. Three judges did not like this. "No, no, those days are gone. Mr. Seervai says this in his book," quoting a part from the book, but omitting the next paragraph. "In such and such a case Mr. Justice Untwalia went back on the Full Bench judgment" — he did not. Read Justice Untwalia's judgment, he affirmed the judgment of the Full Bench. And that is another and second source of delay. Because it is the duty of responsible Counsel not to ask people to embark on a litigation if the law as it stands is against them, and Counsel are of opinion that the law has been rightly laid down. The whole theory of our law is that the ignorance of the law is no excuse. Why? No judge knows all the law, no Counsel knows all the law. All that it means is that by seeking competent legal advice you can be told what your rights are or what your liabilities are. For once you know your rights or your liabilities, the first thing you think of is: Come, come, put an end to the matter by a settlement. What does Counsel say in all this "dynamic" theory of the law, law must "evolve", "must move with the Society?" Is there one law when Mr. Morarji Desai's government is in power, another law when Mrs. Indira Gandhi's government is in power, and a third law and the values of the Constitution when Mr. Rajiv Gandhi's government is in power, a government which repudiates largely doctrines once considered to represent the values of the Constitution? But judges forget that it is the duty of Counsel to advise clients, and the unpredictability of the Supreme Court encourages litigation which is indulged in as a gamble. If you think I am taking too low a view of the Bar, let me remind you that the whole review procedure in the Supreme Court, which took the form of a hearing in open Court had to be given up because Senior Counsel, who were required to give a carefully reasoned opinion justifying a review, gave certificates which in blunt language can only be described as false. So the whole procedure had to be altered. Now how does Counsel advise? Suppose in this fee matter a man comes to you and says, " Well, Sir, what do you think we should do?" I would tell him this: "There are five judgments of the Supreme Court in your favour and you should win. But I ought to tell you that I can give you no guarantee what the Supreme Court will do by "clarifying", "modifying", "explaining" the 5 earlier judgments." The whole postulate on which our system proceeds, that you must give fair and honest advice, is destroyed. Let me give a personal example.

A former Advocate–General of Orissa came and discussed a matter with me. He said: "This is a preliminary discussion. Shall we issue a certificate that the matter is a fit one for review by the Supreme Court?" We discussed the matter and he came again. I said, "I take it that the facts are correctly stated in the judgment." He replied, "Yes." I asked: "Is the law correctly stated?" We both agreed that it was, and we both agreed that we could not reasonably ask that the law should be reconsidered. So we refused to issue a certificate for review. An adventurous Advocate gave the certificate and the petition was admitted. And though we were clearly right, an invitation to gamble and fill the Supreme Court Board, which is congested, with one more matter, was accepted.

And this brings me to another point. You may feel that I have stated certain points categorically — but it is difficult to sum up 50 pages of my book in one hour. You will find reasons given for those points in the printed pages.

One further point. Chief Justice Chandrachud said to me, "It is all wrong that an Advocate of a day's standing should come along to the Supreme Court. He does not know the law, but we have to read his Special Leave petition. Now, surely, democracy does not require that Courts should be flooded with incompetent practitioners." The original rule was that nobody could be an Advocate of the Supreme Court unless he had ten years' standing. If you are really anxious to prevent accumulation of cases, is it not time that we give up populist notions and say, what the Supreme Court has now said in another context: that when it comes to M. D., or Ph.D. examinations, which require skill of the highest kind, merit should be the only test? If it is your experience that incompetent people come and flood the Court with petitions why don't you provide an appropriate period of standing at the Bar before an Advocate can practise before the Supreme Court?

Well, I think I have said enough. If I have not said anything about the lower courts, it is because I agree with my Lord Chief Justice Bhagwati that judges of those Courts are singularly ill-paid, ill-housed and proper Courts are not provided for them. Accordingly, it is the imperative duty of Government, which professes to have the welfare of the people at heart, to give judges who do invaluable service and with whom the common man comes into direct contact, proper terms and conditions of service. But I think it is to the credit of these judges that ill-housed, ill-paid, many of them do their work remarkably well. But if corruption gradually creeps in, for a person must live before he can live well, and if corruption touches, or is said to touch, even the higher courts, it is time we realized that the administration of justice is a first charge on the State, for without justice there can be no freedom and without freedom there can be no justice.

JUSTICE HURRIED IS JUSTICE BURIED

*In **The Seervai Legacy** I reproduced a secret and confidential letter of Seervai's addressed to the Chief Justice of India, (1979). Mention is made in that letter of an accompanying Memorandum, which was not published alongside. Having been told by some readers that it should have been reproduced, I am reproducing it below.*

The Memorandum was in Seervai's hand.

A MEMORANDUM
ON
Rule 7, O.XLVII of S.C. Rules

1. This memorandum is being submitted to the Chief Justice of India, because as the head of the judiciary he, more than any other person, is concerned to see that any rule or practice which impedes or perverts the course of justice is set right. It is with that object that this Memorandum has been prepared. For convenience of reference a typewritten copy of Rule 7 is annexed as Ex. No. 1 to this memorandum.

2. The value of any rule of procedure depends on how far it subserves the ends of justice. And the rule must be judged by reference

to the Court to which it applies. The Supreme Court is the final Court of appeal in India, and Article 141 of our Constitution makes the law laid down by the Supreme Court binding on all courts in India. It is generally known that well argued cases lead to well reasoned and well considered judgements which lay down the law with reasonable certainty, cases which are badly argued or imperfectly argued result in judgements which lay down incorrect law which must take time, money and grave public inconvenience to set right: Justice delayed may be justice denied; but this requires to be balanced by the less known saying "Justice hurried is justice buried." The time taken up in hearing a case must be set against the time taken by numerous litigants to set the judgements of the Supreme Court right. And this leaves out of account numerous persons who must suffer injury in silence because they find a Supreme Court litigation involving a reconsideration of a Supreme Court decision a daunting prospect.

3. The duty of laying down the law for the whole country imposes a more onerous duty and requires a separate procedure to discharge it adequately. Thus the Court of Appeal in England delivers important judgements but is not a final court of Appeal. Therefore, an appeal is by a notice of motion setting out the grounds of appeal. However, the House of Lords is a final Court of Appeal. Therefore, each side is required to file a statement of the case — a written argument which apprises the Law Lords hearing the appeal, of the case of either side, the House of Lords having announced that Counsel drawing the statement of the case should assume that their Lordships will have read the judgements of the lower Courts **and the relevant statutory provisions.** Further, the House of Lords has ruled that it is the duty of Counsel to bring every relevant authority of which Counsel is aware to the attention of the House, whether it is for him or against him so that the law is not laid down in ignorance of relevant authorities. Such information as I have, shows that Counsel discharge this duty.

4. In considering the time taken in hearing an appeal it is not enough to think of justice to the parties alone. For, under our system, the determination of a private dispute between parties by the Supreme Court would determine the rights of and impose liabilities on, an indefinite number of persons including government and public authorities. Hence, the extreme anxiety of the House of Lords and the Privy Council that the law is laid down as accurately as is humanly possible. I need hardly add that justice to the public must of necessity secure justice to the parties before the final tribunal.

5. Before dealing with the actual working of the new Rule 7, I may add that I approve of, and have publicly suggested ways for, eliminating needless delay and expense. The reintroduction of the practice of hearing special leave petitions every Monday is a long step in this direction. Presiding over a lecture given in the Bombay High Court Library by the present Law Minister, I suggested that the delay caused in the subordinate Courts and in the High Court in obtaining certified copies of judgments, decrees and orders — delays which extend to months and at times years, and are a source of corruption — can be eliminated by the State Governments setting up a central Xeroxing organisation, if necessary by assistance from the Centre. And in the Setalvad Memorial Lectures, I have suggested ways and means of speeding up proceedings before the Supreme Court: See Chapter II Supreme Court. I have said this because I am as well aware as judges, of the evils of delay and the need to eliminate delay. But the price which ought not to be paid to save time is by sacrificing justice to time and by so doing, reducing the weight which ought to attach to the judgments of the Supreme Court that they no longer command — the respect due to the judgments of the highest Court in India. In the context of the new Rule 7, I was shocked to hear a judge of the Supreme Court say in open Court — "We are living in an age of mass produced judgments" and so were several lawyers and laymen present in Court. My ingrained respect for our own judiciary prevents me from drawing out the grave implications of "mass produced judgments." I will only say that if there is one thing which "judgments" cannot be it is that they cannot be "mass produced". Nor can justice be mass produced.

6. Before reverting to general considerations, I would like to refer to the actual working of Rule 7 in a heavy appeal involving difficult questions of law relating to the Companies Act and the Foreign Exchange Regulation Act, in relation to documents which occupied over 360 pages in Vol. III of the appeal paper book. The judgment under appeal dealt with the fiduciary power of directors to issue shares, by considering English and Indian authorities in 33 pages of its judgment. Senior Counsel for the appellant did not deal with this part of the case in his opening. In my reply I dealt with the fiduciary power of the directors in Note No. 1 and said that the omission of the Appellants' Counsel had put me in a difficulty as I did not know what he had to say on those authorities and therefore could not reply to his argument. The Appellants' Counsel got up and said that he did not deal with them because time was limited — it would have taken 2 days. I said that time was important, but justice

was more important, and I was entitled to reply to his argument since I had opened the appeal on that point. This was agreed, but as it turned out, this meant that he could reply to my argument orally, but I was to be relegated to a written note. Weighing my words, I thought it an outrage then, and think it an outrage now, that a Counsel whose duty it was to open on a vital issue should not do so, pleading lack of time, that I should have to open on the point as it was central to my argument, that he should reply to me orally and I be relegated to a written Note in reply. But for Rule 7 I would have protested, but when judges are armed with the legal power to order Counsel to stop, responsible Counsel do not put themselves in a position where they can be ordered to stop. In fact, I was told on Wednesday 7th February, 1979, "you must accede to our request to stop tomorrow within one hour, and if things are left out put in a note". An hour's oral argument, bringing together the effect of 10 different notes running into several pages and dealing with different questions of fact and law, would have been reduced to a small fraction of an hour. So it became necessary to tell the judges not to take notes, and that a written note would be put in from brief points jotted down for oral argument. This involved preparing Note No. 12 running into 17 cyclostyled foolscap sheets. During the oral argument of one hour there was one objection on a point of pleadings, which had been dealt with, in the judgments of the lower courts. A reference to those judgments would have involved about 10 minutes extra, and I was driven to ask, "Will you give me 10 minutes extra?" to be told: "You can have 10 minutes". I had booked my air ticket for the Saturday morning plane — this was cancelled, and I spent about 12 hours on Saturday with two steno typists working most of the time, and spent Sunday, 11th February from 8 A.M. to 4 P.M. likewise to put in 4 notes. I need hardly add, this was not an exception. Throughout the argument, time and energy were consumed in dictating written arguments to 2 steno typists, supplementing them by written argument when they were busy, instead of making short notes and addressing the Court orally. Working rarely less than 12 hours a day, this was possible only because I declined to accept special writ petitions on Mondays and for two weeks there were only 3 working days each week. That Counsel should be called upon to work in the conditions I have described above, is degrading and as far as I am concerned I have decided never again to accept a brief in the Supreme Court subject to one absolute commitment to argue for the respondents free of charge.

7. Nor is it only the Counsel for the Respondents, who is handicapped. When the Court told me to stop in one hour on Thursday, 7th February and put written notes on matters which could not be compressed into one hour, it was overlooked that Counsel for the appellant must be able to reply. But such notes could not be ready before the arguments were concluded on Friday 9th February — the notes were handed over to the judges on Monday the 12th February. Advocates are constantly reminded that they are a part of the administration of justice. Rule 7 makes them a part of a system which leads to injustice. They no longer perform their traditional role.

8. A power to impose a time limit is conferred on all judges regardless of their equipment and capacity. Some judges catch a point quickly, remember submissions on fact and law accurately and are able to hold an overall picture of a party's case throughout the hearing, so that incorrect statements are promptly noticed and corrected. Other judges may not catch points quickly or remember things accurately, and are unable to hold an overall picture of a party's case, so that incorrect statements are not noticed and are not corrected. It is obvious that very different time limits are required according as the judge belongs to the first category or the second, or occupies a midway position. And the facts of the appeal I have been speaking of, prove the obvious. Before the Appeal Court in Madras — Mr. Justice Ismail and Mr. Justice Sita Raman — I opened the appeal on 9 written notes (about 92 pages). As soon as the first Note had been completed the presiding judge gave a flawless summary to show that he had followed the argument and that things need not be repeated. There were not more than 3 or 4 questions asked, and I finished the whole argument in about 12 hours. Before the Supreme Court I replied for the Respondents in 10 Written Notes (about 124 pages) *which did not cover the whole ground.* It took me 23 hours. It put me in mind of an appeal I opened before Mr. Justice Lokur in Bombay. I finished my argument in four and a half hours. He intervened only thrice. He referred the matter to a division bench to avoid a Letters Patent Appeal. It took me 12 hours to open the Appeal, or rather four-fifths of the appeal. To ask the Bar to co-operate with the Bench in saving time overlooks the fact that both the Bench and the Bar contain members of varying capacities. And where disposals become the principal desideratum in the administration of justice, justice is perverted. For, human nature being what it is, few Benches would admit that the delay in the disposal of cases is due to them and not to Counsel.

9. I may add that when I was in Delhi, I spoke to several Counsel. They fretted and fumed at Rule 7 and its absurd results. But with characteristic fatalism they said: "What can we do?" I am not a fatalist, and I believe that in the end reason and truth prevail: in any event a duty is laid upon every one of us to try to make them prevail.

10. The example of the Supreme Court of the United States where there is a time limit of 1 hour for either side is misleading and is not in *pari materia* for the following reasons.

11. The U.S. Supreme Court is almost exclusively a Constitutional Court and all the judges sit to hear every matter. By an Act of 1925, the Supreme Court has been given a power to dismiss summarily applications for *Certiorari* or review. The applications filed annually exceed 3000. Of these, about five sixths are summarily dismissed by circulation. Encyclopaedia Britannica (1970), Vol. 21, p. 436 "Supreme Court".

12. The consequence of the Supreme Court being almost exclusively a Constitutional Court and all the judges of the Court sitting as a single bench is that the judges acquire expertise in Constitutional Law which obviously speeds up the disposal of cases. Our Supreme Court is a final Court of Appeal in all matters except appeals from Courts Martial. By special leave it hears appeals against the judgments and orders of courts and tribunals. It has original writ jurisdiction under Art. 32. Rights of appeal are conferred by the Constitution. The judges of our Supreme Court sit in separate benches to hear all kinds of matters so that the question of developing expertise in any subject does not arise.

13. The way in which the Supreme Court functions in the United States is radically different from our Supreme Court. First the Court sits for 4 days in a week (Mondays — Thursdays) for two weeks and then goes into recess for two weeks, so that the sittings are for 8 out of 28 days. Each judge has a legal assistant who helps to digest the elaborate written briefs filed by Counsel for the parties. The institution of the judges' legal assistant has been much criticised, but it does lessen pressure on the judge. The assistant's post is held only for one year. For preparing constitutional briefs in important cases large law firms are engaged. Thus in the landmark case of *Baker V Carr* (1962) 369 U.S. 186, "An army of attorneys prepared briefs for the Supreme Court argument, attesting to the importance of the issue which at last was to be given the attention of the Court" [William A. Swindler's *Court And Constitution in the 20th Century, The New Legality 1932-68* p. 315]. No such army of attorneys is available for our Supreme Court, nor are the

resources of advocates on record comparable to the resources of big law firms in the U.S.A.

14. A study of briefs filed before the Supreme Court of the United States shows that this method is quite unsuitable for oral arguments on complicated questions of *fact and law,* and the method adopted by the Privy Council and the House of Lords, which are final courts of appeal in all matters, namely, a Statement of the Case for the Appellant and the Respondent, is the right one. The Federal Court of India adopted the method and it worked successfully; and so did our Supreme Court in its early days. The method was given up because the statements of the case were found unhelpful, or in blunt language, Counsel did not spend the time required to draw a proper statement of the case. If this is the reason for giving up a method which would put judges hearing an appeal in possession of the case of both parties and thus avoid interruptions, which take place because the judges do not know the case of the parties before them, then the requirement of Rule 7 that Counsel can supplement their oral by written arguments can only be described as grotesque. For if Counsel, in the quiet of their chambers cannot draw or settle a written argument in the form of a statement of the case, it is incredible that they could prepare helpful notes of argument when the case is going on and even more after the case is over, and they are busy with another case.

15. Certain factors which lead to delay are beyond the Chief Justice's control. Jawaharlal Nehru said in the Constituent Assembly that judges should not only be first-rate but should be acknowledged to be first rate. He did nothing to secure first rate judges by improving their terms and conditions of service nor has any subsequent Prime Minister done anything to improve those conditions. As long as the Bench fails to secure leading lawyers, judicial proceedings cannot be speeded up. No Court is in a position to control Counsel's arguments if the gap between leading lawyers and able judges is very great. I have again and again spoken out for the urgent need to improve the conditions of judges, but the demand would come with greater effect from the judges themselves.

16. I have not attempted to list all the factors which lead to trials being prolonged. But they can be briefly referred to. The length of Supreme Court judgments and the difficulty of reconciling different judgments on the same point; the suggestions from the Bench that Counsel should check up a particular line of inquiry; prolonged discussions between members of the Bench in the midst of Counsel's arguments; lengthy arguments with Counsel, and, as

happened to the Solicitor General in the *Fundamental Rights Case,* constant interruptions of Counsel's arguments. One or more of these factors make it impossible to give estimates of the time Counsel will take.

17. One final consequence of asking Counsel to give written notes even of their oral arguments, must be mentioned here. The keen attention which an oral argument requires from a judge to make his own notes is unconsciously impaired by written arguments, especially in a Court which reserves its judgments as our Supreme Court almost invariably does. A written note of Counsel's oral argument is no substitute for the judge's own notes of that argument, for it requires great concentration to formulate briefly an argument urged by Counsel. Lord Denning spoke of the intense concentration required of judges in the Court of Appeal, when it is remembered that in 95 per cent of appeals, judgment is delivered as soon as arguments are concluded.

18. I have a complete set of the 14 notes submitted to the Court and if it is desired I can forward them to the Chief Justice.

19. This memorandum has been prepared before the result of the appeal in which I appeared is known. But the memorandum cannot be forwarded to the Chief Justice till the appeal is finally disposed of. I am therefore arranging to keep the memorandum (and its covering letter) in safe custody and they will be forwarded as soon as the appeal is finally disposed of.

In conclusion, I would like to add that it has given me no pleasure to prepare this memorandum. But I felt that however unpleasant the task, it must be done as it affects the administration of justice to which I have devoted nearly fifty years of my life.

H. M. Seervai

JUDGMENTS : NEED FOR CLARITY AND ACCURACY

The occasion for this speech was the 125th Anniversary Celebration of the Bombay High Court on 14th August, 1987.

Seervai's concern for the administration of justice was never far from his thoughts and his heart. He was nearly 81 years old, when this speech was made. The reader will appreciate the hard punches he gave and the deeply felt effort he made towards the establishment and perpetuation of the highest standards in India's system of justice.

I AM GRATEFUL to My Lord the Chief Justice for inviting me to speak to you on this great occasion because ever since I joined the Bar in 1929 I have been proud of our High Court, been devoted to its cause and not only that but I have felt great affection for it.

Today we are celebrating three anniversaries. The first is the 125th anniversary of the High Court; secondly, with our fellow citizens all over India, we are celebrating Independence Day; and, coming nearer home, almost to a day we are celebrating an event which gave to this High Court the greatest Chief Justice it has ever had since Independence — Mohammedali Chagla. Eleven glorious years of his Chief Justiceship have enhanced the great reputation of the Bombay High Court, and the public felt fully confident that in a Court over which he presided, justice would be done to the limit permitted by law. It was fit and proper that a tribute should have been paid to him this morning outside the Court over which he presided with such distinction. But we pay that tribute in vain if we do not — judges and lawyers alike — take inspiration from his conduct as Advocate, as Judge and as Chief Justice, to enhance the reputation of this High Court.

I have been at the Bar for 58 years. It is a long time in a lawyer's life, but it has enabled me to take part in two celebrations, in celebrating the Centenary of the Bombay High Court and in celebrating the 125th Anniversary of that Court. On the occasion of the Centenary, and as part of the celebrations, speeches were made, or rather read out, by Chief Justice Chainani, by the Governor of Bombay Shri Sri Prakasa, by the Attorney General for India, Mr. Motilal Setalvad and by the Chief Justice of India Mr. Justice Sinha. As Advocate-General I was assigned the task of making a brief extempore speech proposing a vote of thanks to the distinguished guests. I concluded my speech with some words which I would like to repeat to you today. I said:

"My Lords the Chief Justice of India and the Chief Justice of Bombay have looked into the future, and have asked the question : What will people say of us in the year 2062? It is not given to us to look into the future; but we have been told that:

> "Where the safe ways end,
> Known and unknown divide,
> God's great uncharted passes upward tend,
> And the spirit of man undaunted is undenied."

"If Judges and lawyers show the undaunted courage for which the Bombay High Court has been so famous in the past, if Judges not only stand up against the executive but against passing fashions of the day, if they refuse to be bludgeoned into sacrificing the *real* necessities of the times by the *felt* necessities of the times, then we may be confident that in the year 2062 they will say that we, and those who came after us, have done worthily and well."

Well, the courage and resolution of which I spoke — both of the Bench and the Bar — was put to the test during the Emergency, and that test was passed with flying colours. The High Court of Bombay stood firm as a rock for the rule of law, and it refused to countenance the argument, seriously urged by the Government Pleader, that if a detenu was starved to death and shot, this court could offer him no relief. To the credit of the other High Courts, they also stood firm as a rock and they upheld the rule of law. One of the Chief Justices said that "if I accepted Government's argument the ghost of Hitler would haunt the whole of India". Therefore, our High Court and eight other High Courts reached their finest hour. But it was the Supreme Court which in the supreme moment failed to discharge its duty. It delivered a judgment which in substance said that any one of us could be picked up and shot, and our widows may have the comfort of filing a criminal prosecution for murder after the emergency was over! That judgment has few defenders now. Two of those who wrote it are heartily ashamed of it, and one has said that the order was incorrect and did not conform to the judgment.

Now, reverting to the Centenary celebrations, I wish to read to you a passage from the speech of the Attorney General Mr. Setalvad. He had been the Chairman of the Law Commission and had personal experience of various Courts, had met Counsel, examined and cross-examined them, so that his opinion on the subject was worth having. He wrote:

> "The completion of the record of useful and distinguished service for 100 years is undoubtedly an occasion for celebration and jubilation. Is it not also an occasion for taking stock of ourselves? Here one perceives distinct indications which cause anxiety and even alarm. There has been unmistakable evidence of the decline in the standards of efficiency and correct behaviour at the Bar that necessarily postulates a corresponding decline on the Bench, for the Bench and the Bar are the wings of the same profession, the profession of the law. Appointments to the judiciary based on political or communal considerations still hold the field. Patronage in the matter of these appointments is being exercised at high level. Should not then the Bar and the judiciary stand firm against these practices instead of succumbing to them and themselves becoming tools of the exercise of power by the executive?"

I agree with Mr. Setalvad and I share his view that in celebrating anniversaries we should not merely take pride in the glories of the past and its achievements. We should look with a steady eye and an unshaken nerve to the situation as we see it today and see whether it cannot be improved; and plan hopefully for the future so that the future may reproduce some of the glories of the past.

I have referred to the Supreme Court of India and I would like to refer briefly to the great change which took place in the judicial hierarchy from 1929 when I joined the Bar till today. At that time, except for the brief interlude of the Federal Court, the judicial hierarchy was broadly speaking, this : The Subordinate Judge, the District Judge with practically unlimited jurisdiction, the Chartered High Courts with Appellate and Original Side jurisdiction and finally the Privy Council. The Privy Council was manned by Judges of the highest distinction. Its personnel was practically interchangeable with that of the House of Lords. Being the final Tribunal for what was then the whole of the British Empire, Boards of the Privy Council took the utmost pains to see that the law was stated briefly, accurately and clearly. Mr. Justice Venkatarama Aiyar has gone on record in a judgment as saying that in constitutional matters there is no instance of the Privy Council having reversed itself except in one case from Ireland where the Board reversed its earlier decision because facts not available to the first Board were available to the second. You will see with what certainty the law was laid down. No "may be's", no "might be's". Sir Dinshaw Mulla told his son-in-law that a draft judgment was scrutinised line by line, and word by word because the Boards were conscious that they were laying down the law for the whole Empire. The impact of such a final Court on the High Courts and the subordinate Courts was great, for every Judge knew that his judgment would have ultimately to stand the scrutiny of the Privy Council; and no Judge wished to do anything but his best because at no time would he realise when a matter would be carried in appeal.

All that changed with Independence. First, the Federal Court for a few years, and then the Supreme Court of India, took over as the final Appellate Court in this country. It had the widest jurisdiction of any Court in any country. It had the residuary jurisdiction of the Privy Council to grant special leave to appeal. The law declared by it was made binding on all Courts in India, just as the Government of India Act, 1935 had done earlier for the law declared by the Privy Council and the Federal Court. Therefore, a change took place in our legal system. During early days with two of the most distinguished lawyers from Bombay, the Attorney-General and the Solicitor-General Mr. Setalvad and Mr. Daphtary, the early Benches of the Supreme Court were the strongest; and though they might have been unfamiliar with judicial review of legislation and fundamental rights, their reasoning showed clarity, cogency, and deep learning. They talked as lawyers to lawyers and they realised that the essence of law is that the Judge is as much bound by the law as anybody else. Gradually the atmosphere changed. The first inroad was made by Mr. Justice Gajendragadkar who propounded what may broadly and loosely be called the philosophy of the left. "Socio-economic" was a phrase which occurred in most of his judgments. But it must be realised that if Judges were free to propound a philosophy of the left, Mr. Justice Subba Rao was equally free to propound a philosophy of the right. He made no secret of it, so that we reached the stage when we came across the great judgment of *Golaknath* which held that no part of the Constitution could be amended. To the end of his days Gajendragadkar told me that I was very wrong to refuse a judgeship of the Supreme Court, for I would have been a Judge and then the Chief Justice for five years and a half, and the tragedy of *Golaknath* would never have occurred. Well, I said to him that one Judge could not do much, and I honestly believed that I had made a larger contribution to the development of Constitutional Law by my book than I could ever have done by being a Judge of that Court.

I have been spending the last 19 months in one of the most painful exercises I have ever undertaken. First a research of 9 months in the transfer of power which replaces a brief discussion in the first Chapter. It is now a monograph of 150 pages; and, secondly in bringing the law up-to-date. And never have I been more distressed in my life than in dealing with the judgments of the Supreme Court. Mr. Justice Shah has given a parable which emboldens me to say that some Judges of the Supreme Court seem to possess a magic wand — the open seasme which solves every problem, — and it bears the name of Directive Principles of State Policy. No matter that the Directives confer no rights on a citizen. No matter that no Judge can enforce them without violating his oath and probably being impeached. But it is seen as a solution to every problem. I do not say this to provoke controversy. But I am convinced that if this trend is not reversed, the respect due to the highest Court in the realm and, therefore, due to the High Courts will be lost.

Let me give you two illustrations. Two judgments of the Supreme Court had rejected Government's argument that pension was a mere matter of grace. A Constitution Bench had held that it was a matter of right, something much higher than any directive of State Policy. One of our ablest Judges of the Supreme Court heard arguments for days on the Directives of State Policy, the misery of the poor, — the poor broken down pensioner retiring at the end of his life. But all that was required was a judgment of one sentence. "The argument of Government that pension is a matter of grace stands negatived by two judgments of this Court with which we respectfully agree". Eight pages of the judgment, as reported in the Supreme Court Reports, are occupied by a discussion wholly irrelevant. The Supreme Court says, that they are grinding to a halt because of delay. Which Judge should permit an argument when the matter was concluded by the finding of a Constitution Bench, especially when the Judge agreed with the decision? That is one illustration.

The second thing which would have filled me with despair but for the fact that I am an optimist, and despair is unknown to me, is a "judgment" of five Judges (I would put the judgment in inverted commas, bear it in mind) in *Vasanth Kumar's Case.* Eight petitions were filed challenging the reservation of seats in educational institutions and in public employment to the extent of 66 per cent in educational institutions and 68 per cent in public employment. The overwhelming weight of authority was that reservations could not exceed more than 49 per cent because reservations were an exception and equality was the rule. The Supreme Court heard the petitions for 12 full days. It reserved judgment. It would appear that similar questions from Tamil Nadu were heard for 7 days and judgment was reserved. Mind you, we are in July and August, and October 1982. All the High Courts were anxiously awaiting the decision of the Supreme Court for it alone could resolve the conflict of Supreme Court decisions. As month followed month, and year threatened to follow year, the aggrieved persons took to the streets in Gujarat and in Madhya Pradesh. Arson, rioting, looting took place. On 8th May 1985, a day before Mr. Justice Desai was to retire, the Supreme Court delivered, what? — not judgments. They said so. The Chief Justice said that this was not a judgment. It was a useful innovation. We are giving guidelines to a Commission to be appointed by the State of Karnataka. Mr. Justice Desai said, this is an essay. It is not a judgment. It is an essay — not exhaustive — and in any event, nothing that I say about the new approach should touch Scheduled Castes and Scheduled Tribes. Mr. Justice Chinnappa Reddy did not say that it was not a judgment but he did not decide the right of parties. So here we have the highest Court in the realm saying and doing what a law student would know to be utterly illegal — delivering an advisory opinion when the only advisory opinion which the Supreme Court can give is to the President of India. What is more, they disregarded the limitations on the Supreme Court's power under Article 145, sub-article

(5) that no judgment should be delivered except by a majority of Judges who heard the matter. There was no majority of Judges for any point and one is struck with amazement that able Judges, eminent Judges should seriously believe that five different sets of guidelines, each set given separately by each Judge could ever help a Commission. Did they not pause to consider the infinite injury which they were doing to thousands of students and to hundreds of thousands of candidates for public employment ? For if the original judgments were right, for every 100 seats in educational institutions, 17 students were deprived of their right to admission and for every 100 posts in Government service, 19 out of 100 applicants were deprived of employment: petitions filed in 1979 to 1981 hanging fire, elaborately argued "judgments" delivered, rights not determined. So, for the first time in my book, I have been driven to remind Judges of the judicial oath and to point out the limitation of the judicial function. My time is up. But I will end this talk with giving you the example of one great American Judge when he came to decide the validity of capital punishment. Mr. Justice Blackmun said that cases such as those before him "provide for me an excruciating agony of spirit because I hold that finite human beings ought not to be responsible for taking finite life. It is against all my philosophy. It is against all my convictions. If I were a Legislator I would vote against capital punishment. But we sit here as Judges and we must remind ourselves that our duty is to administer the law and to resist every pressure to read our own preferences into the laws" — a pressure so great that his colleagues had succumbed to it. I think that this is the true nature of the judicial function, and that is why in speaking in praise of Chief Justice Chagla I said that people were convinced that they would get justice to the limit of the law.

I thank you.

POWER OF THE STATE
1957

I BEG, SIR, to move that the power of the State has increased, is increasing, and ought to be diminished. I am not unaware of the argument that power by itself is neutral and the question whether power ought to be diminished would depend upon whether the power is being exercised for good or evil. However, I am going to discuss the problem of power not in the abstract, but with reference to a State, that is, an organized political community in a defined geographical area.

By now we know a good deal about States; they have a considerable history and that history is one long attempt to regulate and control the power of the State in the interest of human happiness and human dignity. The reason is not far to seek — power in a State can only be exercised by men and women and they are a mixture of good and evil, wisdom and folly. [Moreover, human powers grow, mature and decay, a fact of great importance in a dictatorship.]

So far as the State is concerned, the 19th Century was one of high hopes and high achievements. The abolition of slavery, the freedom of thought, expression and worship; the emancipation of women, the spread of education and a cheap press were impressive achievements. But even more impressive was the growth and spread of representative government with its faith in human reason and human goodness. I recall these things for two reasons: First, because the men who dared all and endured all to make these things come true made a contribution to human welfare as massive, if not more massive, than is boasted by any welfare state today. Secondly because events were to show that faith in human reason and human goodness is not enough, it is necessary to recognize the passions and the pride of man and to take steps to build breakwaters against them before they overwhelm the State.

"Scarce thousand years suffice to build a State, An hour may lay it in the dust".

We know now that in our century these bright lights have gone out over large parts of our world and have been replaced by the darkness of a tyranny, the like of which has rarely stalked across the darkest pages of human history — and it is stalking still.

It is against this background that I invite you to say that you view with alarm the tendency in a large number of countries for the power of the State to increase and that you are in favour of the curtailment of such power. Time will not permit me to deal with a large number of countries, but the points I wish to make can be made as well with reference to our own country and would have the additional advantage of holding greater interest.

In India and with the Indian Constitution I do not have to argue the question of tyranny against freedom — for we have taken our stand by the side of freedom — at least the Constitution has. In this connection, it would be well not to forget the most terrible exposure of tyranny which took place only last year. You will find it in the speech in which Mr. Kruschev explained to his heart's content the misdeeds of Stalin but failed to explain to the world how he himself, and the other leaders of Russia and in fact the whole nation submitted to the regime of Stalin, which Kruschev described as one of brutal violence and terror. I think it well not to forget this exposure for there are some great ones in this country who feel tempted to kindle their lights from the lamps in Moscow, which, seen from a distance and through the climate of "Hindi Russi Bhai Bhai" appeared to shed a rosy light. But the chill winds which have blown from Hungary have cleared the air and the lights are now seen to be, what they always were, blood red.

The Constitution of India, as adopted in 1950 is based on the principle that power must be controlled and limited. Unlike the British Parliament, which is supreme and sovereign, the Indian Legislatures are not supreme and sovereign. The Constitution is supreme and it permits certain laws and proscribes others. The makers of our Constitution were not unaware that the economic problem was to the fore in our century. But they knew that a Constitution is built on dust if it is not founded on an enduring philosophy of life, instead of the passing fashions of the day. They rejected the gospel that the end of man is economic. They held fast to the enduring lesson of history and philosophy and religion that the end of man is moral and religious. The word 'religious' need cause no lifting of the eye-brow; for though our State is secular, the freedom of religion is a guaranteed fundamental right. In other words, the makers of our Constitution refused to see the glory of man in his being a well fed and well groomed animal, for a slave well looked after by his master answers that description; they saw it rather in man's unconquerable mind and in man's indomitable spirit (which because it is indomitable is undenied). They saw no necessary opposition between economic and moral ends, but they made sure that in cases of conflict, in times of peace, the moral ends prevailed. Hence the grand division between fundamental rights and directives of State Policy. Fundamental rights secure basic human freedoms by the simple expedient of making any law or executive action contrary to them void, and arming the Supreme Court and the High Courts with the power to declare it void. In a society thus made free, social and economic ideals embodied in the directives of State Policy can grow and flourish.

If the Constitution had stood, it could not be said that in India the power of the State had increased and required to be diminished. But the fourth amendment to the Constitution has raised the question of power in a most acute form and has manifested tendencies which if not checked and reversed are going to put our basic freedoms in jeopardy. The fourth amendment abrogated valuable fundamental rights in the supposed interest of economic growth. The right to hold property subject to reasonable restrictions, the right to claim compensation in respect of property taken for the public good, have been taken away and withdrawn from the protections of the Courts. But that is not all. Equality before the law or freedom from unjust discrimination has also been abrogated and withdrawn from the Courts so far as acquisition of property is concerned. Never has a more formidable weapon been placed in the hands of a party in power: the power over men's wills by acquiring power over their property.

You will search Parliamentary debates in vain for any coherent justification of powers so injurious to freedom. Appeals were made citing the Sovereignty of the British Parliament, without anybody realizing the incongruity of such a concept in federal legislatures under a written Constitution. There was thinly concealed disparagement of judges who have done a magnificent job. There was the claim that the legislators, as the chosen representatives, were more to be trusted than judges who are sworn to administer justice without fear or favour, forgetting that for the State to be prosecutor, judge and jailor might almost be given as the very definition of tyranny; it was forgotten that in history the fight for freedom has been a fight for independent and incorruptible judges. There was resentment at confiscation being called confiscation although any intelligent child can see that if a bar of gold worth Rs. 10,000/- was acquired by the State for Rs. 2000/-, four fifths of the bar was confiscated.

Great as is the danger of unbridled power conferred by these amendments, the damage done to the democratic processes is greater still. One should have thought that a select Committee dealing with so grave a matter would hear evidence. Those who had a conviction to state and a claim to state it, let it be known that they were willing to be cross-examined but evidence was not wanted, for cross-examination is a double edged weapon.

Again in order to acquire these powers, it became necessary to treat the Constitution as an ordinary law subject to amendment like any other law. And so, another barrier against passion and pride was lowered, the barrier raised by the reverence and respect and love which a great Constitution commands from people who look upon it as a fundamental law. The American constitution was enacted over 170 years ago: there have been 22 amendments, but with the controversial exception of prohibition they have all enlarged freedom and fettered unbridled power. The very last amendment is instructive. By an act of self denial George Washington refused election after his second term, thus laying down a convention.

Let me turn to the economic problem. The claim is made that in an underdeveloped country the State must have large powers if rapid industrialisation is to raise the standard of living and lift the curse of poverty from the brows of men. It is unfortunate that the economic problem which in its basic outline is simple enough, is so clothed in the mystery of scientific jargon that issues can be clouded and arbitrary powers acquired without a shadow of justification. But the basic facts are these: food, and other material goods must first be produced before they can be shared; and there are not enough to go the round. The production of these goods depends on the much despised words "capital" and "profits". In ancient civilisations capital consisted of lands and animals and slaves, that is, mobile tools. In modern times, machines have taken the place of animals and slaves. But it is not enough to have capital; it must be used to yield profits, part of which must go towards the increase of productive capital goods. I cannot pursue this subject in detail, but you will find a fascinating account in Prof. Lewis's recent book *The Theory of Economic Growth.* You will rise from a study of that book with the conviction that whether the State is Communist, Socialist or Capitalist, economic growth requires capital and profits. You will learn that the fact of the State owning the Capital and earning the profits has not the effect of improving the lot of the people, because great increase in capital goods can and does go with extreme shortage of consumer goods. The exhortations which you hear for austerity during the 2nd five year plan follow from the fact that we are engaged in accumulating productive capital goods and curtailing consumer goods. The process has its limits: Alice in Wonderland was not the only person to be driven to fury by the rule "jam yesterday and jam tomorrow but no jam today". And finally you will understand why the current notions of economic equality are mistaken and unreal in a world where men possess unequal skills and the will to use them is unequal.

It is unfortunate that the economic problem which in its basic outline is easy enough to understand, is so clothed in mystery that issues can be clouded and powers acquired without a shadow of justification. Such was the fourth amendment to our Constitution, which gravely impaired the rights of property — as is generally known.

Let me state very briefly why the wide powers claimed by the State over economic processes are based on unwarranted assumptions:

(i) There is no justification for the assumption that civil servants and political theorists will run business with greater efficiency than business men who have spent their lives in doing business. Experience shows that they don't.

(ii) There is no justification for the assumption that the whole business community is corrupt and government service is pure, because a business man can only corrupt a person in authority and power.

(iii) One of the historic arguments for free trade and free economy is that licenses, controls and quotas confer such immense patronage on persons in authority that corruption in public life and service is inevitable. An ill paid public service and vast industrial projects go ill together. Government claimed to be the model employer and believed in paying its servants well. Mistaken notions of equality have made government service an ill paid service greatly to the detriment of public good.

ON NOTHING

It is known that for ten long years at the Bar, Seervai was briefless. His mother's moral support, his own optimistic and philosophical nature, and his love of literature, on which he depended, kept him from being unduly unhappy — kept him cheerful. During those years his light articles appeared in the Sanj Vartman Press and in the college magazine of Elphinstone College. Here is one of them, from the College Magazine.

The courts had just broken up for the day as I sat in the Bar Library gazing dreamily on a fat, dirty volume of Mayne's *Hindu Law.* I was vaguely conscious of the busy gossip of legal luminaries, but today it had no charm for me. I continued to gaze at the volume before me, for in it was locked up a whole dreary month devoted to analysing and tabulating facts and fictions which belong to a world now buried and forgotten. And yet must we toil over it, and resist the allurements of genuine books which belong not to any time or age ! And that, too, in the name of study!. . . How different will it be to-night ! Yes, for to-night I shall read books — real books. May the dust lie thick on Mayne!

I replaced *Mayne* on its dusty shelf, got a sympathetic nod from a 'senior' standing near by, returned a knowing smile, and walked out with a quick step and a light heart. As I went along I tried to think of the one great book I would prefer to any other. 'An impossible thing to decide off-hand,' the reader will say, and so I found it to be. Don Quixote and Gulliver, Plutarch and Boswell, Tacitus and Gibbon, and a host of rival claimants overpowered me with a sense of my own impotence. And so it was that with a most confused mind I dropped into my favourite seat in the Opera House tram-car, a picture of misery fit to excite the laughter of the Lucretian gods. I can't say how long I had been vexing myself with this increasingly complicated problem when my attention was drawn to a violent disputation between the two passengers in front of me. Both of them were dressed in *khaddar* and spoke a language which was a quaint but happy mixture of English and Gujarati. They were discussing, so I gathered, the nature of free political institutions; and as 'freedom' to each meant freedom for his ideas and way of life, it was not surprising to hear the dire threats which each hurled at his opponent 'if only the government of the country were to be entrusted to him'. But this future exercise of possible power did not long satisfy either side, and each loudly proclaimed his instant readiness to box the other if he persisted in expressing his 'dangerous, reactionary, and unpatriotic views'. (A dozen adjectives, spoken in racy Gujarati, are omitted as likely to offend sensitive ears.) I had promised myself a really serious boxing match when more conscientious and law-abiding citizens intervened, for, said they, they were bound to preserve the peace of His Majesty. Their voluble arguments did not convince the two disputants who, nevertheless, agreed to keep His Majesty's peace, with suppressed references to a nice quiet spot at Chowpatty.

During the next few minutes I heard old men wondering what young men were coming to; and some practical young men wondering what 'highbrow, educated men' were coming to; and almost every-body wondering what everyone else was coming to. But this wonder subsided as quickly as it was roused, and I was once more free to puzzle myself with the best book in literature.

I have got it, at last ! Not absolutely the best, perhaps, but the best one for me tonight. My fellow-passengers made the choice inevitable. The poverty of their talk precipitated a long felt conviction that we had lost the art of good conversation, and this naturally made me turn to the great talkers of the past. But where can I get better talk than that which the genius of Boswell has made immortal? So, tonight, I shall sit at the Club and hear Johnson laying down the law. I shall love to see him worsted in an argument for then will he emerge the supreme dialectician that he was. 'There is no use arguing with Johnson; for when his pistol misses fire, he knocks you down with the butt-end of it.' Burke will be there, and will call forth all the powers of the Sage. And there I'll see the wistful face of Oliver Goldsmith whose attempts at fine conversation the Doctor will tenderly protect from everybody but himself. Of course Boswell will be there, acting the Socratic midwife to the rich, full mind of Johnson, and gathering those subtle observations which will delight untold generations . . . I have resolved to touch nothing but *Boswell* tonight.

A word from the tram-conductor told me that I would be carried back to the Flora Fountain if I continued my reverie. So I hastily got down, hurried along to my house, ran up to my room, changed, and had all but taken down a well worn copy of *Boswell*, when a monogram letter, lying about on the book-case, caught my eye. Now as monogram letters are rare with me, I scanned this one eagerly, tore it open, and found—

An invitation from the editor of a Magazine to write an article for his New Year Annual. Here it is:

'For the last fifty years, writers of distinction from almost all parts of the world have contributed to its columns.

'May I request you on the present occasion to be good enough to contribute to its columns on any subject of human interest.'

Now I can't say that I was insensible to the double compliment of being fit enough to join the company of 'writers of distinction' and being ripe enough to write on 'any subject of human interest'. But what with *Boswell* at my elbow and a disinclination to work— a month of Hindu Law will convert the most hardened sinner to the gospel of laziness — I dismissed the idea of accepting the invitation. I told myself that the company of 'writers of distinction' was too exalted for a person who had won no such thing, and that the attempt to bend so mighty a bow must end in dismal failure. I took up my *Boswell*, but could not let go the editor's letter. Something within me cried out that my conduct would justify those grumpy, disillusioned old men who periodically tell an attentive world that modern youth has lost the spirit of enterprise and is suffering from a most acute 'inferiority complex'. Besides, if the editor thought fit to place me alongside 'writers of distinction' he surely knew what he was about. Perhaps some hints of my budding genius had reached his ears and, with characteristic enterprise, he meant to secure so promising a contributor before his head was turned by success! Yes, I must reluctantly give up *Boswell* for a time and justify the editor's estimate of me.

But what should I write on? A writer cannot be too careful in choosing the subject of his first article especially if he means to awake one morning and find himself famous. Think of the pleasure it would give a malignant critic to point out that the first attempt of 'so delightful an essayist as Mr.—, would do little credit to a boy in the fifth form'.

So I tried hard to find a subject, my treatment of which would make the reader say 'Ah ! this is what I call a great article. Clearly this young man is the writer for me'. I held my pen in readiness for transcribing the inspiring thoughts which seemed to stir my very being. But the subject would not come. After half an hour's illegible scribbling, varied by geometrical designs, a great light dawned on me. I saw at once that my fellow-passengers in the tram-car had again rendered me a signal service. They had talked of free political institutions; it was for me, now, to write about them. Here I can say the apt word which will be taken up in those numberless homes where now it is but silently felt. And here will I unfold a tale such as was never told, for it is the tale of man's endeavour on earth.

I was gathering the threads of a thousand imposing associations which came crowding upon me when I realised that this subject would never do. For if I but uttered the word of wisdom, quite a number of politicians would find their occupation gone. They would discover in their followers a sudden development of the historic sense which is fatal to shallow enthusiasms. Even the magic word liberty will avail them nothing with men who have learnt the outstanding lesson of History, that freedom and order have very seldom been reconciled, and that 'most of those who have the word liberty on their lips are despots at heart'. I see politician after politician go down before audiences to whom I had brought home 'the desolating sentence of Gibbon that history is indeed little more than the register of the crimes, follies and misfortunes of mankind'. No, the editor would never expose himself to the fury of unemployed politicians. 'Beware the awful avalanche,' I hear him mutter to himself as he consigns my cogent discourse to the dust-heap of rejected articles.

After the first feelings of bitterness at this unexpected rebuff had passed, I smiled. Why, I said, if I can't fight the politician out of the field I can laugh him out. He, poor man, has never known what laughter is, and will be taken unawares by this insidious onset. For what a fine comedy can be made of the brawls of the big-endians and the little-endians ! And what respect can they hope to command once they have been held up as mere puppets, actors in a comic drama who take themselves too seriously ? Yes their audiences will dissolve in laughter, and they will awake one day better and humbler men.

But as this great comedy developed I saw clearly that it would be a tragedy in the end. For if my first impulse was to laugh at the blind presumptions of men, my second was to weep over them. Self-centredness is the source both of comedy and tragedy, and often we laugh only to conceal our tears. And here I could not help musing on the familiar problem of man's destiny on earth : how he comes into it, and how little he can make of it, and how he leaves it for he knows not what. I recalled a famous passage which compares the life of man to a shadow, the shadow not of a tree or a tower that standeth but of a bird in its flight. 'Away flieth the bird, and there is neither bird nor shadow.' We may admit this to be a superb crystalization of our inmost feelings but serving only to deepen the mystery of things. For what is the meaning of this flight? The literature of power and the literature of thought bewilder us by their conflicting answers. Which one shall we accept and act upon? But these queries carry me dangerously near philosophy, that searching of the head and the heart which mankind at large professes to treat with contempt. Besides, even the thoughtful reader may complain that he is in no humour for a searching of the heart in this season of joy and good cheer. Be it so; but as I gave up this congenial inquiry, I lingered for a while over those terrible landscapes of Hardy in which man is seen to be but an insignificant phantasm flitting across the unchanging face of nature. And Hardy's central faith may be right, after all. The early cheerfulness of man's childhood is gone beyond recall; his face is seamed with ages of strife, and pain, and defeat; and he looks through eyes dimmed by suffering and sorrow. But he has a beauty of his own, a haunting beauty. And there I may leave him.

It now strikes two in the night. All is quiet except for the merry play of rats in the adjoining lane. A mass of writing lies before me, but the article remains unwritten. In my attempts to please the reader I find that there is no subject that will please him. But perhaps he will like to see the tangible record of such strenuous endeavours after his delight and so this mass of writing may as well go to the editor.

The writing has gone and now I am at the Club with Boswell for my companion.

Nusserwan

Homi

With father on an outing. Homi on the left

Brothers ordained priests. Homi on the right

The Seervai family with Meherbai's cousin Dhunbai Wadia. Homi on mother's lap

Seervai receiving the Padma Vibhushan award at the hands of President V. V. Giri

Meherbai Seervai with Homi (left) and Nusserwan

Seervai receiving the Dadabhai Naoroji Prize

Seervai and Nani Palkhivala 1995

Seervai and Rustomji Andhyarujina 1986

Seervai with grandson Jehangir P. Madon 1983

Seervai with J. P. Thacker at 80th Birthday Felicitation

Seervai's famous birdie whistle

Seervai happy with grandchildren Shirin and Cyrus Pocha and Jehangir P. Madon. Portrait of J. C. P. d'Andrade on wall

Seervai's family picture by Hamilton Studios 1992 (from left) Shirin P. Madon with Sherna and Jehangir, Homi, Mona and Navroz Seervai with Shanoor and Riyad, Feroza, Meher and Jehangir Pocha with Cyrus and Shirin [Pheroze Madon not in picture as he was abroad]

TRIBUTES BY SEERVAI

THE BOMBAY LAW REPORTER - 1898-1973

A Recollection

More than twenty years were to pass before the Bombay Law Reporter resumed publication. This Recollection of Seervai's tells us what a loss its cessation was. I draw particular attention to the last para and the last sentence.

My acquaintance with the Bombay Law Reporter began in 1927, when I joined the Government Law School. But it was the journal part which first attracted my attention. Articles by competent lawyers, addresses delivered by eminent judges, like Lord Macmillan's address on "The Art of Writing a Judgment" and "Gleanings" from two versatile writers L.J, and S.J, who later turned out to be — the Law Journal and the Solicitor's Journal — gripped my attention. In the pages of the back numbers of the journal I became acquainted with the great judges and great lawyers of the past who had brought fame and distinction to the Bombay High Court. The tributes paid by the Chief Justice, Sir Norman Macleod, and by the Advocate-General, Jamshedji Kanga, to Inverarity have lingered in my memory ever since. I understood the admiration which the Bar felt for Inverarity when I read the "Advocate-General's description of him as a lawyer of sure and enormous knowledge on whose mind as on a photographic plate facts fell in their true legal relations."

It was only when I joined the Bar in 1932 that I came to know the spirit in which its founder editors Ratanlal and Dhirajlal had launched their Bombay Law Reporter on its long and successful career. Ratanlal and Dhirajlal had the gift of friendship : both had the humility of scholars who had written standard legal textbooks, for their *Law of Crimes, the Law of Evidence and the Law of Torte* had long been standard books. Besides, they possessed the friendly feeling with which senior members of the Bar extend a guiding hand to raw juniors. I treasured their friendship, and profited by their talk on fine points of legal scholarship. I learnt also what it meant to report month by month the decisions of a great High Court — a meticulous attention to details; attention to the language of the oral judgments which those who delivered them did not always correct; personal attention to the accurate reporting of counsel's arguments in important cases and, finally the preparation of head notes. As the years rolled by, they were ably assisted by Ratanlal's son, Manhar, the present editor of the Bombay Law Reporter.

The friendship which Ratanlal and Dhirajlal showed to young lawyers brought them capable young advocates who volunteered, from time to time, to report arguments of Counsel in important cases when the editors' pre-occupations prevented them from attending to the case personally. For example, those who read the special bench judgment in *Fram Balsara* v. *State of Bombay* 52 Bom. L.R. 799 will not know that on the suggestion of the Bench, counsel for Balsara argued new points in his reply to the reply — but they will find the new arguments recorded in the Bombay Law Reporter.

This invaluable feature of the Bombay Law Reporter is no longer available to the readers of the Bombay Law Reporter — a misfortune which it shares with unofficial and official series alike, including the official Supreme Court Reports. Rising costs and the changed social conditions at the Bar have made it impossible for unofficial Law Reports to report arguments of counsel; and it would seem that the resources of Government have proved equally inadequate to the task.

But the pioneering spirit which inspired the founders has remained with the Bombay Law Reporter. A new feature was introduced some years ago which provided the reader with notes on Recent Supreme Court Decisions.

I would not like to conclude this Recollection without reference to one striking incident. Several young lawyers approached me with the proposal that I should persuade the editor of the Bombay Law Reporter to introduce a new feature by publishing critical Notes on recent decisions on the lines of such critical Notes in the Law Quarterly Review. They pressed upon me the imperative need of such critical notes for the orderly development of case law, and they promised that they would themselves undertake the task. Armed with this youthful mandate I met Dhirajlal, then well past ninety years of age. His eyes gleamed with delight as he heard my proposal and he instantly agreed to introduce the new feature — he said that the young men were clearly right. If critical Notes on recent decisions have not become a regular feature of the Bombay Law Reporter it was not because of the failure of the veteran editor to keep his promise but because of the failure of the young men to keep theirs.

MOTILAL SETALVAD

In The Seervai Legacy I published Seervai's speech at the Golden Jubilee of Motilal — 50 years at the Bar.

The speech here published was made at the unveiling of Motilal's portrait in the Bar Library, on 1st October, 1963.

The reader will see how Seervai could speak on the same person, but make a very different speech each time.

That is because he gave much thought and time to all his speeches.

My Lord the Chief Justice, Judges of the High Court, Members of the Bar, Ladies and Gentlemen:

It is a great pleasure to me, on behalf of the Setalvad Memorial Committee to invite the learned Chief Justice to unveil the portrait of one of the most distinguished lawyers who practised in this Court, Mr. Setalvad. He completed 50 years of practice in 1961 and it was felt by the Bar throughout India that a Memorial should be raised to him. Various High Courts set up committees, and with his own approval we decided that after a portrait had been painted, the rest of the funds should be handed over to the Central Committee in Delhi. Accordingly, a portrait has been painted by an eminent artist Mr. Deouskar. You will see the result when it is unveiled. The committee is thankful to all of you for coming here on this occasion and to My Lord the Chief Justice for readily agreeing to unveil the portrait.

As I look around me at the portraits which are already there, it is remarkable what a wealth of legal talent and other talent there is. It started with the portrait of Mr. Inverarity, who by common consent was the ablest lawyer, but never became a Judge or a law officer. There are two other distinguished lawyers who had taken to politics and distinguished themselves in various fields, Sir Chimanlal Setalvad and Mr. Bhulabhai Desai: Sir Chimanlal being an educationist, Vice-Chancellor, Corporator, leader of a party, distinguished advocate, for part of his time, a Judge, and Mr. Desai an acting Advocate-General for a little while and later on the leader of a very big party. We then come to three lawyers who are lawyers pure and simple, Sir Dinshaw Mulla,

Sir Jamshedji Kanga and Vicaji Taraporewalla. All of them held judicial office and law offices for some time, Sir Jamshedji holding Law Office with great distinction for 13 years, Sir Dinshaw Mulla had a career which was unique: Solicitor, advocate, acting Advocate-General, acting Judge, Law Member of the Viceroy's Executive Council, Member of the Judicial Committee of the Privy Council, writer of books read everywhere, winning for Bombay, for the first time, the Blue Ribbon of Legal Scholarship by his Tagore Law Lectures on the Law of Insolvency. It is this distinguished company, of which any country may be proud, that Mr. Setalvad enters today and even to that company he adds distinction because there is something fresh which he adds to it. Unlike the men whom I have mentioned, he became the Attorney-General for India, an office first created in 1950. He resembled Sir Dinshaw Mulla in that rather late in life he turned to scholarship, edited Mulla's Contract Act at the ripe age of seventy, and is now busy editing Mulla's Transfer of Property Act. And just as Sir Dinshaw Mulla won the Blue Ribbon of Indian Scholarship, Motilal won for India the Blue Ribbon of English Scholarship, being invited to deliver the Hamlyn Lectures in England. When it is realised that the previous lectures were by Lord Denning, Lord Devlin, Lord MacDermott, Prof. Cheshire, Prof. Hamson, all scholars of the highest distinction, the honour is something of which any one may be proud. It is a fact which I cannot help noticing that none of these eminent Lawyers I have been speaking of became a permanent Judge of the High Court of Bombay. But life is full of surprises, and to Motilal Setalvad was assigned the task of sitting in judgment upon Judges and the Bar in the labours which he undertook while holding the great office of Attorney-General, namely as President of the Law Commission. It is difficult to say which of his services will be most highly appreciated. Speaking for myself, I think that the work he did for the Law Commission as its President is outstanding. There was every sort of pressure not to tell the truth. In fact some members of the Commission inquired, "Can we say all these things about Judges and is it proper and respectable?", and the answer which they got was "If the Law Commission cannot tell the truth, who can?" It is to this distinguished lawyer that the Bar desires to pay its tribute by presenting this portrait to the High Court. Chief Justice Chagla unveiling the portrait of Sir Jamshedji dwelt nostalgically on the past and spoke of the shadows falling on the Bar. I would like to end on a more optimistic note. These portraits are an inspiration, but they ought also to be a challenge, namely, are we going to fall very far short of what these great men have done before us? It is true that the tendencies are discouraging, but the Law Commission has indicated that there are counter tendencies which can be set in motion provided one is sufficiently resolute and does not attach too much importance to human frailty, but attaches once in a while some importance to human strength.

In conclusion, I should like to thank all the members of the Bar who have contributed to the memorial fund, to the artist who, I gather, has done extremely good work, and once again to thank My Lord the Chief Justice for readily consenting to unveil the portrait. May I now request him to unveil it.

JUSTICE M. C. CHAGLA

Seervai admired Chagla enormously and was equally fond of him.

In The Seervai Legacy I published two speeches of Seervai's on Chagla — References in Court at his retirement and at his death. The speeches were quite different, as may be expected of Seervai. This third speech will be seen to be different again. The speech here published was made when the memorial Freize outside Chagla's Court was opened.

My Lord the Chief Justice, Honourable Judges, my brothers on the Chagla Memorial Trust, Members of the Bar, Ladies and Gentlemen:

It is a great honour to be invited to speak on this historic occasion. As the learned Advocate-General and my Lord the Chief Justice have reminded us, Chagla assumed office on Independence Day. And this day reminds us that we are all citizens of India, that whatever State we may belong to, whatever religion we profess, whatever community, caste, section or creed claims us as its own, we are first and last citizens of India. India has only one soil, the soil of India, and we are all children of that soil. Independence reminds us that we must so bear ourselves that just as a Roman of old said, and was proud to say, "I am a citizen of Rome", so also we must all be proud to say, "we are citizens of India", or if you would prefer a more modern example, then, as a great American said: "My country, right or wrong, if right to keep right, and if wrong, to set right". Chagla's life and work was a variation of this one simple theme.

I believe I am the only lawyer in practice who met Chagla at the bar in 1932 and worked with him in the Bar Association and its various Committees. We soon became friends and I met him almost every day. I saw him when he waited for briefs which did not come, and then I saw him on the full tide of a fast rising practice, when, at the call of duty, he became a judge of this Court and later a Chief Justice. My admiration for his work as a judge and Chief Justice is unbounded, though not uncritical, and I gave expression to that admiration in a reference to him in this very Court when he retired in 1958. The reference was attended by a number of people unprecedented in the history of this Court. This room was packed to capacity, the gallery was packed to capacity, the corridors outside the galleries and the Court were packed to capacity. That was the tribute which people wanted to pay to the greatest judge this High Court has produced since Independence.

To those of us, who heard that reference, the echoes of his voice seem still to linger in this Court, as he spoke of the work which he had done for 11 long years as Chief Justice of this Court. He recalled that when he became Chief Justice, he made a prayer that he should be able to uphold the traditions of this Court. Well, his prayer was answered and more than answered, for not only did he uphold the traditions of this Court, but he left this Court with its dignity, its authority and the absolute confidence of the public in the Court, enhanced.

As we dispersed after the reference, we said to ourselves that the reference was a fitting climax to his finest hour, the eleven long years during which he had been Chief Justice of this Court. We did not know, we could not have dreamt that his finest hour was to come much later. It came in 1975 when the Emergency was proclaimed. He was an old man nearing his 75th birthday; his health had been undermined by two severe heart attacks, and he believed that the third was not far off. But the Emergency seemed to have rejuvenated him, or in the words of his friend, Jai Prakash Narayan, he showed "the youthful vigour of a full blooded crusader". It was difficult to state the truth in those days but he stated the truth without regard to consequences to himself, for he knew that without courage there can be no truth and without truth there cannot be any virtue.

He delivered a speech in Ahmedabad which he himself said he was proud of, and which is one of the finest speeches delivered by any citizen or certainly by himself. In that speech, he stood up for freedom and liberty and justice for which he had stood up all his life. Reading and re-reading the speech, I would like to read to you the concluding portion in which he said:

> "I refuse to believe that my country which has had a civilization going back to centuries, my country where the Constitution was drafted for a democratic State, will always remain in the shadow of dictatorship. There is a saying in English that 'when the night is darkest, the dawn is not far'. I see the night

very dark. I am an old man and I have not got long to live. But, you, younger people will see the dawn. The dawn is bound to come. This country cannot go under. For thousands of years we have survived invasions, we have survived all sorts of troubles and I think that we will survive both the Prime Minister and her dictatorship."

On the statue which my Lord the Chief Justice is going to unveil, we have put the words : "A great judge, a great citizen and above all a great human being". He was all that and more. But reading and re-reading the concluding words of his speech, it seems to me that the inscription which he would have prized the most can be given in one simple sentence: "He never lost faith in his country". Well, the magnificent ending is only a variation on that simple theme.

It seems to me that the two finest periods of his life sprang from the same source. He believed, rightly, that without freedom, there can be no justice, and without justice there can be no freedom. As Chief Justice, he bent all his energies to see that this Court became a great Court of Justice and a guardian of fundamental rights and freedom. When the Emergency came, he saw, equally rightly, that without freedom there can be no justice and you saw that exemplified as he pointed out in what he described as "the effete and subservient Supreme Court".

Well, you will notice that in dealing with the two finest periods of his life, I have leaped over a period of about 17 years. After he ceased to be a judge, he held high offices. He was Ambassador to the United States, High Commissioner in the U.K., he became a Minister of Education and a Minister of External Affairs. I pass this period by because I am not competent to judge his work. Besides, my learned friend, Mr. Palkhivala, who himself has held the distinguished office of Ambassador to the United States, is better qualified than anyone of us to tell us of the value of Chagla's work in the United States.

After he resigned from office, he made a decision to practise before the Supreme Court, a decision which caused some controversy. This is not the time, or the place, to go into that controversy, but once he decided to join the bar, he devoted all his energies to the affairs of the Bar. He was President of the Supreme Court Bar Association for two years ending 1st April, 1973. However, it fell to him to lead the opposition to the supersession of three judges of the Supreme Court on the 25th April, 1973. He took his stand on the independence of the judiciary, which he said had been gravely assailed, and he did it regardless of consequences to himself. How unpleasant those consequences were and could be is recorded by Chagla when he said that Chief Justice Ray was vindictive and rude to those members of the Bar who had taken an active part in the agitation against the supersession of judges. So, as he began, so he showed in this crisis that the independence of the judiciary was with him a fundamental article of faith and belief.

Well, I have spoken of the great things which Chagla did, but I have not spoken of the great man that Chagla was. Anyone who met him could see that he possessed kindliness and grace, the result of a broad and humane culture. He had innate courtesy and consideration for all, particularly for those whom fortune or fate had treated harshly or unkindly. But I am absolved from drawing a picture of his personality because he has done it with remarkable candour and power in a Chapter of his Autobiography entitled "Personal". It is the finest chapter in that book, and in it he pays a moving tribute to his wife, which probably is the finest thing he ever wrote. On this occasion, she requires an honourable mention, not only for the support which she gave to him in his ardous work as a Chief Justice, but also because of the pains which she took to preserve every newspaper cutting, every document, every letter which referred to the manifold activities of her husband. Without her loving care, his great autobiography could never have been written.

Let me briefly tell you that you should read this Chapter and I believe that you will rise from reading it, refreshed and strengthened. He says that he had been all his life a serious person, that reason was always too much with him, that he was denied the consolations of faith and he says that he had not planned for old age and so he had let go by the pleasures and joys of youth. He says the one thing that life had taught him was compassion and kindliness towards others and he says that after all, all that a man can do is to do the right as he sees it and leave the rest to chance or God or whatever powers there be.

I would like to say that this Chapter takes too pessimistic a view, and is the result of a passing mood of depression caused by the loss of his wife, which left a wound which time did not heal. But it seems to me that had he to live his life all over again, he would equally choose the straight and narrow path, and his Epilogue on the Emergency and the "Emasculation of the Judiciary" shows he would take an even narrower and straighter path if that was demanded of him.

I think if my learned friend Palkhivala and I have been asked to speak today, it is because we knew Chagla personally and I think it would not be inappropriate if I spoke personally about him.

When he died, his loss was, so far as I am concerned, irreparable. As long as he was alive, in all questions of doubts and difficulties — and a writer who ventures to criticize judgments of the Supreme Court and the High Courts must have doubts and difficulties — I used to walk up to him, in the sure belief that I would get wise and truthful advice. I remember one occasion when I carried to him what I had written in criticizing the style of a judge of the Supreme Court, and what I had written on the injury done to the Supreme Court by judges persisting in error which had been demonstrated. He went through what I had written line by line and word by word. We had a discussion at the end of it, and I asked him: "Is there anything you would like me to change?" and the answer was : "No, what you have said is true and it must be published as it stands."

One other thing about him I must mention, and he himself has recorded it in the Epilogue. By the by, I ought to tell you, that the Epilogue tells in its sombre pages his work during the Emergency, though in the end, the triumph of his convictions and beliefs clearly appears. He claimed freedom of thought and expression for himself and the right he claimed for himself as his birthright, he conceded to others. He knew, and he has said so, that he and I did not see eye to eye on many matters, but that did not affect our personal friendship. Honest opinion freely expressed, secured his respect and we remained friends to the end, though I had publicly criticised two of the fashionable theories which he referred to : The inarticulate major premise and the felt necessities of the time. I did so because in the hands of lesser men than Chagla, they have done, and are doing, incalculable harm to the administration of justice.

One final word, because I have taken enough of your time. What would he have felt about the judiciary in India had he returned to the scene of his efforts? It is idle to pretend that the Courts command the confidence which they did before. We want, according to Chagla, a strong and respected Bench and a strong and respected Bar. But an eminent judge of the Supreme Court has told us that the relations between the Bench and the Bar have reached their lowest point. Rumours, canards, character assassination, he said, flourished in the grape vine. I regret the loss of Chagla because I would have greatly desired that he should read what I have written on the work of the Supreme Court, though I believe it would have met with his approval. But may I on this day say that we do not sincerely pay tribute to Chagla unless each one of us, lawyer, judge, asks himself : What are we doing to have a strong and respected bar, what are we doing to have a strong and respected Judiciary? Internal divisions, divisions on idological lines, judges attacking their brother judges in language that can only be described as unseemly, is in my judgment destructive of the judiciary which Chagla built up and which he fought for. But like him, I am an optimist. If he did not lose faith in his country, he would not have lost faith in the judiciary, and he would have exhorted them to remember that the cause for which all judges stand, all lawyers stand, is greater than themselves and that they ought so to behave themselves that the respect for the Bar and the Bench are restored.

There is one tribute which I have left out because the tributes which I have mentioned were paid by members of the Bar on the occasion when he died and on the occasion when he retired. But there is one tribute from a distinguished brother judge, which strikes so true a note, that I must read it to you. It came too late, for it came when Chief Justice Gajendragadkar's *Autobiography* appeared in 1983. He said:

> "Chagla was endowed with almost all the qualities necessary to make a brilliant lawyer, a successful judge and then as the events proved to the satisfaction of everyone, a successful, efficient, powerful, popular and independent Chief Justice. He was a very good leader of his team, helped to create a democratic, friendly, co-operative atmosphere amongst his colleagues, tried his best and succeeded in carrying his colleagues with him in all major administrative decisions. So far as judicial work was concerned, he was undoubtedly a judge of the first order. No one could say that Nehru's choice was not fully justified and it was best proved when, during Chagla's tenure, the Bombay High Court retained its prestigious position in the judiciary of India."

I would sum up what I have said with some beautiful lines which were applied to a great man of the 17th Century and which are applicable to Chagla:

> "He was beside of spirit passing great,
> Valiant, and learn'd, and liberal as the sun,
> Spoke and writ sweetly, or of learned subjects,
> Or of the discipline of public weals;
> And 'twas Mahomadali Chagla".

JUSTICE P. B. GAJENDRAGADKAR

Welcome Speech by Mr. H. M. Seervai, Advocate-General, at the Bombay Bar Association's Party in honour of Mr. Justice P. B. Gajendragadkar Chief Justice of India on 29.3.64.

My Lord the Chief Justice, Ladies and Gentlemen,

It is a pleasure and a privilege to welcome Mr. Justice Gajendragadkar in our midst, to offer him our heartiest congratulations and to tell him how greatly we rejoice that he has become the Chief Justice of India. In welcoming him we are welcoming not a stranger but a distinguished member of the Bombay Bar and a judge who adorned the bench of our High Court for eleven years. Today is a day of reunion, for this gathering holds many of his friends who have come to do him honour.

It is not necessary for me to describe the quality of his work as a Judge of our High Court because the large gathering which assembled in the Central Court in January, 1957 and the tributes paid to him there bear unmistakable testimony to the high quality of his work.

In a thoughtful and moving Inaugural Address he expressed his regret that he never sat as a judge on the Original Side. May I say that the Original Side shares this regret? I say so because judges of the Appellate Side who came to the Original Side rather liked it and to many it has come as an agreeable revelation. For till they came to us they saw us darkly through the refracting medium of the dual system. A closer look showed us as we really are, and the system to be what it is: a powerful instrument for the adequate preparation of cases and for their effective presentation in Court.

However, Mr. Justice Gajendragadkar met us when he was a member of one of the strongest constitutional benches in our court — that consisting of himself and Chief Justice Chagla. Day after day Senior and Junior Advocates of the Original Side appeared before him. I know that it was a happy experience for the Advocates and I believe that it was a happy experience for him.

Mr. Justice Cardozo has said that a judge should never lose touch with the Bar and Mr. Justice Gajendragadkar said much the same thing when he bid us farewell in 1957. He himself has never lost that touch as his presence among us today clearly shows. But he cannot keep in touch with us if we do not tell him our hopes, our expectations, our fears and our difficulties.

Till he became the Chief Justice he has had to discharge the heavy responsibilities which fall on a judge of the Supreme Court. The time has not come to evaluate his work in that Court. But his past colleagues on the Bench are under no such restraint as we impose on ourselves at the Bar; and a retired Judge of the Supreme Court, for whom I have unbounded admiration, has been known to declare that in Mr. Justice

Gajendragadkar he had one of the ablest colleagues he ever had on the bench.

Now that he has become the Chief Justice he will be called upon to discharge duties more exacting and more onerous than any he has hitherto been called upon to discharge. For not only does the Chief Justice set the tone of the Supreme Court Bench and the Bar; his presence is felt on the Bench and Bar of every court. In this great task we wish him every success; and if our efforts can assist him ever so little in that task he knows that they are at his disposal. For the cause of which the Supreme Court is the guardian is after all also our cause: and the cause of every citizen of India — an incorrupt, efficient and fearless administration of justice.

His public pronouncements, and his pronouncements from the Bench, show that he is aware of the grave problems we are facing today and is ready to meet them with an open mind which is full of resource. It is a pity that his inaugural address, of which I spoke earlier, is not easily available; for it shows the spirit in which he will discharge the functions of his high office. It seems to me that in that address he has put his finger on the greatest single handicap judges in India suffer today — an almost complete absence of competent and informed professional criticism of their judgments. In that address he said that wise judges welcomed criticism and never misunderstood it; and he appealed to the Bombay Bar to take a more active part in the affairs of the Law Institute one of whose objects is to provide a forum for such criticism. In echoing that appeal may I say that it will come to naught unless scholarly and learned criticism is treated with respect by the Bench and is not brushed aside as the work of "mere theorists". The love and respect which the Chief Justice bears to learning and scholarship are well known and I believe that his approach and his appeal will bear fruit.

In a recent judgment of the Supreme Court, in language of unmistakable strength, Mr. Justice Gajendragadkar has taken a firm stand on what the Bar looks upon as the greatest reproach to the administration of justice today. A High Court judge disregarded the plain requirements of the law because they did not square with his ideas of fair play and equity. Mr. Justice Gajendragadkar reminded him, and other like-minded judges, that Courts administer justice according to law; that however important fair play and equity may be, they must yield to the clear and express provisions of the law. He said that otherwise it would introduce in such decisions "an element of disconcerting unpredictability which is usually associated with gambling, and that is a reproach which the judicial process must constantly avoid". If he will permit me to say so, I think that these words ought to be framed and placed in every court and before every judge. They have been uttered not a day too soon; for the reproach of which the Chief Justice spoke is on the increase and is driving even highly trained lawyers very nearly to despair. We may be sure that the warning he has given will be resolutely enforced.

I have said enough to show that on some of the central issues of the day the Chief Justice has taken a firm stand on the side of right. There is one topic to which I would like to refer because it is of great importance to us and is of great importance to him as the head of the Judiciary and that is the passion for disposals so fashionable today. To us at the Bar judicial medals seem reserved not for judgments which deal with fact and law with satisfying finality; nor for a demeanour on the bench which makes even the losing party feel that justice has been done. They seem reserved for so many disposals per day or per month without too close a scrutiny of how they are obtained, or of what festering sense of injustice they have left behind. If I have ventured to refer to this topic it is because anguished voices of litigants in the Courts of first instance are rarely heard in the highest court of appeal, and because it is necessary that the Chief Justice of India should not be left uninformed of what is common knowledge in every Bar room and every association.

The Americans have a happy phrase for describing a period of judicial history by calling it after the Chief Justice of the Supreme Court and they speak of the "Marshall Era" or the "Tanney Era" and so on. Well, in that happy phrase we have entered on the Gajendrgadkar era, and on behalf of all of us I can wish him nothing better than to wish that the era will be a bright one, that it will add lustre and glory to the Supreme Court and will enhance its dignity, and that it will see the fulfillment of his visions and his hopes as a judge. For the accomplishment of this grand design, on behalf of us all I wish him health and strength and happiness.

G. N. JOSHI

Court Reference to G. N. Joshi, Advocate

May it please you My Lords,

On behalf of the Bombay Bar Association and on my own behalf, I would like to associate myself with all that has been said by my Lord the Chief Justice and by my learned friend, the Advocate-General.

In G. N. Joshi's death, I have lost a personal friend. I met him for the first time in 1939 under queer circumstances. I had assisted Sir Chimanlal Setalvad in drawing up a Memorandum objecting to the proposed abolition of the dual system as beyond the power of the State Government. The Memorandum went to Motilal Setalvad as Advocate-General, and he passed it on to G. N. Joshi and asked him to discuss it with me. Joshi met me and said: "I am quite clear that the Memorandum is wrong, but give me a day's time." He came the next day, and we discussed the matter and I made some answer to his criticism. But I realised at once that he was a complete master of Constitutional Law, and I expressed that view when we entertained him on his completing 50 years at the Bar. I said that his knowledge of Constitutional Law was second to none in this country, because he could deal with any new tendency or any new problem by fitting it into the existing jigsaw puzzle. Odd as it may seem, Constitutional Law was not my favourite subject for the First LL.B., and, therefore, I did not read his books till I appeared for Government in Constitutional cases.

The glittering prizes which he won to which my Lord the Chief Justice has referred, were a presage of what was to come. His book — *The Wealth of India*, written in collaboration with Prof. Wadia, commanded respect. And when he went to the Second Round Table Conference in 1932, the greatest economist of the day, John Maynard Keynes, offered to him a Lecturer's post in one of the Cambridge Colleges. It was a matter of good fortune for him and for our country that the offer was declined.

My Lord the Chief Justice has said that everybody knew at the Bar that Joshi was a favourite Junior of Motilal Setalvad. I shared that knowledge, but when I met Joshi, I realised that it was not merely favour. Joshi's joining Motilal Setalvad's Chamber in 1932 was a happy event for himself, for Motilal and for the Bar, because the two of them made a formidable combination, and achieved results which neither of them could have achieved singly. Motilal's' ability to see a point quickly, and to present his argument persuasively to the Court, was supplemented by the immense knowledge of Constitutional law which Joshi brought to bear on the matter. I have been reading Motilal's *Autobiography*. In it he has paid a great tribute to Joshi, and has said that when he became Advocate-General, he would have felt lost but for the very great help given to him by G. N. Joshi.

I have read Joshi's book on Constitutional Law because we used to exchange books which each of us had written. He was kind enough to say that his book was written mainly for students and for the intelligent general reader, whereas my book was written on very different lines. I valued his opinion, because he was not given to flattery. He was open to new ideas and was ready to revise his own ideas.

I am personally convinced that had he tried to master the art of persuasive speech in Courts, he would have succeeded. But he had a Professor's contempt for intelligence less active than his own. It is reported of Sir Frederick Pollock that he opened an Appeal before the Privy Council to which there was a reply. He did not reply to it, and when asked why he had not done so, he said — "the reply was so full of obvious fallacies that it required no reply". At times Joshi got irritated and annoyed, not against the Judge, but because a point which was clear to Joshi was not clear to the Judge. If a trap question was put to him, as trap questions had been put to him at times, instead of quietly giving an answer by dismantling the trap, he would say : "Your Lordship will not put me a trap question".

He had intellectual interests of the widest kind and that was a common bond between us. It was a joy to me to see him on Saturdays reading at lunch time the *Times Literary Supplement, The New Statesman and Nation,* and *Punch;* I used to cross over to him and we discussed with pleasure all sorts of subjects; for he was willing to teach and he was willing to learn.

There was another bond between us. His nephew, our friend Ramanlal Joshi, had joined my Chambers and G. N. Joshi was happy to see the rapid progress his nephew was making at the Bar. He was proud of his daughter to whom his intellect had passed in full measure. And he was proud of his nephew who carried on the tradition of honest, straightforward and able advocacy at the Bar.

My Lord the Chief Justice has spoken of Joshi's practice for 20 years before the Income-tax Bench. It seemed to me unfortunate that he should have got involved in Income-tax matters, because what the Income-tax Bench gained, the Constitutional Courts lost. For, however great his knowledge of Income-tax, his knowledge of Constitutional law was immeasurably greater.

During the last few years he suffered from a grave infirmity, because his hearing had been seriously affected. And it was a matter of regret to some of us that we could not visit him because communication with him was possible only in writing. Looking back over his life, I think that as his departure drew near, he could have truthfully said of himself: "I have fought a good fight, I have finished my course, I have kept my faith".

With these words, my Lords, I would like to convey to the members of his family the esteem in which we held him during his life, and the esteem in which we hold him after his death.

R. J. JOSHI

Court Reference to R. J. Joshi, Advocate

May it please you My Lords,

On behalf of the learned Advocate-General and on behalf of the Bar, I have been asked to associate myself with the words which have fallen from Your Lordship and I need hardly add that I associate myself with the moving words which have fallen from Your Lordship.

By a strange irony, we assembled in this very room on the 19th June to mourn the death of Mr. G. N. Joshi. He had died full of years and honour, but he could little have dreamt that his nephew would pass away so soon.

My Lords, as My Lord the Chief Justice has said, Joshi overcame severe educational handicaps. He has recorded in a brief note which he has made that when he joined the Elphinstone College, he found it difficult to speak in English, but with the gifts which he possessed and his inexhaustible industry, he passed with a high First Class in Mathematics. He had a distinguished career in Law and in a moment of inspiration, he just walked into the Chamber of Sir Jamshedji Kanga and said: "I want to read with you". Kanga was a shrewd judge of character. The smiling face, the sparkling eyes, the broad forehead made Kanga realise that here was a presage of future greatness. When a medal had to be presented by the Chief Justice, Kanga, as Your Lordships might expect, accompained him, introduced him to the Chief Justice and when the medal was pinned on, he said that Joshi will be a rising member of the Bar. Within a month or two, Joshi proved his mettle, and I remember Kanga walking into the Chamber saying in his loud voice, "This little boy, Joshi, even at the last moment, he finds the crucial case" and in one of the biggest cases before Mr. Justice Blagden, Kanga openly said that he owed the reference to one crucial case, to Joshi.

He appeared for the Advocates O.S. Examination. He and other candidates were in great trepidation that the examiners (who are not unnaturally maligned) will never pass five students at the first shot. In fact, all of them passed with outstanding marks. He worked for Sir Jamshedji Kanga to Kanga's satisfaction. I do not know at what point of time, he gravitated towards me. I think, within five or six years, we began to work together. It was a joy to me when he was briefed in any case with me, because, as My Lord the Chief Justice has said, his preparation was thorough and one could trust his judgment as to what a case had really decided. But My Lord I would like to refer to the turning point in his career. There was a famous matrimonial case: *Nandini Mehta* v. *Bhagwan Mehta,* son and daughter-in-law of a very rich mill magnate and industrialist; and he was given a docket of four guineas to find out authorities. He did his work, as you would expect, thoroughly, and he was not paid for conferences, but he had a right, as my junior, to attend, and I saw that the client was visibly impressed, and what is more important, the solicitor Petigara was being impressed. Joshi had two paid briefs. I have never made my junior return a paid brief, but I told him that his work was being so much appreciated that I would ask him not to leave this Court, "because when the case is won, as assuredly it will be, work will flow in". He attended every conference. It was made a little difficult by the Chief Justice telling us in our opening that if possible he would decide against us, because he knew the position of women. Joshi's nerves did not give way, neither did mine. The case was won, the prophecy made good — work began to flow in from Mulla & Mulla and there was no looking back. I think, it ought to be mentioned that he had obstruction from a quarter from which it was least expected. One Judge of the High Court for reasons of his own, publicly insulted him, offended him in the hope that a rising lawyer would be put down. But he didn't know the tough fibre of which Joshi was made, nor did he realise that the whole Kanga Chamber was there to support him. My Lord, when I shifted as Kanga's neighbour in 1954, getting Coyajee's Chamber, we used to go back to Kanga. We had the pleasantest association, and when I became Advocate-General, he came to my Chamber. I think, I can say truthfully that not once was any harsh word said by one to the other. We discussed things, we held strong views, but never was there any personal difference, and I looked upon him as though we were members of the same family.

My Lord, a time came when he was in very large practice and he and Atul Setalvad said to me, "Do you mind if we occupy the Chamber of Motilal because it is being offered to us." I said, "Not only do I not mind, your decision is the right one because once I cease to be the Advocate-General I'll be without a Chamber myself. So, your decision is the right one." But for my absorption in my book, a book which I used to tell him had done him a serious disservice, because thereafter he ceased to think out questions of constitutional law; he said to me, laughing, "why should I take the trouble when the argument is ready to hand". It was characteristic of him. So My Lord, this was his capacity at the Bar.

I have seen him arguing cases in the High Court, in the Supreme Court. He argued, as Your Lordship has said, with firmness, with tenacity. He was not easily put down. He disliked a scene in Court, as Kanga disliked it, as I disliked it. But his response was different. If it was forced on him, he would not go back. I remember his coming and telling me with laughter that as soon as he opened an appeal, a Judge lectured him for 40 minutes on what the correct law was and what the law ought to be, at the end of which Joshi said : "My Lord, I want to cite a case". There was no answer to the case, and the Judge said, "Why didn't you tell me at once?" Joshi replied, "Well, I could only tell you if you would let me". This was the man at the Bar. He won universal respect and, what is more, universal affection. He endeared himself to his colleagues and his loss will be felt as a personal loss by a large number of people with whom he worked.

But My Lord, more even than the lawyer was the man himself. As a son, as a brother, as a husband, as a father, he walked with firm and unfaltering step, and in his personal life, he felt no temptation to be a man of the world in the sinister sense of the term, namely, a person who must share what is supposed to be common frailties and common vices in order to prove his manhood.

Your Lordship is right in saying that our thoughts turn at this moment to the members of his family in a loss which is irreparable but which is made more painful by the manner of his death. But My Lord, I think, it will be some comfort to them to know that their loss is shared by a large number of people, and when time has softened the sense of loss, they will think proudly of a man who was not only a great lawyer but was very great as a man, whose smiling face, whose cheery manner will be an abiding memory with all who had anything to do with him. There is little we can say except that there were some lines which I mentioned in a reference, which he liked very much, and which can be truthfully applied to him and I think I would end with the lines which he would have liked me to repeat:

> "His virtues walked their ample round,
> Nor made a pause, nor left a void;
> And sure the Eternal Master found,
> His shining talents well employed".

KARL J. KHANDALAVALA — A TRIBUTE*

Read at the Condolence Meeting on 22.1.1996, by Mrs. Seervai

I first met Karl Khandalavala in the Elphinstone College, and although he was two years my senior, we met in the Debating Society and in Dramatic Competitions. He won the first prize by his performance as Mathias in a play called "The Bells", a part which was to bring Henry Irving fame. Karl's performance was an unforgettable experience. He was a powerful speaker, with a beautifully modulated voice. He told me years later that he wanted to be a professional actor, but his father advised him to take to the law, and he never regretted that he had followed his father's advice. For he brought to the law his gifted speech, a first class mind and an immense capacity for hard work.

After a desultory practice, in 1940 he joined the Royal Air Force as a navigation officer. He was one of the crew when a Lancaster bomber crashed in the sea. The impact dislocated one of Karl's shoulders and some time thereafter he was permitted to return to civilian life. On reverting to the Bar, he accepted the post of a Presidency Magistrate, in which he impressed Advocates and Solicitors who appeared before him, with his complete mastery over their cases. When the City Civil Court was established he accepted a Judgeship in the belief that he would have time to carry on his studies in Indian Sculpture and Painting. However, when he found that a faithful discharge of his duties left him no time for such studies, he resigned as a judge, and reverted to the Bar. During the time I was Advocate-General, we appeared together on an important matrimonial appeal and in a number of land acquisition references. It was clear to me that he was a first class civil law lawyer, and but for the accident of the Union of India briefing him in gold smuggling cases, he would have been one of the leaders of the Original Side Bar.

Reverting to Art, he was an expert photographer and won numerous prizes in Photographic exhibitions. This skill was of help to him when he came to publish his authoritative books on Indian Art. I was connected with the first book *Indian Sculpture and Painting, An Introductory Study*. In his preface, he wrote: "My colleague at the Bar, Mr. H. M. Seervai, not only corrected the proofs but carefully revised the manuscript and suggested many changes which have resulted in simplifying the text". I value this acknowledgement of my assistance, because he knew that I had little or no knowledge of Indian Art. But his total dedication to the

*Seervai wrote this tribute four days before he expired.

study and preservation of Indian artistic inheritance, did not shut him out from the vast treasure of English literature. In presenting this book to me on my birthday, in 1958 he wrote the following beautiful lines from James Elroy Flecker's poem Old Ships:

"It was so old a ship, who knows, who knows?
And yet so beautiful, I watched in vain
To see the mast burst open with a rose,
And the whole deck put on its leaves again".

He and I shared a love of English poetry and to the end we capped each other's favourite lines.

His complete dedication to preserving and protecting in India her priceless works of Art is well brought out in a letter he wrote to the *Indian Express*. A person who was well known in political and artistic circles, whom I will call J, gave an interview to its representative stating that Karl had been connected with the cultural policy of the Government of India and was connected with the exhibition sent out by it, including the ones that sent the Yakshi. Karl replied: *"I have never been connected with the cultural policies of the Government of India nor was I ever consulted, officially or unofficially, on the exhibition which went to Paris . . . . . . The only role I have performed after the National Museum was founded was to acquire for it, all its most important collections through my personal friendships and with private collectors and others."* He specified 10 such collections, adding *"there were many other acquisitions made through my efforts." "The difference between J. and me is that if a plane carrying the Yakshi and other such irreplaceable antiquities of ours were to crash J. would not shed a tear because according to J, a risk has to be taken for international cultural diplomacy, whatever that may mean. I however would be heartbroken."*

He has left behind him memorials on Indian Art which will endure. The last and most enduring memorial was the gift of his own priceless collection of Indian Art to the Prince of Wales Museum.

In his death, I and others like me, have lost a dear and warm-hearted friend the like of whom we will not see again.

DR. ERNEST BORGES

A renowned cancer surgeon

Ex-tempore speech at Dr. E. Borges's funeral, March 1968.

Dr. Ernest Borges died of cancer in March, 1968. He had cured untold numbers of patients and saved many lives. My husband and

I became closely acquainted with him and his family, after he treated our revered teacher, Prof. d'Andrade.

At Dr. Borges's funeral, we were standing in an enormous queue, when someone came up to my husband requesting him to speak when the coffin was lowered, which he did ex-tempore.

The speech is printed here as subsequently written out by my husband, from memory, for Mrs. Borges, who wanted to have it.

Reverend fathers and friends,

The last time I spoke in this cemetery was when we laid to rest a beloved professor. Dr. Borges was there. He had come to the professor as a doctor and remained a devoted friend. Of few can it be said, as can be said of Dr. Borges, that wherever he entered a home as a doctor, he left as a friend. His great skill saved many lives and cured many people. And his kindliness and sympathy soothed and comforted those who were beyond the reach of his skill.

The letter from the Cardinal, which has just been read, expresses the feelings of all of us. Dr. Borges would not have cared only for fine words; but he would have valued the sorrow that beats in your hearts, and is expressed in your faces, as a recognition of all that he has done. I have never seen a funeral like this. Prelate and peasant, the head of the State and the humblest worker, men and women of all communities have paid their homage to Dr. Borges, who gave himself without stint to relieve human suffering.

Quite unaccountably, during the last three months, I have been haunted by some lines which I learnt as a school boy, and which you will permit me to quote because they apply to Dr. Borges:

"So nigh is grandeur to our dust,
So near is God to man;
When duty whispers low, thou must,
The youth replies, I can".

But the dreams of youth can fade away. Dr. Borges gave that reply in his youth, he gave it in middle age and he gave it till the last moment of his working life.

One of the most extraordinary demonstrations of affection for him was witnessed during his illness last year — a demonstration which did credit to the hearts, but not to the heads, of simple people. Persistent rumours went round the city that Dr. Borges had passed away; and people rushed to this cemetry to pay their last respects. The reason for the rumours was that simple people thought that if the rumours were believed, he would live, and continue the beneficent work which had endeared him to thousands. What is it that so endeared him to all? It was simple Christian charity, that is, a genuine love for all his fellow men, which made him treat high and low alike, and with the same care.

No doubt, memorials will be raised to him, though the Tata Memorial Hospital is a memorial to his dedicated service; and the men whom he has trained and inspired by his own spirit are also his memorial. It is right that a memorial should be raised to perpetuate his memory. But there is a second memorial, which is harder to raise, which he would have liked even more. It is that we ask ourselves whether, like him, we are giving more than is strictly required of us. For it is that more which makes the difference between a good doctor and an ordinary one; between a good man and an ordinary one. Dr. Borges gave himself unreservedly to relieve distress and suffering. After his recovery from grave illness last year he worked full time till he could work no longer.

Our thoughts turn to his bereaved family. At a time like this, words of comfort and words of praise must appear to them to be alike unavailing. His death is harder to bear for he was at the height of his powers and had so much to give to suffering humanity. But that is not how he would have looked at his death. There are some famous words in a great book of English devotional literature which are applicable to him. The Pilgrim was at the end of his journey and he said:

"I do not repent me of all the trouble I have been at to arrive where I am. My sword I give to him that shall succeed me in my pilgrimage, and my courage and skill to him that can get it".

What more can we say?

THE FLAVOUR OF SEERVAI'S LIFE IN LETTERS OVER 70 YEARS

Seervai's correspondence published here, is with friends, acquaintances and even strangers; and there are some family letters, although, persuaded by our son, I have not published a selection of family letters, or letters written to me before our marriage. Our son said to me that Homi was, by nature, a private man, and that I should reconsider my first idea to include several family letters.

Selecting letters for this book exercised me greatly. Mainly what I have done is to select letters to reveal Homi's personality through the spontaneously expressed perceptions of others, or through his voice. Thus different aspects come to view. But I have also included letters whose contents hold interest in what they say, or which reveal the wide range of the correspondence, and the distinction of the correspondents. A number of letters relate how much Seervai's example has influenced the correspondent to high standards of conduct in his life.

Among the readers of this book will be persons who personally knew some of the correspondents, or who know them by repute or by their works. These will find those letters more interesting than will other readers.

In most cases, I do not have the other side of the correspondence. Homi's personal letters were handwritten, and no copies exist, except perhaps with the recipient. In a few cases, I have typed copies of letters which were not personal.

The major portion of some letters, concerns the personal matters of the correspondents, or formal greetings, and then I have made extracts. Generally addresses are omitted for brevity's sake. Where a date does not appear, it is because the letter is undated. As many letters were handwritten, there may be words that could not be deciphered, and if so, I have indicated that. The letters are not edited. They are not published in any particular sequence, but I have tried to keep the order of dates.

The writer's identify is disclosed in a word at the top of the letter, or the first letter of a person. The designation stated is then current, if not otherwise indicated.

A few letters after January 1996 are included, as also letters not written by or to Homi where they hold some interest, or are about Homi.

Homi's friends were many, yet all friends' letters could not be included, nor more from the same writer, because this is not a book of letters, and constraints of space guided my selection, combined with the main object of publishing the correspondence, as stated above. There already seem to be too many letters.

The letters are not page identified in the contents: I expect them to be read through as one would read a chapter in a book, and if the reader thinks he would revert to any particular one, he will make a note of its page.

Finally, I can only hope that the correspondence serves its purpose: that Homi is seen through many eyes; that the letters reveal or emphasise different aspects of him, so that interest in reading is held.

H. J. Bhabha
[Subsequently Chairman,
Atomic Energy Commission of India]

Duff House,
North Wales.
21.9.1927

My dear Seervai,

I have not upto now read any work of Pater's. My father is most enthusiastic about him, and so I will kill two birds with one stone — it is an obsession with me — and read *Plato and Platonism*. My father tells me that his *Marcus Aurelius* is a more famous work, so I will read both if I have the time. Time is, I think, a positive nuisance, and the sooner mathematicians and philosophers find a way of overtaking it the better. Vain hope! This shall never be. For it is obvious, that if such a thing as motion existed, then there must be such a thing as time, time in this case being a matter of comparative speeds, a function of velocity and distance, velocity and distance being our fundamental quantities, and time a derived quantity. At present, velocity is considered a function of time and distance.

This leads to another interesting point. Our fundamental quantities, space, time, and mass, are arbitrary, since it is possible to take any other such as velocity or force or acceleration as our fundamental quantities, and express space, time and mass, or any other in terms of these. Instead of space, time and mass, as fundamental quantities, I think it would be much better to take space, mass and energy, time being expressable as a function of these; since energy work = force × distance = [M] [X] [L]. [M] represents mass, [X] = [L] = [T]2 acceleration and [L] length. See Intermediate textbook of Physics. Please excuse this digression.

To return, even if I lived to a hundred, I would not have time to do all that I wish to. Specialization is the curse of modern times, and it is absurd to say that a man cannot excel in many things. Behold Leonardo da Vinci, Angelo, in fact most of the world's great men.

Punch made a hit at it in one of his cartoons "The specialist who puts his finger on the knot."

I wonder if you would mind beginning your letter with Homi instead of Bhabha. Bhabha sounds to me a bit strange. Of course if we write letters to each other beginning My dear Homi, and signed Homi, centuries hence, when people will eagerly read this correspondence of the two great philosophers etc. of the age, they will find it hard to make out which is from whom.

I must close now. Hope you will keep writing. It is always a pleasure to hear from you. I am feeling much better and stronger.

Your sincerely,
Homi J. Bhabha

H. J. Bhabha

Cambridge.
14.11.1928

My dear Homi,

Thank you very much for your interesting letter. I did not know that Dastur had distinguished himself so much. I also thank you for pulling me up for having used extravagant language in my letter from (illegible). But my feelings were rather roused at the time.

I am working hard this time. My singing is getting on very well. I am conducting the C.U.M.S. Junior Orchestra on Friday week in the overture of Fidelio, instead of King Stephan as originally intended.

By the way, I have read two books by Bertrand Russel called *What I Believe* and *Icarus*. I suppose you have read them, but in case you haven't, do read them. They are both very small books, which could be got through in about 2 hours each, and are well worth the time. I quote from the second: "Icarus, having been taught by his father Daedalus, was destroyed by his own rashness. I fear that the same fate may overtake the population whom modern men of science have taught to fly."*

Besides, my point of view has been rather misunderstood by you. I do not object to a steam engine as such, but because of the type of mentality it represents, the vulgar and exceedingly common type of mind, to which nothing is interesting unless it promises to be of commercial value, or to further material comforts. I like knowledge for knowledge's sake and not for any other reason. If I intend to do research in atomic Physics, it is because I love the subject, not because I hope thereby to project an airship to Mars, though I would also welcome any man who did this because of the field for investigation it would open up; but if anyone saw in this the probability of colonization, or further markets for his goods, I would be up against him.

We go and chat on Sunday nights with Dr. Rootham. This time we had a very interesting discussion about civilisation, on the basis of a book by Spengler called *The Decay of the West*. I must stop now. Hoping that you are quite well, and with love.

Yours v. sincerely,
Homi J. Bhabha

* How ironic that Bhabha died in an aircrash, Ed.

H. J. Bhabha

5 Woodlun,
Highgate 6,
London.
3 July, 30

My dear Homi,

My exam is over, and I am now in my holidays, and have some time on my hands for writing letters. As you have probably heard, I have got a first in my exam. But my relations seem to be far more pleased about it than I am. I don't think about these things, and I attach no importance to exams as a test of original ability, and that after all, is what interests me.

Before I proceed further, I must thank you for your last letter with the cutting of your article. Your literary style is very good. I unfortunately have not the cutting with me at the moment, and have to write from memory. Incidentally, I liked your essay *On Nothing** very much, for substance as well as style. There are just one or two places where you have used sentences that perhaps would not have been written by an Englishman. They are by no means wrong or incorrect. It is difficult to express what I mean; perhaps it is that those sentences are not easy in their idiom. I showed the article to a friend whose opinion on these matters I value more than my own. He thought the same about the whole essay as I did. As to the political opinions expressed in the last article, I agree with you as to their soundness in the abstract. That I sympathise with Gandhi rather than with you in practice is a matter of temperament and outlook.

In the last three years, I have changed enormously in outlook, values and beliefs. I am far older than three years even at my time of life, would warrant. I have no longer that faith in the level headedness or goodness of men. I am very conscious of the insignificance of man in the Universe, either in space or time. One cannot dwell for long in the realms of Physics and Astronomy without realising it. It is true that this does not affect men in their dealings with one another, but it diminishes my estimate of the value of human life and of the importance of his sufferings. I look upon these political events in a semi-fatalistic light. The worst that can ever happen is not much. Nature will inexorably pursue its path. As Prof. Eddington says, "In the old conflict between free will and predestination, modern Physics has come down heavily on the side of predestination." Then he quotes Omar Khayam, "Yea, the

* Printed elsewhere in this book.

first morning of creation wrote, what the last dawn of reckoning shall read."

And seeing that ultimately our conduct depends on our system of values, who shall dictate our conduct to us short of dictating our relative valuation of things?

Nobody can accuse me in my life of being sluggish or inactive, or of being a dreamy and vapid "Megalo". I am determined, to the best of my ability, to try and excel in Physics, Painting and Music. Nor is this inconsistent with what I have written above — I think my outlook is rather similar to that of the great Mozart. Towards the end of his life, he seems to have realised the ultimate futility of doing anything, and to have wasted his time in tippling flirtations. He never took the trouble to write his music down on paper in later life except when forced to. He merely carried it about in his head. That he still mentally composed music is due to the fact that such a great artist cannot help it. Similarly, in a small way, I do what I do because I must. I could no more sit inactive like a "Sadhu" than a sadhu could put forward the mental energy that I do. But let me leave these vague subjects in which I am merely expressing my beliefs and opinions and come to something more useful.

It has struck me for some time, that if one would engage in vital art work one must be in the centre of things. I feel more and more strongly that if one would create European Art, one must live, at least for a part of each year, in Europe. An active intellectual society is as necessary to the full development of an artist as food is to his body. Cut off from this, he would merely put forward a few unimportant creations, and artistically end his life. The painting such as one sees in the Bombay Art Exhibitions, is certainly not Indian Art, or as European Art it is absolutely useless and worthless. It has no vital importance, no significance, no place in the development of Art and mind. It is for these things that one must be in the centre of things, or within reasonable distance of them.

Under the present development of communication, India is too far away. It is one of my hopes, that Indian Science may remedy this. That soon all countries of the world will be immeasurably closer. Of course, there is no obstacle to creating Indian literature or Indian art in India, that can only be created in India.

One of the reasons for my coming to India for a month soon, is to see for myself how the atmosphere will suit the further development of my talents and abilities. He who would pursue Science or Art must give up thoughts of wife or home, country or race, and do whatever he may, not for any small part of the race, but for Man. I am driven to pursue Science and Art at all costs. Science shall be my wife, Art my mistress.

With love,

Yours
Homi J. Bhabha

H. J. Bhabha

28 Obstgarten Str.
Zurich, 16.11.32

My dear Homi,

I am sorry I have not written to you before since I left India. But travel and inertia has made it impossible. However I am very loath that regular communication should cease with one whose friendship I value as much as yours, and therefore I propose henceforth to write at more regular intervals, and hope that you will find time to do so too.

I have read half of Boswell's *Life of Johnson*, and it is very interesting. However, when I came to Zurich, I was reading it on the journey. I had to change my train at Paris, and then I lost it. I remember looking in the compartment before I left it, so I have a suspicion that the other people in the compartment put it into their bag by mistake. I went back to the station again as soon as I discovered its loss, but was unable to find it. So much did I value this book coming from you, that I am going to take the liberty of suggesting that you send me another copy with the same inscription written. In the probable event of this letter being destroyed, posterity will be hard put to it to explain the existence of two identical volumes, bearing the identical inscription and date, given by you to me. It would become the subject of academic speculation and controversy. The one man who suggested that it was because one volume was probably lost, would be laughed to scorn. For, they would say, assuming that it was lost, surely it would have been much simpler and quicker for Bhabha to buy another copy himself, instead of sending all the way to India for it and waiting a month atleast. And what would be the point of sending to India for it? The book is a token of the friendship of Seervai for Bhabha, and there is no need for a repetition of it in the case of the book being lost. Again, even granting this most absurd reason, it is even more unlikely that the books would both bear the same inscription and *the same date.* But a brilliant scholar would spend some years of his life reading all the works and letters of Homi

Seervai. He would read his articles, and peruse his library. And he would find that there was a Principle of the Fundamental Duality of Nature in which you tentatively believed, and which you had invented. He would also enlarge upon the mystical tendencies of the Indian and Oriental mind. He would point out, that the two friends had further both the same name of Homi. It is now obvious that the great philosopher had dedicated with characteristic originality, two identical books to his friend as a symbol of their friendship, and a mystical expression of the "Principle of Fundamental Duality." In this he would be given his doctorate with distinction.

Continued on 21 Nov.:

Looking through some old letters yesterday, I found one of yours which I had preserved. I know the letter well for I have read it more than once. It contains a quotation from Bradley. What came to me as a surprise was that this letter was dated 1928. It is this terrific rate at which time flies which is so appalling. Things which one remembers as happening yesterday turn out to have happened years ago. I reflected a few days back that I was 23 years old already, and that more than one third of my useful life had already passed.

Then there is this question. I have mathematical ability. I am handicapped by having spent some years doing Engineering instead of mathematics, but in the long run that is not serious, though it may affect the immediate future. But there is nothing to show so far that this ability is of an outstanding nature. I think that life spent in being a second rate mathematician or scientist is useless, especially when there are other things one can do much better. For one neither earns money to be comfortable in this life, which one might (through Engineering in my case,) nor does one do anything outstanding that would justify one's putting up with hardships. Then, in my case, there is the fact that I can paint. My artistic talent is certainly of an unusual order. That is not only my opinion, but the opinion of people qualified to judge. Here I am quite sure that I can produce works of the very first order, especially on a large scale if the occasion arises. I think I have already done things which will hold their own against anything in modern art. How far, then, am I justified in doing things other than this, in, what is tantamount to wasting my life? On the other hand, as things are at the moment, in India, art has no place. Secondly, my people seem to have some disinclination that I should earn my living painting, though if I did it at all, it would have to be in Europe. And then, I do not know when I shall be able to support myself. The kindness and love of my parents has been such that I cannot hope to adequately repay it, but

I do not wish to be a perpetual burden on them. These are merely the main points. One cannot put everything down in a letter. And I hope you will excuse all this egotistical talk. But if one should not write to a friend, whom should one write it to? Perhaps to no one.

There are only 4 people I know in Zürich. I am alone most of the time, and I work. I have been doing a little painting. You perhaps remember those sketches of male nudes that I had in my note book. Two of those I executed in oils on the boat, and they have come out very well; the sketches could give you no idea of that.

And now I hope you will excuse my saying one thing further. It is not meant as criticism. Your superiority in an argument and quickness of mind over any body else is apparent to any one within two minutes, but beware of becoming dogmatic.

How did you like the book on Leonardo I gave you? And now, farewell until my next letter. Write to me soon, my dear Homi, for it will give me great pleasure.

With love,

Yours affectionately,
Homi Bhabha

J. H. Bhabha
[H. J. Bhabha's father]

20.5.36

My dear Seervai,

Thank you so much for your letter of the 15th May giving me the information with regard to Paranjpye and his salary.

I have written at length to Homi myself. Perhaps your letter will also help to guide him. We have greatly appreciated your very kind and sincere interest in Homi's welfare.

With very kind regards from us both.

Your sincerely,
J. H. Bhabha

Arthur Geddes,
[son of distinguished professor, Partick Geddes]

Department of
Geography,
Edinburgh.
17.10.1932

Dear Mr. Seervai,

Your warm and vivid notes on my father (received today) have given me real pleasure, as an evocation must do from one who has felt and thought on such a man, of his subject. — It is good to know — specially at this time, when you in India have so much to trouble you — that his keen thought and love of his students is with them still.

I am yours cordially,

Arthur Geddes

J. C. P. d'Andrade
[Distinguished Professor of Philosophy]

Dear Mr. Seervai,

You will be glad to learn that I am still at the Elphinstone College and that I have not suffered the indignity of having Dhopeshwarkar promoted over my head. I am told, and I think the information is reliable, that Mr. Sorley, Secretary, Educational Department put his foot down and refused to accept the suggestion that D should be brought over to Bombay. You see all is not rotten in the state of Denmark.

Once again I must thank you, Mr. Mehta and all my other pupils, who not only gave me moral comfort in my difficulty but made my case your own and worked for me to the best of your ability. It was worth being in trouble to have such proof of goodwill and sympathy.

I believe there is no longer any danger ahead, at least for some time to come.

With kind regards,

Yours sincerely,
J. C. P. d'Andrade

P. C. Bhatt

8th May 1944

My dear Seervai,

It would be impossible to thank you enough for the good wishes, the fine feed and the best of feelings with which you obliged me on the evening of Friday last. During the last few years, evenings of the fifths of May have become a sublime feature in my life. I doubt whether any body else, excepting of course my elder brother, under whose kind protection I have the privilege of embarking on life's venture, would have such deep sympathy and such sincere feelings as you have been kind enough to have for me.

Ever yours,
P. C. Bhatt

Porus A. Mehta
[Advocate, GOI Ministry of Law]

Bandra.
7-8-45

My dear H,

I hope you will not mind my congratulating you (even if a little prematurely) on your coming marriage but I feel sure you will be glad to receive my best wishes.

You could not have made a better choice of a wife. Feroza has not only fine intellectual attainments and an eager mind but in common with all the other members of her family, a good heart. I have known her for a long time and I do not know of any girl who has a better outlook. She has a beautiful character too and her husband can count on her absolute loyalty and fidelity as well as fruitful companionship through times fair and times dark.

I need not say that if you are lucky to be her mate, she is no less lucky to have a man of your great intellectual vigour and kindly heart. I have known you and loved you too long to be perhaps very impartial but even in my detached moments or at times when I have felt hurt, my esteem and affection for you have not appreciably lessened.

There is one thing on which you will allow me to say a word. The disparity in your ages is bound to raise comment but I see nothing in that. It is the disparity in outlook that may be dangerous but in this case

I think there is a remarkable affinity between you two. She is wiser than her years and has been singularly free from the half-baked ideas of her/our generation. So there will be a fundamental unity in spite of the diversities and differences which are the salt of life and must be there.

I therefore need hardly wish for your happiness, for that is assured. But with all my heart I pray for a long and rich life for both of you.

It also gives me a great pleasure to find that my daughter Shanur will have you as her real uncle !

With best wishes,
Yours Afftly.
P.

H. M. Seervai

9-8-1945

My dear P,

Many thanks for your good wishes and for all the nice things you have said about Feroza and me.

I am determined to bend all my energies to make her a happy, happy woman. If I say nothing more, I hope you will understand.

Yours H.

H. M. Seervai

10.8.1945

My dear Behramji,

I am very glad to have your letter. Yes. I quite appreciate your anxiety for your daughter's welfare.

I am not surprised that you found her news to be a sort of "bombshell". I have certainly no exaggerated notions of myself and it never entered my head that she would love me so deeply in so short a time. On the rare occasions on which we had met she seemed to me to be so fine a girl that I had hoped that a little later I might ask her to be my wife. Her letter of the 27th of July was a most agreeable surprise to me. But I did not hesitate for a moment and I wrote back proposing marriage, in a letter which I did not mark "private", because you had as much right to read it as she had.

Yes, I realize the disparity in our ages. But though I have worked hard I have lived a temperate life and that has its effect on the system. In October last a German doctor was my neighbour at Mahabaleshwar. On the day I was leaving he came to me and asked "May I ask you a question"? I said "Yes". "Would it be impolite if I asked you your age?" "No; I will complete 38 in December". "Are you sure"? "Yes, but why?" "Because I told our neighbour that you could not be more than 30". And a year before, Sir Jamshedji Kanga had told a matron who wanted to palm off her daughter on me (though she reckoned without me) that I was 30. She asked him whether he was sure, for she wanted a son-in-law under 30 ! Sir Jamshedji said he would ask me — I told him I was 37. I do not say this out of vanity; but this has been said to me repeatedly and I was entitled to take it into consideration when I proposed to Feroza. For age is not merely a matter of years, but of how they are spent. Some men are old at 40; some, like Sir Jamshedji Kanga, are young at 70.

Feroza and I think alike on things which really matter. This is not an idle fancy for she wrote things to me which I had written or spoken, when I was her age, in an article here, a speech there. With me they were no idle words of an immature youth. I have put them in practice all these years and they have made me happy. I felt confident then that Feroza and I can be supremely happy together. She is very, very dear to me and I should not have asked her to marry me if I had the slightest doubt of my capacity to make her happy.

In considering her welfare I hope it will not be overlooked that my happiness is also involved; and that if I made a foolish decision, I have a good deal to lose. I love a home and am happy nowhere else. For the last 2 or 3 years my practice at the Bar has been rapidly increasing. I imagine that at the rate of these 4 months I shall be making Rs. 2,000 a month or a little more and those competent to judge think I'll soon rise to the front rank. In any event, barring Acts of God, I believe I'll do well. During long and weary years of waiting at the Bar I have not allowed myself to be kidnapped into matrimony by irrelevant considerations of money, connections or social position or the more natural desire to get rid of loneliness. I say this in proof of the fact that in matters of marriage, I do not take a light-hearted or selfish view and am not to be swept off my feet except by a girl of such fine character as Feroza.

When Feroza met me on Saturday the 4th, she said to me "Supposing my parents consent, when shall we marry?" I replied, "Give me some time to find a flat and get some furniture and then name your day and time." I suggested December and her face showed that I had put it off too long; but she said "Yes, that will be all right". For her sake, more than for my own, I hope you'll approve of December; I don't think she will be really happy if it is put off even by 2 or 3 months. If a delay of 2 or 3 months would please you she will certainly agree. She loves you devotedly and has drawn so fine and moving a picture of you that I too would much rather displease myself than you. I believe she will complete her thesis sooner and more successfully if she is married than if she is not. She has discovered, to her surprise, that I have read more books on the subject of her thesis (and I read them for pleasure) than her professor is likely to teach. And my help is at her service.

I know it seems bold for a man who has not the good fortune to know you to ask for the two most precious things you have: your daughter and your blessings. When you have given these, we shall ask for nothing more than for opportunities to make you and your wife as happy as we can.

I shall be happy to meet you when you are in Bombay.

Yours very sincerely,
H. M. Seervai

Extract from H. M. Seervai's Letter, 1945

The death of my cousin has been a great grief .... she was a doctor and practised in Ahmedabad for over 17 years .... we had stayed together for years and years, and I never met a woman more absolutely generous. She seemed incapable of keeping money for herself — she spent it all on her patients or her poor relations. When nearing 60 she went to Persia — not to Tehran or any big city, but to Yazd, a poor place where the largest number of Parsis in Persia (mostly very poor) have their home. She was in charge (without pay) of a maternity hospital, and she came to Bombay, under great pressure from her brother, who rightly thought that extremes of heat and cold were not good for her. Here she was welcome in every home which had known her — her relatives claimed a sort of prescriptive right to her presence, if anybody was ill! .... You'll understand why I like and expect women to be capable as well as kind — I was brought up by three women, my mother and my two cousins, who had both capacity and kindliness.

Ever yours,
H.

Nani A. Palkhivala
[Subsequently a famous Counsel and authority on Income-tax Law]

6th Dec. 1945

My dear Homi,

Nargis and I have one dear wish for you and Phiroza today. Some day when both of you are very old and grey and full of sleep, you may say of your unclouded wedded life, what W. W. Gibson said of his:–

"Going my way of old,
Contented more or less,
I dreamt not life could hold
Such happiness.

I dreamt not that love's way
Could keep the golden height
Day after happy day,
Night after night."

There is no blessing in life that we do not wish you both.

Yours ever,
Nani A. Palkhivala

H. M. Seervai

Mon Repos, Bandra, Bombay.
4.7.1946

My dear Meherbai & Freny,

Many thanks for your kind letters of sympathy. Yes. I loved Dhunju dearly, having spent 21 years of my life with him and thereafter having met him once a week. He was such a generous and kindly man and at the same time so able that one couldn't help loving and admiring him and I never left him in doubt that I was very proud of him. From him and from my mother I acquired the intellectual and moral virtues I possess. Their example made goodness and intellectual capacity attractive and necessary for a happy life and I owed to them a debt I could never repay. He died childless; but he passed on his fine personal gifts to me and his 3 nephews who loved him as much as I did — though none of us have his capacities in as full a measure.

The manner of his death was agonizing to his dear ones, for he sustained a fracture at the base of the skull and was instantly unconscious. He lived for 14 hours but he was unconscious all the time. For him the form of his death was merciful. He had gone to his sister and had spent a happy evening; his sister had to pay a mourning visit and his last words to her were characteristic of his thoughtfulness for others. He said " If Dinoo wants to go she'd better do so now, otherwise she'll be drenched in rain". She went. 20 minutes later he got down to go with Prof. P.A. Wadia and his sister. He slipped on the staircase and never regained consciousness. So that for him it was like heart failure. He would not have liked a slow and gradual decay of his powers.

He went about life cheerfully but he was not anxious to live very much longer. He told his sister, who died last year, that there was not much point in living longer unless it be to see his cousin become a judge. My relative success at the Bar and my marriage to Feroza brought him great happiness and satisfaction and I am glad, that he lived long enough to see both. My mother saw neither of these things.

I am very much obliged to Meherbai for the kind offer of the Bungalow. There's time enough to think about it and I'll let you know what Feroza and I propose to do,

With kindest regards,

Yours affectionately,
H.

Maimoona Hamid

Karachi.
30.11.1948

Dear Feroza,

To remedy some of the common evils, like pugree etc. I am afraid I cannot share the fanatical zeal which the people over here express for Pakistan. I, like several others over here feel that this division has been a curse and it will take generations to wipe out the bitterness which all this political propaganda has caused. The original residents of Karachi, Muslims and otherwise, miss their Hindu brothers with whom they shared their soil and resent the goonda element that has crept in and I am sure the people in India feel the same.

It was a relief to learn of my father's acquittal. Please thank Homi on my behalf for having so kindly consented to help him. Tell him I have preserved his two coins and kept them as souvenirs of good-luck. Perhaps some day they will attract some more of their kind and I will have a regular collection. Give my love to Dolly and tell her I am very sorry for not having met her before coming. I miss you all very much. Give my regards to your mother and Homi. Love to little Meher and Shanur.

Yours affectionately,
Mammy

Freny P. Mehta

Bandra.
6-6-49

My dear Homi,

Thank you for your kind letter. We are glad to know you are having a well-earned rest and a well-deserved holiday. Father may come to Poona tomorrow, but Manifui may not come, as she has to see a dentist and have herself examined further.

I am reading *The Life Of Dadabhai Naoroji*. Is Masani reliable as an author? Perhaps a man may have intellectual integrity and have himself accused of commercial dishonesty — do you think? Like Bacon, I think many have a split personality. August 4, 1949 will be the centenary of "the day on which was laid the foundation of female education in the city of Bombay," when the stalwarts of the line decided to go round house to house teaching Parsi girls ! You know Katherine Mayo says the superior position of the women of Bombay is due to the influence of Parsis. What strikes me most so far is the dauntless resolution of Dadabhai to serve India by accepting the position of Minister to the Maharao in Baroda. He knew the Maharaja was a feckless weakling — a degenerate, a dissipated sot — the court was composed of vicious sycophants — yet there he laid the foundation of a good system of Government. Dadabhai resigned as Divan, the king was deposed — Dadabhai fought the Resident and the Court — and was lucky to escape — but the next Maharaja carried the torch of good government. That is heroism. How can men say they won't enter politics as times are perverse? Considering all, when were they not worse? 'tho most politicians be dishonest, for some, politics is a mission.

Thanks for the supplements. I await further information you promise.

Yours Afftly.,
Freny

H. H. Wadia,
[cousin of Seervai, and formerly High Court Reciever in Bombay]

London.
9th November 1949

My dear Homi,

I have your letter of 4th November and am delighted to know you are getting on very well at the Bar. Apart from your own efforts and perseverance, you owe it to M. L. Manecksha and J. B. Kanga. I hope your retainers will increase as months roll on. I have heard of one man at the Bombay Bar (now dead) whose certain 13 *retainers* at Rs. 5,000/- each brought him Rs. 65,000/- a year.

The Telephone shares were originally purchased by your maternal grandfather. Indirectly they proved a very profitable purchase for his grandson, for your conduct of the case relating to their valuation started your career at the Bar. I understand, however, that the Appeal Court substantially diminished the valuation of the shares below what would have been arrived at under the judgment of the Court of First Instance.

I keenly regret your mother did not survive long enough to see you established at the Bar. Sir Dinsha Davar's parents, Mr. Rustomba Patel's father, and Temulji Nariman's father all lived long enough to see their sons prosper.

Dinoo wrote to me some time back that you had secured a flat opposite the Oval. I replied on 5th November and asked her to give my regards. And today I have received your letter. As you no longer have to travel every working day from Bandra to Court and back, I should think you will be saving at least 1½ hours which is the greatest advantage.

It is pleasant to know that you are happy with your wife and daughter. May you always remain so.

I enclose some newspaper clippings which may interest you.

Wishing you and your family a Merry Christmas and a Happy New Year.

I remain,
Your sincerely,
H. H. Wadia

P.S. :

Just fancy, the gentleman in this newsclip* and the writer were the only persons called to the Bar at the same Inn of the Court on the same day, years ago. Whether any other persons were eligible for call to the Bar at the same Inn of the Court on that day, the writer does not know.

* Wadia attached a picture of Lord Chief Justice Goddard. It is not reproduced here. Ed.

Jaya S. Haidrabadi

6th October 1950

To,
Homi M. Seervai,
Bar-at-Law

Dear Sir,

Hoping to be excused for this encroachment upon your valuable time, I am writing this to thank you for the great favour you have done to me by not only fighting my case to a very favourable conclusion but also for being so considarate as to exempt payment of your fee.

Being what I am, I have neither the words nor the means at my disposal by which to express to your goodself how deeply indebted I am to you for this very generous act of yours.

Allow me to assure you Sir, that you have rendered this great service not to me alone but also to my three innocent children. I had lost all hopes of getting the decision read in my favour and if it was not for you I do not know what my children and myself would have had to face.

Thanking you once again.

Very truly yours,
Jaya S. Haidrabadi

H. H. Wadia

London.
4th January 1951

My dear Homi,

I am glad to learn you are now the tenant instead of allottee of the flat you occupy. I can't understand how a person in your category came to be an allottee in the first instance. I thought that in Bombay only a person in Government Service could become an allottee of residential accommodation with perhaps an exception in the case of a few refugees from Pakistan.

Years ago the interests of the then Durbhunga in Bombay were looked after by Messrs. Jehangir, Gulabbhai, and Bilimoria, Solicitors — or, to be more specific, by Jehangir Vimadalal of that firm, and after his death by Cawasji Bilimoria. You talk of the appeal you refer to, coming on for further hearing in March or April before the Supreme Court in Delhi. I am under the impression that the Supreme Court does not sit in Delhi in April as the shade temperature then is over 110°. If the Court were to sit in Ootacamund in that month that would be another matter. Probably it is closed for about 10 to 12 weeks in the hot weather. By the way, is the Supreme Court Building in Delhi air-conditioned throughout ? and are there microphones set up near the witness box, — in case they require additional oral evidence taken before themselves?

Yes, the extension of jurisdiction of the City Civil Court will affect the practice of attorneys and advocates on the Orignal Side of the High Court. But you have to bear in mind that in a *test case* even if the stake be under Rs. 25,000/-, the plaintiff would consider it prudent to engage attorneys and advocates as on the Original Side, knowing fully well that even if he won he would have to bear his own costs in excess of the scale prescribed for the City Civil Court. I know that in the Parsee Chief Matrimonial Court parties frequently appeared by attorneys and advocates — sometimes at the top of their profession — although the scale of fees prescribed for lawyers in that court was, and probably is still, extremely meagre. I am only referring to this as an instance, without implying that there is any common basis of comparison between a matrimonial suit and a money suit even if it be a test case.

So in India there are 5-year National Savings Certificates. Here there are 10-year Savings Certificates. The holder at the end of 10 years gets interest at the rate of 3% per annum. He can cash his certificate at any time during the 10 years. If he cashes at the end of 5 years, he will get interest at a rate somewhat less than 3% per annum. The interest is free of income-tax and supertax.

I am glad Government have nominated you as member of the Board of Visitors of the Government Law College for 3 years, I know you are or were a member of the Bombay Bar Council.

Two weeks at Simla must have been a good change for you and your wife and daughter.

The enclosed clippings from newpapers may interest you.

With best wishes to all for a happy and prosperous 1951,

I remain,

Yours sincerely,
H. H. Wadia

The following letter pertains to the Parsi Charities Schools, sought to be thrown open to non-Parsis.

Sir N. P. Engineer,
[former Advocate-General,
Federal Court of India]

21st September 1953

My dear Seervai,

I have been pondering over the substance given by Sir Jamshedji of his interview with Lady Jahangir. It appears the Petitioners feel that as Dinkerrao Desai asked them to apply to the Court they do not feel themselves at liberty to withdraw. This to my mind is meaningless. The sole ground on which the petition purports to proceed is that the withdrawal of the grant makes it impossible for them to carry on with the school. As we have been able to produce the necessary funds, to my mind the petitioners can, without losing face, say that in the altered circumstances they do not desire to proceed with the petition. We are prepared, if necessary, not to object to the petitioners saying that the withdrawal is without prejudice to their right to apply again, if and when necessary or if so advised. It must, however be made clear that this would be without prejudice to all our rights, contentions and submissions.

It appears that Lady Jahangir is prepared to withdraw the petition if we agree that the petitioners should be at liberty to admit non-Parsis if there are not sufficient numbers of Parsi students seeking the benefit of an Institution. It is impossible for us to agree to any such suggestion.

I understood from Sir Jamshedji that they are not keen upon receiving the grant. They say they are prepared to do without it. But they are worried over the fact that the number attending the School has dwindled and they are therefore unable to run it. If such be the fact it appears that the petition is based on a ground which does not exist. It is surprising that in these days a school of this kind is not able to attract sufficient students. Without knowing all the facts it is not possible to say with certainty what the cause of this can be. I would not be surprised if it is due to the fact that they follow all the directions of the Educational Department particularly as regards the medium of instruction with which, to my knowledge many Parsi parents do not agree. Any way the discussion confirms my conviction that the petitioners are not able to discharge their duty to the Community as trustees. I am sure, if the petitioners resign, the Parsi Community can produce many respectable and responsible members who will carry on the Institution without sacrificing either the efficiency of the education or the interests of the real and only beneficiaries.

What I have written above is strictly confidential. My only object in writing this is to express my feeling that I do not think any useful purpose will be served by holding a meeting with the other side. If, however, you, Sir Jamshedji and our other friends think otherwise, I am willing to give my co-operation in the matter.

Yours sincerely,
Naswanji

Dinoo Bastavala

October 25, 1953

Dear Mr. Seervai,

My most sincere thanks to you for so kindly sparing time, among your multifarious engagements, over my trivial personal problem. It was more than good of you to do so and I am very grateful indeed. I am even more grateful for your gesture of foregoing the fees since I really had no call upon you for such a favour and I can only repeat my gratitude for everything.

I hear you may prove successful in the matter of the Parsi schools. No one will be more delighted than us if this comes to pass, and we are sure that it will be your brilliant handling of our side of the case that will bring it about as much as the law itself. More power to your elbow!

With kindest regards,

I am
Yours sincerely,
Dinoo B. Bastawala

Mehran N. Moos

Bombay.
21-1-54

My dear Homi,

We all miss you so much. The house is so quiet without the hustle and bustle of your departures and arrivals to and from work and the servants must greatly miss the generous tips for the loads of bags and briefs. The house does seem like a wheel without its pivot on which and around which it revolves, so we all eagerly look forward to your return and I am sure your chambers too will be glad to see "the conquering hero come" !

Feroza and Meher are gay but their gaiety is a little subdued by your absence. I went with Feroza to Shirodkar's and all is o.k. he says. Aloo Davar got twin boys yesterday and Feroza told Shirodkar, Meher would like a pair also ! and he laughed.

Weekends at Bandra are nice for Feroza except for the chance of overfeeding by Goola, which F. tactfully avoids ! Now come soon and have a good time.

Love from Mehran Masi.

Extract from letter dated 30-6-55 from Mehran N. Moos.

I am amused that you are having "a nice holiday" at home. That speaks volumes for a contented and happy mind to find joys of life with one's dear ones.

Freny P. Mehta

New Delhi.
1-4-1954

My dear Homi,

I was shocked to hear the news about your dear friend Boman Sethna. He seemed such a good friend of yours, one you fully trusted, so fine and helpful, one who did not do things to show off, but I think out of genuine love of humanity. He will always live in your memory, perhaps that was his keenest wish — to live in the minds of trustworthy people who will carry on the purposes he cared for.

It is really not too warm here yet, but I feel so languid, I don't even read much, wrapt in domesticity.

How are darling Feroza, Meher and her new sister? I am told you are just as glad as you may be for a boy.

With kind regards,

Yours Afftly.,
Freny

Freny P. Mehta

New Delhi.
5-5-1954

My dearest Feroza,

Happy Birthday to you — Best wishes to attain what you deem the Best. My present will come with me.

....

We met dear Homi again yesterday.

Dhurandhar was in high praises of him. "We have standing instructions to engage him if available" he said. "Not only is he clever — he is the coming man". He often says, "I like him much".

Dhurandhar himself is judged to be a very able man. Of course this opinion will not be anything new for you. It is so well known among those who know Homi, that I wonder if I need repeat it. But a loving wife always feels it is a fresh laurel she has won for herself !

....

What are you reading? I have a biography of Wells.

With love,
Freny

Sir Jamshedji Kanga, Bar-at-law

Hotel Rembrandt,
London.
17.6.1954

My dear Seervai,

I received your very kind letter for which I sincerely thank you. You have been one of my very distinguished devils and I am very proud of you. My chamber has been considered lucky because of the distinction attained by advocates like you who worked there. I am glad you are my neighbour and we shall often meet. Though I am now practically on the retired list, I mean to attend the Chamber so long as I live. You are now a first class Counsel and any post in our profession is within your reach. It will be for you to accept it or not. Your industry, knowledge and eloquence have easily placed you in the front rank. I wish you good health, prosperity and happiness. May you live long to enjoy the fruits of your honest work and labour. I am quite well. The weather has not improved. Time flies and we shall soon meet.

With best wishes and kindest regards,

Yours sincerely,
J. B. Kanga

Barjor J. Dastur

10th September, 1956

My dear Homi,

Forgive me for taking the liberty of addressing you by your Christian name, but I feel I can express myself much better if I write to you this way.

I really do not know how I can ever thank you for all that you have done for me. In spite of your various engagements you took up my case and did full justice to it. All along your advice has been so helpful and although the things you told me did not seem true at that time, time has shown that I was wrong and you were right and I am glad that I have followed your advice.

I assure you that the interest you have taken and the hard work you have put in, has completely changed the whole aspect of the case and the final verdict that has been recently passed by the Committee is due to your sincere and wholehearted efforts.

If I am grateful to you, let me tell you that Navazbai is still more grateful in that, the husband of one of her pupils has done so much for her. Phiroza has really been so good to us, she has taken a keen interest in my case and had it not been for her, we would not have had the good fortune of having one of the ablest counsels on our side.

I am writing this letter to you, since I have not been able to see you still, but I can assure you, that at the first opportunity I will come and see you.

Navazbai sends her kind regards to Meher, Phiroza and yourself and kindly accept the same from me and convey them to the family.

Yours v. sincerely,
Barjor J. Dastur

Justice N. H. C. Coyajee

Bombay High Court.
30th December 1955

My dear Seervai,

Among the numerous letters I have received, your letter was the one I have appreciated most and it is a satisfaction to know how widely he was held in high esteem for my father's character and professional (sic). I know that no lawyer of eminence could have made the mark as he did without a personality which was not only striking but in a way which had its own individuality, all its own.

We at home saw another phase of the same character on a higher plane and we are all grateful he was given to us for so many years, cheerful and serene to the last moment of his life.

Will you please convey our thanks to your wife for her kind message.

Yours very sincerely,
N. H. C. Coyajee

H. M. Seervai

22.2.1957

My own sweetest one,

Mehera Masi gave me the good news about the arrival of the baby and that you were both well. I need hardly add what a relief it is to know that all is well and I wish you and all our little ones all the blessings which it is good for men to have. You will have got my letter in which I told you how I spoke with the desperation of love. No one foresaw so early an arrival of our little one. My first impulse was to keep the news to myself, but I felt it would be wrong not to let the Chief Justice and Mr. Justice S. K. Das know the position. So I phoned up S. K. Das, thanked him for having altered his programme for me, and told him of the new arrival. He was very nice. Then I phoned up the Chief Justice; he was very nice but he said that the programme would stand, namely 3 days next week and then Monday.

You know how much I have wished to be with you, but dearest love as a result of my efforts yesterday, valuable days have been gained to bring me to thee as soon as possible.

Kiss the little baba for me and take care of thyself and him.

Give my fondest love to Meher and Shirin. I imagine Meher would sum up the situation by saying "God bless us — everyone".

With fondest love -

Ever your own heart
H.

P.S.: Meher told me on the phone "I was so excited".

J. S. Warden,
[Solicitor]

7.10.1962

My dear Seervai,

It was so kind of you to send me the reprint of your article in the Law Quarterly Review — many thanks for it. I read the article with pleasure not unmixed with some pain, for it brought back to my mind many old, unhappy, far-off things. I don't know whether it was a desire not to go into details irrelevant to the object of your article or a desire not to go into details that were bound to offend most of your readers, which made you write: "the hopes which had been aroused by the Cabinet Mission Plan had vanished and the shadow of partition which, for a time, seemed to have lifted, fell heavily in India" and made you refrain from explaining why the shadow fell again or alluding to Nehru's speech in Bombay in July 1946, in which he went back on the acceptance of the Plan by the Congress and seemed to say that the Constituent Assembly would be free to decide which subjects would be central and which provincial.

I suppose you will be having a brief holiday at Matheran or elsewhere during the October vacation and hope it will be enjoyable.

9.10.1962

P.S.: I wrote the above intending to continue the letter yesterday but didn't, not feeling too bright, and this morning I learnt that my last surviving Uncle, Jamshed Lam had died in Calcutta by heart failure.

With regards to you and your wife,

J. S. Warden

H. M. Seervai,
Advocate-General

<u>Confidential</u>

March 1, 1963

My dear Chief Justice,

I have hesitated long to write to you on the subject of this letter, but a time has come when I think it would not be proper to hesitate any longer.

The passing over of the claims of practising lawyers for appointments to the Bench of the High Court, and to the Benches of Subordinate Courts, particularly the City Court, has been causing the most acute discontent among members of the Bar, and it seems to me that the expression of that discontent cannot be long delayed. The rumoured appointment of a magistrate to the City Court, when highly competent practising lawyers would be prepared to accept such appointment, has brought such discontent to a head.

As you know, members of the Bar have behaved with a sense of responsibility, even when their feelings have been most deeply stirred, as when Shri Gogte was appointed Principal Judge and you know that it was as a result of my advice that a meeting of the City Court Bar Association called to protest against the appointment, dispersed without any resolution being moved. I value the dignity of the Bench highly and at all times I have desired to see it upheld. Any conflict between the Bench and the Bar, and any lack of mutual respect and confidence, is in my opinion an evil which everyone should do much to avoid. Even when members of the Bar have been most excited and agitated and have brought their grievances to me, I have succeeded in soothing them by the reminder that it is unwise to take steps which would provide a remedy worse than the disease. But a stage has been reached when it is clear to us that almost any remedy would be better than the disease.

It is true that the Constitution gives no voice to the Bar in the appointment of Judges, and in that sense, such appointments are not the concern of the Bar. But in a very real sense, such appointments are a vital concern of the Bar, for it is the Bar which argues before the Bench. The whole development of the law and the due administration of justice are dependent upon a judiciary equal to its tasks and the Bar is very much concerned with all these things and can command highly competent professional judgment in regard to all of them. I may therefore respectfully say that if the trend of the last few years continues, a demand which might well prove irresistible, will arise for such competent professional judgment to be brought to bear upon the problem, which the judgment of the judiciary has failed to solve. I have discussed these things with you before, and believe I have sent you the relevant material about the successful working of the judicial committee of the Bar in the United States. The success of such a method in the United States shows that competent professional opinion is able to secure satisfactorily the appointment of a suitable judiciary. One thing is clear that the Bar cannot resign itself fatalistically to the pernicious doctrine that the state gets the judiciary it deserves.

I have written this letter with complete freedom, because I gathered from Chagla C. J. and from you, that the Chief Justice is entitled to expect that the Advocate General will keep him informed of matters which affect the Bench and the Bar and the administration of justice. I need hardly add, that if a personal discussion is desired, I am at your disposal.

With kind regards,

Yours sincerely,
H. M. Seervai

P.S.: My views on Articles 233 and 234 have been publicly expressed, and we have discussed them. I have conveyed them to several judges of the High Court, and will be conveying them to others.

H. M. Seervai
Advocate-General

To the Law Minister

3.4.1963

My dear Minister,

I have already spoken to you about the anxiety felt by several members of the Bar about judicial appointments. It relates both to the appointments in the High Court and in the City Court. As regards the High Court, the State Government is only one of the 4 authorities responsible for making the appointments. As regards district judges (and City Court judges are included in the expression Dist. Judges by Art. 236 of the Constitution) under Article 233 the responsibility is that of the State Government though consultation with the High Court is obligatory. In view of this responsibility, I think it is right to bring to your attention, as the Minister for Law, certain facts and considerations which appear to me to be relevant.

Ever since the attempted supersession of Shri B. J. Divan, the senior-most city court judge, for the Principal Judgeship, members of the Bar have been increasingly worried about judicial appointments. As a result of the strong protest from the Bar, and the knowledge that such action would result in the resignation of 3 judges of the city court, Shri Divan was in the end appointed as a Principal Judge. Now again, the reported or rumoured appointment of an Additional Chief Presidency Magistrate to the City Court has raised serious questions. I am informed that the City Court Bar Association will be meeting within a week or so to consider the matter and a copy of any resolution passed will be forwarded to you.

I came into the picture under the following circumstances: Shri Cooper, the Government Pleader in the City Court, spoke to me of the distress felt by several members of the Bar at the reported appointment of an additional Chief Presidency Magistrate in preference to first class legal practitioners. He said that the repeated statements that members of the Bar in good practice were not willing to become judges of the City Court, was not correct, for he had made enquiries and he mentioned to me two names of lawyers in good practice, who he found were willing to accept the post if offered. One of them was the Asst. Govt. Pleader in the City Court, Shri Parikh.

I have not the pleasure of knowing him, but I found from several judges of the High Court and the City Court that they consider him first class. He has completed 35 years of age. As the question thus raised not only affected the Bar but also the general public, and as both are entitled to as good a judiciary as can be obtained, I felt that I ought to take up the matter. I had a long discussion with the Chief Justice; but after reflecting for over a week, I wrote to him to say that it seemed to me that further steps were necessary and would have to be pursued. I wrote to the Chief Justice, because I had told him that if we, at the Bar, considered further action necessary, I would apprise him of it.

The relevant considerations, as I see them, are these: the City Court is both a civil and a criminal court. The additional Chief Presidency Magistrates were appointed magistrates in 1947 and 1948, and would be out of touch with the practice or administration of civil law for nearly 15 or 14 years, and it is difficult to see how they can be preferred to a first class civil law lawyer who has built up his practice in those years. Secondly, experience shows that a first class civil law lawyer very easily becomes a first class criminal law lawyer, but a first class criminal law lawyer, rarely becomes a first class civil law lawyer. Thirdly, a magistrate appointed a judge of the City Court cannot be confined only to criminal work, for when he finds some judges doing both civil and criminal work, he feels that to be confined to criminal work is a stigma on his capacity. Fourthly, if a practising lawyer is not offered a post when he is inclined to accept it, increased practice will make him decline the offer. And lastly, the crying need of the City Court is for a first class civil lawyer to be a judge, for there are heavy arrears of nearly six thousand cases.

I have written to you because the falling standards of the judiciary are causing grave anxiety, and unless remedial steps are taken it will not be possible to maintain the restraint which the Bar has shown so far, or to prevent a demand that if the judiciary is unable to solve the problem, competent legal professional opinion be brought to bear on its solution.

I need hardly say that I am not interested in any particular person. I have told the judges that if there are abler lawyers than Mr. Parikh, the ablest ought to be appointed.

With kind regards,

Yours sincerely,
H. M. Seervai

The Hon'ble Shri S. K. Wankhede,
Minister for Industries, Law & Judiciary.

Dr. G. N. Lawande
[Professor of Philosophy (Retd.)]

20.9.1967

My dear Feroza,

I write this just to say how delighted I was to read a review of Homi's book. It was a grand review, 'tho in my opinion it was rather short. It was good that Homi has spoken out even against the Supreme Court. This is what should be and I am glad that Homi did it. We are living in a world where everybody flatters everybody for no reason whatsoever and it is so refreshing to have a man like Homi who does not follow this line of the least resistance. The reviewer appeared to be rather shrewd. He pointed out some differences with Homi, but I did not understand what exactly he wanted to differ on. But of course it is my ignorance. The impression which the reviewer gave was that he was not quite upto the mark in reviewing a book such as Homi's. It is by all accounts a book in the tradition of Mulla, who is supposed to be the most scholarly writer on Law. Anyway, I am glad that Homi did a grand — indeed very grand — job of it. My congratulations to him.

I wanted to go to his chambers last week, but for some time I have been suffering from bronchitis with tremendous cough. I told the doctor to give me something drastic but he has given me some antibiotic tablets. The cough has subsided, but I am in consequence down and out. I hope to be alright by the end of the week, and then I want to see Homi next week in his chambers and offer him my congratulations in person, and have a cup of coffee with him. In the meantime, my best regards to him and love to the children.

Yours very sincerely,
G. N. Lawande

Dr. G. N. Lawande

28.9.1967

My dear Feroza,

Thank you for your letter. It arrived on Tuesday, but I had already gone to Homi's chambers on Monday. I saw his book there and I must say that it is a magnificent thing. He showed me the last paragraph of his preface where he thanks you for all the assistance which he received from you. Almost immediately I was reminded of Kalidasa's description of Queen Indumati, where he says through the King, A (illegible) that she was (Sanskrit sentence). I won't translate this verse for you. You must get it translated from someone who knows Sanskrit. It appears to me, after reading Homi's reference to you, that you approach the ideal of a true wife as envisaged by Kalidasa. I wish you both the best of everything. May God bless you.

I was so happy to read that Homi is elected Setalvad Lecturer for the next year. He did not mention the fact to me, though. His book is of such a high order, that I should not be surprised if similar honours come from all the quarters of India and even abroad. He deserves all that. Probably now that he has done so great a thing, he does not care for such honours. I wish there were more reviews and longer ones.

Though it is a great pleasure to meet you and Homi and the children over a cup of tea, I don't think I should come to you so soon, that is to say, until I finish the second draft of my book. It may be over by the end of October. You must read it and then suggest corrections. Homi has agreed to go over it but not necessarily to read it.

So I'll come to you a little later. Kindly excuse me.

Yours sincerely,
G. N. Lawande

The background to this letter was the Constitutional crisis resulting from the confrontation between the Legislature and Judiciary in UP, both branches asserting their respective privileges. The crisis was sought to be resolved by a Presidential Reference to the Supreme Court under Article 143 of the Constitution. The UP Legislature had great difficulty in engaging a Counsel who was willing to represent their case against the Judiciary and assert the supremacy of the privileges of the Legislature conferred upon it by the Constitution. It was therefore, contemplated to engage the services of an English Q.C. The U.P. Legislature was however, represented before the Supreme Court by Seervai, who being approached, readily agreed to represent the cause of the Legislature. Seervai in no uncertain terms told the Judges hearing the matter that his clients did not recognise the jurisdiction of the Supreme Court hearing the matter but that without prejudice to this submission, the arguments would be advanced on behalf of the UP Legislature. The Judgment is reported as Presidential Reference No. 1 of 1964: AIR 1965 SC 745. Seervai has dealt with this case and its background, in Volume II (pgs. 2169-71) of the 4th Edition of the Constitutional Law of India.

M. M. Varma
Speaker,
U.P. Legislative Assembly

19 Mall Avenue,
Lucknow.

My dear Sri Seervai,

Let me first apologize to you for not having conveyed to you and your junior, Sri Andhyarujina, earlier, and with all speed, my personal sense of gratitude and appreciation of the scholarly and effective manner in which you presented our cause before the Supreme Court. I convey this sentiment to you on my behalf as well as on behalf of the Legislators of the Uttar Pradesh Vidhan Sabha and indeed on behalf of all those who have met me and have followed your arguments.

There is appreciation all round not only of your high forensic merit, but also of the unflinching courage which you displayed in the course of your argument and which, unhappily, more often than not, is lacking in many a lawyer practising at the Bar.

I shall convey your appreciation of many of us to my staff and my colleagues that attended the hearing of the case in Delhi. I am also addressing the Speaker of the Lok Sabha to thank him for all the courtesies, cooperation and sympathies that he and his staff extended to us and to you during the arguments.

In the march of life, success and failure, to my mind, are not of as great a moment as the honesty, the vigour and the perseverance with which one pursues a cause which he considers to be just. Therefore, the result of the case is not important. We all of us raise our hats to you for all the high merits that you have displayed.

With the kindest of regards and good wishes to yourself, Sri Andhyarujina, Smt. Seervai and your children.

Yours sincerely,
M. M. Varma

H. M. Seervai

22.8.1964

My dear Mr. Speaker,

I thank you very much for your letter and for the very high praise which it gives to my argument for the U.P. Vidhan Sabha. Both you and the Speaker of the Lok Sabha have rightly said that the strength of the argument is derived from the fact that I believe that your cause is right and just.

That truth must be told when the occasion demands. It is what I learnt from my mother and father; both of them would have said exactly what I said had they been called upon to do so. That lawyers should hesitate to say things which may be unpleasant to judges is unfortunate. But when I think of the courage which countless persons showed to make India great, and the dauntless courage which our beloved Prime Minister, Jawaharlal Nehru showed throughout his life and the example he set before the country, I am able to set my own effort in its proper place.

Yes, success and failure do not matter. The thought you have expressed in your letter has been with me since college in the following favourite lines:

"What the day wills, enough for thee to know;
What the day wills, the day itself will tell.
Do thine own task and be therewith content:
What others do, that shalt thou fairly judge.
Be sure thou no brother mortal hate,
And all beside, leave to the Master Power."

My wife and children join in thanking you for your kind letter and in sending our best wishes and kindest regards,

Yours sincerely,
H. M. Seervai

P.S.: I realize how heavy must be the demand on your time as a result of what is happening in the House.

To Shri M. M. Varma,
The Speaker of the
Uttar Pradesh Legislative Assembly
I9 Mall Avenue, Lucknow.

Shantilal H. Shah

Minister for Public Health,
Law & Judiciary,
Government of Maharashtra,
Sachivalaya, Bombay-32.
The 8th August 1966.

My dear Seervai,

There is a proposal from the ex-Chief Justice of the High Court to appoint Shri _________,* as a Judge of the High Court. I recollect your having told me some time ago that you had adverse reports about him. I shall, therefore, thank you to let me know in writing what these reports are before I deal with this matter further.

Yours sincerely,
Shantilal H. Shah

* name omitted by editor.

To Shri H. M. Seervai,
Advocate-General,
High Court, Bombay.

H. M. Seervai

Advocate-General's Chambers,
High Court,
Bombay - 1.
9th August, 1966

My dear Shantilal,

I have received your letter marked 'secret' dated 8th August, 1966. Your recollection is correct and as desired by you I give below the adverse reports about __________.*

At the end of May 1966, I had arranged to meet Mr. Justice H. R. Gokhale at his house. As I was about to leave my home, an oral message was conveyed to me from some lawyers in Poona that the appointment of __________ was being considered for a judgeship of the Bombay High Court and that those lawyers considered that such an appointment would be most unfortunate. Since I was leaving home, I just slipped in the name in my pocket. I met Mr. Justice Gokhale and we discussed various matters affecting the Bench and the Bar and I happened to mention the appointment of judges to the High Court. He said that things which might have seemed inconceivable at one time might happen in the future and he mentioned that the name of __________ was seriously being considered for appointment to the High Court. I checked up the name with the name on the slip which I had got and I told him that by curious coincidence, that very evening I had received adverse reports of __________ purporting to come from Poona lawyers. He replied that he himself thought it inconceivable that such a person could be a judge of the High Court. He had personal knowledge of the judge and apart from the fact that the judge had been passed over several times for that appointment on the ground that he was not competent enough, his reputation was not high and there had been a complaint against him by a judge subordinate to him that __________ had tried to interfere with that Judge in his judicial work.

I told Mr. Justicc Gokhale about the message which I had received from Poona and said that since the purport of the message was confirmed by a person as responsible and as well qualified to judge as himself, I would take up the matter as the leader of the Bar with you as the Law Minister, for, we at the Bar were very worried at the appointments to the High Court. As the Advocate General, I was also worried on the additional ground that today Government was the

* name of proposed judge omitted by editor.

biggest litigant in the State and the principal sufferer from poor and mediocre judges was Government itself. After I went home I realised that without his express authority I could not mention the above conversation to you. So I rang him up and told him that if I were to take up the matter with you as the Minister of Law, I must have his authority to tell you what he had told me and also to mention his name, for you would wish to be satisfied that the adverse opinion was expressed by a Judge who was both competent and qualified to express it. He gave me the authority and authorized me to mention his name. It was after that, I spoke to you on the matter as the Minister of Law and it is to that talk that your letter under reply refers. Some time later I received a telephone message from Mr. Justice Gokhale that he had personally expressed the same opinion to you.

I have mentioned these matters to you because there is great dissatisfaction at the Bar at appointments of persons whose qualifications are inferior and whose integrity is not beyond doubt when compared with the qualifications and integrity of persons who would be available and ready and willing to be appointed. I do hope that the proposed appointment will not be made as it will cause great dissatisfaction among all responsible members of the Bar.

Yours sincerely,
H. M. Seervai

To
The Hon'ble Shri Shantilal H. Shah,
Minister for Public Health,
Law & Judiciary,
Sachivalaya,
Bombay.

C. K. Daphtary was one of the most brilliant and distinguished members of the Bombay Bar, having been the Advocate-General of Bombay and later the Solicitor-General of India and Attorney-General for India for a period of 20 years from 1950 to 1970. As recognition of his very high eminence in the legal profession, and as a tribute to him, his portrait was placed in the Library of the Bombay High Court in 1968. Seervai as Advocate-General took a leading role in this, and Daphtary's response is conveyed in this letter.

C. K. Daphtary
Attorney-General for India

13.8.1968

My dear Seervai,

The Bar Association Secretary has sent me a copy of the invitation card and intimation that I was duly 'hung'. I feel happy and proud that my Bar Association and my High Court should have done me that special honour.

The very great personal interest you have taken in the matter, I consider a token of the very kind regard you have for me, which has always made me happy.

With kind regards,

Yours sincerely,
Chandu K. Daphtary

C. K. Daphtary

August 13, 1968

My dear Seervai,

I should have spoken to you about a particular matter when I saw you. My private secretary Mr. Bhattacharjee has been with me both as Solicitor-General and as Attorney-General for seventeen years and as such, having regard to his excellent work I got the Finance Ministry to increase his salary to a higher scale which he will be entitled to so long as he is secetary to the Attorney-General. The fear is that the Attorney General is entitled, if he so wishes, to bring his own secretary. I did not do so. If, as I hope, Government asks you to take up the Attorney-Generalship I do earnestly request you, unless you have anyone you prefer to bring with you, to continue Mr. Bhattacharjee as your private secretary, so that he has not to revert to a post where his earnings will be considerably less. He is a qualified lawyer and thoroughly acquainted with all the work and also knows stenotyping. The reason for my writing immediately is that I have been given to understand that an approach may be made to you on behalf of some other person. It is not right for me to express comparisons on paper nor, indeed, to decry any approach whereby someone who has held the post with complete satisfaction of everyone for the last few years may be deprived of it. I have a particular peron in mind on whose behalf, I am told, you may be approached, but I shall be extemely grateful if you will take no steps in the matter until you have put to me whatever you may think.

This is all on an assumption which, I trust, may become a reality.

With kind regards,

Yours sincerely,
C. K. Daphtary

J. B. Wadia

Geneva.
3rd April 1969

My dear Homi,

Bad news travels fast and though Sir Jamshedji Kanga's health was failing and he had lived to a ripe old age, the news of his death — which was sent to me in one of my friend Suru's letters — did come as a shock! Few men in their lifetime become an institution, few men received the esteem, love and affection and deep respect of his colleagues which Sir Jasmshedji had so richly won and though he had ceased active practice and though his health was failing, his presence in his chamber in the High Court lent tone and colour and (illegible) to that building.

Piloo has written to his niece, Alan: Whom could I write to better fitted to receive a letter of sympathy? Though you so worthily represent the Bar — which he did for years — you were also close to him, and held him in affection and esteem, and so I send this letter of sympathy to you. His passing marks the closing of an era of pensive eloquence and great legal learning, and he will be remembered for years and years.

Every year I came to Bombay I'd made it a point to see him more than once. Latterly he might for a moment lose his trend of thought, but soon did gather them up and go on. I shall miss seeing him — how much more will you all !

Jehangir

R. A. Gagrat
[Solicitor]

Personal 21st March 1973.

My dear Homi,

On behalf of my partners Mehta, Jangoo and myself, I take this opportunity to thank you most sincerely for all the help, advice and guidance, at considerable sacrifice of your valuable time, you ungrudgingly gave to us in connection with the recent arbitration proceedings of our firm. I have no adequate words to express my thanks for your constant and kind concern for me personally.

On this auspicious Nowroze Day, let me wish on behalf of Mehta, Jangoo and myself to you, Feroza and your dear children a very happy Nowroze and many more to come with continued happiness and as a token of our regards and appreciation, kindly accept these flowers and a small present from us. We can never adequately compensate you for all you have done.

Yours sincerely,
R. A. Gagrat

W. A. Wynes
[Authority on the Australian Constitution]

North Adelaide,
Australia 5006.
25/5/70

Dear Seervai,

Thank you so much for your letter and the Lectures, including the one on the *Bank Case*, where, from this distance, it looks as if your Court took a wrong turning on several counts and I should be strongly inclined to agree with your very excellent reasoning.

I found the main lectures so interesting and informative (I like your style, not tilted, or as a critic of my first edition said, "angular" like mine) that I read the whole lot in two sittings. I was very taken with your survey of judicial review in the U.S.A. — while aware of its shortcomings, I have never read a concise and connected account such as yours: it is as well, as I said in 1936 (then 28, brash and very unaware of the world of politics), that we departed from any slavish adherence to their decisions and bases of reasoning in the *Engineer's Case* in 1920.

It pleased me that you have stressed the fundamental truth that adherence to British tradition is the best protection for all — fortunately, as you must know from our C.L.R., we have followed it here and it applies equally in our State Courts — the impartiality of the Judiciary is accepted as part of the law of nature. I would not think that the Rule of Law had been conceived in Australia as comprising any more than the *legal* concept; it is very rarely mentioned (*c.f.* Dixon J. in the *Communist Party Case* 83 C.L.R. at p. 193, the only reference I know of).

A small point — you suggest supply to all the Judges of an index to all S.C. judgments. Is this not available now? We have an index-digest to C.L.R., also the *Australian Digest* 1825-1968 or 69 with annual volumes (like Mews or E. & E. Digest) in some 25 volumes to which all have access and I assume that their Honours are supplied with this.

My Publishers (in Melbourne, not in Adelaide) have sent you a copy of my fourth edition; I hope it will be useful — it is shortened in many places and this means that to a student like yourself the third edition is still handy (I use it myself — in fact I've been back to the 1st and 2nd editions for some out-of-date references). No. I'm not doing any legal work just now (too lazy I fear) but must write an article on our Sec. 92 (freedom of inter-State trade) becoming somewhat confused again.

In the meantime, we send your wife, and you our best regards and hope that you have (or by now have had, no doubt) a good rest at Simla.

With all of the Best, I am,
Yours ever,
Anstey Wynes.

S. A. de Smith
[Professor,
The London School of
Economics and Political
Science and eminent writer on law]

Houghton Street,
Aldwych, London W.C.2.
24th June, 1970

Dear Mr. Seervai,

I received your Setalvad Memorial Lectures yesterday, together with a copy of the lecture on the *Bank Nationalisation Case*. Today, I received your letter.

I may say that I have already read your lectures with the greatest of interest. They are extraordinarily interesting and I have learnt something from them even outside the main area with which they were concerned.

Allow me to congratulate you on a splendid achievement.

With kindest regards,

Yours sincerely,
S. A. de Smith.

T. L. Venkatarama Aiyar
[Retd. Supreme Court Judge]

81, M. Road, Alwarpet,
Madras-18
Dated 19-12-1970

My dear Mr. Seervai,

It is with great pleasure that I read your letter. It reminds me of those days when we spent happy evenings in the Gymkhana Club in the parties given by you and your wife. I hope I'll have the pleasure of meeting you again in Bombay. I have read both your books on Sir C. Setalvad Lectures and the Bank Nationalisation case. They are full of valuable information and stimulate thought. I am, in general, in agreement with your views.

Thanking you once again,

Yours sincerely,
T. L. Venkatarama Iyer

Dolly Masani
[President, Women Graduates Union]

15th May 1971

My dear Homi,

I am enclosing herewith a receipt for your very kind donation. The inscription on the plaque will be according to your wishes.

Many thanks for wishing me success in my "selfless efforts for the Hostel" but who should know better than you that these efforts would be of no avail had it not been for your much greater selfless efforts? We do not have adequate words to express our gratitude but you know our sincerity when we say thank you very much for all you have done for us and for what you are still doing for us.

Yours,
Dolly

T.R. Andhyarujina was Seervai's junior from 1957 to 1974. He was Seervai's junior both in the Krishna River Water Dispute between Maharashtra, Andhra and Karnataka before the Krishna River Water Tribunal and in the Kesavananda Bharati Case. The Tribunal's hearings took place between 1969 and 1973 interrupted for six months when Seervai along with Andhyarujina represented the State of Kerala before the Constitution Bench of 13 Judges in the landmark case of Kesavananda Bharati. Both these cases kept Seervai and Andhyarujina in Delhi on a weekly basis for a period of about 4 years.

H. M. Seervai

Room No. 209, Ashoka Hotel.
7.3.1972

My dear Tehmtan,

I have thought over your request on the plane and I have come to the conclusion that you are right, and that if in all respects I was in your position, I would also ask to be relieved.

I could give a list of all your difficulties and I believe that my list would tally broadly with yours. If I appear not to understand them, it is because I shrink from discussing other people's personal matters unless asked to do so.

Although the case will take many more months, the most difficult part will be over by Thursday or Friday and when we return to Bombay on Friday you can remain in Bombay. I will write to the Legal Department that for compelling personal reasons you have asked to be relieved from the case and that I have agreed to relieve you since the matter had already lasted beyond anybody's outermost expectations and especially as the most important part of the case is over.

I would like to say that my admiration for your great capacities and my warm regard and affection for you remain undiminished, if anything they are increased by your making the right decision. No need for you to feel uneasy on my account, for now that almost the whole of the work has been done, no greater burden will be thrown on me than I would have borne anyhow. You know my methods of work: the case engages almost all my time and attention, and rationally speaking there is no additional time and attention which I can give to the case.

With best wishes and kindest regards,

Yours sincerely,
H.

Justice S. R. Das
[Retd. Chief Justice, Supreme Court.
Vice-Chancellor, Vishvabharati]

7.8.1972

Dear Mr. Advocate,

Many thanks for the autographed copy of the article entitled "The Privy Purse Case: A Criticism" which you had contributed to the Bombay Law Reporter Vol. LXXIV (journal). I offer you many more thanks for the kind thought that actuated you, even at this distance of time, to send the copy to me. For this kind remembrance I am, indeed, beholden to you.

Immediately on receipt of the copy I started reading it. Imperceptibly I fell into a trance. As I went on reading it, I felt I was sitting in Court presiding over the Bench hearing the case and I saw you arguing the case before me. The vision was extremely vivid and I could see the earnestness in your face and the piercing thrusts of your slender fingers! The trance lasted only a few minutes and I woke up at the sound of my own voice as I had started reading the article aloud! I have experienced a curious phenomenon, quite a pleasing sensation.

I have been living in this quiet corner of the country in complete retirement. There are 3 or 4 lawyers here who are not overburdened with legal literature. I don't think any of them has even a copy of the Constitution, not to speak of any law reports. In fact, I have not been able to read a copy of the judgment in the *Privy Purse Case* or of the *Golak Nath's Case*. In these circumstances, it is not possible for me to express any intelligent opinion on the correctness of your comments. All I can say is that your reasonings have a ring of rational plausibility. You have successfully kept the two aspects of the matter — legal and moral — entirely separate. I certainly liked the concluding sentences of your article. Indeed you might have added that the Government's law was stronger than their morals. Your article has been to me very pleasant and interesting reading.

I trust you are keeping well and fit. Please accept my most cordial compliments and best wishes, for your health, happiness and prosperity.

Thanking you again.

Yours sincerely,
S. R. Das

S. P. Kotval
Chief Justice
High Court
Bombay.

26th September 1972

My dear Seervai,

I was very happy to receive your letter and thank you for the generous terms in which you have referred to my work in the High Court.

It was a pleasure to work in the High Court at Bombay and imbibe and uphold its rich traditions.

I considered myself very fortunate that during the time that I was the Chief Justice (indeed most of the time that I have been a Judge of this Court also), I had you as the Advocate General. During these last six years and more, whenever I have turned to you for the solution of my problems, not merely on questions of propriety, decorum and good behaviour but in important matters of administration, you have given me unreservedly valuable advice and correct guidance, for which I must say I am deeply grateful.

With warm regards and best wishes for the future,

Yours very sincerely,
S. P. Kotval

B. P. Dalal
[R.L.A., Maharashtra]

D. O. No. 194228/L-2
Law and Judiciary Department,
Maharashtra.
Sachivalaya, Bombay-32.
Date: 11th August 1972

My dear Seervai,

Please refer to your D. O. letter No. 4041, dated the 22nd June 1972.

I am to convey to you the profound appreciation of the Chief Minister and Law Minister of the further generous gesture on your part in surrendering in favour of the State of Maharashtra, a sum of Rs. 1,599/- out of your salary of Rs. 1,600/- for 8 months from June 1972 to January 1973.

With kindest regards.

Yours sincerely,
B.P. Dalal
Secretary.

A. N. Ray
Chief Justice of India

27th July, 1973

My dear Mr. Seervai,

Thanks for your letter of 23rd July. I had no doubt that you would start reading the matter during your journey. It is gratifying to know that you have chalked out your method of completing the second edition of your *magnum opus*. If I may repeat what I had told you once before, your work will be known in the same manner as Dicey's treatise.

During the last two months I have had two most interesting letters. One was yours. The other was your junior's. I shall always value the kind sentiments and thoughts expressed by you. You have lavished on me things which I do not know whether I deserve.

During my stay at Delhi it has always been most refreshing to spend a couple of hours with you. Our introduction was through philosophy. Both my wife and I looked forward to seeing you and Mrs. Seervai. She was here only once. We hope both of you will come again in the not too distant future.

Perhaps, you do not know how often we have talked of both of you as perfect companions in life. This is one of the reasons of your dedicated life of a lawyer. You will perhaps recall what Lord Macmillan wrote about his wife in *A Man of Law's Tale.*

Some day I hope I shall see your son and daughter who are familiar to me through my mind's eye.

With kindest regards from my wife and me to you and Mrs. Seervai and greetings to the children.

Very sincerely yours,
A. N. Ray

Justice S. R. Das

19-11-1973

My dear Seervai,

I am in receipt of the copies of (1) your address on the Directive Principles of State Policy and (2) your article on the Fundamental Rights Case—At the Cross Roads, reprinted from the Bombay Law Reporter. I thank you for the same. It is a matter of great gratification for me to find that even at this distance of time you have me in your thoughts. May God bless you for this kind remembrance.

I have gone through your address on the Directive Principles and am half way through your article. My trouble is that in this place I have no access to any law books, not even a copy of our Constitution as amended up to date, not to speak of any Law Reports. As you know I finished with the law nearly 15 years ago. So it is not possible for me to express any opinion on any serious question of Constitutional law which you have dealt with so adroitly. I am, however, free to confess that I am thoroughly enjoying the reading of the two articles. The feeling is like that of an old and decrepit war horse which suddenly hears a bugle. As I go on reading your article my mind goes back nearly 17/18 years to the days of the *Chamarbaugwala Case.* I can distinctly see you before my mental eyes addressing me and my learned colleagues. Your eyes shining with lustrous keenness and your lanky fingers emphasising your points. This vision, by itself, is ample recompense for me in reading the articles. I thank you for affording me this pleasure.

I trust you are keeping well and fit. I am fairly well for my age. With kind regards,

Yours sincerely,
S. R. Das

H. M. Seervai
To Prof. C. J. Hamson

16.2.1974

My dear Hamson,

We were shocked and dazed to learn of the passing away of Prof. de Smith when we read the obituary in the "Times". It's a great loss not only to Cambridge or to England, but to legal scholarship and studies in all English speaking countries. His books are standard books in India, and a reference to de Smith in Courts is received with the respect due to a most distinguished writer.

I shall never forget meeting him in Cambridge on May 10, 1973. We had hoped to meet again — for he wrote to me about coming to India. I have received nothing but kindness from him and after our meeting at Cambridge we corresponded, sometimes about his writings, sometimes about mine. He sent me his recent books on Constitutional Law and Judicial Review of Administrative Action, and I wrote to him about the help and guidance I had obtained from them.

Mrs. de Smith has been very much in our thoughts since we read of the untimely passing away of her husband. As I do not know her address, and it would take too long to find it out, I have ventured to enclose a letter addressed to her and I would be most grateful if it is sent to her.

With kindest regards to you and Mrs. Hamson from all of us,

Yours very sincerely,
H. M. Seervai

H. M. Seervai

16.2.1974

Dear Mrs. de Smith,

It was with a sense of shock that I learnt of the passing away of your dear husband from the obituary in the "Times", and I, and the members of my family, would like to send you our deepest sympathy on this irreparable loss. The loss is harder to bear because he has been taken away at the height of his powers.

There must be many like me to whom his death comes as a personal loss; who can speak of his personal kindliness — for since 1967 I have received nothing but kindness from him. I am thankful that I was able to meet him personally at Cambridge in May last. I treasure the two books he kindly sent me, and I wrote to him to say that I had turned to him for guidance for my own book, and got the guidance I wanted.

Words of comfort are unavailing at a time like this, but it must be some comfort to you to know that his loss will be felt not only in Cambridge or in England but throughout the English speaking world where his remarkable books have left a deep impress and helped in developing the law. Courts in India refer to his books with the respect due to a most distinguished writer.

With regards,

Yours sincerely,
H. M. Seervai

A. N. Ray
Chief Justice of India

7th March 1974

My dear Seervai,

It was indeed a great joy for my wife and me to spend some time with your son Navroz. He reminded us a lot of you. The saying 'a chip of the old block' is apposite in this case. What pleased us most was that Navroz had his head screwed on the right way in this age of anger and challenge of boys and girls.

I am grieved to know of the sudden death of Professor de Smith. It will be difficult to find one of his type. His contribution to Administrative Law is no less than Dicey's to Constitutional Law.

Kenneth Clark's book is admirable. It gives us an insight into values of human reason. The illustration is Leonardo da Vinci's inquiry into man and Nature.

With kind regards from us to both of you and our very best wishes to the children.

Yours very sincerely,
A. N. Ray

Seervai, as Advocate-General, and Divekar, as the Government Solicitor felt similar revulsion to the theory espoused by Antulay, that Government lawyers must be committed to the Government's philosophy.

Mr. Divekar's following letter was sent to Seervai in 1977, two years after he wrote it, when they had happened to meet and talk about their respective resignations.

I publish the Government Solicitor's letter to show that men who maintained high standards found it impossible to continue in office under the regime of Mr. Antulay; that it was not a matter of inflexibility in the pejorative sense, (as alleged) that led to Seervai's stand, but inflexibility in the best tradition and in the best sense of the term. Divekar's letter lends support, (if support were needed) to Seervai's conduct.

M. C. Chagla wrote and congratulated Seervai for resigning. In his reply, Seervai wrote: "I regret it on public grounds, but if I had been free to consult my own inclination, I would have resigned months ago." (16.9.1974)

G. M. Divekar

Divekar & Co.,
Solicitors & Advocates,
14/Ambalal Doshi Marg,
(Hamam Street), Fort,
Bombay-400 023.
Date: 20th September, 75

Dear Shri Antulay,

I had the honour to attend the Government Law Officers' Conference held on Sunday the 14th instant at Sachivalaya.

In the course of your inaugural address you made it very clear that every Government Law Officer must be a committed Lawyer committed to the philosophy of the Government (which in turn according to me means the philosophy of the party in Power) and those who do not accept this position should better leave their office.

My Firm, of which I am the sole Proprietor, has been appointed as Government Solicitors since 5th June 1974 and at the time of such appointment no such condition was laid down or even mentioned.

I do not belong to any Political Party and I have never joined any Political Party at any time. In other words I am not a politician at all and therefore I am not committed to the policies or programmes of any Political Party.

I have accepted the job as a Government Solicitor only as a Lawyer and I believe I have been doing the work of the Government as honestly and diligently as possible irrespective of my personal views on any subject either political or otherwise.

I believe that one of the principles of Lawyers' profession is that a Lawyer should never identify himself with the client he represents, although he is supposed to work for his client honestly and to the best of his ability. Therefore a lawyer while attending to the work of his client, including the Government, need not have the same view on all subjects which the Government or the Political Party which runs the Government may be having, and he is entitled to have his own views on any subject and to express the same in private, if not in public.

In fact I do not appreciate the concept of a committed lawyer or a committed Judge. Such concept, in my opinion, is the very antithesis of the concept of an independent bar or independent Judiciary in a democratic set up.

I have been working for the Government honestly and to the best of my ability but, I would not like to accede to the position of being a committed lawyer, particularly when I do not indulge in Politics. Of course, this does not mean that I am necessarily against Government Policies. But I do not want to masquerade as a committed lawyer. I shall therefore thank you if you kindly let me have your clear direction in the matter and if you think that I must be a committed lawyer and hold the same views as the Government does on all subjects, as you seem expecting every Government Lawyer to do, I may be permitted to resign as Government Solicitor.

Yours sincerely,
G. M. Divekar

To:
The Hon'ble Shri A. R. Antulay,
Minister of Law,
Government of Maharashtra,
Sachivalaya, Bombay-32.

The eminence of Seervai at the 5th Commonwealth Law Conference is clear from the Reviews I published in THE SEERVAI LEGACY.

The correspondence and the extracts published here, reinforce the Reviews.

The extract from Prof. Sir T. B. Smith's letter indicates Seervai's extraordinary rectitude as well as indifference to the high style of life generally adopted by dignitaries abroad. It shows his optimism in travelling to Scotland without any foreign exchange, depending on £5 for his taxi from airport to the place where he was put up, which £5 were mailed to him by his friend!

At first he had declined the invitation from the Conference organisers on the ground that although he would gladly spend the money in rupees (for example he paid his fare) he would not apply to the Reserve Bank for a foreign exchange permit, in view of the prevailing stringent foreign exchange constraints in India.

The expenditure for 6 days came to £43 !!

It is difficult to imagine others in Seervai's situation undertaking a trip to a foreign country on these terms, at the age of 71. Frugality was never a problem to Seervai, but even so, to undertake a trip literally penniless, required courage, optimism and confidence of a remarkable nature.

Prof. Sir T. B. Smith
To Seervai's daughter

9.3.1977

"I can now report ..... modest success regarding his financial position during the attendance at the Commonwealth Law Conference in Edinburgh. The registration fee will be remitted in his case which saves some £70 or so. I personally am covering the expense of his attending the dinner dance on the last night of the Conference. The Commonwealth Foundation is making a grant for his accommodation and subsistence while in Edinburgh. This we believe to be at the rate of £16.50 .... It would be inappropriate for a man of Shri Seervai's distinction that he should be accommodated in a student residence .... These arrangements though not luxurious, will I hope be sufficient!" *

* (Arrangements were made at a staff club).

H. M. Seervai
[To his Family]

Edinburgh.
27.7.1977

Dearest Loves,

It was a Roman triumph yesterday. I spoke for 50 minutes without a note. There was complete rapport between the Speaker and the listeners and there was tumultuous applause for half a minute when I sat down and again when the Chairman thanked me. As you wrote to Millar, things got sorted out; and it was as well that there was a misunderstanding. But it did involve 6 hours' work in "putting my thoughts in order". A delegate who met me in a bus as I was returning from Lord Wylie's said to me yesterday "when we met yesterday I did not realize that I was speaking to such a distinguished lawyer"!

I was invited to dinner by the Dean of the Faculty of Law — a leading lawyer. It was excellent and everybody there was very handsome about my address. Lord Hunter, the Chairman of the Sc. Law Commission said it was very good. I have written this because I know it will please all of you and will be some reward for mum's labour.

With fondest love,

Ever yours,
H.

Lalit Bhasin
[Advocate, Supreme Court of India,
Hon. Secretary of the
Supreme Court Bar Association]

3.8.1977

It was really a thrilling experience to hear your address at the Plenary Session of the Fifth Commonwealth Law Conference. It was in fact the highlight of the Conference, as, unlike others you did not read your address but spoke ex-tempore. I had heard you in the Supreme Court but this was the first occasion to hear you out of the Court precincts and to know your personality. It is indeed an honour, Sir.

Sincerely,
Lalit Bhasin

K. T. Faud
Director, Legal Division.

Commonwealth Secretariat.
10.10.1977

May I respectfully say that I was very greatly impressed and deeply moved by your address, and entirely agree with the author of the article (in the Journal of the Law Society of Scotland, Sep., 1977), that it was "both in content and delivery, a masterpiece."

K. T. Faud

R. S. Bachawat
Chairman,
Krishna Godavari Water Disputes Tribunal

29th Sept. 1973

Dear Mr. Seervai,

Many thanks for a copy of the "Fundamental Rights Case at the Cross Roads". You have given an excellent summary of the Keshavananda case and made a brilliant critical analysis of the minority and majority judgments. Your memorable contribution to the shaping of the case will be long remembered by those who participated in it.

The Krishna case is nearing completion and it will be concluded soon. You have retired from the case, but looking from the dais, I always feel your presence in the seat usually occupied by you. Mr. Andhyarujina is doing his work extremely well.

I hope you are well. With best regards,

Yours sincerely,
R. S. Bhachawat

S. K. Das
[Retd. Judge, Supreme Court]

8.11.1973

Dear Mr. Seervai,

It is indeed very kind of you to send me a copy of your review on the 'Fundamental Rights case' recently decided by the Supreme Court. I agree with most of what you have said. I had said on many previous occasions that Golaknath's case was wrongly decided. It is unfortunate that the mischief created by that decision has snowballed in the manner it has done. I agree with you that the present decision is also not likely to help — it is difficult to find out what is the majority decision. The good of the country demands that there should be a clear enunciation of the legal position or the amendment of the Constitution.

Having said all this, I must also add that I do not very much appreciate the way Government has gone about it in the matter of the appointment of Judges. I strongly hold the opinion that two wrongs do not make one right.

I only hope that greater wisdom will dawn on us. It is a tragedy to think of the Court now, a Court in which I had the privilege of working.

With regards and best wishes,

Yours sincerely,
S. K. Das

During the emergency of 1975-77, in an attempt to terrorise and browbeat the Judiciary, the Congress Government of Indira Gandhi started transferring independent and fearless judges of the High Courts to other High Courts. Justice S. H. Sheth of the Gujarat High Court was one of the few Judges willing to take on the Government by challenging this policy of transfer. He approached Seervai to represent him in the petition filed by him before the Gujarat High Court challenging his transfer. Seervai readily agreed; and gave Justice Sheth an absolute commitment to see the matter through. The 3 member Bench of the Gujarat High Court upheld Seervai's contention and struck down the transfer of Justice Sheth from the Gujarat High Court to the Andhra Pradesh High Court as being malafide, illegal and unconstitutional. After the emergency was lifted, the Janata Government, whilst reversing the transfer of Judges effected by the earlier Congress Government, shamefully persisted in the pending appeal before the Supreme Court which had been filed by the earlier Congress Government against the judgment of the Gujarat High Court.

In the 1st Judges' Case (Union of India vs. Sankalchand: AIR 1977 SC 2328) the Supreme Court reversed the Judgment of the Gujarat High Court, thereby enabling the Government to transfer Judges.

Justice S. H. Sheth
Judge, High Court A.P.

Himayatnagar,
Hyderabad - 500 029.
August 30, 1977.

My dear Mr. Seervai,

I am -- nay, all High Court Judges are -- deeply grateful to you for bringing to a successful conclusion the litigation which affects all of them very much. Your contribution to the maintenance of the independence of the judiciary will occupy a proud page in the history of India. The posterity will probably realise its value more than we do now. The role which you have played is simply remarkable and deserving of our heartfelt thanks and congratulations.

I have not yet heard from the Central Government. When I leave for Ahmedabad on re-transfer, I shall see you at Bombay if you are there and have not left for England.

With deep regards to you and to Mrs. Seervai,

Yours sincerely,
S. H. Sheth

Morarji Desai
Prime Minister of India

No. 1602-PMO/77.
New Delhi.
November 8, 1977.

My dear Seervai,

I had received your letter of the 13th September, 1977 with which you forwarded a Memorandum on the suggestions for repeal of the 42nd Amendment and a list of actual amendments to the Constitution. The Law Minister had already received a copy and we have given very earnest consideration to the various suggestions that you have made. The material that you have supplied has been very useful and I am glad that you devoted so much of your time and attention to this very important problem. You will, however, appreciate that in the present circumstances, we have to develop a strategy on this matter which would enable us if possible to secure the support of the opposition to as many amendments as possible. This may somewhat hamper us in carrying through everything that we want to put through.

With kind regards,

Yours sincerely,
Morarji Desai

Justice Y. V. Chandrachud
Chief Justice of India

22.3.1978

My dear Seervai,

It is not that I had no leisure to reply to your letter of the 19th February earlier. There is neither explanation nor justification for this lapse. I hope and pray that this will not cause misunderstanding and that I will continue to receive your affection in the future as it has been my good fortune to receive it for over twenty years.

But I am still struggling to find words to express adequately my sense of thankfulness to you for the glowing compliments which you have paid me in your letter. So, if my reply looks cold, you are the one to blame. The warmth of your feelings, the grace of your words and the conviction that nothing that you ever say can in any context be anything less than genuine, rob my response of its full intendment. But I am sure that you will unravel the throb beneath an inadequate exterior.

It is not odd that you, who have not adorned the Bench at any time, should give a recipe for successful Judgeship. During your distinguished career at the Bar you have known Chaglas on one hand and some Toms and Dicks on the other. And your interest in the legal profession has never been of a mere professional but it is the interest of a discerning lawyer, at once critical and appreciative. I value and cherish your kind and timely words of advice. I pray that Providence which has so generously given me this opportunity to serve the Cause of Justice in my humble way will give me the prudence to heed your voice of eminence and experience. One of my foremost ambitions is that in 1985 when I will lay down my office, you will be the first, as now, to say a word of appreciation.

The controversy never affected me, or reviews; I did not permit it to disturb the even keel of my life. I have no anger against anyone and that for two reasons: I genuinely believe that issues of national importance like the appointment of the Chief Justice of India should evoke a national discussion. A vibrant Bar and a wary public are perhaps greater guarantees of fundamental freedom of the people than a judiciary hide bound by the framework of the Constitution. Secondly, I never aspired for the Chief Justiceship though I greatly prize it. I assure you that never shall I permit the echo of that controversy to be heard in my Court. In fact, the public debate which my likely appointment evoked has made me look inwards. I am now more conscious than ever of my failings. The controversy has generated within me an altogether different dimension of humility. Those who critized me had a valid point of view and so I must forget what a few of them said in the exercise of their right of free speech. You cannot put the right of free speech in a golden scale and complain of a word here and a word there. On the whole, it is better that the critics speak out than that their conscience should be muffled. What has Chagla to gain by opposing my appointment except that he felt strongly on a matter of grave public importance? And how can I, who has learnt at his feet, question his bona fides (even if he may now disown me as a disciple)? For me the controversy will endure for the sole and limited purpose of the lessons which I must learn from it. There is and shall not ever be any bitterness or rancour. When that happens, I shall sooner cast my robes aside.

The pressure of work here is tremendous, judicial and administrative. In the High Courts there is a large volume of administrative work but here, one deals with sensitive issues and on a different plane. In regard to Judicial work, the backlog is terrifying. I do not know how best to clear at least a part of it. If, within the next few years, the situation does not improve, the system is doomed to collapse. That has to be prevented. I feel a sense of strength that your good wishes are with me. I deeply value and cherish them.

Prabha and I are thankful to you for your affection and your kind appreciation. May we prove worthy of it, is the prayer of us both.

Kindly give our very kind regards to Mrs. Seervai.

With our regards,

Yours sincerely,
Chandrachud

Note: The letter of Justice Chandrachud is published with permission.

The Rt. Hon. Lord Wylie

House of Lords,
30 Lauder Road,
Edinburgh EH 92JF.
12th January, 1981

Dear Shri Seervai,

Here is just a short note to thank you both for your delightful X'mas card.

I was so glad to learn from your wife of the honour which was recently bestowed upon you for your outstanding work on the Constitutional Law of India.

You may, or may not, have known Professor Mitchell, formerly Professor of Constitutional Law and latterly of European Studies at Edinburgh University. He died last month after a short illness, and I mention this only in case you happened to know him.

I missed you at Lagos, but I hope that we may meet up again in Hongkong in 1983.

With all good wishes to you both for 1981.

Yours sincerely,
Norman Wylie

P.S. Tom Smith delivered a most erudite paper on the Reception of the Common Law, at Lagos.

Niall MacDermot

International Commission
of Jurists,
15th January, 1981

Dear Mrs. Seervai,

Thank you for your letter of 27 November and your kind good wishes for the New Year, which we warmly reciprocate.

I have indeed seen your husband's book on the Emergency in India. It will be most valuable to us for a comparative study we are making on states of emergency.

In this connection, I would be very grateful if you could send me a copy of three articles in the *Indian Express* on the independence of the judiciary, which were referred to in your letter. They would be of great interest to us.

With warmest good wishes to you both.

Yours sincerely,
Niall MacDermot
Secretary-General.

The Governor of Maharashtra, Air Chief Marshall I. H. Latif was called upon to sanction the criminal prosecution of A. R. Antulay consequent upon his role in the cement scandal which led to his downfall and resignation as Chief Minister of Maharashtra in January 1982, after a severe indictment by Justice B. Lentin of the Bombay High Court. Though Seervai had long since ceased to be Advocate General of Maharashtra, and held no public post or office, the Governor sought his advice on the Constitutional position of the Governor vis-à-vis the Cabinet, and whether it was Constitutionally permissible for him to disregard the advice of the cabinet in the peculiar facts of Antulay's case, and to independently consider whether or not to sanction the prosecution of the erstwhile Chief Minister.

I. H. Latif
Governor of Maharashtra

Raj Bhavan.
Bombay 400 035.
25 May, 1982

Dear Mr. Seervai,

Just a line to express to you my grateful thanks for giving me so much of your time the other day. I need hardly add that for me the discussion was invaluable. It was also a pleasure for me to meet such a distinguished citizen of this great metropolis and I do hope there will be other opportunities also to meet you again.

With warm regards,

Yours sincerely,
I. H. Latif
Air Chief Marshal

Feroza Seervai

5th February, 1980

My dearest H,

Thirty-five years ago this day, early in the morning, clad in a grey khaddar skirt and jacket over a blue aertex shirt (which costume met with great favour in your eye) I cycled breathlessly down along my sea-shore to the Bandra Station to keep an appointment to meet you at the Asiatic Library — where you found me, appropriately enough reading *Between Two Worlds.* The memory holds. And as the 5th February comes round again, I dwell on it and feel grateful in my being that because my second world was you, I've had the great good fortune to pass from the happy world of my childhood and girlhood into the happy, happy world of womanhood, and wifehood and motherhood.

Not many days ago, I said to our Meher, God bless you! and she, full of laughter, responded: "He has! He has!"and I can say the same, because of you, and your loving and caring and forgiving and cheering, and lighting my path all the way — 12,775 days!

When Meher was little, sometimes in a peeve — rare as that was — she would say "Oh! Mummy and Daddy always stick together." And it is because you have kept your promise to love me ten-fold that you have stuck to me through those faults and failings that could have made you falter. Your strength and support have sustained me, your faith and fairness kept me free from fear of being myself; to mine own self I could be true, and thus, true to you.

So on the 5th February I must tell you again I love you and I thank you, and I bless you!

Feroza

H. M. Seervai

Room No. 615,
The Taj Mahal Hotel, Delhi.
7.2.1980

My dearest Feroza,

I was very happy and much moved by your most affectionate and heart warming letter of 5th February — I have never ceased to bless that day, for you walked into my heart and have stayed there ever since. Since we are human, at times things will go amiss. And if at times I have mentioned them, it is because I want you to be even happier with your bairns — happy as you already are. You have given me not only love and happiness but firm support in all my work with single minded devotion and I have been more grateful to you than I have been able to convey.

If I had to live my life again, I would bless the day which brought you and me together, for in things that matter we share common ideals and values and a deep affection. It is all summed up in the words which a very great man said to his devoted and loving wife whom he loved deeply; "Life with you has been Sweet, Ferozee." And so it will be to the end.

With fondest love and invoking every blessing on your sweet self.

Ever your own,
H

Justice Ronald D. Wilson

Chambers of Mr. Justice Wilson,
Canberra. A. C. T. 2600
12th January, 1981

Mr. and Mrs. H. M. Seervai,
146, M. Karve Road,
Bombay 400 020
India.

Dear Mr. and Mrs. Seervai,

I was most gratified that you should have remembered to send me Christmas greetings, and particularly delighted to learn that Mr. Seervai has been awarded the Dadabhai Naoroji Memorial Prize, 1980, for his distinguished work on the Constitutional Law of India. Please receive my warm congratulations in respect of an honour which I have no doubt is well deserved.

You will notice that I have been appointed to the High Court. If it should happen that you are ever in Australia, I hope you will give me the pleasure of welcoming you to Canberra, or to Perth, as the case may be.

With warm regards, and best wishes for a very happy 1981 for you both,

Yours sincerely,
Ronald D. Wilson

Professor O. Hood Phillips, QC
[Author]

24 Heaton Drive, Edgbaston,
Birmingham B 15 3 LW.
16th January, 1981

Dear Mr. and Mrs. Seervai,

I was very pleased to receive your attractive Indian card with the season's greetings.

It was also good to hear of the award of the well-deserved prize for Mr. Seervai's work on the Constitutional Law of India, which is just recognition of the outstanding merit of his publications.

You both must be proud and happy also at the very promising start your son is making to what will presumably be a successful career in the law.

I have agreed to collaborate with Professor Swindler (that is actually his name!), of William & Mary College, Williamsburg, USA, in a book on Anglo American Constitutional Law for the American market. The idea is that Professor Swindler will write the American parts in the customary way for American students' text books, and I would put in the English bits. There is no target date for finishing the book!

I hope you will let me know if you come to the vicinity of Birmingham, as it would be a great pleasure to renew your acquaintance.

Yours sincerely,
Owen Hood Phillips

Prof. Sir T. B. Smith, Q. C., F. B. A.
Chairman,
Scottish Law Commission

Kirkton of Morham,
Morham Haddington,
East Lothian Eh41 4lq.
26th Jan., 81

My dear Homi & Feroza,

How very kind of you to write so generously of the conferring on me of a knighthood. Your congratulations are very much appreciated. We have indeed been overwhelmed by the warmth and enthusiasm of very many friends and well wishers on this occasion. It may well be unprecedented that services to Scottish law have been expressly recognised as such, but English & Commonwealth colleagues seem to be as appreciative as the Scots.

Ann has always been well suited for this role. If knights are notionally expected to be proficient in equestrian matters, I must confess that I am notoriously out of practice, having last ridden — to the alarm of myself and the inhabitants of Egypt — about 1943.

I have agreed that if professional support is secured, I shall act gratuitously as General Editor of an encyclopaedia of the laws of Scotland — provided I have complete control on the academic side and am empowered to nominate a much younger Deputy and ultimate successor. Thus my 'services' may be required for the rest of my days.

I am glad that Homi's operation seems to have gone well and was astonished to read how soon he had been in action again.

Warm thanks and most affectionate greetings from Ann & self.

Aye Yours,
Tom

Sir T. B. Smith, Q. C., F. B. A.

Naval And Military Club,
London.
2nd July, 1981

My dear Homi,

I am staying overnight in London so as to attend the Dinner of the British Academy after the A.G.M. Therefore, from the Club I write to congratulate you most warmly on your election today as Corresponding Fellow of the British Academy. This is the highest academic distinction which can be conferred on a lawyer by any British Institution, and your right to such recognition was most warmly acclaimed. Your many admirers in the World of Scholarship will take great pleasure in your election to the Fellowship.

It would be pleasant to think that in a year — or two years — from now you could manage to attend the AGM and dinner. As we are moving presently into new premises near Baker Street Tube Station (and Madame Tussaud's) you might prefer to visit after the move — but there are lectures and special occasions over the year.

Ann joins in sending affectionate greetings and enthusiastic congratulations.

Aye Yours,
Tom

Prof. G.A. Beaudoin
[Law Professor]

Faculty of Law,
University of Ottawa.
X'Mas 1981

Congratulations to Mr. Seervai !

It is well deserved! I am delighted to see that a great jurist has been justly honoured!

I teach constitutional law full time. After ten years as dean I returned to teaching and publishing.

I hope to return to India one day.

G. H. Beaudoin

Sir T. B. Smith, Q. C., F. B. A.

East Lothian.
11.2.1982

My dear Homi,

I am just back to base from London and find your welcome letter of 4th Feb. awaiting my return. Many thanks indeed. Instead of starting to write a Lecture in honour of F. H. Lawson, I have been reading with special interest your contribution to the 'Indian Express' on the *Judges' Case,* and the judgment of Lentin J. in the *Cement Case*. Both are fascinating reading and your contribution has certainly modified the provisional interpretation of the Supreme Court's which I gleaned from the short account in the 'Times'. Many thanks indeed.

Ann is still in the South. Our grandchildren of nearly 15 (grandson) and 14 (granddaughter) were released from their schools near Brighton to visit us overnight in London. The train drivers' strike made life rather difficult for us all at different stages. President Reagan and

Mrs. Gandhi seem to deal more robustly with strikes than is the British practice!

There is, as you will have seen from the 'Times' an uproar over a decision not to prosecute in a rape case in Scotland. The Solicitor-General has had to resign, ostensibly for speaking to the press before the Lord Advocates had returned to make a statement in the Lords. In fact Fairburn had made himself unpopular because of his rudeness in the Commons and imprudent behaviour outside the House. We are now having the interesting legal problem ventilated as to whether a private prosecution is still competent in Scotland. The Dean of the Faculty of Advocates who succeeded James Mackay, is appearing gratuitously for the prosecutrix. Our warm good wishes to you all.

Aye Yours.
Tom

Rustomji Andhyarujina and Seervai were the closest of friends for 80 years and more, the friendship having commenced at the Bharda New High School. Seervai was the recipient of the prestigious Dadabhai Naoroji Prize and Rustomji responded with this letter.

R. B. Andhyarujina
Advocate Supreme Court

My dear Seervai,

It was a Red Letter Day — 21st of December, — in your Life, which I have watched at near quarters from boyhood to manhood, and from manhood to old age, and in varied circumstances of your life and my life — the Life — that Life, that I have watched and admired, has fruited and yielded the richest fruit which the most eligible and the noblest of men could covet.

This happiness is not yours alone, because I am the happiest man today, especially as I carry in my breast the experiences of the noblest qualities that a man possesses of which I was a witness and often a recipient from you. A Scroll of Honour, prepared by rank outsiders, cannot do justice to those qualities.

One peep — only one peep — in the hoary past. When we took walks, almost daily (on the Reclamation) during our college days with you and Banaji, people watched us with a strange gaze, as crazy fellows taking brisk walks and indulging in loud debates. We stand vindicated today. It was more than half a century back, but it is such a heavenly joy to remember those days in the retrospect of the DAY, that we have experienced and are alive today to see with the very same glittering eyes on which our blessed mothers looked and admired.

With love and affection,

Yours Andhyaroo
(signed with actual tears of joy,
which I have just wiped).

John Ll. Edwards
[Professor and author]

Faculty of Law,
University of Toronto,
Toronto, Canada, M5S 1A1.
June 12th 1984

Dear Homi & Feroza,

After so many years' friendship, undiminished by the miles that separate us, I feel happier in addressing you this way. I trust that, in doing so, I do not cause you any offence, for that would upset me greatly.

We were very pleased to receive Feroza's letter which was written at the end of April. When I saw the enclosed wrapper and read what had happened to the 3rd edition of Homi's work, I could not help uttering denunciations of the stupid personnel in the Canadian Post Office. Prior to your letter, and seeing the returned address-label with its various rubberstamps, I had received no intimation that there was a parcel for collection at our local post office. The only mistake — understandable: that many of our UK friends have likewise misread my atrocious handwriting — is the reference to "66 Batry Point Crescent" which should read "66 Baby Point Crescent". But the postalcode "M6S 2 C1" was correct, so that it did not need extraordinary Sherlock Holmes qualities to make the slight adjustment and inform me that a parcel was awaiting my attention.

I can only extend sincere regrets that you have been put to so much trouble, and so unnecessarily to boot, but it may be wiser to send the 3rd edition to the address on this letter-head. This is my academic base and this is where the earlier editions occupy a proud place on my shelves. Not only do I make reference to Homi's *Constitutional Law of India* but I have drawn its importance to the attention of many of my academic colleagues, law and political science. In particular, I shall be interested in the new historical introduction and Homi's treatment of recent controversial events in India that have been reported upon in the Canadian and English newspapers and journals.

It must be a matter of pride to you that Navroz is following in his father's footsteps and sharing the same commitment to the cause of civil liberties and integrity in government. Would that I could sit with father and son to discuss again, in the light of recent episodes, the range of questions that we covered during my very happy and productive visit to Bombay.

John

D. C. Wadhwa
[of the Gokhale Institute of Politics & Economics]

Pune 411 004 (India).
No. 12.5/2664/1984
October 20, 1984

Dear Mr. Seervai,

I am writing this to express my profoundest gratitude to you for writing a lengthy and appreciative note on my book in your monumental book. I was greatly moved by your greatness in doing so. Soon after the publication of my book, I wanted to send a copy to you for your comments but Mr. Majmudar advised me not to do so. He told me that you were extremely busy and therefore will have no time to have a look at it.

As I have been a great admirer of your prodigious work on the Constitution of India, it was a real great pleasure for me to meet you and listen to you on a variety of subjects. I am grateful to you for sparing more than two hours of your precious time for me. I benefited immensely from our meeting. On the next day of our meeting, I purchased a copy of Volume I of your book from N. M. Tripathi for our library and now have started reading it diligently.

With best regards to you and Mrs. Seervai,

Yours sincerely,
D. C. Wadhwa

H. M. Seervai

October 24, 1984

Dear Dr. Wadhwa,

Many thanks for your letter of October 20, 1984 and all the kind things you have said about me. After reading your book I was most anxious to meet you and I am very glad that I had an opportunity of meeting you.

The single-minded devotion which you have shown in writing your book and the great public service which you have rendered, will become manifest once the Supreme Court quotes your book and rules that such repeated re-promulgation of Ordinances is a fraud on the Constitution which the Courts will strike down.

With kind regards from my wife and myself,

Yours sincerely,
H. M. Seervai

G. B. Dingal

Judge, City Civil & Sessions Court,
Bombay.

29th April, 1985

To H. M. Seervai

Dear Sir,

How many know that you love Dr. Johnson?

Just as you have read the totality of Churchill (and you read his 'Marlborough' while you were the Advocate-General), you seem to have read the totality of Johnson (except perhaps his Dictionary, because no one can ordinarily read a dictionary through).

You may be wondering as to how I know all this.

I would not keep you in suspense: One day you happened to sit in a row just behind mine in the American Center Auditorium. You had come to see an old movie 'An American in Paris'. To your right was Mrs. Seervai, and to your left another cultured lady who appeared to be your relative and you were carrying on a conversation with her on Johnson. While the lady referred to Boswell's Journal, you were praising Johnson's diction and precision and you were quoting your favourite passages.

I am specially writing to you respectfully to ask you if you have read *Samuel Johnson* by Walter Jackson Bate about which Nigel Nicolson writes: "This biography attracts on the first page, and continues to attract for six hundred more, partly because it is about Dr. Johnson, and partly because it is written by W. Jackson Bate".

After reading Boswell, one does not really feel like reading any other biography of Johnson. I think, we can make an exception in case of Bate.

Bate speaks about Johnson's honesty and courage, his profound moral sincerity — his practicality — and his unrivalled range, whether he is talking about common domestic experiences, childhood and education, single life versus married life, sickness and death — or about the pursuit of money or the hunger of the heart for importance, fame or social standing. Bate says: "To no one since Shakespeare could we more truthfully apply what the ancient Greek epigram said of Plato, 'In whatever direction we go, we meet him on his way back'."

While I was reading this, I thought that honesty and courage and profound moral sincerity can as well be your description.

Yours sincerely,

G. B. Dingal

P. S. How are your eyes now?

H. M. Seervai

3rd May, 1985.

My dear Judge,

It was most kind of you to write to me.

Yes, I am very fond of Johnson after reading Boswell's Life — the 4 Volumes of Birckbeck Hill's edition, which is the standard edition edited by Powell. I have two books on Johnson; but since you speak so highly of *Samuel Johnson* by W. J. Bate, I have ordered the book.

By the by, "The Times" brought out a facsimile edition of Johnson's Dictionary at £45/-. I bought it, because it contains about 107,000 illustrative quotations. It is a very big and heavy book, but I hope to browse over it for the quotations when I have a little time.

Many thanks for the kind words you have said about me.

Now that the cataracts from both my eyes have been removed, I have been restored to complete mobility. And I can read and see without difficulty.

With kindest regards.

Yours sincerely,
H. M. Seervai

H. M. Seervai

31st July, 1985.

To the Editor,
Freedom First.

Dear Mr. Raju,

I have received your letter dated 20th July, 1985 enclosing a cheque for Rs. 250/- for the "Quarterly Essay, Reservation in Education and Public Service — H. M. Seervai" published in the July 1985 issue of *Freedom First.*

There seems to be a clear misconception. I sent no "essay" to *Freedom First*. All that happened was that I gave a talk under the auspices of the Indian Merchants Chamber and the Incorporated Law Society on "Reservation in Education and Public Service". The talk was cyclostyled by the Indian Merchants Chamber (which has a very large membership) and distributed to all its members. Mr. Minoo Masani thus obtained a copy of the talk and he conveyed to me that he liked it very much and wished to use it as a working paper in a Seminar on "The Reservation of Seats" and I agreed.

I have read the talk in the copy of *Freedom First* which had been sent to me. I thought then, and I think now that the correct note to publish at the end at page 33 was "This speech by Mr. Seervai is published by the courtesy of the Incorporated Law Society and the Indian Merchants Chamber" because the words "Based on a speech to the Incorporated Law Society and the Indian Merchants Chamber, Bombay" suggests that I had used the material of that talk for the purpose of contributing an "essay", which is not correct. Slight deletions, which are immaterial, have been made, but the speech has been reproduced *in extenso.*

I am thankful to you for the appreciation of my talk. However, I return herewith the cheque of Rs. 250/- which you have sent me, first, because I have not contributed an essay to your Journal, and secondly because I do not make a charge for publishing a talk (with immaterial deletions) which was delivered on a subject of great public importance.

I need hardly add that I greatly admire the public service which *Freedom First* renders to freedom of thought and expression in our country.

With kind regards,

Yours sincerely,
H. M. Seervai

H. M. Seervai
To
Margaret Drabble,
Editor,
Oxford University Press.

19th August, 1985

Dear Madam,

I have read with interest the 5th edition of the *Oxford Companion to English Literature*. Among other entries, I turned to Johnson, Samuel (1709-84) because I am very familiar with Boswell's *Life of Johnson* and with the writings of Johnson himself. The article on Johnson says: "... another dependant was Robert Levet, an obscure physician and friend of the poor, on whose death in 1783 Johnson was to write the elegy beginning, 'His virtues walked their narrow round'."

I felt that you would like this statement to be corrected in any future impression, because the elegy begins with the line "Condemned to hope's delusive mine". No doubt the stanza beginning with "His virtues walked their narrow round" is the finest in the poem and might account for confusing it with the opening line.

Yours sincerely,
H. M. Seervai

The Oxford Companion to English Literature
Editor Margaret Drabble

52 Regents Park Road,
London NW1
September 6, 1985

Dear H. M. Seervai,

Thank you so much for your letter, and for your point about the Johnson poem. You are of course absolutely right: although the Johnson entry has been extensively revised from Harvey, this mistake was carried over, no doubt for the reasons you suggest. I am sure you will be pleased to hear that the mistake has been corrected for the first reprint. It was very kind of you to write, and if you spot any more errors do let me know.

Again, thank you for your help.

Yours sincerely,
Margaret Drabble

H. M. Seervai
To
V. M. Tarkunde, President, P.U.C.L.

4th October, 1985.

My dear Tarkunde,

I ought to have written to you earlier but have been busy with legal work. Navroz and I listened with the greatest interest to the interview which you gave to George Arnee of the B.B.C. and which was broadcast in the South Asia Survey on the morning of Saturday, 28 September. We both felt that your answers were absolutely first class, and no one could have put the case of the P.U.C.L. and its work better than you did. You rightly brushed aside the absurd suggestion that the P.U.C.L. was an arm of the C.I.A. by pointing out that no one took such allegations seriously, and that the P.U.C.L. consisted of people dedicated to the ideal of Civil Liberties.

If you have a script, or can get it from the B.B.C. we would like to have it, so that we can make it widely known.

With best wishes and kindest regards.

Yours sincerely,
H. M. Seervai

H. M. Seervai
[To Arun Shourie, eminent writer
and later Union Minister]

11th November, 1985

My dear Shourie,

Navroz and I were heavily engaged in a Writ Petition which raised the question of reservation of posts for Scheduled Castes which was heard before a Full Bench. I could not therefore write to you earlier.

You will find Maulana Azad's stand on the partition in his autobiography *India Wins Freedom* in the Chapter entitled "The Mountbatten Mission", at p. 181. There, he describes that "It must be placed on record that the man in India who first fell for Lord Mountbatten's idea was Sardar Patel. Till perhaps the very end Pakistan was for Jinnah a bargaining counter. . ." (ibid. p. 183)

He adds that since Sardar Patel was convinced, Lord Mountbatten turned to Jawaharlal Nehru. (ibid.) Azad states that when he became aware that Mountbatten was thinking in terms of dividing India and had successfully persuaded Jawaharlal and Sardar Patel, he (Azad) was deeply distressed. He tried to persuade his two colleagues and he records "I was surprised and pained when Patel in reply said that whether we liked it or not, there were two nations in India". (ibid. p. 185)

Azad then records his meeting with Gandhi and he says that Gandhi's first remark was "Partition has now become a threat. It seems Vallabhbhai and even Jawaharlal have surrendered. What will you do now? Will you stand by me or have you also changed?" (ibid. p. 186). Azad replied, *inter alia,* "My only hope now is in you. If you stand against partition, we may yet save the situation. If you however acquiesce, I am afraid India is lost". Gandhiji said: "What a question to ask? If the Congress wishes to accept partition, it will be over my dead body. So long as I am alive, I will never agree to the partition of India. Nor will I, if I can help it, allow Congress to accept it." (ibid. p. 186)

Azad then recalls Gandhi's meeting with Mountbatten. "I received the greatest shock of my life, for I found that he too had changed. He was still not openly in favour of partition but he no longer spoke so vehemently against it." (ibid. p. 187).

He then recalls the A.I.E.C. Meeting on 14 June, 1947. He said that Pandit Gobind Ballabh Pant moved the Resolution and after Sardar Patel and Jawaharlal had both spoken on it, Gandhiji himself spoke. He added: "It was impossible for me tolerate this abject surrender on the part of the Congress. In my speech I said clearly that the decision which the Working Committee had reached was the result of a most unfortunate development. Partition was a tragedy for India and the only thing that could be said in its favour was that we had done our best to avoid division, but we had failed." (ibid. pp. 196-197)

On the second day Gandhiji intervened in the debate. "He appealed to the members to support the Congress Working Committee. He added that he had always opposed partition and no one could deny this fact. He felt however that a situation had now been created where there was no alternative. Political realism demanded the acceptance of the Mountbatten Plan and he would appeal to the members to accept the resolution moved by Pandit Pant." (ibid. pp. 197-198).

He records the result of the debate in the Working Committee as follows: "When the Resolution was put to vote, 29 voted for it and 15 against. Even Gandhiji's appeal could not persuade more members to vote for the partition of the country !" (ibid. p. 198)

Since the crucial decision was taken by the Working Committee and the Resolution was passed by a majority, it is clear that had Gandhi opposed partition, he had a fair chance of success. Your article reports that he wanted the proposal of 16 May to be accepted. But the published documents show beyond any doubt that he was the person principally responsible for smashing up that proposal.

Knowing how busy you are, I thought I might give you in some detail the views of Maulana Azad as I see no reason to doubt his views. On such points, as confirmation can be had from the official records, Azad's statement finds confirmation, except when he did not have knowledge of what actually passed between the Viceroy and the high Officials in India and the Secretary of State or the Prime Minister and other Ministers in England.

It is clear therefore that it was left to Azad, among the leading Congressmen to oppose partition. He recounts on the last para at p. 185 and the first two paras at p. 186 that Jawaharlal Nehru tried to dissuade him from opposing partition, but he refused to do so.

With kindest regards and best wishes for a happy Divali and the New Year.

Yours sincerely,
H. M. Seervai

Nicholas Mansergh
Editor-in-Chief,
The Transfer of Power

St. John's College,
Cambridge CB2 1TP.
7 January, 1986

Dear Shri Seervai,

I am writing to acknowledge with many thanks your letter of 5 December last and, separately, the copy of the Introduction to the 1st Volume of your critical commentary on the *Constitutional Law of India* (3rd edition).

I have read your introduction with interest and the extract to the Supplement to Volumes 1 and 2 which you have reproduced in the second paragraph of your letter with much appreciation. I am glad our editorial work was helpful and only regret that the two concluding volumes were not earlier available to you. But these things determine their own time-table and, as I mentioned to you, I was myself surprised at the extent of the records especially in April-May 1947 which resulted in there being a need for the twelfth volume. It was, however, mostly of absorbing interest. At times I now feel at something of a loss having no correspondence to unravel or minutes to consider! If I say so I appreciated especially your all too generous tribute to our impartiality.

Without giving our readers confidence that we had sought at all costs and at all times to preserve that, the enterprise would hardly have been worth undertaking.

My New Year Greetings to yourself and to your wife. I recall with pleasure the evening you both dined as my guests in College.

Yours sincerely,
Nicholas Mansergh

Dr. D. K. Jumani
President, Society for the Preservation of
Medical Ethics

15th April, 1986

Dear and Esteemed Sir,

Worlds and worlds of congratulations to your dynamic self for being elected as the President of People's Union for Civil Liberties.

We are aware of you as a man who is self made, a magnetic personality bestowed with great intelligence and a superb sense of humour. Your sheer hard work, great dedication and positive approach towards any problem make every one feel proud of you. We are proud of you.

I, as the president of the Society for the preservation of medical ethics, congratulate your kind self once again and pray May Lord shower upon you the essence of all the choicest things you usher in life.

I remain,

Yours affectionately,
Dr. Deepak K. Jumani.

Prof. Sir Thomas Smith, Q.C., F.B.A.

Edinburgh.
28th April, 1986

My dear Homi,

I think that you might be interested — and possibly amused to know, that as I was shaving yesterday morning, I listened to a trailer — to a 'Raj in India' programme to be broadcast at 5.05 pm. Ann was listening to the radio in the bedroom at the same time. When we met we immediately commented 'That must be Homi', and when we listened at 5.05 our opinions were confirmed. We greatly enjoyed your contribution. This indeed is why I write now. Congratulations!

You may have attended the last British Academy Dinner, as this year there will only be a Reception. Ann accompanied me to the B.A. Reception in January, but it was too crushed for comfort and one could not converse at any reasonable level. I shall not go in July. In the old days, Arthur Goodhart, who was very rich through the Chase Manhattan Bank, subsidised the Dinner substantially, but no Croesus has succeeded him. I should be prepared to pay for my dinner and contribute to guests, but that solution has yet to be considered.

Since, contrary to all medical expectations, I reached an 'allotted span' last December, Ann and I celebrated by going on a Swans Art Treasure Tour of Jordan and Israel for 15 days concluding on 2nd April. It would seem that we chose time wisely — or providentially. Though the tour was very hard work and we rode into Petra, it was a memorable experience. Our efforts were perhaps more engaged in

Jordan than in Israel. In Israel we were repelled by the superstition and commercialism of the 'holy places'. The Inn of the Good Samaritan strained credulity and the Stone of the Good Shepherd — 'Lab and Speciality' seemed in dubious taste.

In June we hope to visit our daughter and family in Brussels and stay for about a fortnight in her small house in Provence. The weather in the U.K. from autumn until now has been definitely depressing. However, that has kept me hard at work on the encyclopaedia. Prince Charles has accepted as Duke of Rottisery — Stain having escheated his Institution to Charles II. Recently, I have drafted a section on Judicial Review of Fundamental Law and have quoted the great Seervai on the Supreme Court and the 'Emergency'.

Ann joins me in sending most affectionate greetings to you and yours. We felt that you were almost one of our Company when we listened to the broadcast.

Best Wishes,
Aye Thomas

Naval Gamadia
[Advocate]

6th December, 1986

My dear Homi,

It gives me great pleasure to congratulate you on your 80th birthday. My mind goes back 40 years, when I joined Sir Jamshedji's Chambers and came to know you when you were relatively a junior at the Bar and have happy memories of those days. Then came the Bombay Telephone Co. Case which you argued and your capabilities were recognised and from that time onwards there was no looking back.

You have attained distinctions not only as an advocate and as a Constitutional jurist but also in other spheres of life.

All I can wish you now on this occasion is good health and happiness for years to come.

I had looked forward to attend your function, but am sorry could not attend for reasons of health.

Wishing Pheroza and you all the best.

Yours sincerely,
Naval Gamadia

H. M. Seervai

14th October, 1988

To
The Indian Express Newspapers
(Bombay) Pvt. Ltd.,
Express Towers,
Nariman Point,
Bombay 400 001

Dear Sir,

I received to-day a letter No. AC. 1002 dated 6.10.1988 from your Delhi office enclosing a cheque for Rs. 500/- drawn on State Bank of India, Indraprastha Estate, New Delhi, for my contribution in the "Indian Express" on September 20, 1988.

The article on "The Supreme Court and Ms. Sheela Barse — Children rotting in Jail" and the second article "When is a Court dysfunctional?" which appeared on 10th October 1988 in the "Indian Express" were not written for a fee.

Ms. Barse spent three years of her life and large sums of her own money in order to secure release of children illegally detained in jail. Her cause was just. However, the Supreme Court in effect turned her out of the Court. Believing her cause to be just, both legally and morally, and the decision of the Supreme Court wrong, I thought it was my duty to aid the cause of Ms. Barse. Under the circumstances it is impossible that I can charge any fee for the articles written in September 1988 and October 1988.

I therefore return the cheque herewith. Please note that I cannot accept any fee for the two articles.

Yours truly,
H. M. Seervai

H. M. Seervai

11th December, 1989

To
The Accountant,
Indian Express Newspapers
Express Building,
Bahadurshah Zafar Marg
New Delhi 110 002

Dear Sir,

I have received your letter No. 2728 dated 6.12.1989 enclosing a cheque of Rs. 500/- for an article which I wrote and which appeared in the "Indian Express" on 25.11.1989.

I do not make any charge for writing on a topic of public importance and accordingly I am returning the letter and the cheque herewith.

Yours faithfully,
H. M. Seervai

Ann, Lady Smith

Edinburgh.
November 12th, 1988

Dear Homi,

Thank you very much indeed for your particularly kind letter of sympathy, which was a great comfort to me and to the family. Tom had been ill for a long time as you know, but he managed to get a great deal of enjoyment out of his work and meetings with family and friends during this past year. I feel very grateful that although he had some frustrations and discomforts he never had any pain, and was able to die at home in the wonderful care of our doctor and the nurses who looked after him. Indeed, he was working happily at his desk up to the last 2 days of his life.

Tom always admired you greatly and was glad when you received the honours you so richly deserved. He valued the books you sent him, all his contacts with you over the years, and much appreciated the opportunities he had to meet you, here and in India. Of course, the birthday party you so kindly gave for him was a very special memory.

Thank you again and with our love and wishes to you and Feroza.

Ann

The Rt. Hon'ble Lord Denning P.C., F.B.A.

The Lawn,
Whitchurch, Hants.
25 Jan. 1990

My dear H.M. Seervai and your dear Feroza — and Navroz your good son,

Thank you greatly for your letter and good wishes for my 91st Birthday. It was very different from my 90th when we had a Royal Banquet in Lincoln's Inn Hall. This year we had it at home here — with a musical evening — 3 dear children and their mother (an Indian lady) — played on their bassoons and flutes for us. Their father is the local Doctor here.

I have had hundreds of Birthday Cards from London and all the world over — but I appreciate most your own letter from India and your paperback on *the Partition of India*. It is the best account that ever was — telling the truth about Mountbatten's responsibility. My family are so closely connected with the principal characters that I find it fascinating.

We are so old now at 91 — and near 90 — that I am at home in the country all my time — and do not get to London. My hearing, eyesight and walking are very poor — but my mind clear as ever to recognize good and valuable contributions to law and to history — and of these yours, my dear H.M., are outstanding.

Yours very sincerely,
Tom Denning

Granville Austin
[Author]

157, Jor Bagh, New Delhi 110 003.
5th August, 1990

Dear Mr. Seervai,

I am researching Indian Constitutional developments 1950-1985, to follow up my Cornerstone book on the framing of the Constitution.

I shall be in Bombay from the evening of 7th September arriving from Ahmedabad by train, until the 13th morning, when I shall go to Pune for a conference there.

Some time with you would be very valuable to me. I would be most grateful for it.

I shall ring your residence or your chambers upon my arrival to find if you can have time for me. I do hope you will.

Yours sincerely,
Granville Austin

Professor Sir William Wade QC, LLD, FBA
[The Master of the College
and Legal Authority]

Gonville and Caius College,
Cambridge CB2 ITA.
15 August, 1991

Dear Mr. Seervai,

Once again I am most grateful to you for sending me a copy of your latest volume, Vol. 1 of the Fourth Edition of your Constitutional Law of India. Like the earlier editions, it is a monument — and a large one — to your learning, your industry and your devotion to scholarship.

I have been reading parts of it with especial interest, since I hope to come to India again next January to give the M.K. Nambyar Lectures, one of which will I think be given in Bombay. I am planning to incorporate some Indian material and I have already started work on it, so that your third edition had already come down from my bookshelf before your new volume arrived. It is a great advantage to have your full and penetrating account of the vicissitudes through which the Constitution of India has passed.

The British constitution has also taken a knock recently. You may well have heard of the Spanish fishery case *(R. v. Secretary of State for Transport ex parte Factortame Ltd. [1990] 2 AC 85)* in which the House of Lords held that a minister must be restrained by injunction from obeying an Act of Parliament of 1988 if the Act violates European Community law, since the European Communities Act, 1972 provided that Community law was to prevail over Acts of Parliament, both past and future. So Parliament has succeeded in binding its successors, contrary to the principle of sovereignty which ordains that where two Acts conflict, the later must repeal the earlier. Forbidding a minister to obey an Act was of course unprecedented. I commented on the case in the Law Quarterly Review for 1991, January.

I will mention it also in my lectures in India. But are there any Indian parallels? Have any of the legislatures attempted to tie the hands of their successors? And has this produced any litigation? India of course has the Constitution, but the same general rule ought to apply. The British case is an interesting example of the way in which basic constitutional rules can change in new situations. The House of Lords did not even mention the fact that they were making a revolutionary innovation.

Thank you once again for your splendid book, and for the kind inscription in it. I hope that I may be able to see you next January.

Yours sincerely,
H. W. R. Wade

H. M. Seervai

20 August, 1991

Dear Prof. Gadbois,

Many thanks for your kind letter of 25 July 1991. I am glad to hear that in spite of your early retirement you have a very full programme of research and scholarly work.

I will be sending you by air mail a copy of the first volume of the 4th edition of the *Constitutional Law of India*. The first Chapter includes my monograph of *Partition of India: Legend and Reality* which has been printed as a paper back. As a reprint was called for, I put in a New Introduction. The 1st volume to be sent to you includes that New Introduction as an Appendix at pp. 948 to 967.

I appreciate what you say about Journals reviewing one volume of a multi-volume work. I have printed on the inside flap of the paper jacket of the *Constitutional Law of India* a review of the first volume of the 3rd edition. The first was by Frank Wooldridge in *International and Comparative Law Quarterly*, January 1984. The extracts from the review which I have reproduced run thus:

"The first volume of this outstanding work should maintain the reputation which this treatise has established as the leading commentary on the Constitution of India.... The introductory first Chapter has been greatly enlarged and benefits considerably from the enlargement. ... The former Advocate-General of Maharashtra writes in a clear and elegant style . . . his capacity for very rigorous, detailed and searching legal analysis, concern for preservation of legal and constitutional values . . . and immense scholarship are evidenced throughout this magisterial work . . . It will prove an indispensable tool to everyone interested in the Indian Constitutional Law, or comparative human rights."

Prof. D. G. T. Williams reviewed the first volume in the *Cambridge Law Journal*, March 1985. He wrote:

"H. M. Seervai's new edition of his established work, *Constitutional Law of India*, is a massive undertaking. Volume 1 alone has increased in size by 325 pages . . . ; and the second volume which appeared in 1984... has increased in size by some 500 pages. The importance of the subject matter more than justifies the care and the detail . . . Mr. Seervai offers trenchant criticism of individual judgments and individual judges in a variety of cases. . . . Such criticisms, however, have to be seen in context. Mr. Seervai is anxious to delve deeply into constitutional issues, and inevitably he has strong and committed views to expound or defend. These views give the work a special vitality, and there are illuminating discussions of numerous topics in the course of Volume I . . . His approach throughout is thoughtful and humane, and he is determined that India's own brand of constitutionalism should, with all its faults and failings, stand the test of time. He has managed to write a commentary which must be of great importance, professionally and academically, in India. . . . The third and expanded edition of Vol. I is a work of recognised scholarship. We should be grateful for the manner in which Mr. Seervai has wrestled with the constitutional quandaries of a great democracy and for the optimistic tone he adopts."

I accept your suggestion to leave the matter of the review of Vol. I to your judgment in consultation with Prof. Mansfield and Marc Galanter. However, if my view is relevant, I would like to say that for the first time the Preface includes a 14-page account of the practical working of the Indian Constitution from 1950 to 1991. Secondly, the Addenda contains a very full account of a sensational case relating to the former Chief Minister of Maharashtra, Mr. A. R. Antulay, who was found guilty of abuse of power and mala fide conduct in distributing a scarce commodity with the result that he was forced to resign from his office. The Supreme Court judgment is a travesty of justice and therefore a large number of legal authorities, including those on the exercise of the Writ jurisdiction of the Supreme Court have had to be dealt with.

With many thanks and kindest regards from Feroza and me to Donna and you.

Cordially,
Homi Seervai

George H. Gadbois, Jr.
[Professor and Author]

520 McCubbing Drive,
Lexington, Ky 40503.
December 15, 1991

Dear Mr. Seervai,

Your letter of November 21st awaited us upon our return from a trip.

The book review process in this country, particularly with the best journals, is a very slow one. It may take the book review editor a few months to take the first step, then the selected reviewer is given a couple of months to complete the review, and, finally, the journal may schedule publication of the review six-to-nine months later. If you look at the book reviews in, e.g. the Fall 1991 issue of a major journal, you would find that the publication date of most of the books reviewed would be 1989. I have long thought the process was unnecessarily slow, but that is the tradition.

I took the initial steps in September, and have not heard anything. But now that I have your letter, I will make some informal inquiries, and try to nudge those who are involved. Once a quantum leap is made, I will let you know. But please tell the Tripathi people that it would be a mistake to delay publication of the second volume until a review from this side of the globe is completed.

During the past few months, I have made rather good progress with my book on Indian judges. Largely because I am privy to so much information told to me in confidence or otherwise off-the-record (especially about the process of selecting the judges), it is a difficult book to write. But it will get done, and it will be in good taste.

Donna and I send our warmest wishes to all the Seervais during this holiday season.

Cordially,
George

H. W. R. Wade

The Taj Mahal Hotel,
Bombay, India.
5th Jan. 1992

Dear Mr. Seervai,

Many thanks to you and Mrs. Seervai for your kind hospitality yesterday. It was a pleasure to have a talk with you.

I am worried that you may not have received the enclosed letter, since you did not reply to the question in the 4th paragraph. I would be extremely sorry if you had not received my thanks for your generous gift of Vol. 1 of your Fourth Edition, which of course I greatly prize and which I have used in preparing my lectures.

Please do not trouble to reply now, since I am in touch with plenty of Indian lawyers who can answer my questions.

Yours sincerely,
H. W. R. Wade

Professor Sir David Williams
President, Wolfson College

Wolfson College,
Cambridge CB3 9BB.
21 January, 1992

Dear Dr Seervai,

First of all, Sally and I would like to send to you and your family our warmest greetings for 1992. We often talk about you, and it is my regret that, when we visited India in January 1991, we were unable to get to Bombay. The occasion for that visit was the conference of the Association of Executive Heads of Commonwealth Universities, and I was representing Cambridge University, where I have been Vice-Chancellor since 1989 and will probably continue until 1996.

The arrival of the new edition of your book was immensely welcomed, and once again I can only marvel at the scholarship and commitment which you have shown. It is really a tribute to you that you have maintained the impetus over so many years, and you have undoubtedly contributed immensely to the knowledge and body of Constitutional Law throughout the Commonwealth.

Please accept our warmest greetings for 1992.
With kind regards.

Yours sincerely,
David Williams

Lord Denning, F.B.A., M.P.

House of Lords.
1st February, 1992

My dear Homi & Feroza,

We are greatly pleased with your letter for my 93rd Birthday and a nice letter from your daughter Meher Pocha — Thank you. All went very well — no big parties like my 90th — just family parties for 4 days.

Your cassette proved an attraction to everyone. We played it on our record player — with everyone listening to you. We managed to get some of the words, especially the opening words. We think the tape must have been damaged in transit. We think your friends must have put it in a suit case which was X-rayed for security and the X-ray damaged the tape. But we made it out. I got the text from the library of the House of Lords of which I enclose a copy.

I told everyone of you and of your great qualities — of your magnum opus — the Constitution of India — But all were most interested in your account of Mountbatten's mistakes — your assessment of him fascinated all. It was at Birthday parties which my step daughter gave for us. Lord Goff (one of our Law Lords) was there.

Joan and I are very frail — I am very deaf — we cannot walk very far — but a few steps in the garden — but we carry on able to read and write still and to enjoy your letter. Love from Joan and me to you all.

Yours ever,
Tom Denning

Seervai along with 11 others was the recipient of the Living Legend of the Law Award, presented by the International Bar Association in March 1994. Justice R. S. Pathak and Nani Palkhivala were amongst the Awardees on that occasion. Seervai was at that time 87 and declined to travel to Delhi to personally receive the Award which was therefore received on his behalf by our son, Navroz.

R. S. Pathak
[Hony. Master of the Bench, Gray's Inn (London)
Former Chief Justice of India
Former Judge, International Court of Justice (The Hague)]

10 May, 1994

Dear Mr. Seervai,

It was a great pleasure to meet Navroz during the Award Ceremony organised by the International Bar Association. I am thankful for your good wishes and consideration of regard conveyed by him. Coming from one whom I regard as a great lawyer and jurist and the embodiment of the noblest principles of the legal profession, I respect and value these greatly. I consider it a privilege to be included with you among the Awardees.

I was in Edinburgh last year as a Distinguished Visiting Professor at the Institute for Advanced Studies in the Humanities, and I was delighted to find a set of your work on Constitutional Law in the Bar Association Library as well as one set with one of the retired Judges of the Court at Edinburgh.

With warm personal regards.

Yours sincerely,
Raghu Pathak

S. D. Vimadalal
[Advocate]

8.6.1994

My dear Homi & Feroza,

Rarely lately have I been so delighted with a gift from friends like you both and the loving care exercised in its choice, as when getting your gift of the J.R.D. biography, the other day.

For years J.R.D. and I have been friends in my practice and have had close contacts in Air India, as well as his various enterprises.

For a long time the book will give me delight and bring home delightful contacts. Thank you both very much.

Please forgive me for the delay in sending this.

With kind regards,
Sohrab

H. M. Seervai
[To Nani Palkhivala]

29.11.1994

My dear Nani,

I was delighted when Navroz told me that the Original and Appellate Side Bar have combined to entertain you at a tea party on your completing 50 years at the Bar. I wish I could have joined the tea party, but with an eye problem and a leg problem I find it unsafe to come to the Common Room on the 3rd floor.

I send you my best wishes and affectionate regards on your completing 50 years at the Bar. The "Living Legend of the Law Award" to you in April this year was a well deserved recognition of one of the most outstanding careers at the Bar. But it has not been recognition enough, because, apart from a wide and varied practice at the Bar, you have been the author of the leading text book on Income Tax. Side by side you have been a captain of Industry for many years; and last but not the least, you have expressed forcefully and fearlessly unpopular views on current political issues.

Our great leader, Sir Jamshedji Kanga completed 60 years at the Bar which celebrated the event with well deserved tributes to him. I hope and pray that you also will complete 60 years at the Bar, and the Bar will celebrate the event with éclat.

I send my love and best wishes to Nargesh. It is a proud day for her and she can look forward to even prouder days to come.

With love, Yours always
Homi

Nani A. Palkhivala
[Senior Advocate]

November 29, 1994

My Dear Homi,

How very gracious of you to have taken the trouble to write me in your own hand your most heartwarming letter of date. I am deeply touched by the generosity of your words.

May I take this opportunity of acknowledging your earlier letter of the 14th instant, along with the second edition of your book on the *Partition of India: Legend and Reality* with your kind inscription. I am very glad that this edition has the Index which would make it so much easier to trace your observations upon any topic.

This book represents a signal contribution to historical reality dealing with the partition of India. As *The Economist* rightly says, your account "must remain the most authoritative version", you have been so thorough in research and in the marshalling of details. The recent revelation about the Radcliffe Award which you have referred to in the Preface of the second edition is truly startling. I am looking forward to the third edition of your book which will no doubt incorporate more facts culled from the two biographies of Mountbatten published this year.

Nargesh joins me in sending you and Feroza our most affectionate regards, and best wishes for many long years of good health and happiness spent in the warmth and comfort of your family.

Yours ever,
Nani

H. M. Seervai

9th February, 1995

Dear Prof. Wade,

I thank you very much for directing the Oxford University Press to send me a hard-bound copy of the 7th edition of your book on *Administrative Law*. Feroza and I would also like to thank you and Lady Wade for sending us a very beautiful card of New Year Greetings which has been greatly admired by everyone who saw it. I am glad that the controversy between us as authors has not affected our personal relations. Feroza and I have the happiest memories of twice meeting you and Lady Wade at Cambridge and enjoying your generous hospitality.

In view of my criticism in the Post Script to Chapter XVI of Vol, II (4th edn.) of my *Constitutional Law of India* and in the Preface of it, I felt that I ought to read your book so that if any of my criticisms required correction I would make such correction in the Preface to the 3rd Volume and in an Addenda. Merely as a matter of information, and not by way of raising a controversy, I find that no change requires to be made in my criticism.

With best wishes to you and Lady Wade from Feroza and myself.

Yours sincerely,
H. M. Seervai

Nani Palkhivala

July 24, 1995

My dear Homi,

Thank you so much for your telephone call the other day.

I admire you as a human being as much as I admire you as a lawyer. I am glad you are continuing the writing of your books which, as you rightly said, cannot be edited by anybody else after you.

I have never met a man who lived in his own life, so truly and fully, the admonition of the great Law Lord who said, ". . . It is of supreme importance that, on this short day of frost and sun, we do not sleep till the evening".

With affectionate regards, in which Nargesh joins, and sincere good wishes for many more years of good health and happiness.

Nani

H. M. Seervai

April 28th, 1995

To,
The "A" Ward Officer,
Bombay Municipal Corporation,
134, Mint Road,
Bombay 400 001.

Dear Sir,

I am 88 years old and make two return trips daily from my home opposite Oval Maiden to my Chamber at 40, New Marine Lines (Vithaldas Thackersey Marg). Occasionally I use Marine Drive and "B" and "C" Roads, Churchgate or Cuffe Parade, to visit friends who live at "C" Road or Cuffe Parade.

The drive in each case is a punishment to my system and especially to my back, because the Municipal authorities are not maintaining the roads so as to keep them motorable. This results in jerks and bumps, which are distressing and also harmful to health.

Such neglect is causing a public nuisance, harmful to human beings and to vehicles. The dug up portions of roads are never properly re-surfaced, there are deep pot-holes, ridges are created where the trenches were hastily and badly closed, and there are unmarked speed-breakers.

Section 61 of the Bombay Municipal Corporation Act, 1888 prescribes the obligatory duty of the Corporation. Section 61 (m) runs: "the construction, maintenance, alteration and improvement of public streets bridges, culverts , causeways and the like"; Section 61(o) provides for "the removal of obstructions and projections in or upon streets, bridges and other public places"; Section 3(w) defines "street" as "street" including any highway and any causeway, bridge, viaduct, ... over which the public have a right of passage or access or have passed and had access uninterruptedly or a period of twenty years . . . and Section 3 (x) defines "public street" as "any" street heretofore levelled, paved, metalled, channelled, sewered or repaired by the corporation and any street which becomes a public street under any of the provisions of this Act, or which vests, in the corporation as a public street". It is therefore an obligatory function of the Municipal Corporation to construct roads which are metalled, levelled, channelled, etc.

I am writing to ask you to direct that the defects described above be remedied and to thus *abate a public nuisance*. The Supreme Court has held that it is an obligatory duty to abate a public nuisance.

I shall be thankful if you will let me know within a fortnight from the receipt of this letter, what urgent steps are being taken to set things right, bearing in mind that the monsoon will set in in the first or second week of June 1995.

I may add that neither I nor other persons who use the roads can allow matters complained of to continue and it may become necessary to approach the highest authorities so that matters are set right, and/or to adopt appropriate proceedings to see that the Municipality discharges its obligatory duty.

Yours truly,
H. M. Seervai

Ashok Desai
[Bar-at-Law, former Solicitor General of India]

July 15, 1995

Dear Seervai,

I greatly appreciate your note. I am putting it on a computer and shall send you a copy. It was so good of you to spare some time and thought on free speech under the election law. The cases about the nature of the statute itself including *A. S. Krishna* and *Ranganth Reddy* will be particularly useful. I will absorb the whole reasoning in the course of arguments which begin on Tuesday, July 18th. I must express my admiration for the way in which you devote yourself wholeheartedly to a public cause.

Suverna and I missed both of you during the wedding feast. We are concerned about your problem. But I am sure that with your fortitude the problem will not impede the important work you are doing.

With warm personal regards to you both.

Yours sincerely,
Ashok

Personal & Confidential

H. M. Seervai

12 December, 1995

My dear Chief Justice,

I read with interest your interview in which, if I may be permitted to say so, you rightly defended Supreme Court judgments enforcing anti-pollution laws in cases in which the State neglects to enforce them.

In the same interview you observed that practising Advocates do not accept a High Court judgeship because their professional earnings are much larger than the remuneration of judges. This might have been true when judicial salaries fixed in 1950, were frozen till 1986 with small increase in allowances after the sixties.

It is no longer true today after the Constitution Amendment raising the salary of High Court Judges from Rs. 3,500 per month to Rs. 8,500 per month, read with the Judges' Condition of Service Act which provided for tax free perquisites. I asked two very senior Judges whether it would be correct to say that the total emoluments of High Court Judge would come to between Rs. 30,000 to 31,000 and they say that it would be correct to say so. Further, the maximum pension of a High Court Judge which was Rs. 1,330 per month, or thereabouts has been raised to Rs. 4,800 per month. A Chief Justice of the Bombay High Court told me "For the first time we are able to save and are no longer forced to live on overdrafts". This was about five years ago and I gather that the amount of some perquisites has been increased having regard to the rise in the cost of living.

If in this letter I take the liberty of differing from your diagnosis as to why advocates in good practice do not accept High Court Judgeship it is because I am convinced that broadly speaking, if the present policy of transferring Judges is continued, great High Courts like the High Courts of Bombay, Calcutta and Madras will be reduced to the level of District Courts. Four new Judges have been appointed to the Bombay High Court. *Not one of them* was an Advocate in good practice.

In my opinion, no self respecting Advocate would accept a High Court Judgeship for the simple reason that he can be transferred against his will to another High Court, because transfer without consent is essentially punitive. When the Third and the final volume of the 4th edition of my *Constitutional Law of India* is published, hopefully by February or March 1996, it will show that for reasons there given the majority and the two concurring judgements in the *Second Judges' Case* reached the lowest level of judicial incompetence. But so great is the power of truth to assert itself that in proposition 9 of para 508 of his judgement Verma J. observed that "Any transfer made on the recommendation of the Chief Justice of India is not to be deemed punitive and such transfer is not Justiciable on any ground". In other words, although such a transfer is in fact by way of punishment, by way of legal fiction *created by the Court* (!) such a transfer is not to be looked upon as a punishment. No euphemism can disguise the fact that the underlying basis of compulsory transfer of one-third of the number of Judges including Chief Justices of High Courts is that a fair number of High Court Judges and Chief Justices are believed to be corrupt, and by transferring them to other High Courts the mainspring of corrupt connections would be broken.

Now that the result of the policy has become manifest in the appointment of Judges to the Bombay High Court, I am sure it was never the intention of the sponsors of the policy to eliminate for practical purposes practising lawyers in large practice from the High Court Bench.

I have written this letter to you because it would be a sad day for the State of Maharasthra and for India if one of the premier Courts in India sank to the level of a District Court. The Chief Justice of India carries great weight not only with his colleagues in the Supreme Court but with High Court Judges. And if the Chief Justices and his colleagues feel that the policy requires to be reversed in the interests of the High Court and the administration of justice, his voice would be heard.

This letter requires no reply. I realize that any discussion of the question between the Chief Justice and the concerned authorities is confidential, and no responsible person would wish to break into that confidence.

As a number of letters sent from Bombay to Delhi have miscarried, this letter has been sent by Registered Post.

With kind regards.

Yours sincerely,
H. M. Seervai

The Hon'ble Mr. Justice A. M. Ahmadi,
Chief Justice of India,
Supreme Court of India,
New Delhi 100 001.

P.W.H. Brown, CBE, D Litt.

The British Academy,
20-21 Cornwall Terrace,
London, NW1 4QP.
26 March, 1996

Dear Mrs Seervai,

I was very sorry indeed to hear of the death of your husband, our distinguished Corresponding Fellow. The news was reported to the most recent meeting of the Council of the British Academy and was received with deep regret. May I express to you especially, and to the other members of your and his family, our condolences on your loss.

The Corresponding Fellowship of this Academy is reserved for scholars of the highest academic distinction and we were proud to number H.M. Seervai among them. He was most generous in sending copies of his publications to the Academy, and indeed as I write I have before me Volume 2 of the Fourth Edition of his *Constitutional Law of India*. It is very good to know that before he died he had dictated the end of the final chapter of Volume 3. The volumes, in their successive editions, stand as a vastly impressive monument to a famous scholar.

His election to the British Academy in 1981 paid tribute to his outstanding contribution as Jurist, Law Officer and Advocate to Constitutional Law, primarily in India where he fearlessly and dispassionately maintained the Consitution, of which he was the principal exponent and interpreter; but also as a comparative scholar recognized as of outstanding merit throughout the Jurisdictions which participate in the British and American constitutional legacies. We greatly mourn his passing.

Yours sincerely,
P. W. H. Brown
Secretary

N. G. Thakar
[Principal (Retd.)
Bombay International School]

24th July, 1996

Dear Mrs. Seervai,

Shashi tells me that you have invited me to an anniversary meeting in memory of Homi on 26th July. It is good of you to remember me and I shall try to come to Pune.

I have always felt that Homi was too great a man for India to sustain. India, at this juncture, needs persons like him — honesty, courage and forthrightness have almost totally disappeared and we are as good as living in dark ages.

The companionship I enjoyed with him (and you) is unforgettable. Your sojourn in Pune in the Turf Club, the evenings I spent there with you, all come back to me. I definitely want to meet you, your family and Navroz. But my age (I am ninty two) does not allow me to do what I want to do and as I want to do it.

Please bear with me. If I am in Pune I definitely want to see all of you.

If I cannot make it to your house, could you please spare some time and meet me in my house?

With deep remembrances and affection.

Yours,
N. G. Thakar

Maimoona Hamid

Karachi.
Dec. 18, 1996

My dear Feroza,

Thinking of you a great deal. I wish I could come to see you, but the visa has become difficult and we have to go to Islamabad to apply. May be I will try in the summer vacation.

They say time heals but it only reconciles. Yes. It is your loss and in your case, it is not only a personal one but a national one. India has lost a brilliant man.

May be you should write your memoirs. It will be good for posterity. With good wishes for the coming year and lots of love.

Mammy

Jean Kalgutkar

26.1.1997

To,
The Seervai Family,

This reading from "The Prophet" by Khalil Gibran and the painting by Tang Yun titled "Loquat & Bird" is a tribute of love from a friend who considered it a great privilege to be associated with Mr. Seervai. Though we disagreed on many subjects I always came away from a meeting with him having learnt a great deal from him. I miss him and think of him often.

With much love,

Jean

Lakshmi Sreenivasan

Bangalore.
19.4.1997

Dear Feroza Aunty,

Malathi and I wish to convey to you our heartfelt sympathy and it is so difficult to believe that Uncle is no more. He was a dynamic personality, very friendly and generous, in short a wonderful person.

His tremendous contribution to the Constitution of India will always inspire generations of aspiring lawyers. He was a beacon light in the legal field.

We'll always remember our visits to your beautiful home, and on one particular occasion, Uncle entertained us with a recitation of the "Owl and the Pussycat" and put us at ease immediately. The visit to Uncle's office and chambers will also be in our memories forever. My late father always had the highest regard for Uncle, and felt that Uncle always embodied the noblest aspects of human nature. Though not in our midst any more, he has left behind a part of himself in all of us. Kindly convey our sympathies to Meher, Navroz and Shirin and their family.

Yours,
Lakshmi

Justice Michael Kirby, A.C., C.M.G.
[Judge
High Court of Australia]

11 April, 1997

Mr. T. R. Andhyarunjina,
Solicitor-General of India,
18 Teen Murti Lane,
New Delhi 110 001 India.

My dear Solicitor-General,

Thank you so much for arranging for the copies of Seervai's Constitutional Law of India to be sent to me through the Australian High Commission. They have just arrived and they represent a peerless analysis of your remarkable constitutional document. I will be plunging into the pages often.

I am going to try to get something equivalent — although there is nothing now quite the same in Australia since Dr. Wynes died. Other texts are much more temporary and this is doubtless a reflection of changing attitudes to constitutional law itself.

Your act of friendship is greatly appreciated by me.

Warm regards and thanks.

Forever Sincerely,
Michael Kirby

Lord Denning

Hazelbrook,
Winterbourne Dauntsey,
SALISBURY,
Wiltshire, SP4 6ET
25th April, 1997

Dear Solicitor General,

Lord Denning has asked me to enclose with his dictated letter his own handwritten letter which reads:

"Dear T. R . Andhyarujina,

I can only write a little but this is to send you my warmest congratulations and good wishes. More in the typed letter which I have dictated."

Because he is registered blind and aged 98 he has dictated the following letter to you:

"Dear Mr. Solicitor,

That is the way I would have addressed the Solicitor General in England whenever he argued a case before me.

I am very proud and delighted you should have become the Solicitor General of India and I congratulate you sincerely for attaining this great office which I am sure you will do very well and I wish you every success and happiness in it. But I also want to thank you for the friendship and regard you had for my dear friend H. M. Seervai. He was a great personality and one of the most learned I have ever met. His daughter wrote to me on his death and I have written to her, but I would like to add this word in regard to him and his memory.

I am most interested to have your quotation from my book *The Closing Chapter*. They are so apt that I am having the whole chapter reprinted for the Lawyers' Christian Fellowship of which I used to be the President (now followed by the Lord Chancellor) and am now the Patron.

Yours sincerely,
P. D. Post
(for Lord Denning)

T. R. Andhyarujina
[Senior Advocate, Supreme Court,
former Solicitor General of India.]

8th December, 2000

My dear Feroza,

I was very sorry to miss the function to release *The Seervai Legacy* on December 5, much as I tried, I could not persuade my opponents to consent to an accommodation for that day. I am delighted the event was a huge success.

I would like to tell you how much I have admired your and Novroz's effort in publishing Seervai's papers. Everyone who has read the book so far has told me that after reading his speeches and writings they could not help remarking what a man of character Seervai was. Indeed this is what comes out so strikingly from the publication. Seervai had said that he would not commit the folly of writing his memoirs in his old age. He was right. His autobiography would have never been so convincing of the man's character, exemplary integrity and commitment, as the publishing of his writings and speeches as you have done.

For me who knew and admired and loved him from my infancy, the collection is partly familiar but what was not, or forgotten, has made me more conscious than ever of his rare qualities of mind and heart and intellect. Some of the pieces such as his oration in college at the early age of 18 shows the qualities of his later life — a gift of literary style, fearless approach to a problem and a powerful intellect. His affection and love for his mother is one of the most touching pieces in the miscellany! Who in the wide world would be so committed to his life's work of writing a book as to refuse an offer of the highest position in the legal profession. With what felicity he speaks in his speeches. We in the Chamber know how much he thought and ruminated over a speech which when it was delivered without a scrap of note appeared so easily delivered. Another aspect of his life which comes out forcefully is his transparent honesty and sincerity. Indeed it was this quality more than any other which made him so liked in the very carping and critical atmosphere of the profession. In all my acquaintance I never knew him to do a mean thing, though of course he was quite wrong in his perception of men and things at times, as who is not. Generations hence those who read this legacy will wonder how a man like him did exist in this very earthy and practical profession.

Your editorial comments and Introduction could not have been more apt and revealing of Seervai. You never reveal your great love and affection for him though his for you and the family is so evident in his writings. Only once in the lovely lines of Stevenson you reveal it "Steel-true and blade straight, The great artificer, made my mate."

How true! What a void his sudden passing away must have meant to you. What a blow it must have been to you that fateful night of 26th January, 1996. I saw how nobly and bravely you took up the task of the next day's arrangements. Homi would have admired you for that as he always did for all you did. That evening, I broke down before his body lying in bed and wept unashamedly in the presence of Navroz!

Your publication has made me realise more than at any time what a truly noble and powerful intellect he was. I am grateful to Providence for having known him and received from him the abundance of his help and affection.

With affectionate regards to you and Navroz, and the entire family,

Tehmtan

Avinash Rana
[Advocate]

12th Dec. 2000

Dear Mrs. Seervai,

I was browsing through the book, *The Seervai Legacy*. I liked it immensely. It was news to me that Hormasji was offered Attorney Generalship. I am sure he would have enhanced the prestige of the high office with his erudition, dedication and high integrity.

At the function on 5th December everybody mentioned about Hormasji's phenomenal memory. Both Fali and Atul referred to the quality of his head and heart. Both of them spoke very well — straight from the heart. Only change I would have made in Atul's speech was replacing the word "generous" with "magnanimous." I can vouch for it. Hormasji was simply magnanimous. Whether I was opposing him or assisting him. Sometimes it would be embarrassing when one realized that we did not deserve the lavish praise he was showering on us. One hardly meets with a person of Hormasji's qualities; a very fine human being with rare sense of integrity and commitment.

Yours sincerely,
Avinash

UNESCO

C-109, South Extension,
New Delhi - 110 049.
19-12-2000

Murlidhar C. Bhandare
[Senior Advocate]

My dear Feroza,

I was very happy and touched to receive *'The Seervai Legacy'*, with your good wishes. The book symbolises ethical values which Homi practised more than he preached.

The book has instantly revived innumerable memories of Homi — remembering my sitting in the court to listen to his erudite and eloquent arguments, appearing in any cases against him. I found him to be one of the fairest opponents always encouraging the juniors. I did also appear with him in few cases.

His first volume *Constitutional Law of India* I read from page to page and line by line. That has been the foundation of my Constitutional law with little effort to improve on it later.

Above all I remember the affection and warmth with which he treated me when I was a briefless, friendless and penniless member of the Bar appearing for the poor litigants in our society. I owe my present position in no small measure to the encouragement he gave me in those days. I also remember vividly you, Feroza walking with Homi across the oval maidan.

The Publication is timely because it brings out vividly and brilliantly the ethical values of the noble and learned profession of law at a time when the image of a lawyer is fast sagging and the confidence of an average litigant in the Justice delivery system in our country is rapidly sinking. The lawyer's profession will cease to be able and learned unless the lawyers cease to lack independence, integrity and industry.

Seervai's true legacy — "Cherish values — do not chase money" will continue to inspire young lawyers.

Once again hearty congratulations to you and Navroz for the superb publication.

With love to you, Navroz and your loved ones.

Yours sincerely,
M. C. Bhandare

Anil B. Divan
[Senior Advocate]

22nd December, 2000

Dear Feroza,

It was very kind and thoughtful of you to have remembered us and sent us *The Seervai Legacy* even though we are mostly in Delhi.

Seervai's words and example have inspired many of us at the Bombay Bar. In my formative years at the Bar, Motilal Setalvad as Attorney General and Homi Seervai as Advocate General were two shining examples of independent fearless advocates who had reached the top of the profession without indulging in unethical practices or without fawning on politicians and developing rapport with the powers that be. Unfortunately, it is a different world now.

It was a revelation to me that Seervai is derived from 'Sher-vai' "like a lion". Homi was undoubtedly a lion at the Bar, but he was more, he was a role model for the young and rising advocate.

It is a sad commentary on our leaders that after 17 years of his distinguished tenure as Advocate General, he received no word of appreciation from the Government. I am reminded of what M.C. Setalvad has written in his autobiography, *My Life* about a similar experience when he demitted office as the first Attorney General. He was treated similarly by the then Prime Minister Nehru. In contrast he mentions the courtesy and appreciation shown to him by a letter written by Sir Roger Lumley then Governor of Bombay when Motilal resigned as Advocate General of Bombay as a result of the freedom struggle. So Seervai was in good company.

Seervai's views on the duties of a Law Officer, be it Advocate General or Attorney General are refreshing. He regarded the duty of a Law Officer to represent the public interest and acting independently of the government. Current practices in India, are now more tailored to the practices of what Seervai has referred to as Mr. Worldlywiseman and Mr. Facingbothways.

It was a wise decision on your part to have published this Collection even though it is only a part of the Seervai Legacy. As you have said in your introduction, the book recalls the man and his mind. And what a man!

I recall vividly and with pleasure my meeting with Seervai and you at the PVM Gymkhana during the Emergency. Seervai came to know that I was going to address the Supreme Court in *the Habeas Corpus Case* (A.D.M. Jabalpur) and he was kind enough to contact me on phone and advise me on the points to be made. It showed his commitment to freedom and the Rule of Law.

Smita sends her affectionate regards to you, Navroz and the family.

With Warm Regards,

Anil Divan

BRIEF EXTRACTS FROM LETTERS/CARDS

The following pages contain extracts from Homi's letters to me from Delhi between 1949 and 1961 and a Telex message of 1973.

1986, Homi's 80th birthday, was the occasion for the next lot of letters, from which extracts are published.

Of the last published seven letters, three are very early ones, Navroz's letter is of 1991 on Homi's 85th birthday, and the last ones were written after Homi died, to me or to Navroz.

Delhi, 18.4.1949

My darling,

I do not require to look at your and Meher's sweet photographs because your faces are always before me. But I am glad you put them in because they adorn my mantelpiece.

With love,

Yours,
H.

Delhi, 1.5.1951

My own sweet Ferozee,

....

No, I am busy but not extended and there can be no doubt of a letter to you each day, no matter what the work.

I look forward to the group photo. But whether it is there or not, the thought of your dear self walks beside me. I think of you and dear Meher and look forward eagerly to hear your voices on the 4th.

Ever your love,
H

Delhi, 8.2.1953

Darling Feroza,

....

In the train I met Prof. V.K.R.V. Rao whom I knew in my college days. He spoke to my companion thus: "Since his college days, the logic of Seervai was merciless and he showed no temper. He is exactly the same — style, manner and all."

....

Your love,
H

Delhi, 7.3.1957

Dearest Love,

....

Talking to thee and the little ones makes this exile bearable. The little one was expected a day or two hereafter, and I would have fretted and fumed if I could not have returned.

....

With love, Ever your own
H

Delhi, 10.3.1957

Dearest Ferozee,

....

The habit of giving parties to new judges seems to have spread from Delhi to Bombay. Murz gave a party to K. K. Desai; of all persons M. L. Manecksha did likewise! I imagine this was also in thankfulness for the calamity escaped — of your husband becoming a judge!!

....

Ever yours,
H

Delhi, 8.2.1960

My dearest Ferozee,

.... Sir S. M. Bose told me the latest Daphtary story: On being asked how long the case would take, he said: "I'll take 2 hours, my learned friend will take 1 — the case will take 10 hours!".

....

Ever your own,
H

Delhi, 7.9.1960

Dearest Love,

....

I was so glad you looked up Sir Jàmshedji. Yes, he is not alone in the view he expressed about the judgement. It's like him to talk of my kindness to him after having me in his chamber for 22 years and shown me the utmost kindness. Only today Daphtary (the Solicitor Gen.) said to me "I still maintain that Sir Jamshedji is the greatest lawyer I have seen".

....

Ever your own,
H

Delhi 31.8.60

Dearest Love,

.... The time has not been wasted for I have done a good deal of reading. As you know, I'll take "the next train home" with the delight of a schoolboy welcoming a vacation.

....

Ever your own,
H

Delhi, 1.9.60

Dearest Love,

......

We will reach in an hour tomorrow — that is definite, so we can rejoice that the day of deliverance is not long distant.

....

Ever your sweetheart,
H

Delhi, 4.9.61

My own sweet one,

....

S.K. Das said at the end, referring to the other advocates general: "I hope they will only add to your argument". I replied: "Some of the Advs. Gen. have been kind enough to say that my argument has lightened their burden." He said, "Yes, but the more they add, the greater is our burden." I replied promptly: "It only shows that of him to whom much has been given, much will be required", on which they rose for the day, pleased and smiling.

Ever your own,
H

Delhi, 3.9.1961

Dearest heart,

....

I dream of you at times, and think of you all the time. "Since to be loved endures, to love is wise", and since "a little warmth, a little light, of love's bestowing", is what we most desire, to be away from love and life must be folly, made bearable only by a sense of duty and self-discipline.

....

Ever yours,
H

Delhi, 9.9.61

Dearest Love,

....

I am enclosing herewith a dedication for my book for opinion, criticism and comment, both of its form and content.

I am glad you said no to Lalit Walawalkar, for I will be starting from here when you would have been expected to start from there. We have been away from each other long enough; I have very heavy work ahead of me in Bombay and I need you.

It is good to know from the children's letters that things are bright and gay. And I am longing to be back home to bask in this sunshine.

Ever your own,
H

Delhi, 25.8.1961

My own darling,

....

Viswanath Sastri, who is for the Respondent, whom we support, began late yesterday ...... Sastri's argument was excellent and he made an excellent joke in reply to Hidayatullah, who said, "If you are right you might as well put Art. 301 of the Constitution in your pipe and smoke it!" Sastri (who does not smoke) replied, "That shows the extreme unlikliness of such a thing happening." to the merry laughter of everyone in Court.

I have invited Jimmy Dadachanji to dine here on Sunday. I'll have deserved a little holiday as I work most of the time — with afternoon sleep bunged in on holidays.

Your own sweetheart,
H

Enclosure with letter.

" Lincoln, . . . might have recalled a remark he once made to a lawyer who had asked him to go in a case he didn't believe in, and he said "You'll have to get some other fellow to win this case for you. I couldn't do it. All the time I'd be talking to that jury, I'd be thinking, 'Lincoln you're a liar' and I believe I should forget myself and say it out loud."

Telex Message Delhi, 30.1.1973

Attention of Shri Chokshi, Little Co. Bombay

Please give Mrs. Feroza Seervai the following message:

As expected, the Reading of Summary a triumphant success. Not a single question asked. Most grateful for your invaluable help and also to Chokshi for his whole hearted assistance. If possible I'll phone today, Tuesday at 9 p.m. I work till 11 p.m.

Seervai

A birthday card from our daughter, Shirin Madon

"A Dad is someone special, who always finds a way
To give the kind of strength and love his family needs each day.
He's firm but understanding as he teaches what is right
And a problem seems much smaller when he smiles and hugs you tight.
A Dad is always busy, but he loves to share your laughter.
So he finds the time for fun.
A Dad is someone wonderful, who's thought the whole world of
And no one can replace him because he's love — a wonderful Dad."

Arvind V. Savant
Advocate General of Maharashtra

....

Your life has been full of glorious and enviable achievements. Your contribution to the growth of Law in this country and particularly the Constitutional Law is peerless. The pages of the Law Reports in this country bear an eloquent testimony to what I am saying. You have left an indelible mark on the sands of time whether it was in your capacity as a lawyer, an Advocate, the Advocate General for the State for the record period of 17 years, and as a champion for the cause of civil liberties in the country.

Your reputation as a jurist has been acknowledged not only in this country but also abroad. Your treatise on the Constitutional Law of India is unparalled in the commentaries on the subject. It shows your industry, deep scholarship, analytical mind, your zeal for research, and above all your originality. Your shining integrity and transparent honesty is a virtue for we youngsters to try to emulate. It is very difficult to find adequate words to measure your greatness in all walks of life.

....

R. B. Andhyarujina

....

Our friendship, the peculiar boon of heaven, to men and angels only given, which had started from our school days in Bharda New High School, and has been happily continuing today, when our hair has turned beautifully grey, and our friendship, as Samuel Johnson has said, has become noble mind's delight and pride, how lucky we are!

How do I know what friendship is? I know because you, Seervai are my friend, and you are all these things to me. It is feeling completely natural with another, shedding all pretence, just being yourself; it is sharing with another, both big and little things, joy and sorrow, laughter and tears; it is counting on another to understand your moods, to put up with your feelings, to be there when needed most with a word of encouragement, a smile, a look, a deed, about which you can write a book, especially when our friendship has lasted for more than sixty years, through ups and downs of life.

I may truthfully say about my *contact* with you, as Firdousi has sung in his sweet verse:

"If you happen to pass by the seller of ambergris
Your clothes will emit the perfume of nothing else
Except ambergris, ambergris, ambergris."

....

Reginald Mathalone
[Retd. Chief Presidency Magistrate,
Retd. High Court Receiver,
Retd. Official Liquidator]

....

You have been a good friend to me throughout my career and I appreciate it very much. One has very few real friends in life. I am 88 now.

....

H. C. Dhagat, C. A.

....

It may, perhaps, satisfy you to know that your example in strict pursuit of Integrity, Honesty and Professional Competence has inspired many a lesser man like me to follow suit. I may confide in you though that, in the prevailing atmosphere, it is not an easy task. Your shining example alone fortifies us to continue.

Maj. R. A. Mehta, Ex. I.M.S.

....

Few persons can boast of highest quality of head and heart together with good health and maintenance of sound body at 80. An open mind with sharp razor's edge intellect, with qualities of honesty and straight forwardness and compassion for others, I have always found in you.

....

Dr. Kamalimi Parpia

....

It is said that one who has lived 80 years has seen a thousand full moons and is always to be venerated.

Age has nothing to do with my veneration for you. Your profound knowledge, your sincerity and honesty and above all, your fearlessness have had me awestruck . . . . . .

Perviz M. Dubash, Bar-at-Law

....

Your extraordinary ability, sincerity and high integrity are well recognised and appreciated by all . . . Few men earn such credit in their later times. You are one of the lucky few. But of course you have earned every bit of it. ....

B. B. Chinoy

....

I was very happy to read these richly merited tributes to Homi. There might be many brilliant lawyers like Homi, but I sincerely doubt if there is any who could be as scrupulously clean, as dedicated, as comprehensive yet precise, as thorough and as humane as Homi. It is this rare blend of special excellences that make him a Titan among men. ....

K. S. Cooper
[Senior Advocate]

....

A tiny tribute to a Colossus, who is a living proof that great achievements and total integrity can go hand in hand and that true greatness and worship of Mammon are incompatible.

"Well done. Well hast thou fought the better fight, who single hast maintained the cause of truth."

....

Dr. P. B. Umralkar
[Principal, Law College]

I highly appreciate your erudition and the presentation of matter. I have often quoted from your Commentary on the Constitution of India in my speeches and articles. You represent the best in legal tradition.

Roda Mehta
[Business Consultant]

I felt proud and honoured to have had the opportunity to meet and know you. I can only hope that we can look back, as you do today with even a small measure of the satisfaction and fulfilment that you must know for all your contribution and achievement.

Anil B. Divan
[Senior Advocate]

It is given to a few only to achieve high honours while not compromising the highest standards of integrity and independence at the Bar. Your example and career have been an inspiration to members of the Bar and particularly Lawyers of my generation.

Yogesh Kamdar
[Engineer and Human Rights Activist]

For some queer reasons, the society that we live in acclaims and even idolises an 'AJAT SHATRU' (a person having no enemies). In such a set-up it requires a rare blend of courage and honesty to be an individual with your philosophy of life..... In felicitating you, we dedicate ourselves to the values you have lived by and fought over.

Sharda Joshi
[widow of Seervai's Junior, R. J. Joshi]

Since forty years of my association . . . . . I have always admired your sense of honesty, sincerity and loyalty . . . . . You have always been kind and considered us your family members. My husband had always tried to follow in your footsteps. Today, in his absence, we are all the more grateful to you both for the wonderful LOVE you had bestowed on him.

I have always seen both of you performing your tasks in life so naturally and wonderfully. Your motto seems to be 'ACTION'. This reminds me of the advice Shri Krishna gave to Arjuna. (Bhagwat Gita Chapter 3. Verses 4, 6, 7 and 8):

(4) Not by refraining from action does man attain freedom from action. Not by mere renunciation does he attain supreme perfection.

(6) He who withdraws himself from actions . . . . . is a false follower of the Path.

(7) Greater is the man who, ... with a mind ruling its powers in harmony works on the Path of Karma Yoga, the Path of consecrated action.

(8) . . . perform therefore thy task in life . . .

Maj. R. A. Mehta, I.M.S.

From letters to Feroza from the war front, Burma.

28.4.1945

. . . . .

In army language Seervai is 'first class'. The greatest pleasure which I derive during my short leave is when I go for a walk with him. There is no person who has any influence on me except Seervai.

25.8.1945

. . . . You are a very lucky girl in getting the nicest man on earth as your husband.

N. M. Seervai

8.5.1957

My dear H,

. . . .

I am glad to learn that your son is improving in health and when the rainy season steps in, the weather will also help him and automatically he will start gaining weight.

Thank you very much for your cheque . . . . I don't know what I would have done without you, and I am thankful to God that he has given me a brother like you, one in a crore. In fact when you went to Delhi and stayed there for over a month, I, so to say, felt myself completely lost and on occasions did not know what to do . . . .

Your loving brother
N

Navroz

5.12.1991

Fifteen years ago you had quipped that you had completed your biblical span — and that every year more was a bonus! But at 85 you are going strong with hardly a hint of the passage of those 15 years . . . . Aspi Chinoy once told me, in response to a comment of mine: "If we were to live to be 84, we'll be blithering, babbling, bed-ridden men. Your dad has just completed arguing a very heavy constitutional matter and put in more time and effort than all of us put together." Yes. I marvel at your capacity and ability to carry on working at 85, on what is the monumental work on our Constitution.

On a personal level the past 15 years have seen you become the proud and happy grandfather of 6 grandchildren. If they have given you joy, the same has been reciprocated in full measure. It is not for nothing that Shanoor says "I am going to grandpa and grandma". In due course Riyad will be saying the same.

Justice Deepak Verma

Dear Madam Feroza,

. . . . .

The high standard of advocacy with sincerity and honesty adhered to by Mr. Seervai has been well recognised and well known to all. I only wish it could be followed by practising lawyers and by Hon. Judges too, so as to revive the degrading image of Indian Judicial System. I am not only sure but confident, even if some percentage of it is followed by all, then it would be an entirely different scenario of our system and would be a positive step towards improvement. Unfortunately, he is not with us to read what has been written by me, which comes from the deep corner of my heart. ....

A. R. Wadia
Solicitor,
[Seervai's second cousin]

14.12.2000

. . . . .

I first turned to the chapter on "Distinguished advocates". I think the finest tribute is the one to Sir Jamshedji Kanga. It is not only a moving and outstanding tribute but is a miniature work of art and indirectly tells us much about Homi's character and qualities.

Justice M. H. Kania
Former Chief Justice of India.

29th Dec., 2000

Dear Mrs. Seervai,

. . . . .

Looking at the Bar today, it is difficult to believe that only a few years ago there was someone like Homi, with his strict adherence to principles and remarkable indifference to money, as a leader of the Bar .. . . . .

Justice Kamal M. Mehta
[High Court of Gujarat]

3rd March, 2001

Dear Navroz Seervai,

In 1976 when your father came to Gujarat High Court at Ahmedabad for arguing Writ Petition regarding transfer of Shri S. H. Sheth, Judge of the Gujarat High Court, for about 15 to 20 days, I had an occasion to see and hear his arguments closely — his preparation, his courtesy towards court, his courtesy towards other side advocates and other advocates who were assisting and hearing his arguments .....

P. D. Sirdeshmukh

20th August 2004

Smt. Feroza H. Seervai

Respected Madam,

You may feel a little surprised at this letter because we are not personally known to each other.

The main purpose of this letter is to convey to you my sense of deep gratitude for bringing out *The Seervai Legacy* in a very elegant form. Not only the students and practitioners of Law but also the students and teachers of English in schools and Colleges will remain ever grateful to you and your son Navroz for making the priceless thoughts of the great Jurist and a great legal genius H. M. Seervai, available for the perusal of the lay readers.

The book evinces a very wide range of Seervai's interests and pursuits, and his deep knowledge of each of his pursuits.

I had read a review of this book a couple of years back in The Maharashtra Times and was tempted to read the book in original. But looking at the forbidding price of the book I had almost lost hopes of laying my hands on the book. My friend, Advocate Shivprasad Page, who practises in the Mumbai High Court, knowing my love of books and also my deep veneration for H.M. Seervai, lent me his copy in May 2004 and allowed me to keep the book to my heart's content.

Madam, Seervai Sahib's empire of thoughts is both imperishable and invulnerable. His tributes to Prof. J. C. P. d'Andrade, the distinguished lawyers and judges, his mother Meherbai Seervai, his views on

Goodness, True Charity and Widow Re-marriage are not only edifying but are a perennial source of intellectual pleasure.

I now forget the count how many times I read his articles 'A Common Civil Code', 'The Legal Profession and the State', 'Religious Freedom under our Constitution' and 'The Rule of Law'. Each reading gave me fresh joy and opened before me a grand vista of new meanings. His 'Poetry and Life' is simply miraculous. His encounter with the then Law Minister conclusively proves that there was something of a lion in him. I carefully read his preface to the Critical Commentary on Constitutional Law and that has aroused my curiosity to go to all the three volumes of his Magnum Opus. I am confident beyond the slightest shadow of a doubt that this small volume of about 211 pages has assured H. M. Seervai of immortality in the World of letters. Not only your 'Steel-true and blade-straight' mate but all of you in the family seem to have fully imbibed the well known Zoroastrian Vispa Humata (Good Thoughts), Vispa Hukhta (Good Words), Vispa Hvarshta (Good Deeds). May all of you live long and drench the World with the moonlight of your kind words, good deeds and noble actions. I trust this finds yourself in quite good cheer and the best of spirits. Thank you. A line in reply will extremely oblige.

P. D. Sirdeshmukh

REVIEWS OF THE SEERVAI LEGACY

At a court reference to Chief Justice Chagla, Seervai said "Your work has been woven into the texture of other men's lives, where it will continue to stir them to speech or action as occasion may come by." The same tribute can be paid to Seervai. His principles, his exacting standards and his humanism have truly become part of the immortal Seervai Legacy.

(*Soli Sorabjee in* India Today)

The Seervai Legacy is best summed up in the last piece in the book .... his letter to the then Law Minister, declining his offer to make him the Attorney General of India, easily the ultimate ambition of every lawyer .... His evidence before the Law Commission in 1957 and two letters to the Chief Justice of India .... contain effective cures for the chronic maladies afflicting the justice delivery system .... The collection brings out the multi-splendoured personality of Seervai as a philosopher, scholar, orator, writer, jurist, lover of poetry, seeking perfection in everything he did and, above all, striving to be a great human being. The publication of this volume is timely because it brings out vividly and brilliantly the ethical values of the noble and learned profession of law ....

(*Murlidhar Bhandare in* Sunday Indian Express)

What he wrote in 1981 is a devastating indictment of our judicial system. He covered many topics .... The 'evidence' that Seervai would have given in 1981 is some of the rare material included in the book .... Quite obviously (the editor) wants the reader to embark upon a personal journey and deduce the Seervai

Legacy from his writings. It is a journey that every reader will delight in undertaking, at the end of which he will feel quite enriched. The Seervai Legacy consists of a collection of values which he stood for .... Seervai's personal honesty gave him the courage to speak on issues where most people would prefer to maintain a cautious silence. Seervai could fearlessly express his views on PARTITION, and the BABRI Masjid.

(*Goolam Vahanvati in* The Asian Age)

The Seervai Legacy is an excellent collection of Seervai's essays, speeches, tributes and letters .... and Constitutional Perspectives *is a collection of essays (a festschrift) in memory and honour of H. M. Seervai edited by Dr. Venkat Iyer of the University of Ulster. The hardbound books are very reasonably priced and are well worth buying .... Of particular interest to us of a later generation who by and large are condemned to encounter mediocity at the Bar and on the Bench, is the section in* The Seervai Legacy *wherein are collected Seervai's tributes to distinguished lawyers and judges of the past .... All of us can see for ourselves, how low we have fallen, but if you wish to have a glimpse of the peaks of yore, I recommend* The Seervai Legacy ....

(*Raju Moray in* The Indian Express)